The Autism Spectrum in the 21st Century

Exploring Psychology, Biology and Practice

First published in 2010 by

Jessica Kingsley Publishers, 116 Pentonville Road, London N1 9JB, UK
and
400 Market Street, Suite 400, Philadelphia, PA 19106, USA

www.jkp.com

in association with
The Open University
Walton Hall, Milton Keynes
MK7 6AA
United Kingdom

Edited and designed by The Open University.

Typeset by The Open University.

Printed and bound in the United Kingdom by Latimer Trend and Company Ltd, Plymouth.

The paper used in this publication is procured from forests independently certified to the level of Forest Stewardship Council (FSC) principles and criteria. Chain of custody certification allows the tracing of this paper back to specific forest-management units (see www.fsc.org).

This book forms part of the Open University course SK124 *Understanding the autism spectrum*. Details of this and other Open University courses can be obtained from the Student Registration and Enquiry Service, The Open University, PO Box 197, Milton Keynes MK7 6BJ, United Kingdom (tel. +44 (0)845 300 60 90, email general-enquiries@open.ac.uk).

www.open.ac.uk

Library of Congress Cataloging-in-Publication Data

Roth, Ilona.
The autism spectrum in the 21st century : exploring psychology, biology, and practice / Ilona Roth ; with Chris Barson ... [et al.].
   p. ; cm.
Includes bibliographical references.
ISBN 978-1-84905-087-6 (alk. paper)
1. Autism spectrum disorders. I. Barson, Chris. II. Title.
[DNLM: 1. Autistic Disorder. WM 203.5 R845a 2010]
RC553.A88R68 2010
616.85'882--dc22
              2010001551

British Library Cataloguing in Publication Data available on request

ISBN 978 1 84905 087 6

10 9 8 7 6 5 4 3 2 1

About this book

The Autism Spectrum in the 21ˢᵗ Century: Exploring Psychology, Biology and Practice is an accessible, wide-ranging and up to date introduction to this field for all who are professionally or personally interested in it, including students and researchers, clinical practitioners, teachers, social workers, healthcare professionals, individuals on the spectrum and their families. The book has been specifically designed as a self-contained volume for a wide range of readers, either as part of an educational programme or for general interest and self-directed study. It is also part of a course about the autism spectrum for students studying with The Open University. No previous knowledge of science has been assumed, and new concepts and specialist terminology are explained with examples and illustrations.

The book comprises nine chapters written by academic staff from the Open University Department of Life Sciences, together with other professionals in the autism field. The titles of the chapters reflect the multidisciplinary nature of this book and the wide range of topics related to autism. Chapter 1 considers milestones in the history of autism, including developments in research, diagnosis, clinical practice and public understanding which have influenced how the concept of autism has evolved since its first description in 1943. The chapter also explains some key scientific methods and principles used in autism research and practice. Chapters 2 to 8 all deal with theory, research, and practical issues in the recent and contemporary period. The topics range from psychological and biological explanations of autism to diagnosis, intervention and family life. Chapter 9, the concluding chapter, reflects on the key themes and issues that have emerged, and looks forward to some of the challenges that lie ahead in the autism field. In such a wide ranging and complex subject area, we have had to be selective, and we have sought to balance a solid foundation in background and issues, with accessible explanations of relevant methods and approaches, and introductions to the most recent work.

A huge amount of information about autism is available from newspapers and magazines, as well as online via databases and other resources, but it is often difficult to know whether it has been carefully checked for authenticity and accuracy. The information in this book, by contrast, is drawn from reliable and authoritative sources. These include scientific articles which have been through the peer scrutiny system known as 'refereeing', textbooks and chapters by experts in the autism field, and material from specialist organisations such as the American Psychiatric Association and the UK National Autistic Society. Personal accounts by individuals on the spectrum also play a very important role in understanding autism, and the book quotes extensively from such material.

Throughout this book you will be engaging with information about the autism spectrum. You will be invited, for instance, to consider descriptions of the characteristic symptoms, difficulties and skills presented by people with autism, to relate these to diagnostic criteria, to try out examples of test items used by researchers and clinicians, and to reflect on the value of different interventions. If people on the autism spectrum are part of your work, family or social life, or if you are yourself on the autism spectrum, we certainly encourage you to build upon the insights you will gain from this book. However, it is very important to remember that the book alone does not equip you to make diagnostic judgements, or to take specialist decisions about topics such as intervention and care. As you will see, these are fields which involve experienced professionals, very often working in teams, in collaboration with affected families and individuals.

The special format and presentation of the material in this book is designed to encourage active engagement with the subject matter, develop your understanding and confidence, and provide a stepping stone to further study. At various points in the text you will find material in boxes. Boxes are used for purposes such as accessible overviews of key concepts, research methods and studies, case studies and other special topics. Throughout the text you will also notice terms displayed in **bold**. These key terms are the most important terms in the text. Quite a number of them come up repeatedly (though only in bold when they first appear), and they are also in bold in the index at the end of the book. Understanding of these terms is essential (i.e. assessable) for Open University students. To assist all readers in their assimilation of these terms, a glossary of definitions is provided for Open University students via the course website, and for other readers, via the Jessica Kingsley Publishers website at: http://www.jkp.com/catalogue/book/9781849050876/resources/. A list of further reading and other autism-related resources is available via both websites.

Active engagement is further encouraged by numerous 'in text' questions, indicated by a purple square (■) with the answers directly below, marked by an open square (□). It is good practice always to cover the answer and attempt your own response to the question before reading ours. Many chapters also contain activities to help you reflect on particular issues, and/or to explore them more widely. Where relevant, comments on these activities are provided at the end of the book. Each chapter includes a summary of key points after each section, and at the end of the chapter, a list of the main learning outcomes, followed by self-assessment questions to enable you to test your own learning. The answers to these questions are at the end of the book.

Authors' acknowledgements

As ever in The Open University, this book combines the efforts of many people with specialist skills and knowledge in different disciplines. The Open University authors, Ilona Roth, Rosa Hoekstra and Terry Whatson, who were joined by Greg Pasco (Research Associate, Autism Research Centre, University of Cambridge) and Chris Barson (Consultant, The National Autistic Society), would like to acknowledge the critical comments of their colleague Claire Rothwell (Science) and the additional critical feedback from parents, and others with specialist knowledge, all of whom made numerous comments and suggestions for improvements. We are most grateful to our External Assessor, Professor Aline-Wendy Dunlop, Lead Director, National Centre for Autism Studies, University of Strathclyde, whose detailed comments and evaluations have made important contributions to the book, and have kept the needs of our intended readership to the fore.

Special thanks are due to all those involved in the production process, especially Anisha Davé, our excellent course manager, whose outstanding commitment and efficiency, and unflagging good humour sustained us throughout the endeavour, and who was ably assisted by course team assistant, Yvonne Royals. We also warmly acknowledge the contributions of Bina Sharma (editor), Jon Owen (graphic artist), Chris Hough (graphic designer), Martin Keeling (picture research and rights clearance) and Corinne Owen (media assistant). Judith Pickering (media project manager), coordinated the production process.

For the copublication process, we would especially like to thank Helen Ibbotson of Jessica Kingsley Publishers and, from within The Open University, David Vince (Copublishing). As is the custom, any small errors or shortcomings that have slipped in (despite our collective best efforts) remain the responsibility of the authors. We would be pleased to receive feedback on the book. Please write to Dr Ilona Roth at the address below.

Dr Ilona Roth, SK124 Course Team Chair
Department of Life Sciences
The Open University
Walton Hall
Milton Keynes
MK7 6AA
United Kingdom

Contents

Chapter 1 Autism: an evolving concept

Ilona Roth

1.1 Introduction

Alison was a happy, chubby lively little girl, totally dependent on us for all her needs. Living in a world of her own, she took little notice of her surroundings, but was used to the routine we had formed. We noticed that she would constantly rock herself backwards and forwards, and seemed to get some sort of relief from this … because she responded to music, the radio used to please her, and the record player was in constant use.

(Betty Cole writing about Alison aged 3, born in the 1950s, 1987, p. 3)

During our first hour on the road, Elijah rifled through hundreds of stickers I had brought along to keep him busy in the car. He feverishly peeled them and pasted them onto a large piece of cardboard like a small machine with his strict and narrow concentration. In the rear-view mirror, I saw the waxy paper backings of the stickers piling up in the back seat like fluffy patches of snow surrounding him. When he had peeled the very last sticker from its paper he let out a screech. Quickly, I popped the Pinocchio soundtrack into the tape player to redirect him, but to my dismay, I had forgotten to rewind it.

… 'REEE…WIND' he bellowed when he suddenly heard Pinocchio's voice singing mid-song.

(Valerie Paradiž writing about Elijah, aged 5, 2002, p. 132)

Jessy's social understanding remained, and remains, radically incomplete. Such simple lessons. 'We can't ask them to move because they were there first.' The difference between irritation and hurt feelings. Making sense of people, 'grasping the general significance of situations'. What the autistic adult, like the autistic child, finds hardest of all.

What is it like to have a mind that picks 'remembrance' out of the newspaper yet must struggle to comprehend the most ordinary vocabulary of social experience? What is it like to have to learn the myriad rules of human interaction by rote, one by one? By rote, because the criterion of 'how would I feel if' is unavailable, since so much of what pleases (or distresses) her, does not please others, so little of what pleases (or distresses) others pleases her.

(Clara Claiborne Park writing about Jessy, aged 42, 2001, pp. 16–17)

I must mention that the boy loved to watch the different calendars of different rooms and then recall the numbers. He also compared them. He thus spent a lot of time, gazing at the numbers. He wanted to know what they meant. He found a kind of pattern in them. He wondered how the figures bent and straightened up, curled and sometimes broke!

(Tito Mukhopadhyay aged 8, writing about himself as an infant, 2000, p. 19)

Words were no problem, but other people's expectations for me to respond to them were. This required my understanding what was said, but I was too happy losing myself to want to be dragged back by something as two-dimensional as understanding.

'What do you think you're doing?' came the voice.

Knowing I must respond in order to get rid of this annoyance, I would compromise, repeating 'What do you think you're doing?' addressed to no-one in particular.

(Donna Williams aged 29, writing about her childhood self, 1992, p. 9)

These extracts about children and adults with autistic conditions have been selected to provide a quick initial snapshot. Given the range and variety of behaviour you may be wondering how such different cases could possibly belong to the same group. If so, notice that there are also similarities: misunderstanding of, or isolation from the social world, unusual use of language, obsessions with particular sounds, sights or activities. Notice too that some of the accounts are written by parents. Even as they grow older, many people severely affected by autism seem to lack the capacity for self reflection and/or the communication skills necessary to describe their own experiences. Yet others, like Tito Mukhopadhyay and Donna Williams, communicate for themselves, and strikingly, describe their insights into their own condition.

Autism is of worldwide concern. Recent estimates suggest that as many as 1 in 100 children in the UK have a form of autism, while estimates for the USA are 1 in 150. In this book, you will learn about the characteristics of autism, and about how these vary between individuals and sub-groups. You will be introduced to the way in which people with autism make sense of the world around them, and to some of the underlying psychological and biological causes. You will consider the criteria by which experts diagnose the different variants of autism, and learn about the factors that influence the rising estimates of how many people have these conditions. You will also read about the effects of autism on the family and the implications for education and adult life. Box 1.1 introduces some key definitions and terms which you need to grasp before reading further.

Box 1.1 Key definitions and terms

People with **autism** have moderate to profound difficulties in communication and social interaction and show inflexibility and repetitiveness in their activities and interests. These three areas of difficulty, often known as the **triad of impairments** (see Figure 1.1), frequently go with other problems. For instance, people with autism may have **intellectual disability** (marked difficulty in tasks involving thinking, logical reasoning and problem solving), **sensory hypersensitivity** or **hyposensitivity** (heightened or reduced sensitivity to sounds, tastes, visual and other sensory stimuli) and/or **perceptual difficulties** (difficulty in making sense of sensory stimuli). People with autism may also have special interests and skills in highly specific areas such as memory for facts about dinosaurs. Autism quite often occurs together with another medical condition, especially **epilepsy**. This co-occurrence is known as **co-morbidity**.

The varying expression of these problems, depending on the individual, their age, the severity of their condition and other factors, means that autism is usually considered as a 'family' of sub-types – including **'classic autism'** the prototypical form, with full expression of the triad of impairments, and **Asperger syndrome (AS)**, a form with less pronounced communication difficulties, and intellectual abilities in the normal range. This variation between individuals and sub-types lends itself to the concept of an **autism spectrum**.

Unfortunately the appropriate terminology for talking about autism is not universally agreed. In general discussion the term autism is frequently used to mean both the spectrum as a whole, and one specific sub-type within this spectrum. In the context of diagnosis and clinical practice many specialists use the term **autism spectrum disorders (ASD)** to refer to the sub-types making up the autism spectrum. Some individuals on the spectrum and their families reject the implication that they have a disorder, as do some researchers. They favour the more neutral term **autism spectrum conditions (ASC)**, though others feel that this underplays the seriousness of autism.

The terms 'autistic individual' or 'autistic child' are also unacceptable to some, and the **National Autistic Society (NAS)** advocates 'person with autism', 'person on the autism spectrum', etc. However, others on the spectrum object equally to this 'people-first' language on the grounds that autism 'is not an appendage that can be separated from who we are as people, nor is it something shameful that has to be reduced to a sub-clause' (Sainsbury, 2000, p. 12).

Clearly there are no easy solutions to these 'labelling' issues! In this book, the terms 'autism' and 'the autism spectrum' will be used interchangeably to refer to the spectrum as a whole. Where specific sub-groups within the spectrum are being discussed, this will be made clear by using terms such as classic autism and Asperger syndrome. This book will also adopt the NAS guideline for 'people-first' language, wherever possible. When comparing the characteristics of children with autism with those of non-autistic children, as happens in many research studies, the term **typically developing children** will be used in preference to 'normal children', which carries the implication that the contrast group is 'abnormal'.

Epilepsy is a group of neurological disorders characterised by recurrent seizures, which reflect abnormal or excessive activity in one or more brain areas.

The National Autistic Society is an organisation for people with autism, their families and carers. It acts as a forum for exchange of ideas and information, pioneers national and international initiatives and raises public consciousness.

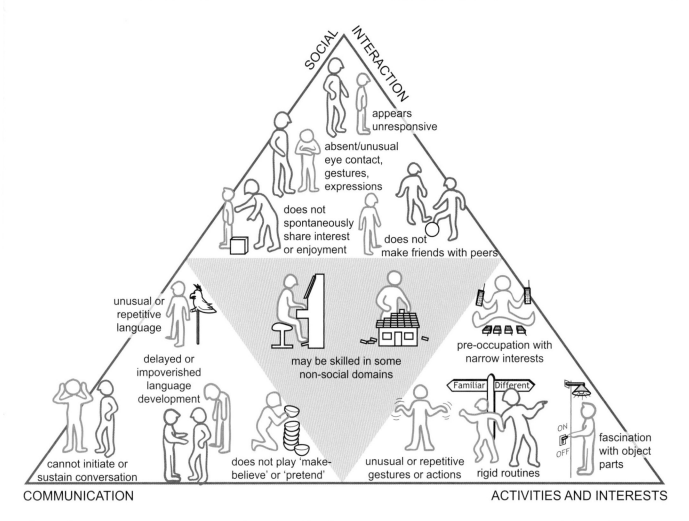

SOCIAL INTERACTION

appears unresponsive

absent/unusual eye contact, gestures, expressions

does not spontaneously share interest or enjoyment

does not make friends with peers

unusual or repetitive language

may be skilled in some non-social domains

pre-occupation with narrow interests

delayed or impoverished language development

Familiar   Different

cannot initiate or sustain conversation

does not play 'make-believe' or 'pretend'

unusual or repetitive gestures or actions

rigid routines

ON OFF

fascination with object parts

COMMUNICATION

ACTIVITIES AND INTERESTS

Figure 1.1 The triad of impairments in autism. Special skills in some domains (central triangle) are also quite common.

Figure 1.2 Dustin Hoffman gave a convincing performance as an individual with severe autism and special talents in *Rain Man*. (Photos 12/Alamy)

Hardly a day goes by without autism being mentioned in media. It has been the subject of several well-known films (such as *Rain Man* (1988): Figure 1.2) and books (e.g. *The Curious Incident of the Dog in the Night-Time* (Haddon, 2003)), and there has been intense speculation and controversy surrounding the claim that the **MMR** (measles, mumps and rubella) vaccine plays a role in causing autism.

If your ideas about autism are drawn largely from such sources, how accurate do you think they are? Of course, if you have first-hand contact with autism – perhaps you have a child or sibling with autism, work with people on the spectrum, or are on the spectrum yourself – you will have many ideas and insights. Even so, your views may be influenced by your particular experiences. Activity 1.1 offers you the opportunity to test and update your knowledge of the autism spectrum.

Activity 1.1 How much do you know about autism?
Allow 15 minutes for this activity

Decide what you think about each of the statements in Table 1.1. Some of them are known to be true or false, while for others the answer is uncertain even to the experts. Tick the answer that you think is most accurate or 'DK' if you really don't know. Answers and comments are at the end of the book.

		True	False	Uncertain	DK
1	Autism is more common in boys than girls.				
2	Autism can be caused by emotional deprivation.				
3	People with autism are all eccentric geniuses.				
4	Autism is on the increase.				
5	Autism has the same rate of occurrence worldwide.				
6	Autism can be detected before a child is 2 years old.				
7	People with autism don't easily understand other people's thoughts and feelings.				
8	Autism runs in families.				
9	There is a gene for autism.				
10	Autism can be caused by the MMR vaccine.				
11	A person with autism can grow out of it.				
12	People with autism all have below average intelligence.				
13	People with autism always prefer being alone.				

It is likely that you answered some questions correctly, but found others where you had misconceptions, or were unsure. If you answered all the questions correctly you already have some sound knowledge of autism. Whatever your performance in the quiz, the aim of this book is to enhance your understanding of the areas covered by the questions, and many others besides. You may like to return to Activity 1.1 later on, and see how you have updated your knowledge.

Continuing this learning journey, another question is whether autism has occurred throughout history. The answer is 'yes and no'. In one sense, it could be said that autism (let alone the autism spectrum) did not 'exist' before 1943, because that is the year when the condition was first identified as such. Without doubt though, before that date there were children and adults with the difficulties now known as autism. Some would have been supported by their families, but sadly many were probably in-patients in psychiatric hospitals.

Even after the first description of autism in 1943, ideas about what it means, and exactly to whom it applies have changed, and are still evolving. This chapter describes some key historical milestones, showing how developments in research, diagnosis, clinical practice and public understanding have all contributed to the evolution of the concept of autism. You may find some areas of discussion challenging when you first encounter them. But each of the milestones contributes important ideas and principles to the contemporary work on autism addressed in the rest of the book – the ideas will fall into place as you read later chapters.

1.1.1 Summary of Section 1.1

- Autism is characterised by a triad of impairments including difficulties in communication, social interaction and inflexibility and repetitiveness in activities and interests.

- People with autism may also have intellectual disability, sensory and perceptual difficulties and special interests and skills. A number of individuals have co-morbid conditions such as epilepsy.

- The varying expression and severity of these characteristics means that autism is differentiated into sub-types and also considered as a spectrum.

- Concepts of autism have evolved and opinions about terminology vary somewhat.

1.2   Leo Kanner, Hans Asperger and their syndromes

> Since 1938, there have come to our attention a number of children whose condition differs so markedly and uniquely from anything reported so far, that each case merits – and, I hope, will eventually receive – a detailed consideration of its fascinating peculiarities.
>
> *(Kanner, 1943)*

With these words, the child psychiatrist Leo Kanner (Box 1.2) introduced the first description of the condition that for almost seven decades has challenged and perplexed doctors, psychologists, families and individuals working and living with this problem.

In some ways Kanner's original idea of autism has proved remarkably accurate. But advances in research and clinical practice, especially since the

Figure 1.3   Leo Kanner (1894–1981). (US National Library of Medicine/Science Photo Library)

1980s, have generated many new insights into the nature and causes of autism, as well as improvements in **interventions** (techniques for helping people with conditions such as autism). Public understanding of autism has developed and with this has come an improvement in attitudes, and better provision for individuals with autism. Inevitably the concept itself has undergone considerable evolution.

Box 1.2 Leo Kanner

Leo Kanner (Figure 1.3) was born in Austria in 1894. He studied medicine at the University of Berlin, and emigrated to the USA in 1924. He pioneered the application of **psychiatry** (the branch of medicine that deals with the mind) to psychological disturbances in children, setting up the first child psychiatry service at the Johns Hopkins Hospital in Baltimore, and publishing the first English language textbook on child psychiatry in 1935.

Kanner's paper entitled 'Autistic disturbances of affective contact', published in 1943, comprised individual **case study** material drawn from careful observations of 11 children whose parents had sought his help.

Kanner's observations convinced him that there were some key patterns of behaviour which all the children shared in common. It was the first of these – the children's apparent aloofness and isolation from the human world – that led Kanner to coin the phrase 'autistic aloneness'. 'Autism' comes from the Greek word *autos*, meaning 'self', and means being absorbed into oneself. The term autism had previously been used by the psychiatrist Bleuler, but in relation to the different case of schizophrenia.

A case study involves in-depth observation and description of the specific characteristics of a selected individual. Pooling of case study material across individuals may permit identification of general features. The method is used by clinical practitioners, and in some forms of research.

The core features observed by Kanner are explained in Box 1.3.

Box 1.3 Kanner's core features of autism

Autistic aloneness

There is from the start an extreme autistic aloneness that, whenever possible, disregards, ignores, shuts out anything that comes to the child from the outside.

He has good relation to objects; he is interested in them, can play happily with them for hours ... The children's relation to people is altogether different. ... Profound aloneness dominates all behaviour.

(Kanner, 1943)

Narrowly restricted interests and desire for sameness

The child's noises and motions and all of his performances are as monotonously repetitious as are his verbal utterances. There is marked limitation in the variety of his spontaneous activities. The child's behaviour is governed by an anxiously obsessive desire for the maintenance of sameness.

(Kanner, 1943)

Language problems

Kanner noted problems ranging from '**mutism**' (absence of speech) to 'a kind of language that does not seem intended to serve interpersonal communication'. Other characteristics were **echolalia** and **pronoun reversal**: a child asking for a biscuit might simply echo his parent's question, using 'Do you want a biscuit' to make the request, and making no attempt to substitute 'I' for 'you'. Children with better developed language and vocabulary would tend to use it monotonously and repetitively, taking no account of whether the topic was of relevance to others.

Islets of ability

By this Kanner meant isolated areas of special skill: for instance, in memorising words or pictures, or doing mental arithmetic.

For Kanner, working within the framework of medical psychiatry, the shared features of the children's behaviour were indicative of a **syndrome**, a specific disorder with a characteristic set of **symptoms** (observable characteristics that may indicate a clinical problem or disorder). Even today his descriptions of autism remain remarkably fresh and up to date. What has changed, however, is the interpretation of the substantial variation in the expression and severity of the key symptoms between different individuals. Rather than representing a single unified condition, autism is now considered as a range or spectrum of problems. Curiously, evidence consistent with this rather different interpretation can be found in the observations of another Austrian-born doctor, Hans Asperger (Box 1.4), working in Vienna during the same period as Kanner was active in the USA.

Figure 1.4 Hans Asperger (1906–1980). (Asperger Estate)

Box 1.4 Hans Asperger

Hans Asperger (Figure 1.4) was born in Austria in 1906. He studied medicine in Vienna, and eventually specialised in **paediatrics** (the specialist branch of medicine dealing with children). He joined the staff of the University Paediatric Clinic, which treated psychologically disturbed children through 'remedial pedagogy', an intervention combining medical and educational principles. A child's medical problems (e.g. the effects of brain damage or epilepsy on mental function) were always evaluated and addressed, alongside a daily routine of educational, creative and physical activities. Asperger eventually became clinic director, working with Sister Viktorine Zak, a gifted nurse and teacher, who was tragically killed when the clinic was bombed in 1944.

Like Kanner, Asperger observed a particular symptom pattern among some of his child patients. In a paper published in 1944, just one year after Kanner's, he called this 'autistic psychopathy' (Asperger, 1944). 'Autistic', as for Kanner, referred to the children's aloneness and self-absorption, while by 'psychopathy' Asperger meant a psychiatric disorder affecting the personality.

These days, two clinical scientists such as Kanner and Asperger would almost certainly be aware of each other's work. But in the environment of war-torn Europe, it is not so surprising that they were unknown to each other. If Kanner came to know of Asperger's work later, he never acknowledged it, whereas Asperger published a paper in 1979 in which he referred to Kanner's. Kanner quickly achieved international recognition, while Asperger's work was not widely known outside Austria until the 1980s, when the psychiatrist Lorna Wing highlighted the remarkable similarity between his and Kanner's clinical observations (Wing, 1981).

Asperger's key features were essentially the same as Kanner's listed in Box 1.3, and the two also agreed on some additional features listed in Box 1.5 (adapted from Wing, 1991).

Box 1.5 Additional features observed by both Kanner and Asperger

Both conditions involve:

- presence in many more boys than girls
- lack of imaginative play
- atypical eye-gaze, gesture and other 'non-verbal' forms of communication
- atypical reactions to sensory stimuli such as extreme sensitivity to noise, and obsession with the texture of materials
- clumsy movements, though special skills show dexterity
- behavioural problems including aggressive and destructive tendencies.

Yet the children described by Asperger seemed less disabled. They were more likely to have developed fluent speech and vocabulary, even if they used it oddly. Asperger used to refer to them as 'little professors' because of their tendency to talk at length about their favourite topic or interest. Rather than seeming unaware of the existence of others, their reactions to others appeared strange and antisocial.

Note that the extent of this discrepancy may have been accentuated by the two clinicians' different perspectives and methods. Kanner emphasised the disabling features of the children's behaviour, while Asperger is said to have seen something of himself in the personality and behaviour of his patients, and believed that their development might have positive outcomes.

Several children, whose progress Asperger followed into adult life, were gifted individuals, who achieved outstanding success. One, Elfriede Jelinek, was awarded the Nobel Prize in Literature and another became a brilliant scientist:

> Even as a toddler, one could see in him a most unusual and spontaneous mathematical talent. Through persistent questioning of adults he acquired all the necessary knowledge from which he worked independently. ... Not long after the start of his university studies, reading theoretical astronomy, he proved a mathematical error in Newton's work. ... In an exceptionally short time he became an assistant professor at the Department of Astronomy.

> *(Asperger, 1944, translated by Frith, 1991, pp. 88–89)*

Kanner also conducted **follow-up studies**, in which he documented how 96 of his child patients had developed by their twenties and thirties (Kanner, 1973). Twelve had made reasonably good social adjustments – one, a successful music composer, was married with a child. So while Kanner's group seems to have mainly comprised profoundly affected children, and Asperger's group were predominantly less disabled, there was also an overlap between the two groups.

■　Why are both the similarities and differences between Kanner's and Asperger's accounts important?

☐　The similarities suggest a common factor underlying the disorders described by Kanner and by Asperger. The differences suggest that the disorders are not exactly the same.

To conclude, Kanner and Asperger were apparently dealing with 'variants on a theme'. This established an initial basis for the modern idea of a spectrum including sub-types such as Asperger syndrome. But, as you will see, it was to be another 40 years before the ideas of spectrum and sub-types really replaced the single syndrome approach.

1.2.1　Summary of Section 1.2

• In 1943, Leo Kanner published the first account of autism, based on 11 case studies of children.

• Kanner identified 'autistic aloneness', narrow, obsessive and repetitive interests, problems with language and 'islets of ability' as core features.

• Kanner interpreted his findings as a syndrome, a specific disorder with a characteristic set of symptoms.

• In his 1944 paper, Asperger outlined a syndrome (autistic psychopathy) that both resembled and differed from Kanner's.

• Forty years on, the range among Kanner's and Asperger's cases was reinterpreted in terms of a spectrum and sub-types including Asperger syndrome.

1.3   Biology and environment: early views of the causes of autism

> We must then assume that these children have come into the world with **innate** inability to form the usual, biologically provided **affective** contact with people, just as other children come into the world with innate physical or intellectual handicaps.
>
> *(Kanner, 1943) (bold added by present author)*

Innate refers to a characteristic that is present at birth – usually, by implication, something that is inherited. Affective means emotional.

■   What views do you think Kanner is expressing here about the way typically developing infants form emotional bonds with others, and the reasons why children with autism fail to form them? Think carefully about this before reading on.

☐   When Kanner made this claim, he clearly believed that typically developing infants are already biologically equipped at birth to form emotional relationships with their care-givers. This means that after birth, mechanisms in the infant's brain and other parts of the nervous system spontaneously trigger certain behaviours which promote the development of interaction with other humans.

There is much evidence to support this view of typical development. For instance, experiments suggest that newborn babies have a preference for human faces: they look for much longer at a schematic human face than at a set of scrambled human features, or an abstract pattern. They also prefer the sound of a human voice to other sounds. Such actions initiated by the newborn infant evoke corresponding responses from the mother, and so mutual interactions between mother and baby begin to unfold. Kanner also believed that children with autism are born without this propensity for bonding – their impaired ability to relate to others is there from the start of life, and is caused by a disruption of biological mechanisms, not by the context or environment in which the child develops.

Though Kanner initially favoured this biologically oriented explanation, he was puzzled by his observation that some of the mothers of the autistic children in his care seemed emotionally and socially detached and what he came to term 'refrigerator mothers'. At this time (1940s and 1950s) **Freudian psychoanalysis** was becoming very popular in the USA. This theory, based on the work of Sigmund Freud, saw children's personalities as strongly influenced by their early experiences with their parents. Kanner began to consider that, rather than being biologically vulnerable, children became autistic as a form of withdrawal from the emotional coldness of their mothers – in other words, as a result of their social environment. Although he later retracted this idea, it was enthusiastically promoted by the psychoanalyst Bruno Bettelheim, another Austrian, who fled from the Nazis to settle in the USA. In the 1960s Bettelheim practised a treatment in which children with autism were separated from their parents to live in a special 'therapeutic' environment, designed along psychoanalytic lines. He described apparently dramatic improvements in the emotional adjustment, speech and behaviour of children treated in this way (Bettelheim, 1967). But it is now known that Bettelheim's claims were unsound.

A visitor to Bettelheim's centre in the 1970s stated:

> There were locked doors everywhere – it is claimed, 'to keep the world out' – and I caught only a brief glimpse of a pupil … For the first year the child is completely separated from his parents, and after that only limited visiting is allowed – perhaps 2 or 3 times a year.

(Roth, personal communication)

The views of Bettelheim and other psychoanalysts about the causes of autism, and the treatment regime that Bettelheim pioneered were profoundly distressing to parents. They came to believe that they were responsible for their children's autism, and the sense of shame, guilt and stigma that they experienced stayed with them, not only during the period when psychoanalysis was at its height, but in some cases for decades afterwards.

■ What alternative explanations might there be for Kanner's and Bettelheim's reports of emotional coldness in the mothers of their patients?

☐ One possibility is that Kanner and Bettelheim were observing the *consequences* of trying to care for a profoundly disturbed child. Some parents are known to become depressed by the burden this places on them. Another possibility is that atypical emotional and social responses in parents reflect mild or attenuated autistic tendencies – an idea that will be further explored later in this book.

1.3.1   Summary of Section 1.3

* Kanner initially proposed that autism was due to an innate impairment in the infant's ability to form social and emotional bonds with his or her parents. This explanation of autism emphasises biological factors.
* Observations that some mothers seemed socially and emotionally detached led Kanner to reformulate his theory in line with psychoanalytical accounts of child development.
* The theory that autism is caused by the child's withdrawal from emotionally deficient parenting, and is therefore 'environmental', was promoted by Bruno Bettelheim.
* Bettelheim's 'therapy', based on isolating children with autism from their parents, caused stigma and distress to families, and is now discredited.

1.4   Parents fight back

It is easy to imagine the despair of parents who were not only told that their child was autistic, but were also led to believe that they might be responsible. Fortunately some parents, in both the USA and the UK, had the determination, insight and strength of character to challenge this view. One of the most influential was the American psychologist Bernard Rimland (Box 1.6).

Box 1.6 Bernard Rimland

Bernard Rimland's first child Mark, born in 1956, was very difficult from an early age. He screamed constantly and could not be comforted or placated. Autism was still little known. Since paediatricians expressed themselves baffled, Rimland worked through available textbooks himself and concluded that his son was autistic, a diagnosis that was subsequently confirmed.

Knowing that his own wife was an affectionate parent, Rimland set about assembling scientific and medical evidence to challenge Bettelheim's approach, publishing his own biological theory of causation. He devoted his life's work to exploring the causes of autism, and acting as advocate for children with autism.

In 1962, a group of 12 British parents of children with autism launched the society that in 1965 became the National Autistic Society. Rimland founded the Autism Society of America in the same year. The British group also joined forces with a gifted teacher Sybil Elgar, who had pioneered a method for teaching children with autism, centring on a structured environment, clear and straightforward communication, and use of visual aids. Together (also in 1965) they founded The Sybil Elgar School, the first of several National Autistic Society residential schools. The Society itself has flourished over the years, becoming a major source of information, advice, services and resources for all those with a personal or professional involvement with the autism spectrum.

The National Autistic Society and the Autism Society of America are now joined by others such as the Scottish Society for Autism. Each has an official website, which you will easily find by entering the name into a search engine. Activity 1.2 provides an opportunity to explore, or to extend your current knowledge of, one or more autism societies of your choice.

Activity 1.2 Exploring the work of an autism society
Allow 30 minutes for this activity

Spend about 30 minutes exploring one of the three autism societies above or another one of your choice, and list five different ways in which these societies are involved in supporting people with autism and their families. Comments are at the end of the book.

1.4.1 Summary of Section 1.4

- Rimland's experiences with his own child led him to mount a scientific challenge to Bettelheim's theory and to found the Autism Society of America.

- A group of British parents founded the National Autistic Society in 1965 and together with Sybil Elgar, the first residential school for children with autism.

- Sybil Elgar's educational approach involved a structured environment, clear and straightforward communication and visual aids.

1.5 Experimental studies of psychological processes in autism

Sybil Elgar's teaching methods were guided by years of experience, and also by profound intuitive insights into the behaviour and psychological processes of children with autism. But psychologists soon recognised the need to study these processes using **systematic methods**; that is, studies in which the conclusions are derived from careful objective evaluation of evidence following scientific principles. One of the most widely employed systematic research methods in psychology is the **experiment** used to gain insights into how people remember information, attend to things, recognise people's faces – in other words, how they process information from the environment (Box 1.7).

Box 1.7 Basic principles of experimental research

Consider the following simplified example. Children on the autism spectrum are often good at repeating back what they have heard, and at remembering lists of things. Some people might claim that this indicates 'good memory' in autism. What does this claim mean and how could it be verified? The goal of experiments is to put such claims to a critical test – otherwise people may adopt misguided or unfounded beliefs about autism.

The first step is to formulate a **hypothesis**. This is a statement that one **variable** (in this case having an autistic condition or not) is linked to another (in this case memory ability). To test this hypothesis, you would need to make a prediction about how children with autism will perform on a memory test. You would then need to make a 'fair' comparison of the memory performance of a group of **participants** (volunteers) with a diagnosis of autism, with another 'comparable' group of typically developing children. The first group is termed the **experimental group** and the second group the **control group**. You would need to arrange for all participants in both groups to take part in a test of memory: for instance, seeing or hearing a list of words and recalling them after an interval. The number of words recalled by each child provides a measure of their memory recall. From this you can calculate the **average** score for

---

A variable is something that varies, either along a dimension, such as height or weight, or from one group to another, such as gender (male or female) or eye colour (blue or brown).

An average is the single 'middle' value used to represent a set of observations or measurements. Most often the average is the **mean** of the measurements, calculated by adding all the measurements together and dividing by the number of measurements taken.

the group with autism and compare it with the average score for the control group.

- ■ In this experiment all participants saw or heard the same words. Why do you think this was so?

- □ If some children have a slightly easier list of words to remember than others, this could mask any other differences you are trying to observe. In experiments where different participants receive different lists, the lists need to be carefully matched for characteristics such as word length and familiarity.

- ■ Suppose that, on average, the participants in the experimental (autism) group recalled more words: could you then conclude that this group had better memory for words lists?

- □ No, such a difference could also occur purely by chance.

All experiments therefore involve using **statistical tests** designed to evaluate the **probability** (mathematical odds) that an observed result has occurred by chance alone. A result that is highly unlikely to have occurred by chance is said to be **statistically significant**. If your carefully controlled experiment yields a statistically significant result, you can conclude, with some confidence, that your prediction about memory performance has been confirmed.

- ■ Could you conclude from such a result that children with autism have good memory skills?

- □ Only in terms of the specific type of task they have undertaken. Children with autism might still perform poorly on other tests, as Box 1.8 illustrates.

Some of the first experimental studies of autism were conducted in the 1970s by the psychologists Beate Hermelin and Neil O'Connor (Figure 1.5), who developed a framework for studying many aspects of sensory, perceptual and memory processing (Hermelin and O'Connor, 1970).

Figure 1.5 Beate Hermelin (1919–2007) and Neil O'Connor (1917–1997). (Uta Frith)

An illustrative experiment is summarised in Box 1.8.

Box 1.8 A memory experiment illustrating Hermelin and O'Connor's approach

Hermelin and O'Connor compared children with autism and control participants on their ability to recall sequences of eight words which were either randomly ordered such as 'day-she-farm-when-cat-fall-back-rake', or sequences in which four of the eight words formed a sentence such as 'read-them-your-book', and four were random, such as 'way-spoon-here-like'. The results showed that the groups of participants recalled, on average, the same numbers of words from the randomly ordered strings. However, the typically developing children were significantly better at recalling words that formed a sentence than at recalling randomly ordered words. This was because they were taking advantage of the meaningful relationships among the words to aid their recall. The children with autism appeared oblivious of the meaningful relationships between some of the words: they tended to recall the last words in each presented sequence, whether the sequence was all random, or included a meaningful sentence.

From findings such as these, Hermelin and O'Connor concluded that memory in autistic children is not poorer than in controls if judged purely in terms of the amount of items they can recall: indeed children with autism may have enhanced word for word recall of information – sometimes known as **rote memory** – as in the imaginary experiment in Box 1.7. Yet their memory functions inefficiently, in that it is not structured or guided by meaning. In everyday life we rarely recall information 'verbatim'; rather, we select and structure our recall in terms of the overall meaning or 'gist' of the original information, omitting unnecessary detail.

■ In what sorts of everyday memory tasks would an inability to structure and select by meaning be a disadvantage?

☐ Many! Think of trying to explain the theme of a story or film to someone else, recalling the important bits of a television news report, or revising material you have studied for an exam.

The echolalia observed in the speech of children with autism may occur precisely because they are 'echoing back' words or phrases they have just heard, rather than responding to their meaning.

1.5.1 Summary of Section 1.5

• The experiment is a widely used systematic method for studying psychological processes in people with autism.

- Experiments involve testing hypotheses. They may compare the performance of different groups of participants on the same task and/or the performance of the same participants on different tasks.

- Key stages in an experiment include comparing performance of participant groups on a task, and establishing whether predicted differences are statistically significant.

- Hermelin and O'Connor's experimental studies of memory highlighted autism-specific characteristics of preserved or even enhanced rote memory skills, coupled with difficulties in tasks relying on processing of meaning.

1.6   The first genetic study

You saw in Section 1.3 that having introduced the term 'refrigerator mothers', Kanner came for a time to agree with Bettelheim's psychoanalytical interpretation of this phenomenon. Interestingly, in Kanner's original case reports, he noted a lack of 'warm-heartedness' in both the fathers and mothers of many of the children, as well as in some other family members. His subsequent selective focus on emotional detachment in mothers does suggest that his interpretations of his case notes may have been influenced by the theories popular at the time. Asperger interpreted unusual personality characteristics in both fathers and mothers quite differently. He saw them as **autistic traits** indicating that the propensity to develop autism is **genetic**; that is, it is transmitted from one generation to another via the genes, and is therefore likely to 'run in families', rather than being purely due to influences in the child's environment.

It is impossible to decide between such different interpretations of why autism occurs without gathering systematic evidence. Another important scientific method, involving comparisons of twins, was first applied to autism by Susan Folstein and Sir Michael Rutter (Figure 1.6) in 1978. See Box 1.9.

Autistic traits are psychological or personality characteristics typically associated with autism, such as being withdrawn, emotionally detached, or obsessed with particular objects or interests. They do not necessarily mean that the person meets the criteria for autism.

Figure 1.6   Sir Michael Rutter (b. 1933), a child psychiatrist, has been a leading pioneer in autism research since the 1960s as well as an expert on many other developmental difficulties. (Sir Michael Rutter)

Box 1.9   Folstein and Rutter's twin study of autism

The **twin method** involves measuring how frequently a particular condition or characteristic – autism in this case – co-occurs in identical twins as compared with non-identical twins. Identical twins originate from a single fertilised egg, and therefore have identical genes. Non-identical twins come from two different fertilised eggs. On average non-identical twins share 50% of their genes in common, and in this respect are no different from any two non-twin siblings within a family. Suppose that autism is diagnosed, not just in one member of a twin pair, but in both twins. This twin pair is then said to show **concordance** for autism. The proportion of cases in which twin pairs are concordant for autism is known as the **concordance rate**. If this proportion is much higher for identical twins than for the non-identical twins, this provides strong evidence that the characteristic being investigated has a genetic basis. The logic of this is that what differs between identical and non-identical twins is whether their genetic material is identical or not: it is assumed that the kinds of environment to which twins are likely to be exposed within their family will not vary much according to whether the twins are identical or not. So any differences in the patterns of concordance between the two types of twins can be attributed to genetic not environmental factors.

Folstein and Rutter (1978) investigated 21 same-sex pairs of twins, including 11 identical pairs, and 10 non-identical pairs, between the ages of 5 and 23. The basis for selecting these pairs was that one or both twins were known to have autism. Diagnoses were independently checked for all 42 individuals in the study. Of the 11 identical pairs, 4 were concordant for classic autism. Of the 10 non-identical pairs, none was concordant for classic autism. So the concordance rate was 36% for the identical twins and 0% for the non-identical twins. In addition, the estimated concordance rose considerably when the twins unaffected by classic autism were scrutinised for autistic-type symptoms or traits, such as language and social difficulties. On this looser criterion of concordance, there was concordance in a further 5 identical twin pairs, bringing the total concordance to 9 out of 11, or 82%, for identical twins; one non-identical twin pair also met this looser criterion, bringing total concordance to 1 out of 10, or 10% for non-identical twins.

This pattern of results is depicted in Figure 1.7.

■ Why was it important that the non-identical twins were the same sex?

☐ There are two reasons. One is that many more males than females are diagnosed with autism and so mixing that variable into the study complicates things unnecessarily. Secondly, and more importantly, the assumption of a shared environment may be invalid for twins of different sexes. The boy and the girl of a different-sex twin pair are quite likely to be treated somewhat differently, and therefore to occupy different 'environments' within the family.

Two important conclusions arise from this classic study. First, the high level of concordance for the identical twins, compared with that for the non-identical twins points strongly to a genetic influence in autism.

Secondly the study supports the view that autism is not invariably expressed in the same way or to the same degree in different individuals. The finding that some of the twins had autistic-like traits, without meeting all the criteria for autism, is consistent with the idea that autism is not a single syndrome, but a spectrum, with mildly affected individuals at the boundary of the spectrum.

■ If there is a genetic factor in autism, why is the concordance for identical twins not 100%? And why are there twin pairs where one is more severely affected with autism than the other?

	identical twins 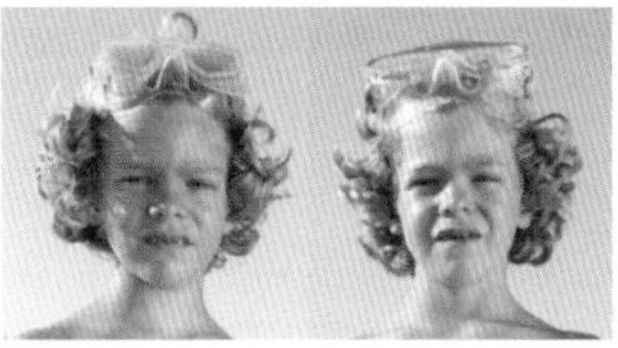	non-identical twins 
classic autism in both twins		
concordance	4 twin pairs out of 11 = 36%	0 twin pairs out of 10 = 0%
classic autism in one twin; language and social difficulties in other twin		
concordance	5 twin pairs out of 11 = 46%	1 twin pair out of 10 = 10%
non-concordant pairs, i.e. classic autism in one twin, typical development in other twin		
total concordance	9 (4+5) twin pairs out of 11 = 82%	1 (0+1) twin pair out of 10 = 10%

Figure 1.7   Visual representation of the patterns of concordance across all twin pairs. (Photos: Daniel Attia/Corbis; Photolibrary)

□   The answer to these questions is still not fully understood. The way in which the same genetic propensities are expressed in different individuals depends on complex factors including gene penetrance. Subtle environmental influences may also play a role here.

By 1978, the year of Folstein and Rutter's study, a number of other studies had reported the occurrence of epilepsy in a proportion of people with autism. All these findings together strongly implicated biological factors in autism, though, as the last in-text question shows, the mechanisms involved are clearly complex.

1.6.1   Summary of Section 1.6

• Kanner's and Asperger's contrasting interpretations of personality characteristics in parents demonstrate the need for objective scientific evaluation of the role of genetics and environment in autism.

- Folstein and Rutter pioneered the use of the twin method to compare concordance for autism in identical and non-identical twins.

- Concordance, the proportion of cases in which a characteristic present in one member of a twin pair is also present in the other member, was much higher for identical twins, especially when autistic-like traits in twins without an autism diagnosis were included.

- This study provides strong evidence that genetic factors, together with other biological influences, play a central role in the causes of autism. The study also supports the idea of an autism spectrum.

1.7   Early interventions for children with autism

With the rejection of Bettelheim's theory, and growing recognition during the 1960s and 1970s, that autism has a biological basis, you might imagine that clinicians aiming to help people with autism would have developed 'biological' interventions. In practice, progress in this area has been very limited, for reasons further discussed in Chapter 6. Another seemingly obvious focus would be to tackle the problems underlying difficulty in communication and social interaction in people with autism. Yet one of the most influential early developments in therapeutic intervention was based on the idea that people with autism have acquired, through learning, a set of 'maladaptive' or inappropriate behaviours, which can be eradicated or 'retrained'. The basis for this approach is introduced in Box 1.10.

Box 1.10   Learning theory and behaviour modification

This approach is grounded in Burrhus Frederick Skinner's influential 1960s theory about how both animals and humans learn new behaviours. He argued that spontaneous behaviour can be 'shaped' or modified using a principle known as **reinforcement**. Suppose that a child with autism who habitually plays with his food, squashing bits of it all over the meal table, one day picks up a knife and fork and eats 'normally'. His mother promptly rewards him by praising him and allowing him extra time on a favourite computer game. The next day the child does the same, and receives more praise and more computer time. In learning theory terms, the child is learning to modify his behaviour, in order to obtain **positive reinforcement** (effectively a reward) from his mother.

Take a slightly different example. A child with autism is constantly disruptive and unruly in his classroom. Every time he behaves like this, his teacher stops what she is doing to reprimand him, thus focusing attention on his behaviour, which gets no better. Closer analysis of the situation suggests that the child is gaining positive reinforcement from his unruly behaviour, because it is gaining him some attention. The teacher starts ignoring him when he behaves badly, and over time the behaviour ceases. The teacher starts rewarding him with praise for sitting quietly and attending to the lesson. Notice that this change does not involve punishing the child's bad behaviour.

These examples illustrate the technique of **behaviour modification**, whereby established principles of learning can be harnessed to influence and improve a child's behaviour. The psychologist Ivar Lovaas pioneered the application of these techniques to modifying difficult and disruptive behaviour in children with autism, and to develop behaviours such as spoken responses in children with little language.

■ Behaviour modification focuses on modifying a child's *existing* behaviour. How does this constrain its usefulness in relation to autism?

□ If the desired behaviour is something that a child has never enacted, such as speaking a few words, then using positive reinforcement to shape the child's existing behaviour will not achieve the desired goal. Another problem is that it is the therapist (sometimes an experienced parent) who decides what is desirable or not. For instance, the therapist might decide that continuous hand flapping is socially undesirable and needs to be eradicated, even if the child finds it soothing or pleasurable.

Some practitioners are sceptical about the value of behaviour modification, arguing that it does not address the underlying psychological difficulties that cause the behavioural symptoms of autism. Nonetheless, the technique is still in use, and the basic principles have been incorporated into other approaches which seek to tackle the core problems more directly. You will read more about this in Chapter 6.

1.7.1   Summary of Section 1.7

• An intervention for autism, developed in the 1960s, involves behaviour modification using positive reinforcement of desired behaviour.

• This procedure can be helpful in shaping behaviours of children on the autism spectrum, but its efficacy as an intervention for core problems in autism is contended.

1.8   The first diagnostic criteria for autism

Despite the rapid proliferation of research and clinical work after Kanner, for 40 years there was no universally agreed definition of autism. Consequently, there was little consensus on diagnosis, the process of applying agreed criteria to identify individuals who come within a clinical category, and to differentiate them reliably from those who don't. By 1956 Kanner, with his colleague Leon Eisenberg, had reduced the essential defining symptoms of autism to just two: 'extreme aloneness' and 'preoccupation with the preservation of sameness'. During the 1960s, other variants emerged: for instance, omitting preservation of sameness as a key feature, including perceptual disturbances, or re-emphasising language disturbances. Suppose that two specialists are asked to identify which of a group of children have autism. One specialist includes children who show sensory disturbances, while the other does not.

■ Why is this problematic?

☐ The specialists are using different inclusion criteria, and it is therefore possible that they will have different children in their 'autism' group. In a real-life setting this could have serious consequences, for instance determining whether or not parents have access to support and help.

For accuracy and clarity of communication in research, and for sound clinical practice, specialists must work with agreed definitions of medical and psychiatric conditions. This involves panels of experts working together, usually over a period of years, to reach consensus on **diagnostic criteria**; that is, symptoms or features that an individual must have for the condition to be diagnosed, and sometimes additional symptoms that should not be present. Once agreed, diagnostic criteria are published as the authoritative guidelines; the most widely used being the **Diagnostic and Statistical Manual of Mental Disorders (DSM)** published by the American Psychiatric Association, and the **International Classification of Diseases (ICD)**, published by the World Health Organisation.

When the first and second editions of the DSM were published in 1952 and 1968, respectively, autism did not appear as a diagnostic category in its own right. Instead, it was included under the heading of 'childhood schizophrenia', a misleading label since it implied that autism involves a psychotic withdrawal from the world, and hallucinations, both symptoms of schizophrenia. In the third edition, DSM-III, published in 1980, formal criteria for autism were included (see Table 1.2). Notice that the criteria appear within a hierarchy or tree. At the top level is the broad heading of 'developmental disorders'. Under this are three different sub-categories. One of these, **pervasive developmental disorders (PDD)**, is an 'umbrella' term for conditions characterised by difficulties in communication, social interaction and range of activities and interests.

'Pervasive' means that the difficulties embrace many key aspects of development, rather than just a specific developmental capacity such as language or reading.

Infantile autism and its specific criteria appear as a sub-listing under this heading. This hierarchical arrangement therefore represented the first formal recognition that autism might have different variants.

Table 1.2 DSM-III classification of autism.

The term mental retardation has been used in the USA, and some other parts of the world, with essentially the same meaning as intellectual disability (see Box 1.1). The term mental retardation is no longer in use in the UK.

Developmental disorders		
Mental retardation	**Specific developmental disorder**	**Pervasive developmental disorders (PDD)**
		Infantile autism: Lack of responsiveness to others Language absent or abnormal Resistance to change/attachment to objects Absence of schizophrenic features Onset before 30 months

Note that the three first DSM-III criteria for infantile autism broadly correspond with three of Kanner's original core features (see Box 1.3): lack of responsiveness to others is similar to Kanner's autistic aloneness, though it is a less broad criterion. Language problems appear in both Kanner's features and DSM-III, and resistance to change and attachment to objects also echo Kanner. The main differences are that DSM-III has an exclusion criterion designed to discriminate autistic disorder from childhood schizophrenia, and makes no mention of Kanner's 'islets of ability'.

■ Why do you think that 'islets of ability' are not picked up in the DSM-III criteria?

☐ Islets of ability (areas of preserved or enhanced skill) do not occur in all children who meet the main criteria for autism. Therefore this characteristic is not considered a good discriminator.

The DSM-III criteria have been revised several times since 1980. The version current at the time of writing (2009), DSM-IV-TR (American Psychiatric Association, 2000), is in fact due to be replaced by DSM-V. Each new version of the diagnostic criteria aims to improve on the clarity and accuracy of the last. Yet at any point in time, experts have to operate with the current version of the criteria, knowing that ongoing research is informing revisions that will take some years to implement. Diagnostic criteria serve as a 'best fit' summary, which cannot fully represent the range of different expert opinions, and which reflect the state of knowledge at the point when they are finalised for publication. You will read more about these criteria, and how they are applied, in Chapter 2.

1.8.1 Summary of Section 1.8

• Diagnosis is the process of applying agreed criteria to identify individuals who come within a clinical category, and to differentiate them reliably from those who don't.

• The purpose of diagnosis is to ensure clarity and accuracy in research and sound practice in diagnosis and treatment.

• Diagnostic criteria are an agreed list of the symptoms or features that an individual must have for a condition to be diagnosed, and sometimes further symptoms that should not be present.

• Widely agreed diagnostic criteria for autism were not available until 40 years after Kanner's original paper.

• The first set of criteria published in DSM-III had a broad heading of 'pervasive developmental disorders' (PDD), with 'infantile autism' as a sub-heading.

• Diagnostic criteria are constantly under review, but each new version takes several years to be formally adopted.

1.9   Lorna Wing: prevalence, the autism spectrum and the rediscovery of Asperger

When autism was first identified it was considered to be a rare condition. The first estimate of **prevalence**, defined as the number of cases of a condition within a population at a particular time, was made by Lotter in 1966. Clear diagnostic criteria are obviously essential for estimating prevalence. Lotter's study preceded the first publication of formal criteria, so he had to rely on the definition of autism available at the time. On this basis Lotter estimated the prevalence of childhood autism to be 4 cases in 10 000. However, as you saw from Folstein and Rutter's twin study, it is sometimes important to consider cases that meet some but not all of the criteria for autism; otherwise, some important and relevant information may be missed.

■   How do you think prevalence estimates might be affected if the criteria are relaxed in this way?

☐   Using a broader set of criteria means that more cases will fall within the category, so the prevalence estimate will go up.

It was with this in mind that Lorna Wing and Judith Gould conducted a large-scale **epidemiological study** (a study designed to estimate prevalence, distribution and causes of a health problem in a population) in the London borough of Camberwell (Box 1.11).

Box 1.11   Wing and Gould's epidemiological study

From a total population of 35 000 children under the age of 15, Wing and Gould (1979) carefully scrutinised medical and social services registers to identify children with diagnoses ranging from severe 'mental retardation' to problems with language, behaviour and learning. A total of 167 children were identified. The teacher, nurse and, wherever possible, the mother of each child was interviewed using a **structured schedule**: a pre-agreed set of topics, which as far as possible is covered consistently with each parent. In addition, the children were observed by the interviewers at school, and if possible at home.

On this basis 17 (or just under 5 children in 10 000) were found to match the diagnostic criteria for classic autism. Note that this is similar to Lotter's estimate. However, a considerably larger group had some autistic-type difficulties in social interaction, typically coupled with communication problems, and an impoverished range of activities and interests. Wing and Gould argued that these children should be considered part of a wider group on a continuum with those meeting the full criteria for autism. (It was only later that Wing introduced the term 'autism spectrum' to reflect this variation on a core pattern of symptoms.) Including this wider group, the estimate of prevalence was more like 21 children in 10 000, a big increase on Lotter's and their own original estimates.

It was also from this study that Wing and Gould identified the triad of impairments (Figure 1.1) as characteristic markers which occur together in autistic conditions.

Wing and Gould's study promoted the transition from Kanner's idea of one discrete and specific syndrome to the variability which was becoming increasingly evident to all involved in the area. Their findings also demonstrated how prevalence estimates increase as the boundaries of the autism category (i.e. the inclusion criteria) are expanded. As you will see in Chapter 2, while Wing and Gould's estimate of 21 children in 10 000 for the spectrum is considered too conservative today, the criteria used in any estimate of prevalence must be clear and explicit in order to distinguish between increased prevalence due to changes in inclusion criteria, and a genuine increase in the number of individuals having autistic conditions.

The evolving concept of autism was further developed in 1981 when Lorna Wing published a paper highlighting the important but relatively little-known work of Asperger (Wing, 1981). She argued that the children described by Asperger represented a relatively 'high-functioning' group, to be distinguished by the sub-classification of Asperger syndrome (AS). Separate diagnostic criteria for AS were formally adopted as part of the diagnostic classification in 1994.

Finally, note that the concepts of sub-types, spectrum and continuum are all now applied to autism. The idea of sub-types suggests groups that are distinguishable from one another; and the idea of a spectrum is sometimes seen as an extension of this principle implying that different sub-types occupy different positions within a wider category. But spectrum also lends itself to an alternative interpretation: as a continuous dimension or scale of difference between all individuals, and an indistinct or fuzzy boundary with those not on the spectrum. You will look at how these ideas have been further developed in subsequent chapters. In practice, many researchers and practitioners work with all of these concepts, using each for slightly different purposes! To understand this, think of the colours of the rainbow. We perceive bands of wavelengths within the visible spectrum as qualitatively distinct categories: red, orange, yellow, green, blue and violet. However, colour variations are, for scientific purposes, different wavelengths on a continuous scale. Beyond a certain point these wavelengths shade to invisibility: ultra-violet and infra-red are not visible to the human eye (see Figure 1.8).

1.9.1 Summary of Section 1.9

- Wing and Gould's epidemiological study (1979) yielded a prevalence of 5 in 10 000 for classic autism, similar to Lotter's earlier estimate.

- On a more flexible criterion, which included children not meeting the full criteria for autism, the prevalence was 21 in 10 000. Prevalence estimates vary according to inclusion criteria.

- Wing and Gould originally proposed that autism should be considered as a continuum encompassing individuals differing in the expression and

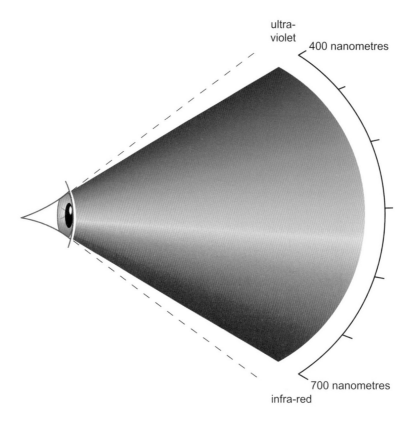

Figure 1.8   The spectrum of visible light is perceived by humans as a series of relatively distinct colours. But the spectrum is also a continuum of wavelengths shading into non-visible ultra-violet at one end, and infra-red at the other.

severity of their symptoms. Wing subsequently introduced the term spectrum to capture the idea of sub-types and relations between them.

. Wing and Gould identified the triad of impairments in autism.

. Lorna Wing brought Asperger's work to wider attention, and introduced the term Asperger syndrome, now a recognised diagnostic sub-category.

. Spectrum, continuum and sub-type concepts of autism are in current use, with slightly different implications.

1.10   Autism in the 21st century

This chapter has charted some of the most significant milestones in work on autism, from its first description in 1943 to the 1980s, and has shown how the concept of autism has evolved as a result of developments in diagnosis, research, clinical practice and public understanding. Recent years have seen many new developments, and this period, from the 1980s to the first decade of the 21st century, is the main focus in the remaining chapters of this book. So this final section of Chapter 1 will provide a brief taste of some of the topics to come.

1.10.1   Diagnostic criteria and assessment

The two international systems of diagnostic classification, DSM and ICD, have included pervasive developmental disorders, and some of the autistic sub-types since the 1980s. But, as you saw in Section 1.8, precisely how this group of conditions should be classified and diagnosed is a complex and evolving question. Chapter 2 explains the basis for the different sub-classifications within the diagnostic criteria, describes, using case studies, the procedures and tools used to decide whether diagnostic criteria are met, and considers the implications for prevalence estimates.

1.10.2   Psychological characteristics and explanations

As you have seen, autism is largely defined in terms of behavioural and psychological characteristics, and much research has been devoted to systematic studies, including experiments, documenting exactly what these characteristics are, and to seeking to explain why they occur. The question of how people with autism process information about the world covers many areas including:

- **cognition**: for instance, how people on the autism spectrum think, understand and use language, plan their activities, and solve problems
- **social cognition**: for instance, how people on the autism spectrum make sense of other people's behaviour and 'mental life' – what they are thinking and feeling
- **sensation** and **perception**: how people on the autism spectrum experience and interpret sounds, visual stimuli, taste, touch, and so on.

Some of the most important advances in understanding autism have occurred in these areas, which are covered in Chapters 3 and 4.

1.10.3   Biological explanations

As you have seen, the case for a biological basis to autism is firmly established. Recent scientific and technological advances have brought major new insights. The mapping of the human genome, and **molecular genetics** (the understanding of genes at the level of the molecules involved) have promoted new theories about exactly which genes are involved in autism, and what role they play. Techniques for studying the structure and functioning of the live brain, known as imaging, have shown that particular areas and circuits of the brain in individuals with autism may be atypical in structure and function. A crucial aspect of this work is the mapping of known psychological deficits to these atypically functioning areas. For instance, it is likely that the areas of the brain involved in language, and in processing emotional information, function atypically in people on the spectrum. These fascinating topics are discussed in Chapter 5.

1.10.4   Perspectives on intervention

Early advances in theoretical understanding helped to challenge Bettelheim's misinformed and inappropriate approach to helping people with autism. Behavioural approaches to intervention, based on the idea of shaping behavioural symptoms, were one of the early alternatives. With the massive growth of different interventions in the last three decades, the major question of evaluation arises. How do we know if a proposed intervention is going to work? How can we be certain that it will not have risky or damaging effects? Chapter 6 introduces the guiding principles which should be involved in evaluating all potential interventions, reviews a whole range of interventions, and the evidence for their success.

1.10.5   Education

Increased understanding of the nature of autism, and of the special educational needs that this implies, has brought improvements in educational provision, and some attempts to tailor the education of the individual child to their particular needs. Individuals with Asperger syndrome or 'high-functioning' autism may cope in the mainstream, while this may be impossible for more profoundly affected children. Legislation has also enhanced the statutory support available. Even so, this is a complex field, and one that many parents find difficult to negotiate. Chapter 7 considers educational options for people on the autism spectrum, and analyses the issues involved.

1.10.6   Family perspectives

Family life is complicated where one or more individual is on the autism spectrum. Though the last decades have brought greater insight into the issues, there is still much to be done. What are the implications for families? How do individuals on the spectrum function within the family setting? How can families adapt to their situation? These are some of the issues covered in Chapter 8.

1.10.7   Challenging issues

The theme of this chapter has been the way the concept of autism has evolved. The last chapter of the book reflects on how far ideas about autism have come, and on some of the major challenges that lie ahead.

We hope you will find the rest of this book as stimulating and thought provoking to read as we have found it to write.

1.11 Learning outcomes

1.1 Define and use, or recognise definitions and applications of, each of the terms printed in **bold** in the text.

1.2 Comment on how concepts of autism have evolved with developments in theory, research, diagnosis and clinical practice.

1.3 Identify the main characteristics of autism including the triad of impairments and other common features.

1.4 Describe key principles of experimental and twin study methods as used in relation to autism.

1.5 Comment on the emergence of diagnostic criteria for autism.

1.6 Explain the basic principle of prevalence studies.

1.7 Comment on changing ideas about the causes of autism.

1.12 Self-assessment questions for Chapter 1

Question 1.1 (LO 1.2)

Kanner and Asperger considered autism to be a syndrome, while nowadays it is thought of as a spectrum. Give one similarity and one difference between the idea of a syndrome and a spectrum.

Question 1.2 (LOs 1.3 and 1.5)

A mother is concerned about her 2-year-old son who has been slow in starting to talk, and also seems fixated with a particular toy train, which he constantly rolls backwards and forwards across the floor. The mother has read some accounts of autism in the media, and starts to wonder if her child might have an autistic condition. Draw on this example to answer the following questions.

(a) What is meant by the triad of impairments in autism?

(b) Which *two* of the triad features might this child's behaviour resemble?

(c) What is meant by the term 'diagnostic criteria'?

Question 1.3 (LO 1.4)

A psychologist conducts an experiment to compare the ability of a group of children with autism, and a typically developing group of children, to recall the same brief story. The psychologist reads out the story to the children, and then after an interval asks them to relate what they remember.

(a) Which is the experimental group and which is the control group in this study?

(b) Why does the psychologist read out the same story to all the children?

(c) Why might recall of a story be an interesting test of how children with autism remember things?

Question 1.4   (LO 1.4)

A researcher conducts a study of 12 identical twin pairs and 12 non-identical twin pairs, in whom one or both twin members are known to have autism diagnoses. Among the 12 identical twin pairs, there are five pairs who both meet the criteria for a diagnosis of classic autism. In a further four identical pairs, one twin has classic autism and the second twin has some language and social difficulties. The percentage concordance for classic autism in the identical twins is $5/12 \times 100 = 41.7\%$. Use this example to answer the following questions.

(a) What is the total percentage concordance (for classic autism *and* other autism-related symptoms) in the identical twin pairs?

(b) Would you expect the percentage concordance for classic autism in the non-identical twin pairs to be higher, lower or the same as that for the identical twin pairs? Give reasons for your answer.

Question 1.5   (LOs 1.5 and 1.6)

Recent studies in the UK suggest that around 1 in 100 children has an autism spectrum condition. Prevalence, frequently expressed as the number per 10 000, is therefore 100 children per 10 000 (calculated as $1/100 \times 10\ 000$). In the USA, the estimate for autism is around 1 in 150 children.

(a) What is the prevalence per 10 000 for the US study?

(b) Does the difference between these two prevalence estimates mean that there are more children on the autism spectrum in the UK than the USA? Give reasons for your answer.

Question 1.6   (LO 1.7)

Bettelheim claimed that autism occurs because a child withdraws from emotional coldness in his or her mother. This social/environmental explanation of autism has since been dismissed in favour of an explanation involving biological influences. Which of (a) to (d) provide supportive evidence for the biological explanation. Give reasons for your answers.

(a) Autism involves difficulties in communication, social interaction, and inflexibility of activities and interests.

(b) A proportion of children on the autism spectrum have epilepsy.

(c) Autism spectrum conditions occur in more males than females.

(d) There is strong evidence for a genetic factor in autism.

Chapter 2   Diagnostic criteria and assessment

Greg Pasco and Ilona Roth

2.1   Introduction and case study of classic autism

This chapter looks in some detail at the way in which the various forms of autism, including classic autism and Asperger syndrome are defined and how this relates to the process of diagnosis. Chapter 1 showed how, over the last four or five decades, understanding of autism has evolved, and the concept of the autism spectrum has emerged, and you will see how the formal definitions used in diagnosis have changed too. The terms used to describe the variants of autism will be discussed, along with some of the issues that surround the use of this terminology. In relation to the clinical diagnostic process, the chapter considers 'ideal' models of good practice, and assesses how well these are achieved in everyday clinical situations. Finally, the chapter considers prevalence studies that have followed those of Lotter, and Wing and Gould described in Chapter 1, as well as appraising the evidence for or against a real increase in the occurrence of autism. But before looking at diagnosis from a technical perspective, Case Study 2.1 describes how one family in the UK experienced the process of diagnosis.

Case Study 2.1   Anton

Anton is now eight years of age. He lives with his mother, Jenny, his father, Damon, and six-year-old sister, Marie, in a three-bedroom flat in a town in southern England.

Early concerns

Jenny first had concerns about Anton's development when he was about 20 months old, as he was only using a few words. He had started using a few single words soon after his first birthday, but his vocabulary did not subsequently seem to be expanding. Jenny approached her general practitioner (GP), but he suggested that boys were often late in learning to talk, and that she shouldn't worry, but should continue to monitor his language over the next six months or so.

Soon after this, however, Jenny became even more concerned. Anton would spend hours tipping plastic bricks onto the floor, and then putting them back into their container – an atypical way of playing for a child at this age (Figure 2.1). He would become extremely upset about some of the changes in the home following the birth of his little sister; and it was often impossible to get him to respond when he was called. Jenny spoke to a **health visitor** at a local 'well baby' drop-in clinic that she sometimes took Marie to.

A health visitor is a qualified nurse or midwife, who works in the community, providing advice and help on health matters, especially to parents with young children.

Figure 2.1   Most typically developing children will use toy bricks to build something whereas children on the autism spectrum often prefer repetitive activities such as tipping or sorting them. (Solus Veer/Corbis)

She wondered whether Anton had a problem with his hearing, which might explain why he often didn't pay attention when called. The health visitor observed Anton briefly. He had been screaming loudly until Jenny gave him his plastic bricks. She noted, however, that he turned round immediately when she rattled a few plastic bricks in a tub from the other side of the room. The health visitor said that she would make referrals for Anton to have a hearing test and also to be seen by a **speech and language therapist (SLT)**, who would assess his language and communication skills.

Initial assessments

The hearing assessment was inconclusive, as Anton did not like being in the unfamiliar room, and would not allow the audiologist (hearing specialist) to put headphones on him. In discussion with the specialist paediatrician who was overseeing the clinic, Jenny identified several situations where Anton's hearing appeared to be very good: he would always run to the window when Damon's car turned into their street, long before Jenny could hear it; and he could hear his parents opening a packet of biscuits in the kitchen, even from the other end of the flat. They agreed that Anton's hearing was probably fine, but they should continue to monitor him.

They had to wait nearly four months for the initial speech and language therapy appointment. It was a group assessment along with three other children and Anton initially sat quietly in a corner, playing with some toy cars. He got very upset when one of the other children came over and took one of the cars, and he was inconsolable until the car was returned to him. The SLT tried to assess how much language Anton understood, as well as his level of expressive language, although this proved difficult as he would not cooperate. The SLT told Jenny that she would refer Anton to the **Social Communication Clinic** at the local **Child Development Centre (CDC).**

Nursery school

Anton started at nursery a month or two before his third birthday. He was fine at the nursery as long as he was left to play by himself. (Figure 2.2). If the staff tried to get him to join in with regular group activities, such as snack time, or singing, however, he would become very distressed, hitting out at others or banging his head on the walls. One day, when Jenny came to pick him up, the manager told her they were seeking funding for an extra member of staff to support Anton: they knew someone who had worked with lots of children with autism, so she would know how to help Anton. This was the first time that anyone had mentioned autism directly in relation to Anton. Jenny and Damon did some research on the internet, and what they read about autism upset them greatly. However, they did find contact details for the National Autistic Society (NAS), who provided them with details of a local parent support group.

Child Development Centres carry out thorough assessments of children who appear to have developmental problems. Social Communication Clinics within CDCs specialise in assessing children with language and communication difficulties.

Figure 2.2   Children on the autism spectrum often prefer to play alone, rather than joining in with others. (Queensmill School)

Multidisciplinary assessment

Ten months after the referral, Anton was assessed at the CDC. The Social Communication Clinic was staffed by a multidisciplinary team including a paediatrician, a **clinical psychologist**, a specialist SLT and a social worker.

The appointment lasted about four hours. Anton was observed and also assessed using the **Autism Diagnostic Observation Schedule (ADOS)** – an interactive assessment tool used in diagnosis, which will be

Clinical psychologists apply psychological methods and theories to helping people of all ages who have intellectual disability or mental health problems such as depression or anxiety. Unlike psychiatrists, they do not have to be medically qualified.

described later in this chapter. Jenny was asked lots of questions, enabling the team to formulate a **case history** – a detailed overview of Anton's development, including atypical behaviour and any other difficulties. On reflection, Jenny realised that Anton's early development was markedly different from that of Marie, now two years old. Anton often seemed like a very quiet and 'easy' baby, but he didn't enjoy being cuddled or comforted like Marie did. Jenny also realised that Anton had very rarely smiled at her, pointed at things that interested him, or brought things that he liked to show her. After the various professionals had met and discussed their findings, the paediatrician told Jenny that they believed that Anton was on the autism spectrum, and that his behaviour and development matched the diagnostic criteria for classic autism, rather than for one of the other variants. They also felt that he had a moderate to severe degree of intellectual disability, meaning that his scores on an intelligence test were low compared with the majority of the population (see Chapter 3 for further discussion of this).

Dealing with diagnosis

Even though Jenny and Damon were fairly certain prior to the appointment that Anton had autism, they found it quite devastating to have this confirmed. They had read that autism was a lifelong condition: it seemed probable that Anton would have difficulty in leading an independent life or in forming relationships. They started to attend meetings at the local parent group and got to know some of the other parents. The local education department said Anton would need a **Statement of Special Educational Needs**, which would help to identify the type of support he would need at school. After a few months a provisional statement was given to Jenny, suggesting that Anton should attend a special school for children on the autism spectrum. Jenny and Damon had hoped that Anton would attend a mainstream school, and have extra support from a teaching assistant, like at nursery. From the parent support group they learned that they could insist on a mainstream placement, but were advised to at least visit the local special school. After visiting the school and discussing the alternatives with professionals and other parents from the group, they accepted that he should go to the special school.

At school

Anton is now in a class with six other children. The class has a regular weekly session run by an SLT, and Anton has been introduced to the **Picture Exchange Communication System (PECS)** to help him improve his communication skills. With PECS, children with autism learn through reinforcement to use pictures or symbols to communicate about objects of interest to them. (PECS is described in Chapter 6 along with other interventions for children and adults with autism.) The school provides some limited **respite provision** during the school holidays, and tries to organise outings for families once or twice a year. Respite provision means that Anton occasionally stays overnight in the residential part of the school, in order to give his parents and sister an opportunity to do some things that they would not be able to do as a family if Anton was at home – a trip to a restaurant or cinema, for example. The school is a primary school (for children aged from 5 to 11), and there is no equivalent for children when they reach secondary school age (11–18 years). Jenny and Damon are trying to decide whether they want Anton to attend an autism-specific secondary school run by a specialist charity, which means that he would have to be a weekly boarder as it is too far away to travel every day. The education department is suggesting that he attend a language unit in a local mainstream school, but Jenny doesn't believe that they have the resources or expertise to support a child with Anton's needs.

Activity 2.1 provides questions and issues for you to consider concerning the case study of Anton.

Activity 2.1 Anton's diagnosis: some questions and issues
Allow 30 minutes for this activity

(a) Do you think that either the health visitor or the first SLT might have suspected that Anton had autism? If so, why do you think they didn't say so to his parents?

(b) Why do you think that Jenny and Damon were upset when the diagnosis was confirmed by the professionals at the CDC, given that they probably already knew that he had autism?

(c) What were the negative aspects associated with the family's experience of their local health and education services?

(d) What were the benefits for Anton and the rest of the family as a result of the diagnosis?

Comments are at the end of the book.

2.1.1 How typical is Anton's story?

The experience of Anton and his family is fairly typical of many children who eventually receive a diagnosis of classic autism in the UK, although the exact circumstances, timing and outcome will vary according to a number of factors, including:

- the degree of impairment and difficulty experienced by the child
- whether the parents have experience of a typically developing child to compare with
- issues relating to local provision, including availability of resources and services such as specialist clinics, professional knowledge, length of waiting lists, etc.

When Jenny first raised her concerns about Anton he was less than two years of age. Even when Anton was referred for specialist assessment, it was well over a year before he was assessed and diagnosed at the CDC. However, it

In other countries, such as the USA, where autism is well recognised, experiences of diagnosis are likely to be broadly comparable, though the agencies and professionals involved will differ somewhat. Experiences may be very different in countries where autism is not well recognised and few services exist.

should be recognised that Anton and his family did receive some support prior to the diagnosis. After Jenny and Damon were alerted, almost accidentally, to the fact that Anton might have autism, they received advice from the NAS and the local parent support group.

Many parents are annoyed when they realise that the professionals they have seen did not mention 'the A-word', when they apparently knew their child had autism. However, professionals, such as the health visitor and SLT who saw Anton early on, have some justifiable reasons to be cautious about discussing autism (or other specific diagnoses) prematurely. First, professionals who are not specialists are often not confident about making such clinical judgements, and they are rightly concerned about 'labelling' the child or raising concerns for parents unnecessarily. Furthermore, as will be outlined later in this chapter, the process of diagnosis should involve a range of different professionals and a number of different assessments: a diagnostic judgement based on a brief and incomplete assessment of a child is inappropriate.

Various research studies have investigated the time between parents' initial concerns that their child's development may not be progressing in a normal way, and the point at which the child receives a diagnosis. In some cases, studies have found the delay to be in the region of several years, although there is evidence that this is reducing as knowledge of autism improves amongst both the general public and non-specialist professionals alike.

A further personal experience of the diagnostic process will be considered later in the chapter, after a look at the way in which the conditions or disorders within the autism spectrum are formally defined and diagnosed.

2.1.2   Summary of Section 2.1

- Parents' concerns about a child later diagnosed with classic autism often emerge in the second year of life.
- Initial assessments, for instance for hearing, speech and language, are often inconclusive.
- Atypical behaviour may stand out when the child joins nursery.
- Referral to a Child Development Centre for assessment may take many months.
- A multidisciplinary team will assess all aspects of the child's development, and take a case history.
- Diagnosis may be accompanied by a Statement of Special Educational Needs.

2.2   Formal definitions of autism

You will realise by now that children and young people on the autism spectrum share some common difficulties and behaviours, but that there are also clear differences between individuals. Chapter 1 introduced the triad of impairments (Figure 1.1) representing the three main areas of difficulty that characterise people on the autism spectrum.

■   What are the three elements of the triad of impairments?

☐ Difficulties with social communication, social interaction and inflexibility in activities and interests.

The triad is a widely agreed concept which has helped many people to understand the fundamental nature of autism, but it is not specific or detailed enough to enable specialists to make clear and definite diagnostic decisions, given so much variation in the expression and severity of symptoms associated with the spectrum. The two official sources for diagnosis, DSM and ICD, both introduced in Section 1.8, contain detailed descriptions of the diagnostic criteria for the disorders within the autism spectrum.

■ What is meant by diagnostic criteria?

☐ Diagnostic criteria (criterion is the singular form) are the standards upon which a diagnostic decision is based. They identify the aspects of difficulty and impairment that must be present in order for an individual to receive the specific diagnosis, together with any that must not be present.

Note that the scope of the two classification systems is different: DSM relates exclusively to psychiatric and mental health conditions, while ICD covers all branches of medicine, including both 'physical' and psychiatric conditions. Definitions of autism in successive revisions of these systems reflect the way in which attitudes towards and knowledge about the autism spectrum have evolved over time. Box 2.1 lists developments in the DSM classification of autism. The current 'text revision' of the fourth edition, known as DSM-IV-TR, was published in 2000, and is due to be replaced by DSM-V in 2013. The current version of the ICD, ICD-10, was published in 1993, and is due to be replaced by ICD-11 in 2014.

Box 2.1 Evolution of the Diagnostic and Statistical Manual (DSM)

DSM-I (1952) and DSM-II (1968)

There was no definition of autism in either of these two versions. Children who would now be diagnosed as autistic were (incorrectly) described as having 'childhood schizophrenia'.

DSM-III (1980)

Autism now included, under the broader category of 'pervasive developmental disorders' (PDD). Criteria for 'infantile autism' were (i) lack of responsiveness to others; (ii) language absent or abnormal; (iii) resistance to change or attachment to objects; (iv) absence of schizophrenic features; and (v) onset before 30 months. (See Table 1.2 for this version of the criteria.)

DSM-III-R (third edition, revised, 1987)

The term 'infantile' was dropped and 'autistic disorder' introduced, defined as (i) impairment in reciprocal social interaction; (ii) impairment in verbal and non-verbal communication; and (iii) markedly restricted repertoire of activities and interests; a specified number of symptoms from each category were also required to be present.

DSM-IV (fourth edition, 1994) and DSM-IV-TR (fourth edition, text revision, 2000)

Distinct types of PDD now defined, including autistic disorder, Asperger's disorder and 'pervasive developmental disorder not otherwise specified' (PDD-NOS) which is often used interchangeably with 'atypical autism'.

As explained in Chapter 1, the term 'autism' is often used informally for all the related conditions within the spectrum. But as Box 2.1 makes clear, autism is also the classic or prototypical variant among several different sub-types of autism distinguished by DSM-IV-TR, and also by ICD-10. Figure 2.3 is a schematic illustration to help you understand how the various sub-types 'sit' within the broader category of pervasive developmental disorders. Details of the DSM-IV-TR and ICD-10 diagnostic criteria corresponding to these sub-types are given in Sections 2.2.1–2.2.3. *In these sections, the term 'autism' is used to mean the classic sub-type, not the spectrum as a whole.*

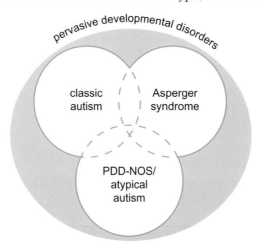

Figure 2.3 In the current DSM-IV-TR criteria classic autism (autistic disorder), Asperger syndrome (Asperger's disorder) and PDD-NOS are treated as diagnostically distinct, but overlapping entities within the broad category of pervasive developmental disorders.

2.2.1 Diagnostic definitions of classic autism

In DSM-IV-TR and ICD-10 the formal terms for classic autism are '**autistic disorder**' and '**childhood autism**', respectively. The criteria in both systems contain definitions of difficulties under the three main areas of (i) social interaction, (ii) communication and (iii) restricted, repetitive and stereotyped behaviours. Although the precise definitions differ, they are essentially focused on the same collection of difficulties.

Social interaction difficulties might include difficulties with 'non-verbal' aspects of communication, such as the use of gestures, eye contact and facial expressions. Other specified difficulties with social interaction might include difficulties making friends with other children, a lack of spontaneous showing and pointing by the child to share their interests with others, and a lack of emotional 'give and take', such as not responding to the changing emotions of other people.

Specific difficulties relating to communication range from the total absence of speech (without the use of gestures to compensate) to the use of language that is excessively repetitive or unusually stereotyped. Speech may also be considered atypical in terms of qualities such as **intonation** (the way speech rises and falls), **pitch** (whether the speech is high or low) and **stress** (the use of emphasis to mark particular words or phrases). Aspects of communication-related difficulties also include an inability to maintain a two-way conversation, as well as a lack of pretend play.

Problems relating to restricted, repetitive and stereotyped behaviours include intense preoccupations and obsessions with specific objects or topics of interest, odd mannerisms such as hand flapping and finger flicking and an insistence on following fixed routines.

Further details of these characteristic symptoms are outlined in Chapter 3.

In addition, there is a requirement that at least one area of difficulty has been present before the age of three years. In all cases, the difficulty should be such that it causes a significant problem with everyday functioning.

Activity 2.2 provides the opportunity to compare Anton's behaviour and difficulties with the diagnostic criteria.

Activity 2.2 Comparing Anton's symptoms with the diagnostic criteria

Allow 20 minutes for this activity

Look back at Case Study 2.1. Can you identify which of the criteria for autism may have been met in Anton's case? Do you think that the diagnosis was appropriate? Comments are at the end of the book.

2.2.2 Diagnostic definitions of PDD-unspecified, PDD-NOS and atypical autism

The current versions of both the ICD and DSM systems include broader diagnostic categories for cases where the specific criteria for autism cannot be satisfied. In ICD-10, the term **pervasive developmental disorder, unspecified (PDD-unspecified)** is used for cases where, although there is clear evidence that a PDD is present, the available information is either inadequate or too contradictory for a specific diagnosis of autism or Asperger syndrome to be made.

■ Can you think of some reasons why this might occur?

☐ First, the parents may not be available to provide a clear description of early development – the child might be adopted or an orphan, for example. Second, information from different sources may be contradictory: for instance, two parents may make different claims about their child's early development. Alternatively, the parents and the child's school might say different things. Finally, the information provided by the parents may not tally with the professionals' observations – particularly if the parents report that the child is definitely unable to do certain things (make eye contact, smile in response to another person's smile, use spontaneous, creative speech, for example) and the professionals have observed the child doing these things.

DSM-IV-TR uses the more widely recognised term, **pervasive developmental disorder not otherwise specified (PDD-NOS)**. Though this sounds very similar to the ICD-10 term, the meaning is subtly different. It is reserved for situations where there is clear evidence that the child has difficulties related to the autism spectrum, but where the full criteria for autistic disorder are not met. For instance, the child may have clinically significant difficulties in communication and social interaction, but show only minor symptoms of stereotyped or repetitive behaviours. Alternatively, there may be no evidence that the difficulties started before three years of age. In DSM-IV-TR, the terms **atypical autism** and PDD-NOS are used interchangeably for this kind of diagnosis. In ICD-10, atypical autism is defined more specifically in relation to either late onset or atypical symptomatology (i.e. that the usual symptoms are not present) or both.

You may wonder how these confusing discrepancies can be allowed to persist! The answer is that the DSM-IV-TR and ICD-10 criteria reflect slightly different views of the 'state of the art' by groups of professionals predominantly based in the USA and Europe, respectively. With increasing consensus about the nature of autism, such differences are likely to disappear.

2.2.3 Diagnostic definitions of Asperger syndrome

As for autism, the DSM-IV-TR and ICD-10 definitions of Asperger syndrome (formally termed 'Asperger's disorder' and 'Asperger's syndrome', respectively) differ in their precise detail, but overlap almost entirely in their broad focus. In relation to social interaction and restricted, repetitive and stereotyped behaviours, the criteria are virtually identical to those specified for autism, but some of the behaviours may be more subtle than those typical for autism. For instance, hand flapping and preoccupations with objects are less likely to occur. However, lining up toys in a repetitive or obsessive way, or an extremely intense interest in a particular topic, such as dinosaurs or trains, is more common.

An important distinction from the criteria for autism is that for Asperger syndrome, the main milestones of speech development, defined as the use of single words by two years of age and the use of simple phrases by three years of age, should have been met. However, as you saw in Chapter 1, this does not necessarily mean that a person with Asperger syndrome uses their language normally in communication, and generally there are also difficulties with the non-verbal aspects of communication (e.g. eye contact, gestures, facial expression and 'body language').

The definitions for Asperger syndrome also specify that there should be no delay in cognitive development. This means that the child or adolescent must be within or above the average range in terms of intellectual ability to meet the diagnostic criteria for Asperger syndrome. In contrast, cognitive or intellectual ability is not a defining criterion for autism, meaning that some individuals diagnosed with autism will have an intellectual disability while others will be in the normal range or above.

Another difference is that the criteria for Asperger syndrome do not specify onset of symptoms prior to three years of age. Age of onset, therefore, may be a distinguishing characteristic between Asperger syndrome and autism.

■   Why do you think that the criteria for Asperger syndrome don't include onset of symptoms before three years of age?

☐   This doesn't mean that Asperger syndrome only develops after three years. However, subtle symptoms before this age may go unnoticed by parents and clinicians. If early onset of symptoms were a criterion, a diagnosis of Asperger syndrome could not be made in cases where no early difficulties were reported.

2.2.4   Distinguishing classic autism from Asperger syndrome

When Leo Kanner and Hans Asperger independently described groups of children with great similarities, but also differing in certain key respects, they unknowingly gave rise to a question which is still unresolved: are autism and Asperger syndrome essentially variants of one condition or disorder, or are they distinct conditions with some similarities? The fact that there are now formal diagnostic criteria for both autism and Asperger syndrome might seem to indicate that there are precise ways of distinguishing them. But this is not always the case. Sometimes an individual's symptoms meet *both* the criteria for Asperger syndrome and those for another pervasive developmental disorder, i.e. autism or PDD-NOS. In this case, the ICD-10 and DSM-IV-TR definitions of Asperger syndrome both state that the diagnosis should not be given – a diagnosis of autism or PDD-NOS should take precedence. This is an explicit acknowledgement that the diagnostic criteria are not always definitive.

This ambiguity is most likely when considering the diagnostic status of individuals within the normal range of intelligence. People with autism who score within the normal range on intelligence tests are sometimes referred to as people with **high-functioning autism (HFA)**. This term is not used in the formal definitions of autism, but is used in everyday situations and research. Similarly, those who have autism and an intellectual disability are sometimes said to have **low-functioning autism (LFA)**. You will read more about this in Chapter 3. There has been an ongoing debate amongst researchers, clinicians, parents and people with autism or Asperger syndrome themselves, about the relationship between HFA and Asperger syndrome.

■ Can you think of a combination of difficulties where the criteria for an autism diagnosis would be met, while the criteria for Asperger syndrome would definitely not be met?

☐ The clearest example would be where the individual in question has an intellectual disability. In this case, the diagnostic criteria for Asperger syndrome would definitely not be met.

■ Can you think of a situation where an individual with some autistic symptoms and an intellectual disability would meet the diagnostic criteria for PDD-NOS, rather than autism?

☐ One situation would be where the person did not have clinically significant difficulties in all three triad areas (communication, social interaction and repetitive, stereotyped activities). Another would be if the person's symptoms did not manifest themselves below the age of three years.

In everyday practice, professionals involved in clinical diagnosis (i.e. those making decisions about the diagnostic status of children, adolescents or adults in the 'real world') may only use the precise DSM or ICD criteria as a broad guideline. Their diagnostic judgements are frequently guided by practical considerations as to which specific 'label' might be most helpful or acceptable to the individual and their family, and they may also take local circumstances into consideration, such as whether a diagnosis of Asperger syndrome might help the person to access a particular school or unit (Sciutto and Cantwell, 2005; Woodbury-Smith et al., 2005). Therefore, many people who meet the criteria for autism with no intellectual disability may actually be diagnosed as having Asperger syndrome, even though this is technically incorrect, according to ICD-10 and DSM-IV-TR. A number of research studies have suggested that the differences between HFA and Asperger syndrome are fairly limited, particularly when considering outcomes such as adults' scores on formal assessments of language and cognitive skills as well as life circumstances such as employment, educational attainment, living arrangements and relationships (Howlin, 2003; Macintosh and Dissanayake, 2004).

One consistent research finding is that parents' initial concerns about their child's development and the age of actual diagnosis both tend to occur at a later age for Asperger syndrome than for autism. This is illustrated in the next case study.

2.2.5 Summary of Section 2.2

• The two official sources for diagnostic classification, DSM and ICD, have evolved over time.

• DSM-IV-TR includes three main sub-types of pervasive developmental disorder: autistic disorder (classic autism); Asperger's disorder (Asperger syndrome); and PDD-NOS, also known as atypical autism.

• The main criteria for classic autism include a range of difficulties listed under social interaction, communication, restricted activities and interests, with the requirement that difficulties must cause significant disruption of everyday functioning, and at least one of these must be evident below three years of age.

- In ICD-10, PDD-unspecified is for cases that cannot be unambiguously matched with autism or Asperger syndrome.

- In DSM-IV-TR, PDD-NOS is used to mean a disorder on the autism spectrum, but not meeting the full criteria for classic autism.

- DSM-IV-TR and ICD-10 criteria for Asperger syndrome differ from those for classic autism in requiring (a) no delay in obvious speech milestones and (b) intellectual ability in the normal range; also (c) symptoms need not be evident before the age of three.

- Real-world clinical diagnosis may be guided by what 'label' is most acceptable or useful for the person and their family.

2.3   Case study of Asperger syndrome

Case Study 2.2 considers the experience of Oliver, who is now a teenager with a diagnosis of Asperger syndrome, and his family. Oliver lives in London with his mother, Hannah, his older sister, Lucy, and younger brother, Noel. His parents are divorced, and he spends alternate weekends with his father, Daniel.

Case Study 2.2   Oliver

Early development

There was nothing remarkable about Oliver's first year-and-a-half: he made good progress in all aspects of development. At 18 months he became very interested in the television and video recorder, and learned how to switch them on using the remote controls. He was mostly not interested in watching the videos or TV programmes, but more in how to fast-forward, rewind or eject the tapes, and how to change channels. This was particularly annoying for Lucy, who could rarely sit and watch the TV without Oliver interfering with it, and this often led to squabbles and fights. Eventually the remote controls had to be kept out of reach, and strict rules put in place about who was allowed to change channels. Oliver generally accepted this, although he still sometimes tried to take control of the TV, video and the other technology in the house.

By the time Oliver was two years old, Hannah's friends and family often commented about how good his language was compared to other children of his age. He had an extensive vocabulary, and Hannah was often surprised to hear him saying a word that she did not know that he knew. He also seemed to have taught himself to read, and would often read out the words printed on cartons, shopping bags and road signs. Oliver's parents were generally very proud of his talents, but his grandparents, uncles and aunts were often more struck by how controlling he could be when he was with his cousins and other young children. They also found it difficult to have a two-way conversation with him, despite his precocious language skills.

At four-and-a-half years of age Oliver would insist on reading the instructions for any new equipment or toys that came into the house, and he would often dismantle machines, including the new DVD player and the toaster. He would spend hours reading through the help and installation programs for their cable TV supplier, and would regurgitate these to anyone who would listen. Although this often drove Hannah to distraction, Daniel felt that it showed just how bright Oliver was, and, as he himself was an electrical engineer, he shared Oliver's interest in machines and technology. Oliver did sometimes play with the other children at nursery, but this was usually a game of his choosing, and he would direct the others to perform very specific roles.

Primary school

Oliver settled into school very well, and the teacher in his reception class (an 'entry' class for four-year olds) regularly commented about how helpful he was around the class, and that he was rarely a problem, certainly compared to some of his classmates. When he moved into Year 1 or primary school at five years old, however, things did become more difficult. His teacher often became irritated that he would tell the other children what to do, and Oliver was often quite insistent on certain things happening according to the usual routine, even if it was a special occasion. When talking to or referring to the other children, he usually called them by both their first and last names. He found it difficult to interact with most of his classmates, particularly as they didn't know how to respond to some of the things he would say to them. He would tell them about the technical details of certain bits of equipment, or describe the plot of one of his favourite TV programmes (such as *Dr Who* or *Star Wars*) (Figure 2.4) even if the other child wasn't interested in them, and would rarely respond appropriately to the things they said to him. Oliver's teachers found that he did respond to clear instructions and rules, and so he was not usually disruptive within the classroom.

Figure 2.4   Children on the autism spectrum often seem to be fascinated by science fiction series such as *Dr Who* and *Star Wars*. (Rex Features; Photos 12/Alamy)

Referral for consultation and assessment

When he was seven years old, Oliver got into trouble because he touched a girl inappropriately. Some boys in the year above had persuaded him to do it, offering to buy him a game for his PlayStation®. The school realised that Oliver was quite socially naive and could be easily led, but decided to make a referral to the **Child and Family Consultation Service (CFCS)**, a service that may be called upon if a child demonstrates problem behaviour at home or at school.

Both Hannah and Daniel attended the first appointment. Daniel became very angry at the suggestion that there was 'something wrong' with Oliver, and accused Hannah and the child psychiatrist of trying to create a problem. After the third appointment it was agreed that Oliver would be referred to the **Child and Adolescent Mental Health Service (CAMHS)**, where his social difficulties could be assessed more clearly. Oliver was assessed by a clinical psychologist, whilst Hannah was interviewed by a consultant psychiatrist about Oliver's developmental history. The psychologist concluded that he had well above normal intelligence, particularly in relation to his verbal skills, but his social reasoning was often quite immature. A week or so later, another psychologist visited Oliver at school and conducted a formal assessment with him using the Autism Diagnostic Observation Schedule (ADOS). At the subsequent appointment, the psychiatrist told Hannah and Daniel that they would diagnose Oliver with Asperger syndrome.

Dealing with diagnosis

Daniel did not initially accept the diagnosis, but a compromise was reached where it was decided not to tell Oliver about the diagnosis for the time being.

Oliver's school was committed to a 'whole school approach' in helping to support Oliver and other children with autism and Asperger syndrome, and two training sessions were run for all staff to explain some of the most effective ways of working with and helping these children. Increasingly, Oliver spent more time with some of the other boys who also attended a 'Communication Group' that was run by an SLT. Oliver and his friends were allowed to spend break and lunchtimes in the library if they felt they needed some time away from all the other children. Figure 2.5. Oliver was still occasionally teased or bullied by other children at the school, but over time he learned how to avoid getting into trouble.

Shortly before Oliver started secondary school, his grandfather died. When he was told, Oliver's only response was to ask if he could have his grandfather's TV, as he 'wouldn't need it anymore'. This even shocked Daniel, who was starting to understand that Oliver didn't see the world in the same way as most other boys of his age. He could also see that some of the support Oliver had received since being diagnosed with Asperger syndrome had helped. One day Lucy told him that he had Asperger syndrome while they were having a row. Oliver didn't really know what this meant, but he looked it up on the internet, and realised that this explained many of the difficulties that he had in dealing with other people as he was growing up. After a few weeks he started referring to his 'Aspergerness', and discussed this with his school friends.

Figure 2.5   Teenagers with Asperger syndrome may find it easier to relate to others who have similar interests and difficulties. (National Autistic Society)

At secondary school

Oliver's start at secondary school was quite traumatic, as he found it very difficult to cope with the constant changes of classroom and teacher. He was also bullied by some older students, and he refused to go back to school for a couple of weeks. The school's **Special Educational Needs Coordinator (SENCo)** and a local educational psychologist devised a plan to help Oliver understand the structure of the day, and advice was given to his various subject teachers, although some were better than others at incorporating this into their teaching. By the second year, things were reasonably stable again and Hannah now feels that Oliver is fairly well supported at school, with just the occasional mishap. Oliver has been enrolled onto a programme for gifted and talented children run across a consortium of local schools, and he has his sights set on a place at university.

Activity 2.3 provides some questions for you to consider concerning the case study of Oliver.

Activity 2.3 Oliver's diagnosis: some questions and issues

Allow 30 minutes for this activity

(a) To what extent do you think that Oliver's behaviour and difficulties are consistent with the criteria for Asperger syndrome described in the previous section? Do you think he could also have met the criteria for classic autism or PDD-NOS?

(b) Why do you think that Oliver was diagnosed at a much later age (seven years) than Anton (three years)?

(c) Why do you think that Daniel was initially against the idea that Oliver had a problem or that he should be diagnosed?

(d) Do you think there were any benefits to Oliver and his family following the diagnosis?

Comments are at the end of the book.

2.3.1   Summary of Section 2.3

- The early development of children later diagnosed with Asperger syndrome may give little cause for concern.

- Precocious development of technical, reading and other skills may mask a lack of social development.

- Social and behavioural difficulties often emerge at primary school, and may lead to referral for consultation.

- Specialist assessment is likely to include tests of intellectual ability, the ADOS and interviews with the parents.

- Children with Asperger syndrome may encounter particular difficulty in adapting to the learning and social environment of secondary school.

2.4   Making a diagnosis: assessment procedures and instruments

Diagnostic practice varies considerably depending on the individual professional, their specialist field or discipline, the type of service where the diagnosis is being considered, geographical area and country. The two case studies earlier in this chapter show that an individual's journey to receiving a diagnosis can involve problems, delays, distress for parents and sometimes conflicting information from professionals. In the UK, most **local authorities** have defined procedures or 'pathways' that specify the process by which children suspected of having some kind of special educational need are referred for specialist assessment and/or diagnostic evaluation. Though these procedures may vary, certain standards are required by statutory authorities (such as maximum waiting times for appointments which are specified by the National Health Service (NHS)). The **National Autism Plan for Children (NAP-C)** is a UK voluntary framework containing guidelines and

Local authorities are regional government bodies with responsibilities in areas such as education, health and social services.

recommendations for good practice in relation to the identification and diagnosis of children with autism (NIASA, 2003). Some of the NAP-C recommendations relating to **multi-agency assessment** are shown in Box 2.2.

Box 2.2 Essential components for a complete multi-agency assessment (MAA)

1   Existing information from all settings should be gathered.

2   A specific autism spectrum developmental and family history should be taken by an experienced team member with recognised training in autism spectrum disorders. In some cases it will be useful to use a semi-structured interview such as the Autism Diagnostic Interview (ADI-R) or the Diagnostic Interview for Social and Communication Disorders (DISCO). If the person taking the developmental history is not medically trained, then the medical history and examination should be completed separately.

3   Focused observations should be made across more than one setting. This could use tools such as the Autism Diagnostic Observation Schedule (ADOS). For primary school aged children, observations should include their functioning in an educational setting.

Assessments should include:

4   A cognitive assessment performed by either a clinical or an educational psychologist with autism spectrum training.

5   A communication assessment including speech and language abilities, made by a speech and language therapist with autism spectrum training.

6   A mental health and behaviour assessment. Co-morbid (i.e. co-occurring) mental health and behaviour problems are common.

7   An assessment of the needs and strengths of all family members.

8   A full physical examination including appropriate medical tests.

9   Choice of medical tests will depend on each child's clinical presentation. Currently certain genetic and chromosome analyses are routine. Clinical evidence of co-morbid medical conditions such as epilepsy should be sought but tests of brain activity (such as EEG) not undertaken unless clinically appropriate. The evidence base for all investigations should be fully explained to parents.

10 Other assessments may be required to investigate unusual sensory responses, movement and coordination difficulties and self-care problems.

■   Which of the features of the NAP-C recommendations listed in Box 2.2 were present in Anton's and Oliver's diagnostic assessments?

☐   (1) The case studies only mention information gathered from Anton's and Oliver's parents, but it is possible that reports were also provided by

Anton's nursery and Oliver's school. (2) It is reasonable to assume that the professionals involved in the two diagnostic clinics had specialist training. It is not specified which, if any, diagnostic interviews were conducted. (3) Both assessments involved the ADOS. It is not specified whether the children were observed at nursery/school. (4) Both children had cognitive assessments to establish their intellectual level. (5) Anton was assessed by an SLT, although this was not the case for Oliver. (6–10) The case studies do not specify which other assessments were conducted.

The NAP-C recommendations provide ideal guidelines. These are not necessarily achieved by diagnostic services across the UK, although many services report that they use them as a framework to guide their practice. In the USA there are no legislated standards for the diagnostic process, although guidelines containing similar recommendations to those of NAP-C have been published by the American Academy of Neurology (Filipek et al., 2000).

2.4.1   Diagnostic assessments

The case studies and discussion in this chapter have mentioned several forms of diagnostic assessment (sometimes also referred to as instruments or measures) which are used by professionals as part of the diagnostic process. In this section, two of these – the Autism Diagnostic Observation Schedule (ADOS) (Lord et al., 2000) and the Autism Diagnostic Interview (ADI) (Lord et al., 2000) – are described in some detail. The ADOS was used in the diagnostic assessments of Anton and Oliver, and both assessments are recommended for use in the NAP-C and American Academy of Neurology recommendations. You should be aware, however, that alternative instruments exist, and are often used, depending (amongst other factors) on the specific requirements of the diagnostic assessment at hand and the preferences and training of the professionals involved.

Professionals carry out diagnostic assessments not only for clinical diagnosis but also for research studies. For instance, in studies evaluating a therapeutic intervention, it may be important to check that participants meet the formal criteria for autism. Alternatively, in studies concerning the prevalence of autism, individuals should be assessed in order to calculate how many people meet diagnostic criteria within a defined population. In many cases, a diagnostic assessment for a research study may be carried out after a child or adult has already been diagnosed clinically, in order to confirm the person's diagnostic status.

■   Why might this be necessary?

☐   As you saw earlier in this chapter, professionals involved in clinical diagnosis may not stick to the precise criteria when giving a diagnosis. Their decisions may be guided by practical considerations which are entirely appropriate in the circumstances. However, in research, where the findings will be read by people from different professions, geographical locations and countries, it is important that the formal criteria are accurately and consistently applied, so that there will be a shared understanding of the precise diagnostic status of the participants.

Another function of diagnostic assessments is to add further to the accuracy and consistency offered by the formal diagnostic criteria. For example, the DSM-IV-TR criteria for autistic disorder include the following definition: 'marked impairment in the use of multiple non-verbal behaviours such as eye-to-eye gaze, facial expression, body posture, and gestures to regulate social interaction'. Suppose that a child makes eye contact, but only from time to time, and uses just a few facial expressions and gestures when communicating. The diagnostic criteria provide no guidance as to whether or not this child meets this criterion. Similarly, the DSM-IV-TR criteria for Asperger's disorder include 'lack of social or emotional reciprocity'. The problem is that two different professionals may have a different idea of what this means.

Diagnostic instruments such as the ADOS and ADI have been designed to help in standardising decisions taken using the formal diagnostic criteria, by enhancing the accuracy and consistency with which they are applied.

2.4.2 The Autism Diagnostic Observation Schedule (ADOS)

The ADOS (Figure 2.6) is an interactive assessment involving the child or adult who is being assessed and a trained examiner (usually a clinician or researcher). The ADOS consists of four separate modules, each of which consists of a number of tasks designed for use with individuals of different ages and levels of development and language. For example, Module 1 is formulated at the level of a typically developing two-year-old, and the activities are appropriate for a toddler, whereas Module 4 is for adolescents and adults with fluent speech. There is also a degree of overlap between some of the different tasks in successive modules.

Because the ADOS is interactive, the examiner may have to modify some of the procedures for administering the tasks and so the assessment is often described as being 'semi-structured'.

Figure 2.6 The equipment used in the ADOS. (Western Psychological Services)

Module I

Tasks include:

- free play – the child is presented with a range of toys including building blocks, a toy truck and 'cause and effect' toys such as a Jack-in-the-box and 'pop-up' toys
- bubbles
- balloons
- a 'birthday party' activity involving a doll and a pretend cake made of 'play dough'
- 'peek-a-boo'.

In addition, the examiner carries out certain actions to assess how the child responds, such as calling the child's name to see if they look round, and smiling at the child to see if this elicits a smile in response. The examiner also shifts his/her gaze to look at a toy, to see if the child follows the gaze to locate the toy (this is known as engaging in **joint attention**).

Throughout the assessment the examiner observes the child's verbal and non-verbal communication and social behaviour, noting how the child makes requests for things (e.g. to ask for more bubbles), and whether they share their interest with another person: for example, by looking at a toy they like, looking at the examiner or their parent, and then looking back at the toy (i.e. initiating joint attention). If a child of two years is observed to lack a particular number of these age-appropriate behaviours, this may indicate that he or she is on the autism spectrum.

Module 2

This is formulated at the developmental level of a typically developing child of approximately four to six years of age, who has the ability to have at least a limited conversation. This assessment includes several of the same tasks and activities as Module 1, but several tasks involve more language demands such as having a conversation, describing a picture and telling a story from a book. As with Module 1, the examiner observes the child's language, communication and social behaviour, but as the child being assessed should use some expressive language, there will be a slight difference in the nature of the difficulties being investigated. For example, the examiner may need to pay attention to the child's use of pitch and stress when they are talking.

Modules 3 and 4

These are very similar to each other in content, and are used with children, adolescents or adults with fluent speech. Module 3 tests for the skills expected of a typically developing child between approximately six or seven years and 13 or 14 years of age, and Module 4 would be suitable for adolescents from about 14 years through to adults. The majority of tasks in these two modules involve conversational exchange, but several tasks also involve materials such as a book, pictures and 'action figures'. In these modules, the examiner attempts to assess a range of social and communicative behaviours, as well as the way in which the person being assessed is able to integrate their use of verbal and non-verbal skills. For example, do they combine their use of eye contact, gestures and other non-verbal skills naturally, or are any of these features stilted or absent?

Administering the ADOS should take between 25 and 40 minutes in total. Following the assessment, the examiner uses their notes and observations to score the responses and behaviours of the child, adolescent or adult within five categories:

- communication
- reciprocal social interaction
- play or imagination/creativity
- stereotyped behaviours and restricted interests
- other abnormal behaviours.

As you can see, these areas, or domains, broadly correspond to the areas of difficulty covered by ICD-10 and DSM-IV-TR. Scores from the first two domains are used to decide whether the individual being assessed is likely to meet the criteria for any form of autism. There are three possible outcomes:

- autism – this corresponds to a diagnosis of childhood autism (ICD-10) or autistic disorder (DSM-IV-TR), i.e. classic autism

- autism spectrum – corresponding to atypical autism (ICD-10) or PDD-NOS/atypical autism (DSM-IV-TR)

- not autism spectrum – either the person's difficulties are due to something other than autism or PDD-NOS, or they are typically developing.

Note that Asperger syndrome is not one of these outcomes. The wide variation in skills and behaviours associated with Asperger syndrome means that the ADOS is not necessarily a definitive assessment for this group. In practice, many children, adolescents and adults with a clinical diagnosis of Asperger syndrome meet the criteria on the ADOS for a classification of autism spectrum, but actually receive an ADOS classification of 'not autism spectrum'. However, experienced professionals base their diagnostic decisions on the full range of information from all of the assessments carried out. The eventual diagnosis does not always tally with the outcome suggested by their score from the ADOS assessment.

- Can you think of any reasons why an individual's behaviour in an ADOS assessment might not be representative of their skills and difficulties in everyday situations?

- The ADOS assessment generally takes place in an unfamiliar location and involves an unfamiliar person as examiner. If these factors cause anxiety, they may disturb behaviour in ways that make it difficult to carry out the assessment, and which would not necessarily occur in a more familiar environment. Also, since the ADOS is a very brief assessment, some relevant behaviours, such as over-reaction to sounds or visual stimuli, or hand-flapping and other mannerisms, may not be observed during the assessment. Finally, for some, particularly the more able individuals, one-to-one interaction with a sympathetic adult may not highlight the difficulties they have dealing with their peer group at school, for example.

The ADOS provides evidence of the child's current level of competence in areas of social communication and interaction. In order to get detailed information about the person's developmental history, as well as aspects of behaviour that may not have been observed directly during the ADOS, an interview is conducted with the parent(s). One instrument designed specifically for this purpose is the Autism Diagnostic Interview (ADI).

2.4.3 The Autism Diagnostic Interview

The **Autism Diagnostic Interview (ADI)** consists of almost a hundred questions about current skills and behaviours, as well as how these behaviours were at age four to five years (or 'ever' in some cases). From the parents' responses, scores are derived for four domains, broadly corresponding to the ICD-10 and DSM-IV criteria:

- reciprocal social interaction
- communication (non-verbal and verbal)
- repetitive and stereotyped behaviours
- age of onset.

If the scores for all four domains are consistent with autism, the child will receive an ADI classification of autism. The only alternative outcome is 'not autism'. As before, an experienced clinician will exercise judgement to make an overall diagnostic decision, taking into account all sources of available information. For clinicians, a considerable disadvantage of the ADI is the extensive time to administer it, usually between two and three hours. One study found that the ADI did not enhance the accuracy of diagnostic outcomes compared to the judgement of experienced paediatricians working in a multidisciplinary CDC setting (Chakrabarti and Fombonne, 2001).

2.4.4 Other diagnostic interviews

Though the ADI is widely used, particularly in research, there are other diagnostic interviews, which are described below.

The **Diagnostic Interview for Social and Communication Disorders (DISCO)** was developed at the NAS diagnostic service by Lorna Wing and Judith Gould. Whereas the ADI results in an 'all-or-nothing' diagnostic outcome ('you've either got it or you haven't'), the DISCO is dimensional, allowing for more subtle or graded evaluation of how far an individual matches the criteria for autism or another PDD as defined in the ICD and DSM systems.

■ What might be the advantages of this?

☐ Some people who are assessed using the ADI may just fail to meet the specified score for a classification of autism, resulting in an outcome of 'not autism'. With the dimensional approach of the DISCO, these individuals will be identified as scoring high enough to probably or possibly meet the diagnostic criteria.

The **Developmental, Dimensional and Diagnostic Interview (3Di)**, devised by Professor David Skuse at Great Ormond Street Hospital, is another diagnostic interview providing dimensional outcomes. The format of the 3Di is similar in structure to the ADI, but uses computer analysis of the responses in an attempt to reduce the time burden on clinicians.

2.4.5 Summary of Section 2.4

- The National Autism Plan for Children has established guidelines on the recommended procedures for a multi-agency assessment of children under scrutiny for autism.
- Diagnostic assessments are carried out within clinical practice and also to confirm diagnostic status within research studies.

- The ADOS is a widely used interactive assessment. Four modules designed for use with different age groups specify observations of behaviour designed to highlight autism spectrum symptoms.
- Diagnostic interviews such as the ADI, DISCO and 3Di specify questions for parents designed to elicit information relevant to any autistic symptoms in their child.

2.5 Screening for autism

As you have seen in both of the case studies in this chapter, there is often a delay between parents' first concerns and the point at which the child is diagnosed.

- What do you think are the main factors that contribute to this delay?

- Parents may take a while before they are sufficiently worried to raise their concerns with a professional; professionals may not initially identify a problem, and may advocate a 'wait and see' approach or dismiss the parents' concerns altogether; there is often a long wait for specialist assessment and diagnostic services, and in some cases local professionals may wish to refer children on to more specialist regional teams.

Currently, children in the UK are usually diagnosed with classic autism between three and five years of age, although some more severe cases may be diagnosed at two years old. Asperger syndrome is generally diagnosed later (as in Oliver's case). Apart from the distress that delays in diagnosis cause for parents and other family members, earlier identification may possibly have direct benefits because it leads to earlier specialist intervention. While it is not definitively proven, this is a widely held and not unreasonable view.

Some specialists therefore argue for **screening**, a procedure for identifying which young children in the population as a whole may be at risk. The approach is similar to that used for screening for medical conditions such as cancer. The **Checklist for Autism in Toddlers (CHAT)** was one of the first assessments developed with the aim of screening for autism in preschool children. As you will see, however, its accuracy as a screening tool is limited.

2.5.1 The Checklist for Autism in Toddlers

The CHAT was designed to be administered at a routine developmental assessment of all children at 18 months of age, generally carried out by health visitors or GPs. There are nine questions for parents, and five items of behaviour for the professional to observe during the assessment. Five key items are:

Parental report

Does the child:

- pretend when playing?
- point in order to share interest?

Professional observation

Does the child:

- look where someone else is pointing?
- pretend when playing?
- point out an object of interest?

The three key items relating to pointing and the two relating to pretend play were selected because children diagnosed with autism almost always show difficulties in these areas (this is further discussed in Chapter 3). A lack of pointing or pretend play in toddlers can therefore reasonably be assumed to be a strong indicator of risk for later diagnosis.

In a large-scale study (Baron-Cohen et al., 1996) the CHAT was administered to over 16 000 18-month-olds. All children who 'failed' were followed up at seven years of age using a variety of screening, surveillance and diagnostic methods – the ADOS, the ADI, ICD-10 criteria and clinical judgement – to determine diagnostic status. Nineteen children with autism had been correctly flagged using the CHAT at 18 months. However, a further 31 children from the original population were also diagnosed with autism, but were not picked up by the CHAT.

- ■ What do you think this indicated about the success of the CHAT as a screening tool?

- ☐ Children who failed the CHAT were very likely to end up with a diagnosis of autism. However 'passing' was no guarantee that the child would not later be diagnosed, and in fact the CHAT missed more cases than it correctly identified. This means that the CHAT is not very 'sensitive', and consequently it has not been adopted as a screening tool for autism in toddlers.

Since the first CHAT study was published, researchers have tried to develop alternative screening instruments, most based, partly at least, on the CHAT. Since there is no longer a regular developmental assessment at 18 months across the UK, some of these more recently developed instruments have been designed as questionnaires to be posted to parents of all children when they reach a certain age.

2.5.2   Recommendations for screening tools for autism

Because no screening instruments have so far demonstrated sufficient accuracy to be used in early identification of the risk of autism, whole population screening is not recommended by the **UK National Screening Committee** or the National Autism Plan for Children (NAP-C).

- ■ Does this mean that there is no way of checking for autism in preschool children?

□   NAP-C recommends training for all key professionals who work with preschool and school-age children, along with regular opportunities for parents to discuss their child's development with relevant professionals during the preschool years. In the USA, Filipek et al. (2000) recommend the use of autism-specific screening following parental concerns about their child's development.

2.5.3   Summary of Section 2.5

- Given the benefits of early identification of autism, and the frequent delays in diagnosis, screening for autism spectrum problems in toddlers seems highly desirable.

- The CHAT, designed as a screening tool, has proved insufficiently accurate to be implemented as a population screen.

- Currently no population screening is recommended in the UK, but training and vigilance on the part of professionals working with young children can enhance identification.

- In the USA, autism-specific screening is recommended following a parental expression of concern.

2.6   Prevalence

These days there are many more people with an autism spectrum diagnosis than when estimates of the number with autism were first made. The press often carries alarming reports stating that autism is 'on the increase'. The implication is that there is an increase in the number of people affected by autism, which is in turn related to the controversial claim that autism is caused by specific environmental factors, such as the introduction of the MMR vaccinations (this is further discussed in Chapter 5).

Understanding why these controversial claims are misleading depends on a clear grasp of the concept of prevalence.

■   Recall the definition of prevalence given in Section 1.9.

□   Prevalence is an estimate of the number of people who have a particular medical or psychiatric condition within a defined population at a particular time. Prevalence may be expressed as how many individuals per 10 000 are affected by the condition and/or as a percentage.

Estimates of the prevalence of autism vary depending on both when and where they were made. For instance, current estimates yield much higher figures than older ones, and estimates made in the UK yield higher figures than those made in other parts of the world. But the higher estimates do not necessarily mean that more people are affected by autism. The remainder of this section considers the factors that may be responsible for these differences.

2.6.1   Is autism on the increase?

As you saw in Chapter 1, the earliest prevalence studies for autism suggested that autism was a relatively rare condition. Lotter's study (published in 1966) estimated the prevalence of autism to be approximately 4 per 10 000, or about 0.04%.

Wing and Gould's later prevalence study (1979) involved children defined as having special educational needs, which meant that virtually all of them had an intellectual disability. From this group, Wing and Gould estimated that about 5 in 10 000 met the 'narrowest' definition of autism, based on the criteria available at the time. So the prevalence estimate for classic autism in this study was very similar to Lotter's original estimate of 4 per 10 000. However, Wing and Gould also identified around three times as many children in the same intellectually disabled group who met some but not all the criteria for autism. Many individuals in this wider group would probably meet the current criteria for PDD-NOS or atypical autism. When they included both the original classic autism group and the wider group, they came up with a combined prevalence of around 20 per 10 000.

A few years later, yet another study (Ehlers and Gillberg, 1993), carried out in Gothenberg, Sweden, was reported, this time focusing just on children without intellectual disability; that is, with IQ scores in the normal and above average range. This study reported a prevalence for Asperger syndrome and high-functioning autism of 36 per 10 000. Ehlers and Gillberg also identified an additional 35 individuals per 10 000 who had social impairment but did not meet the full diagnostic criteria for Asperger syndrome or high-functioning autism. Again, most individuals in this wider group would probably meet the current criteria for PDD-NOS or atypical autism, but this time without intellectual disability.

Wing and Gould's study and Ehlers and Gillberg's study were almost certainly looking at two differently defined groups: in Wing and Gould's study both the narrowly defined and wider group were intellectually disabled, while Ehlers and Gillberg's study considered groups with Asperger syndrome, high-functioning autism and PDD-NOS, but no intellectual disability. It is therefore possible to add the figures from these two studies, in order to calculate a grand total prevalence figure. Given the range of sub-types which the two studies covered, this is likely to represent a prevalence figure for all disorders within the autism spectrum. This total is 91 per 10 000 (i.e. 20 per 10 000 from Wing and Gould's study and 71 per 10 000 from Ehlers and Gillberg's study), equivalent to a little under 1%. The basis for this calculation is shown in Table 2.1.

Table 2.1 Summary of the data from three prevalence studies.

Study	Group included in estimate	Prevalence estimate	Totals
Lotter (1966)	Autism (as defined in 1966)	4 in 10 000	
Wing and Gould (1979)	Autism (similar group to Lotter's)	5 in 10 000	
	Wider group with autistic symptoms	15 in 10 000	20 in 10 000
	Both above groups with intellectual disability		
Ehlers and Gillberg (1993)	Asperger syndrome and high-functioning autism	36 per 10 000	
	Wider group with autistic symptoms	35 in 10 000	71 in 10 000
	Both above groups with no intellectual disability		
	Total prevalence estimate for the autism spectrum	91 in 10 000	

The figure of approximately 1% tallies remarkably well with one of the most recent epidemiological studies carried out by Baird et al. (2006). The latter study estimated the prevalence of autism spectrum disorders as in the region of 116 per 10 000, or little over 1% of the population of the UK. Interestingly, the breakdown into sub-types provided by these researchers also tallied pretty well with the set of figures for each of the sub-types just outlined. At present, therefore, there is no evidence to support the claim that the numbers of individuals affected by autism is rising.

■   In the light of these findings, what do you think is the main reason for the dramatically increasing estimates of autism prevalence over the past 40 years?

☐   The main reason for the change in estimates of prevalence over time is that the identification of cases in early prevalence studies such as Lotter's study relied upon narrow or classic criteria, while those in recent studies such as the one by Baird et al. adopted broad criteria to include the autism spectrum as a whole.

2.6.2 Prevalence estimates from different countries

Different prevalence estimates arise not only for earlier compared with more recent studies, but also from prevalence studies in different countries (see Table 2.2).

Table 2.2 Current estimated prevalence figures for the autism spectrum in selected countries.

Country	Prevalence of ASD	Source	Year
UK	1 in 100 (1.00%)	UK National Autistic Society	2007
USA	1 in 150 (0.67%)	Autism Society of America	2007
Australia	1 in 160 (0.63%)	Autism Council of Australia	2007
Canada	1 in 217 (0.46%)	Autism Society of Canada	2005
India	1 in 250 (0.40%)	Autism Society of India	2007
Hong Kong	1 in 621 (0.16%)	Hong Kong Government Statistics	2008

■ What do you notice about the figures presented in Table 2.1?

☐ The highest prevalence estimates are for the Western countries, with lower estimated rates in Asia.

At first glance, these different estimates might seem to indicate that more people are affected with autism in the UK than, say, in India. But as for the historical variation in prevalence estimates, it is probable that variations in diagnostic practice, or in the methodology involved in these studies, explains most of these differences.

■ What other factors related to diagnostic practice might contribute to varying prevalence estimates?

☐ Even now, diagnosis is not a straightforward matter of matching a person's symptoms to a set of fixed, universally agreed criteria. Current diagnoses may also vary according to which criteria (DSM or ICD) are used, which assessments are carried out, and even what diagnostic label is most likely to be acceptable to the person's family. In different countries there may be differences in factors such as local knowledge about autism, the degree of expertise in identification and diagnosis, cultural variations in attitudes to disability, and local practices in terms of how statistics relating to such disabilities are recorded.

2.6.3 Summary of Section 2.6

• Estimates of the prevalence of autism have increased from 4 per 10 000 or 0.04% for classic autism in 1966 to 116 per 10 000 or around 1% for the autism spectrum in 2006.

• The most likely reason for this increase is the widening boundaries of the autism category and the consequent changes in the diagnostic criteria.

• The different estimates for prevalence from different countries are likely to be due to differences in local information, cultural assumptions and diagnostic practices.

2.7   Conclusion

This chapter has considered diagnosis from various perspectives. It has outlined the nature of formal diagnostic criteria, the way they have evolved over time, and the implications for current definitions of the different variants of autism. It has looked at the use of assessment instruments such as the ADOS and the ADI to compare an individual's symptoms to the main criteria for the different sub-types of autism. It has outlined typical family experiences of diagnosis from two rather different perspectives – that of a family whose child is diagnosed with classic autism, and that of a family whose teenager receives a diagnosis of Asperger syndrome. While the current framework of diagnostic criteria and assessment procedures have more clarity and agreement than those, say, 20 years ago, there is clearly still a way to go. You saw, for instance, that there are some discrepancies between DSM-IV-TR and ICD-10, and that the framework of good practice for assessing children is recommended but not mandatory. Levels of knowledge and diagnostic expertise vary from place to place and country to country, and diagnostic decisions may be informed by what is seen as acceptable to an individual's family. All these factors leave room for differences in diagnostic assumptions and practice, which mean that differences in prevalence estimates are hard to interpret. And last but not least, there is as yet no reliable basis for early screening of those at risk of autism.

The impact of diagnosis on family life is taken up again in Chapter 8. The next chapter (Chapter 3) takes a detailed look at the behavioural and psychological symptoms which form the basis for diagnostic definitions of the autism spectrum – as well as some other key characteristics which lie beyond the diagnostic criteria.

2.8   Learning outcomes

2.1   Define and use, or recognise definitions and applications of, each of the terms printed in **bold** in the text.

2.2   Describe aspects of the typical clinical diagnostic process experienced by children on the autism spectrum and their families in the UK.

2.3   Outline the criteria by which classic autism, PDD-NOS, atypical autism and Asperger syndrome are formally defined.

2.4   Comment on some of the key differences between the characteristics of classic autism and Asperger syndrome.

2.5   Describe some of the key aspects of two of the main diagnostic instruments.

2.6   Comment on the current situation with regard to the use of screening tools for autism.

2.7   Describe and evaluate the current evidence in relation to variations in the estimated prevalence of autism spectrum disorders.

2.9   Self-assessment questions for Chapter 2

Question 2.1   (LOs 2.2 and 2.4)

The case studies of Anton and Oliver described how two families came to experience the process and outcomes of their child receiving an autism spectrum diagnosis. List (a) the main similarities and (b) the main differences between the two stories. (c) Comment briefly on how the differences relate to the key differences in the symptoms of autism and Asperger syndrome.

Question 2.2   (LO 2.3)

The DSM-IV-TR system includes PDD-NOS (also known as atypical autism) as an autism spectrum sub-type, while ICD-10 includes PDD-unspecified.

(a) What is the purpose of these categories within the diagnostic system?

(b) How do they differ from one another?

Question 2.3   (LO 2.5)

What is the role of diagnostic assessment instruments in (a) clinical practice and (b) research? Give examples of observations that are made in Modules 1 and 2 of the ADOS.

Question 2.4   (LO 2.6)

An autism screening tool is tested on a population of 10 000 children aged 18 months. This screening identifies 60 children who appear 'at risk'. In follow-up studies conducted a few years later, 34 of these children have received an autism spectrum diagnosis, while the remaining 26 are now considered typically developing. A further 20 children from the original 10 000 have also received an autism spectrum diagnosis. Why do these outcomes suggest the tool might be inadequate for screening purposes?

Question 2.5   (LO 2.7)

Prevalence estimates for the autism spectrum obtained in the UK and in India in 2007 differ markedly (Table 2.2). This difference does not necessarily reflect a difference in the number of affected individuals in the two countries. Why not?

Chapter 3   Psychological characteristics

Ilona Roth

3.1   Introduction

Most of the diagnostic criteria discussed in Chapter 2 focus on psychological characteristics of autism – how people on the autism spectrum think, behave and interact with the world. Chapter 3 considers the psychological characteristics in more detail, while Chapter 4 looks at the main theoretical explanations of why they occur. For a complete picture, this **psychological perspective** must be integrated with a **biological perspective**, exploring topics such as the strong genetic component, and the likelihood that the brain functions atypically in people on the autism spectrum. This biological perspective is further explored in Chapter 5.

A psychological perspective contributes important insights to both practical and theoretical work. As you will learn in Chapter 6, currently the most successful therapeutic interventions focus on overcoming psychological difficulties: for instance, techniques for improving communication, and encouraging greater flexibility in thinking and behaviour. The psychological perspective also highlights a range of **phenomena** (observable aspects of behaviour and inferred features of cognition) which theories aim to bring together by identifying common underlying factors. Finally, the psychological perspective contributes important information for biological work: for instance, the known difficulties in language function in autism offer clues to where in the brain to look for atypical function. So the psychological and the biological levels of analysis inform each other.

Sections 3.3–3.5 of this chapter consider in detail the three main areas in which people on the autism spectrum experience difficulty: communication, interacting with others, and flexibility of behaviour and interests. These three areas of the 'triad' form the core of the current formal diagnostic criteria, which were discussed in Chapter 2. Section 3.6 considers some characteristics that are not part of the triad, but nonetheless have special significance in relation to autism. Unusual reactivity to sounds, smells, sights and tastes (discussed in Section 3.6.1) occurs so often in people on the autism spectrum that certain specialists have argued that the diagnostic criteria should be revised to include these sensory and perceptual disturbances (Bogdashina, 2003). Special skills and talents (Section 3.6.2), though not universal, reflect one of the most fascinating and puzzling aspects of autism.

The chapter starts by looking at intellectual ability. Autism may occur with or without intellectual disability, so again it is not a defining or diagnostic aspect of autism. However, as you saw from the case studies of Anton and Oliver, the educational implications and outcomes for a child with autism *and* intellectual difficulties are likely to be very different than for a child whose intellectual functioning is comparable to that of a typically developing child. Understanding a little about this topic is essential background for the discussion in later sections.

3.2 Intellectual ability on the autism spectrum

Other students don't think very highly of me at school. A lot of people look at me and assume that I am not very smart. They think I am rude and stuck up … I don't know exactly why people assume low intelligence. It probably has to do with the way I walk or talk. It is probably also due to the fact that I don't socialise much and don't talk much.

(Quinn in Sainsbury, 2000, p. 81)

This statement by a boy with Asperger syndrome shows that people's informal judgements of intellectual ability – the ability to think, reason logically and solve problems – may be influenced by factors that have nothing to do with these skills. Such judgements are subjective: they are the personal opinions of one or more individuals and they sometimes reflect erroneous beliefs about what it means to be bright, or simple prejudice. To ensure that claims about intellectual ability are objective (i.e. independent of such biases), it is often desirable to measure thinking and reasoning skills using an intelligence test. Many people argue that there is more to intelligence than what intelligence tests measure, but nonetheless these tests often provide an effective way of evaluating how individuals compare with one another and with the average for the population. This can be especially helpful in considering the profiles of skills and difficulties in individuals on the autism spectrum. The broad principles are explained in Box 3.1.

Box 3.1   Measuring intelligence

The person undertakes one or more **intelligence tests**. One widely used system includes 'verbal' tests such as vocabulary, comprehension and general knowledge, and 'performance' or non-verbal tests, such as **block design**, using coloured blocks to copy a geometric pattern or **picture completion**, identifying the missing element in a picture of a familiar object (see Figure 3.1).

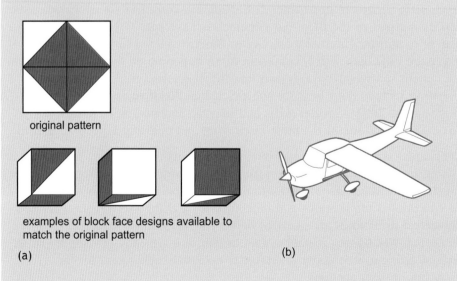

original pattern

examples of block face designs available to match the original pattern

(a)   (b)

Figure 3.1   Examples of (a) block design and (b) picture completion tests.

Test scores are added together to give a separate total for verbal and for performance tests, and each of these total scores is 'standardised' by comparing it with scores on the same tests that have been assembled from a large population of individuals of the same **chronological age** (age in years and months) as the tested individual. The mean of these scores is always set arbitrarily at 100. If the person tested exactly matches the mean for the same-aged population, they are said to have an **intelligence quotient** or **IQ** (verbal or performance) of 100. A score below 100 is below average, and above 100 is above average for that particular age group.

- ■ Why do you think that separate IQ scores are obtained for verbal and performance sub-tests?

- □ Some people are relatively good at verbal tasks, while others are better at tasks where visual or spatial skills are called for. Testing both areas provides a more balanced assessment.

Verbal and performance scores can also be combined, the mean of the two representing the person's overall or **full-scale IQ**. In any large group of people of a particular age, IQ scores will vary considerably, but the majority (95%) will fall within the range from 30 points below 100 to 30 points above 100, i.e. from 70 to 130. This characteristic 'bell-shaped' distribution of IQ scores is shown as a **graph** in Figure 3.2. The **vertical axis** of the graph (the left-hand vertical line) shows numbers of individuals, while the **horizontal axis** (the line from left to right) shows IQ score. IQ scores within the range of 70–130 are considered to be 'normal', those from 70 to 100 being on the low side of the mean, while scores from 100 to 130 are on the high side of the mean. The small proportion of people (around 2.5%) scoring below 70 are considered to have an intellectual disability. Similarly, the minority of people with scores above 130 are considered exceptionally bright or able.

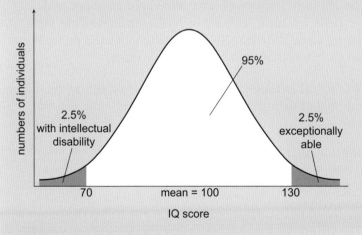

Figure 3.2 Graph showing the characteristic bell-shaped distribution of IQ scores within a population.

Another useful concept, especially when considering any group of individuals with intellectual difficulties, is mental age. Because IQ develops across childhood and adolescence, the full-scale IQ score of a 12-year-old child who scores well below the mean for their own chronological age group will match the mean for a lower age group. The age of this younger group is defined as the child's **mental age (MA)**. For instance, a child of 12, whose overall score on IQ tests matches that of seven-year-old children, is said to have a mental age of seven. This means that they are performing at the level expected of seven-year-olds.

■ If a child with a chronological age of 10 has an IQ score equivalent to the average of a group of 14-year-olds, what is the child's mental age?

□ The child's mental age is 14. That means he or she is performing at the intellectual level of 14-year-olds.

■ If a child has the same chronological age and mental age, what does this mean?

□ It means that the child's IQ is exactly average for his or her age group (i.e. 100). As Figure 3.2 shows, most typically developing individuals in any population score at or near this average.

The measurement of IQ and mental age has several roles in understanding the autism spectrum. First of all, IQ testing helps to assess what proportion of individuals on the autism spectrum have an intellectual disability; that is, an IQ below 70. This was recently estimated as at least 50% for children with a diagnosis of classic autism (Baird et al., 2006). However, in children with severe intellectual disability (i.e. in the IQ range well below 70) precise estimates of IQ may be difficult.

■ Can you think of a reason for this difficulty?

□ One problem is that individuals with extremely poor language and communication skills are likely to have difficulty understanding the verbal tests and may not understand the instructions for the performance tests. Therefore their scores cannot be reliably assessed.

■ The estimate of 50% of individuals with classic autism and an IQ of less than 70 is much higher than the 2.5% quoted earlier for the general population. Why is this?

□ The 50% estimate is for a specially selected group (people on the autism spectrum) and will include a higher proportion of individuals with intellectual disability than the general population.

Specialists often use the term low-functioning autism (LFA) for the group with scores below 70. The term high-functioning autism (HFA) is often used for the relatively able group with scores of 70 upwards. As mentioned in Section 2.2.4, the precise difference between HFA and Asperger syndrome is a matter of debate. Some specialists argue that the HFA and AS groups differ in their language development (see Section 3.3). Others, however, see no clear-cut distinction, and unfortunately, as for other aspects of autism terminology, there is no complete consensus.

Notice that although all IQ scores above 70 are, by convention, in the normal range, a person scoring anywhere between 70 and 85 is still likely to struggle with intellectual tasks. Some specialists have therefore suggested that the term high-functioning autism should be reserved for those with IQs above 85 (Baron-Cohen, 2008).

How a person with autism performs on the two main IQ test components is also interesting. While individuals in the general population may score slightly better, on average, on either verbal tests or performance tests, a *large* discrepancy between these two sets of scores may indicate an underlying problem (in some cases a brain injury) which undermines specific areas of functioning. Such discrepancies are very common in people on the autism spectrum. Individuals with LFA almost always perform better on performance than verbal tests. For people with HFA and AS it is often the reverse. This fits with the observation that highly 'verbal' individuals with Asperger syndrome may be awkward or clumsy, with poor physical coordination.

In people with autism, the pattern of scores on different IQ sub-tests is also distinctive. Whereas most people in the general population score at a similar level across all the verbal or performance sub-tests, people on the autism spectrum often show a very uneven profile with 'peaks' on specific sub-tests such as the block design test, shown in Figure 3.1. Exceptional performance in the context of a low average IQ is consistent with the phenomenon of special skills (see Section 3.6).

Finally, IQ and mental age scores have an important role to play in experimental studies of autism. Section 1.5 described Hermelin and O'Connor's studies comparing the memory performance of children with autism and typically developing children. These researchers were among the first to recognise that using typically developing control groups of the same age as the experimental (autistic) group is not in fact a fair comparison. For children with intellectual difficulties, performance on all ability tests will, on average, be inferior to that of typically developing children of the same age – any differences may reflect intellectual level, rather than being specifically due to autism.

■   How do you think Hermelin and O'Connor matched the experimental and typically developing control groups in their studies?

☐   The typically developing children were matched in *mental* age with the autistic participants, and were thus lower in chronological age. You will encounter this and other approaches to matching, including matching by IQ, in some studies described later in this book.

3.2.1 Summary of Section 3.2

• Intelligence tests offer an objective method of evaluating intellectual ability.

- An IQ of 100 is, by definition, exactly average, with scores between 70 and 130 representing the normal range.

- An individual's mental age is the age of the group whose IQ performance he or she matches.

- Autism with an IQ score less than 70 is known as low-functioning autism. At least 50% of children with classic autism may fall in this range.

- Autism with an IQ score of at least 70 is known as high-functioning autism. Asperger syndrome also applies to people in this IQ range.

- People on the autism spectrum often show a large discrepancy between verbal and performance IQ scores, and an uneven profile of scores on sub-tests.

- Matching by mental age and/or IQ is important in studies of psychological processes in autism.

3.3   Communication

You will recall from Section 1.2 that Kanner observed many oddities and deficiencies of language in his child patients, including some children with hardly any speech and others whose main use of language was echolalic, involving repeating back previously heard phrases. By contrast, Asperger found many of his patients to be highly 'verbal', in the sense that they had a good command of vocabulary and grammar and would converse at length on topics they found particularly interesting. Yet this apparent facility with language masked more subtle difficulties in using language for two-way communication. Asperger's patients often used language eccentrically or idiosyncratically, so sentences that were perfectly accurate in a grammatical sense came over as pedantic or odd. These early findings established the basic pattern that characterises the range and variation of language and communication difficulties across the autism spectrum. To understand this pattern, you need first to grasp some basic concepts and definitions.

3.3.1   Key concepts in language and communication

Language, defined in a narrow sense, means a system of sounds, signs or written items (letters, word fragments and words), together with rules for combining these elements in ways that convey meaning to others who share a knowledge of this language. To decide whether someone was using a particular language correctly in this narrow sense, you would need to consider two main levels: grammar and syntax, and semantics.

Grammar and **syntax** refer to rules governing the correct way of combining words into sequences such as sentences. The sentence 'I puts the flower vase on the table' may be understood, but it is technically an incorrect use of grammar, as the verb should be 'put'. The sentence 'I put the vase flower on the table' is an incorrect use of syntax, as the words are in the wrong order. People learning a language other than their own often make these sorts of mistakes, because the grammatical and syntactical rules of their own language work in different ways.

Semantics concerns the use of language to convey meanings. The two sentences in the previous paragraph do convey meaning, despite their grammatical inaccuracy, but the sentence 'I put the flower vase into the piano key' is effectively meaningless. Of course, someone might be able to devise a completely zany or imaginary situation in which this sentence becomes meaningful – so meaning and semantics are slippery areas to deal with!

Knowledge of vocabulary, grammar, syntax and semantics are by no means all that is involved in appropriate language use. A person must have the capacity to produce language themselves – known as **expressive language** – and, equally if not more important, the capacity to understand language that someone else produces – known as **receptive language**. If the language in question is spoken or listened to, the rules governing how words should sound – for instance, how 'piano' is actually pronounced, and what sequence of sounds that a person hears corresponds to this concept – also come into play. This aspect of expressive and receptive language ability is known as **phonology**.

Suppose that a person is familiar with the vocabulary, grammar and syntax of a language, can produce grammatically accurate, correctly sounded and meaningful sentences, and also extract meaning from sentences that other people produce. Is that all that is necessary to communicate effectively? Unfortunately not, as the following scenario illustrates. A pupil at a school was asked by a teacher (Mrs Patel) to go and ask another teacher (Mr Smith) if he would like a cup of coffee. The child went and delivered the message 'Would you like a cup of coffee Mr Smith?' But he didn't wait for Mr Smith's reply.

■ Can you think of a reason for this?

□ The child had understood that he should carry out Mrs Patel's instruction to ask Mr Smith a question, but he had not understood that the full purpose of Mrs Patel's instruction was to offer Mr Smith a cup of coffee.

The underlying problem here is that the child had not understood the *intention* behind Mrs Patel's request. Most if not all of our utterances can be understood in different ways, depending on the intentions of the communicator. You may be interested to know that the coffee cup scenario is a true event related by the head teacher of a school for children with autism. A child on the autism spectrum dutifully delivered the message, without really understanding or executing its purpose, illustrating the way an over-literal approach to a medium that is full of ambiguity can disrupt normal communication. The ability to produce and receive language effectively for purposes of two-way communication comes under the heading of **pragmatics**.

■ Think of two different meanings for the sentence 'Can you boil an egg'.

□ This could be either a request to someone to put on an egg to cook, or a question about whether they know the procedure for boiling an egg.

So how do most people 'decode' the meaning of ambiguous utterances in everyday communication? This is a very complex field, but some key points are relevant here. First of all, the context in which the utterance is made is

Irony is the use of an expression or phrase to mean something quite different from, or opposite to, what it normally means.

often very informative. If I say 'Lovely day for a walk' and actually it is cold and rainy outside, you are likely to conclude that I am joking or being **ironic**.

You are not interpreting my statement literally, but are taking the context (a rainy day) into account. Suppose that I invite you for a walk (on a really lovely day), and you reply 'What a good idea'. If you are also smiling and nodding your head, your facial expression and gesture convey to me that you really do want to go. But if you say 'what a good idea' while actually looking glum at the prospect, I may conclude that you are not really very keen on going. This illustrates that expression and gesture play a very important part in what is known as **non-verbal communication**.

■   Can you think what other sources of information may help me to decide, from your utterance, whether you genuinely want to go for a walk?

☐   The pitch, intonation and stress with which you say 'What a good idea' can either communicate a genuinely enthusiastic response, or a negative or even ironic response – just think of all the different ways you can make that simple sentence sound.

These non-verbal aspects of speech are known as **prosody**. What people say, the way they say it, and their accompanying expressions and gestures all work together in such a subtle and complex fashion that most of the time we are not even aware that we are processing these sources of information in everyday communication.

3.3.2   Language difficulties across the autism spectrum

People on the autism spectrum may have difficulties with any or all of the aspects of language and communication just outlined. Which aspects are affected, and to what extent, vary considerably. Researchers find it useful to differentiate between the language skills of children with low-functioning autism (LFA), high-functioning autism (HFA), and Asperger syndrome (AS) (see, for instance, Boucher, 2009).

Language and communication difficulties in children with LFA are pronounced, and include many of the aspects outlined earlier. To explain this pattern it is also necessary to specify the stage of development in question. Some young children with autism have no functional use of language at all, and this persists throughout life. For others there is some development over time, though language capacity at any given stage does not match that of typically developing children of the same age, and the outcome, in terms of the final level of language attained, is poor. Comparisons of typically developing children and children with LFA at some key stages of language development are summarised in Box 3.2. Note that this is a much simplified summary of a complex pattern, and it glosses over individual differences. Some typically developing children may be less or more proficient at a given age than is suggested here, while the language skills in some children with low-functioning autism may also depart somewhat from the description.

Each stage described in Box 3.2 gives separate examples of receptive language (what the child understands) and expressive language (what the child says). Notice, however, that even at an early stage in typical development these activities start to work together as part of an ongoing cycle of interaction between the child and his or her mother or care-giver. This two-way use of language involves what is known as **reciprocity** – processes of 'give and take' and 'turn-taking' which are fundamental for communication.

Box 3.2   Stages in early language development in typically developing children and children with LFA

12 months

Most typically developing children will understand simple spoken instructions such as, 'Give me the ball', especially if accompanied by gestural cues such as holding out the hands. They will also have produced their first words, using them appropriately to point out people ('Mama', 'Dada') or objects ('book', 'ball') in their environment. Children subsequently diagnosed with autism often show little response to what is said to them. They may produce a few words, but as their parents tend to recall, these words are not used meaningfully.

24 months

Typically developing children will understand simple phrases such as 'Where's Daddy?' and opposites such as 'hot' and 'cold'. They will have a vocabulary of up to 200 words, will use some pronouns ('I', 'me' and 'you') correctly, and will be combining two to three words into their own simple phrases such as 'more juice'. By contrast, children subsequently diagnosed with autism will show little evidence of understanding what is said to them. They may have a small vocabulary of words, but some of these may not remain in their repertoire. There will be little attempt to combine words into simple phrases, and incorrect use of pronouns if any (such as saying 'you' for 'I').

36 months

Language understanding in typically developing children will have extended to include questions such as 'Who?', 'What?' and 'Where?' Their vocabulary may comprise up to 1000 words and many elements of grammar and syntax will be appropriately used. Their language will extend beyond pointing out present objects, to refer to people and objects that are not physically present. Children with an autism diagnosis may now indicate some understanding of, and response to, things said to them. However, their responses are likely to consist of echolalic repetition of phrases such as 'Do you want a drink' to indicate 'Yes I want a drink'. Their vocabulary will be small and they will still make few attempts to combine words into sequences.

Five years

The language of the two groups is even more divergent: typically developing children will show an increasing understanding of complex or abstract concepts, such as 'family' or 'age', and their now large vocabulary will include number terms and opposites. They will be capable of quite sophisticated use of grammar, recognising when their own or another person's utterances are grammatically incorrect. Above all, they will be using their receptive and expressive language abilities for two-way communication, and showing a grasp of ambiguity and other pragmatic complexities. By contrast, children diagnosed with autism will show little understanding of complex or abstract concepts. Many will use grammar inappropriately, including features such as pronominal reversal, in which pronouns like 'he' or 'she' are used instead of 'I' to refer to self. And most striking of all, they will typically have great difficulty in using language for two-way communication. A child may be able to convey requests and desires to a parent who knows him/her well (e.g. by the echolalic repetition of particular phrases) but will be unable to take turns in conversation: for instance, by asking a question, and then waiting for, and responding appropriately to, the answer.

■ From the description of typically developing children in Box 3.2 pick out examples of (a) receptive and (b) expressive language at 12 and 24 months.

▢ (a) Examples of receptive language include understanding simple instructions at 12 months, and understanding simple phrases and opposites at 24 months. (b) Examples of expressive language include using words to indicate people and objects at 12 months, and using a range of vocabulary, including simple words and phrases at 24 months.

Turning now to more able children on the autism spectrum, high-functioning autism (HFA) is the term used for autistic individuals with IQ in the normal or above normal range, but who have nonetheless shown delayed language development in childhood. Early language development in these individuals would be similar to that described in Box 3.2, but would continue to improve markedly, so that by the early teens, these individuals would have an adequate command of vocabulary, grammar and semantics.

The term Asperger syndrome is reserved for individuals with IQ scores in or above the normal range, but who show no obvious delay in the main components of language. However, this differentiation is less clear-cut if language ability is defined as competent use of language in two-way communication. Individuals with Asperger syndrome, as well as older children with HFA, may make long statements in which they use vocabulary, syntax and grammar perfectly, but yet remain 'literal' in their understanding of others and oblivious of or confused by the subtle nuances and ambiguities of language. Such difficulties usually persist into adult life. Will Hadcroft recalls a childhood experience of interpreting the presenter of *Rainbow*, a children's TV programme, too literally.

My earliest memory of taking things too literally involves Rainbow. It was customary for Geoffrey to end each instalment by saying 'That's all we have time for boys and girls, but we'll see you again soon'. One afternoon I got into my head that 'soon' meant soon the same day. As the afternoon progressed, I kept approaching my mother to ask 'Is Rainbow coming back on yet?' To which she would absent-mindedly reply 'I don't know, love'. It was only when I approached with an alarm clock in my hand, and pointing at the fingers, that she realised I was very anxious about Rainbow coming back. This time she sought clarification. I explained 'Geoffrey said he would see us soon'. Mum smiled, 'No, love. He doesn't mean the same day. He means the next episode in a few days'.

(From Hadcroft, 2005, p. 26)

Over-literal understanding of language is also well illustrated by difficulties many people on the autism spectrum have in understanding **metaphors**, irony and jokes. If a person says that they want to be 'in at the kill', it means that they want to participate in the conclusion of something (often involving financial gain), not that they want to be involved in a murder! Everyday language is full of such familiar metaphors, as well as others that are more individual or original. Difficulty in making appropriate sense of them can make the world a confusing and even frightening place for people on the autism spectrum – so much so that a guide to interpreting metaphors and everyday expressions has been published especially for this group (Stuart-Hamilton, 2007). Inability to understand irony or jokes makes it difficult for people on the spectrum to join in light-hearted social interactions, and lays them open to teasing or bullying, which may be indistinguishable for the person with an autistic condition.

> A metaphor is a word or phrase applied to a concept with which it has no literal relationship.

> I can remember some children chasing me home from kindergarten, telling me that since I liked animals so much they were going to cut me up into bacon. They described the whole process, telling me what they were going to do and how they were going to do it. I didn't eat bacon for about three years, I thought it was made from little kids no one liked.
>
> That was almost 30 years ago … About six years ago I supervised one of them at work. He didn't even remember. He said it was just 'kid stuff' and meant nothing. I still don't understand that.

(Jim in Sainsbury, 2000, pp. 73–74)

Notice that all children misunderstand such 'jokes' at some point and this does not mean that they are on the autism spectrum. It is also important to remember that there are individual variations in the capacity for irony and metaphorical language. The writer and poet Donna Williams, who is a very able individual on the autism spectrum, writes poetry that is replete with ironic references and unusual metaphors. For instance 'Humour has been my life's marshmallow' is Williams' way of saying that humour is her treat or enjoyable experience (Williams, 2004).

- ■ Does Donna Williams' capacity to write poetry with metaphors mean that she has no difficulty with non-literal language?

- □ A person with good expressive language may not have good receptive language abilities. Donna Williams is able to use metaphors in her writing, but may find the non-literal language used by others difficult to understand. Indeed, she mentions this in her autobiography (Williams, 1992).

3.3.3 Non-verbal communication

Facial expressions and gestures are forms of communication occurring either with or without language, while prosodic features (pitch, stress and intonation) are by definition complementary to language. Most individuals across the autism spectrum have difficulty with some or all of these forms of communication. For instance, their gestures and facial expressions may be sparse, awkward or inappropriate. Spoken language in some individuals sounds flat or dull, while in others it may be 'singsong' or exaggerated. In the fluent speech of individuals with HFA or Asperger syndrome, it may be the unusual use of gesture or the atypical prosodic quality of their speech that makes them stand out. Whether the level of impairment in non-verbal communication is related to level of language difficulty is not well understood. However, McCann et al. (2008) tested children with HFA on measures of their receptive and expressive language ability and their understanding and use of prosody, and found **correlations**: that is, children who scored less well on language tests also tended to score less well on tests of prosody.

3.3.4 Summary of Section 3.3

- Language means a system of sounds, signs or written items, together with rules for combining these elements in ways that convey meaning to others who share a knowledge of this language.
- Language ability includes receptive and expressive aspects, and knowledge of vocabulary, grammar, syntax, semantics and phonology.
- Use of language for two-way communication (pragmatics) involves reciprocity, and the consideration of context and the speaker's intentions, in order to understand ambiguous and non-literal utterances.
- Non-verbal communication, including gesture, expression and prosody, works in close interaction with language to convey meanings.
- People with low-functioning autism show marked delays in language development, including vocabulary, grammar and semantics, and poor long-term outcomes.
- People with high-functioning autism show early language delays, with better long-term outcomes, while people with Asperger syndrome do not show obvious delays in early language development. However, both groups have difficulties with pragmatic use of language for communication.
- Most people on the autism spectrum have atypical or impoverished use of non-verbal communication, including expression, gesture and prosody.

3.4 Social interaction

As for language, it is important to take age and developmental stage into account when considering findings about social interaction. The interactions expected of any child – whether typically developing or with autism – are different from those expected of an adult. Note however, that the early difficulties in social interaction thought to occur in autism may change the whole **developmental trajectory**. This is the term for the developmental sequence: in typical development, early 'milestones' lay the foundations for later, more sophisticated skills such as play with siblings, friendships with peers, or the complex relationships of the teenage years and adulthood.

3.4.1 Social interaction in infancy

As you saw in Section 1.3, studies suggest that typically developing children are attracted to social stimuli, such as human faces and the sound of human voices, from birth. Equally, from a strikingly early age, typically developing infants actively encourage social responses from others by their behaviour. For instance babbling attracts a mother's attention and responses in the form of baby talk, which evokes further responses from the baby, and so on. Many psychologists believe that close reciprocal interchanges develop from birth onwards because infants and their mothers are biologically attuned to pick up and respond to each other's cues, this reciprocity promoting **bonding** or emotional attachment (Trevarthen, 1979). See Figure 3.3. Infants later diagnosed with autism may lack social approaches and responsiveness from a very early stage, and therefore fail to engage their mothers in reciprocal interaction and bonding (Hobson, 2002).

Figure 3.3 Close interaction between mother and baby is thought to promote emotional attachment. (Ian Hooton/Science Photo Library)

■ Why is it difficult to know for sure whether these early social behaviours are missing?

☐ Children are rarely diagnosed with autism before the age of two, and are not usually diagnosed until at least three years, but the behaviours being considered here occur in the first year of life.

Some relevant clues may be found in parents' recollections of the early behaviour of children subsequently receiving an autism spectrum diagnosis. In one study (Wimpory et al., 2000), parents described their children as not being 'cuddly': for instance, not showing pleasure in being held or played with. Some reported that their child gazed blankly rather than with interest at other humans, or seemed more fixated on objects than people. Poignantly, some parents recalled that their child had developed normally, and then the development seemed to cease or even reverse, so that the child lost skills he or she had had. A very pronounced reversal of development may reflect an unusual 'regressive' form of autism.

■ What problems might there be with evidence that is based on parents' recall?

☐ Knowing that your child has an autism diagnosis may colour a parent's memory of early life events. Indeed all of us with children may think we have clear memories of how they were early on, yet memory may act to distort or embellish our recollections.

■   Can you think of another everyday source of information, which is not subject to this bias?

☐   Many families have made home videos of their children from soon after birth.

Such videos can provide informative material for researchers. Some recent studies, summarised in Box 3.3, illustrate the use of the **observational method**. Like the experimental method introduced in Box 1.7, the observational method involves systematic analysis of behaviour, but in contrast to the experimental method, observational research examines naturally occurring behaviour, rather than responses to specially devised tests. The researcher often needs to derive categories for evaluating the behaviour from the observations made, rather than determining them in advance.

Box 3.3   Exploring early responsiveness to people and objects in autism: observational studies of home videos

Maestro and colleagues (Maestro et al., 2005; Maestro and Muratori, 2008) explored differences in behaviour between children who later received an autism spectrum diagnosis, and a control group of typically developing children, at ages 0–6 months and 6–12 months. Both social and other aspects of behaviour were considered. (Notice that this study is about early developmental milestones, and in this case it is appropriate to compare children of similar chronological ages.)

Method

Parents of the two groups of children were asked to loan their home videos. The researchers prepared equal length extracts of activities such as feeding and bathing, birthdays and holidays, play with objects and people. For each extract, the child's age in months was recorded, so that observed behaviour could be related to the age when it happened.

The researchers watched each extract, categorising the behaviour under headings or **codes**; that is, phrases providing concise summaries of the behaviour observed. The codings made by two researchers working independently were compared to ensure that they both agreed in their interpretations of what the child was doing. An acceptable level of agreement in such studies, usually at least 75%, is known as **inter-rater reliability**. The numbers of behaviours noted under each code were then counted.

The researchers coding all the videos were also not told whether the child being observed was in the autistic or control group. This procedure is known as **blind rating**.

■   What do you think is the purpose of this?

☐   The procedure helps to ensure that the researchers' analysis of the video is not influenced by expecting particular behaviours (such as less looking at people) from the participants with autism.

The researchers focused on two categories of behaviour:

- **object-focused attention**: looking at objects; orienting towards objects; smiling at objects; vocalising to objects

- **social attention**: looking at people; orienting to people; smiling at people; vocalising (making sounds) to people

Results

Summaries of some key findings are shown in Figure 3.4. This is a graph comparing the amount of behaviour directed towards social and object stimuli shown by the typically developing (TD) children, and those later diagnosed with an autism spectrum condition (A), at 0–6 months and 6–12 months. Along the vertical axis the figures show the mean numbers of behaviours observed. The horizontal axis has points representing the two time periods. Within the graph, the solid lines join up the observations for the TD children made at the different times, while the dotted lines do the same for the children subsequently diagnosed with autism. At 0–6 months, TD children showed far more social attention; both groups showed only limited and approximately equal attention to objects. At 6–12 months TD children were still very attentive to people, and had also developed more attention to objects; children with autism had become particularly attentive to objects (more than the TD children), but had also become more socially attentive.

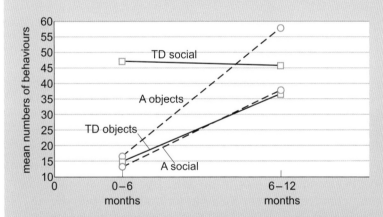

Figure 3.4 Measures of social and object-focused attention for typically developing (TD) children and those with an autistic spectrum condition (A). An increase in object-focused behaviours is present in both groups but is more marked in children with autism, so that during the second time period these children become significantly more attracted by objects than TD children. The graph also shows some increase in socially oriented behaviour by children with autism at 6–12 months. (Adapted from Maestro and Muratori, 2008)

Conclusion

The researchers argued that the typically developing children's early attention to people, which they sustained across the 6–12-month period, together with their increasing attention to objects during this second period, would enable them to begin drawing their parents into shared games involving their toys. This *sharing of attention* becomes a striking feature of behaviour in the second year of life, and a building block for later social interaction. Because the autistic group had little social attention in the first period, and then developed a predominant interest in objects, they missed out on opportunities for engaging their parents in joint activities, even though they developed a bit more social attention at 6–12 months.

- From the graph in Figure 3.4 read off: (a) the approximate mean numbers of socially oriented behaviours by TD children at 0–6 months and 6–12 months; (b) the approximate mean numbers of object-focused behaviours by children with autism spectrum diagnoses at 0–6 months and 6–12 months.

- (a) The mean numbers of socially oriented behaviours (TD) at 0–6 months is approximately 47, and remains more or less the same at 6–12 months. (b) The mean numbers of object-focused behaviours (A) at 0–6 months is approximately 16, and at 6–12 months it is 58.

3.4.2 Social interaction in toddlers

Further evidence for early difficulties in social interactions comes from studies of children in their second year of life. One early difference is in **pointing**, and this features in the CHAT (Section 2.5.1). By the age of 12 months, typically developing children use their index finger to point at things they want – a favourite toy or a biscuit, for instance. This so-called **protoimperative pointing** is a type of request, enabling the child to convey 'I want to have that', before they are able to say this. During the second year, typically developing children also start pointing for a different purpose: to indicate or share their interest in something. Known as **protodeclarative pointing**, this activity is equivalent to the child saying 'Look at that!'

Protoimperative pointing enables the child to gain a pleasurable reward, such as a biscuit or a favourite toy, while for protodeclarative pointing there is no tangible reward or outcome, and the purpose of the pointing is inherently social. The child's aim is to get the adult to focus their attention on the same thing as them – in essence, to influence the focus of the adult's thoughts. Children who are later diagnosed as on the autism spectrum tend to show protoimperative but not protodeclarative pointing.

Imagine that a typically developing 14-month-old child sees a plane in the sky. He might point at the plane, then look at his mother, and then back at the plane.

■ What type of pointing is the child using?

☐ The child is using protodeclarative pointing to draw his mother's attention to something that is of interest to him (Figure 3.5).

■ (a) How do you think the mother is likely to respond?
(b) Suppose it is the mother rather than the child who looks at the sky – what do you think the child will do?

☐ (a) The mother is likely to look where her child is looking, and then to say 'Plane' or 'It's an aeroplane'. (b) If the mother looks at the sky first, the child is likely to look where the mother is looking, and may again have the opportunity to hear the plane named.

Note that these behaviours form part of joint attention – the sharing of a thought process with another person (see Section 2.4.2). The acts themselves may seem simple, but the underlying psychological processes are exceedingly complex. Notice too, how they provide the child with useful opportunities to learn the names of objects. Children later diagnosed with autism initiate joint attention very infrequently, and are also very poor at responding to others' attempts to initiate joint attention (Charman, 2003). Missing out on early social and learning opportunities is likely to have a profound impact on the developmental trajectory.

Figure 3.5 This small boy is engaging his mother's attention: she looks at what he is pointing at. (Photolibrary)

■ Which of the aspects of language discussed in Section 3.3.1 might be affected by missing these interactions?

☐ At the very least, children will have less opportunity to learn vocabulary, phonology, and meanings of words. Poor joint attention will also undermine development of pragmatic understanding.

3.4.3 Social interaction in later years

You saw in the two case studies in Chapter 2 that problems in social interaction take different forms as a child grows up. During the preschool years, children on the autism spectrum typically appear immune to attempts to draw them into games involving reciprocal exchange with other children, and seem uninterested in making friends. They may become strongly attached to their parents, though not in a secure way: for instance, being very demanding or clinging. At school these children may learn to tolerate having other children around them, but without really integrating with them. Some children negotiate adolescence without major difficulty, but also without improvement in their social skills. At this age they may well want to make friends, but have no idea how to go about it. Their clumsy attempts at approaching others will usually put other children off, so they remain friendless and are frequently teased or bullied.

As far as social interaction is concerned, it would not occur to me naturally to do something (or not do something out of kindness, respect, or appreciation of someone). Social rules like saying please and thank you, reciprocating someone else's kind act and so forth, would be beyond me. I would need to be reminded to do some thing or another, or it would occur to me afterwards, usually when it's too late ... There was another student whom I thought resembled a cat, so I 'meowed' whenever she spoke to me, which she thought was strange.

(Sarah in Sainsbury, 2000)

In adulthood, the style of social interaction in people on the autism spectrum tends to fall into one of four different categories (see Wing, 1996):

- **aloof**: these adults continue to avoid interaction with others, remaining withdrawn and apparently unaware of the existence of others.

- **active but odd**: these adults seek people out and try to make contact. But their approaches tend to be inappropriate. For instance, they may talk at length about their special interest, regardless of relevance or interest to others; come up too close to other people; or even touch them in unacceptable ways. Inevitably these approaches will be rejected, unless others are aware of the autistic person's difficulties.

- **passive and friendly**: these adults are able to tolerate the company of others, but do little to interact with them. They may seem quiet and shy rather than autistic, as long as they remain within a familiar and non-stressful environment.

- **overly formal and stilted:** these adults try hard to overcome their social difficulties. They do so by conforming to rigid rules of behaviour, and thus appear formal and excessively polite.

Notice that only the first interaction style evokes Kanner's original description of autistic aloneness (Box 1.3). Some form of social interaction, albeit atypical, is present in the other three interaction styles.

3.4.4 Recognising and responding to emotions

Jessy, who distinguishes the minutest differences between shades – how can we expect her to pick up the subtlest indicators of emotions? And if she can't, how can we expect her to manage the ordinary inescapable interchanges of living?

(Claiborne Park, 2001, pp. 139–40)

Difficulties in engaging emotionally with others features in the DSM-IV-TR and ICD-10 diagnostic criteria, but this symptom does not play a very prominent role (see Section 2.2.1). In practice there is evidence that people on the autism spectrum have considerable difficulty in recognising and responding to emotions. Many studies have built on a method developed (outside the autism research field) by Ekman and Friesen (1971) to study the so-called **basic emotions** – happiness, sadness, anger, fear, disgust and surprise. When Ekman and Friesen showed photographs of faces posing these emotions to people in different cultures, recognition seemed to be universal. That is, allowing for translation, a particular facial expression would evoke the same response across all the cultures tested. This supports Charles Darwin's original view (Darwin, 1872) that the capacity to express and to recognise basic expressions is innate; that is, a biological endowment at birth. An impairment in these innate abilities might explain why parents recall that infants diagnosed with autism did not smile or respond to smiling at an early age.

Hobson (1986) gave children with autism schematic drawings of faces expressing the basic emotions of anger, unhappiness, happiness and fear (Figure 3.6), and asked them to match the expressions with audio or video sequences of an actor portraying the same set of emotions. The sequences were designed to present three types of cues:

- vocalisations: with the screen blank, the actor made sounds appropriate to each of the four emotions

- gestures: with his face obscured by a mask, the actor made appropriate gestures for the four emotions

- context: the actor (still masked) appeared in scenes appropriate to the four emotions: e.g. for happiness, the actor is seen receiving a birthday cake.

Figure 3.6 Schematic drawings of emotional expressions used to match video sequences. From left to right: unhappy, afraid, happy, neutral, angry. (Adapted from Hobson, 1986)

Hobson found that the children with autism performed poorly on all aspects of this task when compared with MA-matched control groups.

Hobson's use of audio and video sequences to provide dynamic cues and contextual information was designed to make this task more **naturalistic** (representative of real life) than one employing still photographs.

■ However, the task is still not completely naturalistic. Why not?

□ The schematic emotions are static and cartoon-like and the video emotions are posed by an actor, not spontaneously occurring; in real life face and voice cues usually occur together rather than being artificially separated.

Studies following up Hobson's findings, including some improving further on the naturalistic qualities of the stimuli, have provided mixed results. Some studies identified recognition difficulties, others found little difference between the performance of autism spectrum and control groups. Some of these discrepancies may relate to the sub-group being tested. Though they may not have the apparently effortless recognition skills of typically developing children, children with HFA may learn special strategies to overcome their initial lack of understanding, by paying close attention to particular cues.

Understanding certain emotions, such as embarrassment or pride, requires more complex understanding than basic emotions. To feel embarrassed, a person needs to be aware that something they have said or done has amused or offended another individual. To feel pride, a person usually takes into account the approval of others. Understanding these **complex emotions** is difficult for all sub-groups on the autism spectrum. Often the person needs to integrate facial expression and voice with other sources of information including gesture, body posture and context. These sources of information may even be ambiguous. For instance, a student receiving an exam result may state that they are quite happy with their mark, while their facial expression or tone of voice suggests that they feel disappointed. For most people, processing these multiple sources of information (known as **multi-modal emotion recognition**) is carried out automatically and with little effort (Herba and Phillips, 2004).

Finally, perhaps the most difficult emotion skill for people on the autism spectrum is to understand what emotions mean, and therefore to respond appropriately. If a friend looks very upset, the natural response is to ask them what is wrong and to try to comfort them. This is known as **empathy**. In many situations, the response may be more subtle than an action: the individual may just feel emotionally affected by what another person seems to be experiencing. They may well experience the same emotion as the other person – known as **mirroring**. The profound difficulty people on the autism spectrum have with situations and tasks calling for empathy is widely documented and some researchers believe that it is fundamental to the psychological causes of autism (see, for instance, Baron-Cohen, 2003). The implications of emotion recognition and empathy difficulties for explanations of autism are explored in Chapter 4.

3.4.5 Summary of Section 3.4

- Typically developing infants show simple forms of social approach and responsiveness from birth.
- Evidence that children on the autism spectrum lack many forms of social responsiveness comes from parents' retrospective reports and observational studies of home videos.
- In their first year, lack of early social attention and growing interest in objects may deprive children with autism of the chance to engage reciprocally with care-givers.
- In their second year, children later diagnosed with autism are likely to lack the capacity for protodeclarative pointing and joint attention.
- Older children on the autism spectrum tend to remain isolated, unable to engage reciprocally with others, and friendless.
- In adults on the autism spectrum, four different styles of interaction have been observed.
- Clinical observations and experimental findings indicate that people with autism have difficulty recognising and understanding emotions, especially in situations involving complex emotions and/or empathy.

3.5   Restricted and repetitive activities and interests; pretend play and imagination

Spinning my body brings some sort of harmony to my thoughts

So that I can centrifuge away all the black thoughts

I realise that the faster I spin

The faster I drive away the black

When I am sure that even the last speck of black

Has gone away from me

Then I spin back in the opposite direction

(From Poem 4 by Tito Mukhopadhyay (2000) in Beyond the Silence: My life, the world and autism, *p. 101)*

This description of stereotyped behaviour is remarkable: Tito was a child when he wrote it, and he is also in the minority of people on the autism spectrum who can describe their own symptoms. This section considers this third triad area – probably the least understood and researched of the three.

3.5.1   Stereotypies, repetitive behaviours and routines

A **stereotypy** is a repeated or ritualistic movement, posture or utterance. Some of the most common in autism are waving, twirling or flapping of the hands. It is possible that these movements may be used to gain stimulation. For instance, moving the hand in front of the face may change the amount or pattern of light reaching the eyes. Some high-functioning people on the autism spectrum even refer to their stereotypies as 'stimming' (or stimulating). On the other hand, some activities, like Tito's spinning, may have a calming effect.

Stereotypies may emerge very early in a child's development – again, according to parental accounts, before a year old. Slightly later, the child may start to repeat rather more complex behaviour patterns: for instance, repeatedly running their hand down a velvet curtain, perhaps because it has a pleasing texture and feel.

Later still, repetition may take the form of strict routines and rituals: for example, always wearing the same item of clothing or putting on clothes in exactly the same order. Notice that many typically developing children have routines which they follow rigidly at certain stages in development. But the autistic routines tend to persist much longer (even throughout life), and have a much stronger hold on the individual. People with autism may become very anxious if they are prevented from executing their usual routines.

The time spent engaged in repeated movements or activities means that the repertoire or range of behaviour in people with autism is likely to be narrower than in a person who freely adjusts their behaviour to each new situation. Extremely focused interests may have the same effect. A person with an obsessive interest in *Star Wars*, for instance, will be engaging repeatedly, and for long periods of time, with the same themes, leaving less time and scope to develop a wider, more varied repertoire of interests. Topics of interest to people on the autism spectrum often lend themselves to the accumulation of facts or lists, such as all the species of dinosaur discovered to date, or names and telephone numbers learned from the telephone directory.

> In fourth grade, I was … interested in both dinosaurs and astronomy, especially since this was the time of the Voyager flybys of Jupiter and Saturn. My appetite for information was voracious and I would clip or photocopy everything I could find on the subject in the newspaper, magazines, academic journals and books. I think my interest in dinosaurs waned at this point, though I remember an occasion when I went to the neighbourhood pool and I went up to total strangers asking them to ask me any question about dinosaurs because I felt I knew everything about them.
>
> *(Sarah in Sainsbury, 2000, p. 68)*

Before moving on to the next section, take a look back at the triad diagram in Figure 1.1. The third triad area, at the bottom right-hand corner of the figure, depicts the inflexibility and repetition in activities and interests just outlined. Lack of pretend play is grouped *separately* with communication difficulties, in the bottom left-hand corner of the diagram, and other imagination difficulties are not included at all. Though this arrangement corresponds with the current diagnostic criteria (discussed in Chapter 2), the original triad of impairments (Wing, 1981) had impairment of creative and imaginative concepts as its third area. Pretence and imagination are discussed here, alongside repetitive activities and interests, because of the possible links between them.

■   In what ways might repetitive behaviour and narrow interests be linked to problems in pretence and imagination?

☐   Engaging in repetitive activities and interests may take up so much time that the child has little scope to develop more imaginative ideas. Alternatively, a lack of imagination might prevent a child from developing new ideas for activities, thus leading to repetition of those activities that are already familiar. Just how these aspects of behaviour are linked merits further research.

3.5.2   Pretend play and imagination

Like joint attention, pretend play is seen as a milestone in typical child development, emerging somewhere between 12 and 18 months. At this stage, pretence is solitary, and fairly simple. For instance, a child may pretend to drink out of a toy cup, talk into a toy telephone, or use a toy block as a car. In each case the child is behaving *as if* the toy had properties it doesn't have. By 24 months, the child's pretence will be slightly more complex: he/she may 'walk' a toy animal across the floor, or enact pretend sequences, such as pouring an imaginary drink into a cup, drinking from the cup, and offering a drink to someone else. Though these examples include toys, you have probably noticed that children will use whatever materials are to hand – including sticks, stones and earth – to pretend. Between 36 and 48 months, children's pretend play becomes more social, involving scenarios in which they role play with other children.

Typically developing children may carry on pretending until about the age of 12. In children on the autism spectrum, pretend play is usually very limited or absent throughout childhood. Baron-Cohen (1987) compared how three groups of children played with a specially selected set of toy materials. The experimental group comprised children with low-functioning autism, with a mean chronological age (CA) of eight years. One control group were typically developing children with a mean CA of four years, while the other were children with **Down syndrome**, with a CA of eight years. The group of typically developing children were selected to match the group with autism in mental age (MA) rather than chronological age.

■ Why do you think the experimenter included a second control group comprising children with Down syndrome?

☐ These children matched the autistic group in both CA and MA. If children with autism and with Down syndrome both showed similar deficits in play, this would suggest a general impairment due to developmental delay, rather than a specific impairment due to autism. The use of two controls, one TD and the other with a different developmental delay, is quite common in research on autism.

Baron-Cohen's results suggested impairments in pretend play that were specific to the group with autism and to playing in pretend mode. The children showed about as much 'functional play' – for instance, turning the dials on a toy cooker – as both of the control groups, but significantly less pretence, such as putting a piece of foam sponge into a pan and pretending to cook a meal.

Baron-Cohen's interpretation was that children with autism lack the **symbolic capacity** for pretence – roughly speaking, the capacity to treat objects and entities *as if* they were something else. However, in common with many experiments comparing autistic and non-autistic groups, the differences were not all or none: the group with autism did show *some* capacity for pretence. Other researchers have demonstrated that children on the autism spectrum can be encouraged to pretend if ideas are provided (Lewis and Boucher, 1988) and can understand if someone else enacts a pretence (Jarrold, 2003).

■ What might these findings suggest about pretence difficulties in autism?

☐ Since the children with autism show some, albeit limited, capacity for pretence, it could be that what they lack is *motivation* rather than symbolic skills – an important difference, since a motivational problem suggests scope for teaching pretence.

These ideas about pretence remain debated, the answer resting partly on how the concept is defined and explained. Craig and colleagues (Craig and Baron-Cohen, 1999, 2000; Craig et al., 2001) further explored the areas where children on the autism spectrum seem to lack imagination. Their experiments are summarised in Box 3.4.

Down syndrome is caused by chromosome abnormality and usually involves a degree of intellectual disability, together with characteristic physical features, and sometimes medical problems.

Box 3.4   Experimental studies of imagination in children on the autism spectrum

Method

The researchers compared the performance of children with classic autism, Asperger syndrome (AS) and control groups on three types of test:

1   'Seeing the possibilities': for example, suggest ways of making a toy more interesting; suggest uses for a piece of foam.

2   Drawing: for example, drawing pictures of familiar creatures and impossible creatures such as a 'fish-mouse'.

3   Story completion: for example, writing a story on a reality-based theme, such as a girl going to school; and a fantasy theme, such as a dragon that lives in a cave and eats jam sandwiches.

Children's responses to the tests were evaluated for the number of different ideas produced and the imaginative quality of content. A blind rating procedure was used (see Box 3.3) to ensure that evaluations were not biased by expectations about the outcomes.

Results

1   Seeing the possibilities: the two autism spectrum groups produced fewer responses, which were also rated as less imaginative, than the control groups.

2   Drawing: the autism spectrum groups drew real creatures as competently as the control groups, but had significantly more difficulty in drawing the unreal creatures (see Figure 3.7).

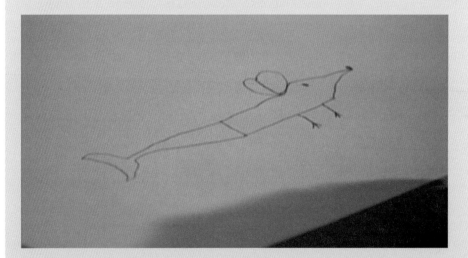

Figure 3.7   A 'fish-mouse' drawn by a typically developing child. Children on the autism spectrum had difficulty drawing such unreal composites, opting instead for separate drawings of real animals. But they could draw composite figures of real objects, such as a houseboat.

3 Stories: the quality of realistic stories was comparable for the different groups; the autism spectrum groups' stories on a fantasy theme included few imaginative elements.

On all three sets of tests, the children with AS performed better than those with classic autism. However, as these two groups had the same CA (13 years), this result is difficult to interpret.

- ■ Why is this a problem?

- ☐ The group with AS would, by definition, have better language skills than the autistic group of the same chronological age. This puts the group with AS at an 'unfair' advantage, especially on the stories task.

Conclusion

The results were interpreted as evidence that children on the autism spectrum have a general difficulty with imagination.

Findings such as these may reflect two different sources of imagination difficulty. For instance in the 'seeing the possibilities' test, difficulty in suggesting really imaginative ideas for the piece of foam may reflect a symbolic difficulty in seeing it *as* something completely different – similar to Baron-Cohen's interpretation of pretend play discussed earlier. For typically developing children, thinking *as if* – about things that don't really exist, and thinking *what if* – about events that might or might not happen, play an essential role in fantasy, and in understanding fictional stories, movies and even some computer games. This may also help adults to make everyday decisions and 'try out' possible solutions to problems. For instance, to choose a holiday, you might try imagining yourself in scenarios such as a hot sunny beach, or a beautiful city.

Difficulty in generating more than a small number of ideas for the foam may reflect an inability to move flexibly from one response to another. This second type of constraint on imagination relates to the executive function theory of autism, which you will encounter in Chapter 4.

3.5.3 Summary of Section 3.5

- Stereotyped movements, such as hand flapping, emerge quite early in children on the autism spectrum, and may serve a stimulating function.

- Stereotyped movements, repetitive activities and rigid routines reduce the scope and variety of behaviour.

- Interests confined to factual topics and lists may reflect an inability to access more imaginative themes.

- Pretend play develops between 12 and 18 months in typically developing children, and is impoverished throughout childhood in those on the autism spectrum.

- The studies of Craig and colleagues suggest constraints on the quality and quantity of imaginative ideas, especially in classic autism.

3.6 Psychological characteristics beyond the triad

With the constantly unfolding understanding of the autism spectrum described in Chapters 1 and 2, non-diagnostic symptoms now play an important role in both theory and practice. For many parents of children on the spectrum, dealing with sensory and perceptual difficulties is as much of a challenge as language and social difficulties. Special skills and talents often provide a source of pride and fulfilment for the individual and his/her family, and have played a major role in shifting psychological theories about autism from focusing exclusively on deficits, to considering strengths.

3.6.1 Atypical sensory and perceptual processing

Sometimes if there was too much commotion around me, either in movement of people or in noise, I would just automatically tune out. In situations such as these, my senses would sometimes not be integrated and each individual sound would be heard as a separate sound and each visual detail would clutter my line of sight. So I would just stare blankly without exactly looking at anything and I would sometimes not be aware if I happened to be looking in the direction towards someone. I would often not be aware of anything during these episodes and would not even notice if someone was trying to get my attention.

(Sarah in Sainsbury, 2000, pp. 101–102)

When Jessy painted her room last year she used, of course, the full spectrum: violet, blue, green, yellow, orange and pink, for these are pastels. Not just any pastels, however, but mixed to her specifications. A friend, an architect, brought her four huge volumes of colour samples. The whole rainbow was there, hundreds of shades, numbered for a fussy client to choose from. Jessy did not deliberate, she knew; her choice was *instantaneous*.

(Claiborne Park, 2001, p. 136)

These two extracts give fascinating insights into the complex and diverse atypicalities of sensory and perceptual processing in people on the autism spectrum. To consider these in more detail, some key concepts need to be explained. **Sensory processing** refers to the means by which we acquire information about the environment through specialised **sense organs**, each of which deals with a different **modality** or dimension of input. The main sensory modalities, and their corresponding sense organs are listed below in Table 3.1.

Table 3.1 Sensory modalities and sense organs.

Sensory modality	Sense organs
Vision	Eyes, including the lens and light-sensitive retina
Hearing	Ears, including the ear-drum, middle ear structures and auditory receptors
Touch	Touch receptors in the skin, specialised for light touch, pressure, hot, cold and pain
Smell	Smell receptors in the nostrils, specialised for different chemical particles in air
Taste	Taste receptors in the tongue, specialised for different chemical particles in food and drink; sense of taste also involves smell
Proprioception (sense of bodily position in space)	Movement receptors in muscles, tendons and joints
Vestibular sense (sense of balance)	Organs of balance in the inner ear; sense of balance also relies on visual and proprioceptive input

■ Which of these sensory modalities are referred to in the two extracts above?

☐ The two obvious ones are vision and hearing. However, Sarah also alludes to sensory disturbance caused by too much movement around her. This could be because the movement is disturbing her vestibular system, similar to the feeling of travel sickness which can occur when watching rapidly moving images on a cinema screen.

Sensory processing is primarily concerned with registering the presence and qualities of sensory stimuli from the environment, and transmitting signals based on this information to the brain. In contrast **perceptual processing** is primarily concerned with interpreting and making sense of these signals, enabling the person to make appropriate responses. In practice, sensation and perception are interrelated stages in the same processing system. Some sensory processing, especially in vision and hearing, involves forms of perceptual interpretation from an early stage in processing stimuli.

Two main aspects of atypical sensory and perceptual processing are hypersensitivity and hyposensitivity introduced in Box 1.1. Hypersensitivity means that people on the autism spectrum may experience sounds which seem quite moderate to others as excessively or painfully loud. They may experience lights, colours and patterns as harsh and disturbing, feel nauseous at tastes which others find appetising, or perceive other people as having an off-putting smell, possibly accentuating their aversion to being approached or touched. Similarly, some people with autism find the feel of particular fabrics next to their skin unbearable, making them 'faddy' about clothing. Temple

Grandin, whose writings offer many insights into autism, described the feeling of wool as intolerable (Grandin and Scariano, 1986). People who are hypersensitive to several modalities may experience **sensory overload**, leading to extreme anxiety and/or 'shut-down', where the person becomes unresponsive to all stimuli as a form of defence.

Hyposensitivity implies that an individual has *reduced* awareness of sensory stimuli, though the evidence for this is usually a lack of *responsiveness*. For instance, in the case study of Oliver in Chapter 2, the fact that he didn't respond when called does not necessarily mean that he did not register the sound; his lack of response might have been because he did not attach any meaning or significance to it. This is consistent with the fact that he picked up the sound of his father's car long before others could hear it. It follows that hypersensitivity and hyposensitivity may sometimes be part of the same difficulty in modulating sensory inputs appropriately, leading the individual to overreact in some situations, and 'tune out' stimuli in others, as described in the quote from Sarah at the beginning of this section.

True hyposensitivity – where the individual does not *experience* sufficient stimulation – may lead to what is known as sensory-seeking behaviour, an active search for more stimulation. This may be one reason for behaviours such as spinning (leading to increased vestibular and proprioceptive input), and flicking the hands in front of the eyes (increased visual input), though the full reasons for these behaviours are not known.

Reduced proprioceptive and vestibular input may also have consequences for **motor behaviour**, that is for the way a person uses his/her muscles in movement. For instance, a person who has a diminished sense of balance, or of the position of their body in space, is likely to be clumsy and uncoordinated. This is well documented, particularly in people with Asperger syndrome.

Bogdashina (2003) suggests that atypical sensory experiences result in atypical styles of perceptual processing. For instance, to avoid overload of sensory information, the person may 'tune out' all modalities except one, focusing in great detail on the perceptual qualities of this modality. This attention to fine detail, which is well documented in autism, is illustrated by Jessy Park's ability to distinguish minute gradations of colour for use in her pictures. Attention to detail is useful in some situations, but may mean that the person has difficulty in integrating information from different sources or modalities to interpret complex stimuli. You will read more about this in Chapter 4.

Among many other sensory and perceptual atypicalities, two which are particularly striking are synesthesia and prosopagnosia. **Synesthesia** means the spontaneous triggering of one sensory system, when another different one receives input. For instance, the person may see a colour when hearing a sound, touching something or tasting something. Synesthesia can also occur when a concept (e.g. a number) triggers a sensory experience. **Prosopagnosia** means face blindness, or the inability to recognise faces. Temple Grandin has described how she fails to recognise people unless she has seen them many times, or they have a very distinctive feature, such as an unusual hairstyle.

Both synesthesia and prosopagnosia occur outside the autism spectrum, and their prevalence in autism is not known.

Sensory and perceptual atypicalities can have as much impact for the person on the autism spectrum as difficulties with communication, social interaction and flexibility of action. Indeed, as touched upon in Section 3.5.1, sensory difficulties may play a role in these other symptoms. You may wonder, therefore, why this group of problems are not included in the diagnostic criteria. One reason is that the prevalence of these problems across the autism spectrum is not known, and this may stem, in turn, from the difficulty of identifying them. Difficulties in communication, for instance, have clear behavioural consequences, such as problems using language. In contrast, detecting a feeling of sensory overload when a child cannot describe what he feels, may well be a matter of guesswork. In this field, in particular, the personal accounts of individuals who can describe their experiences have an invaluable role to play.

3.6.2 Special skills and exceptional talent

Alongside the psychological difficulties in autism, some people on the spectrum have areas of special skill – what Kanner called 'islets of ability' (Box 1.3). The general term for this is **savant syndrome**, usually defined as an isolated, narrow area of ability in the context of profound disability (Treffert, 1989). Probably the best-known savant, the character Raymond, played by Dustin Hoffman in the film *Rain Man*, was partly based on a real-life savant with a phenomenal memory capacity and specialised arithmetical skills. People are fascinated by such special gifts and autistic savants are understandably encouraged to display them publicly. But there are ethical issues about how to celebrate these talents without demeaning or taking advantage of the individual.

■ What psychological characteristics of people with autism make them particularly vulnerable to exploitation?

□ As you have seen, people on the spectrum often don't appreciate subtle nuances of communication, and may also fail to appreciate the consequences of actions proposed to them by persuasive individuals.

Not all people with savant syndrome are on the autism spectrum, but a majority are. Among people with autism spectrum diagnoses, it is estimated that at least 30% have some area of special skill (Howlin et al., 2009). Not all of these are as exceptional as Raymond's in *Rain Man* and they can be categorised by level:

• **splinter skills**: usually a well-developed ability – for example, completing complex jigsaws; or an obsessive hobby, like Sarah's comprehensive knowledge of dinosaurs quoted earlier

• **talents**: more highly developed and noticeable skills, such as the capacity to paint accomplished pictures, or to do difficult mental calculations – for example, **calendrical calculation** is the highly specialised ability to work out the day of the week, given a randomly chosen date such as 20 January 1809

- **prodigious skills**: talents so exceptional or outstanding that they are likely to attract widespread public interest. It has been suggested that there may be only 25 individuals in the world with prodigious skills.

While specialised spatial or arithmetical skills are common, some savants execute their skills in typically creative fields such as art and music. The artist Stephen Wiltshire has a phenomenal capacity to reproduce architectural scenes after glancing briefly at them. On one occasion, after a helicopter trip along several miles of the Thames in London, he drew, from memory, an accurate aerial view of everything that he had seen, all in perfect perspective. Figure 3.8 shows one of Stephen's many drawings of Canary Wharf.

Figure 3.8   Stephen Wiltshire's precise rendering of the buildings at Canary Wharf. (Stephen Wiltshire)

It is often suggested that savant skills depend on highly developed and specialised perceptual or memory skills, rather than creative imagination – this would be consistent with the imagination deficits discussed in Section 3.5.2. But some savant works have imaginative qualities. For instance, Jessy Park, mentioned in extracts by her mother earlier in the chapter, executes meticulous paintings of everyday objects or buildings. They appear photographically accurate, but are transformed by her vibrant and original use of non-realistic colours (see Figure 3.9), evoking a little of the flavour of pop artists like Andy Warhol.

Like Stephen Wiltshire, Gilles Tréhin makes precise line drawings of buildings and complex urban scenes. But Gilles' are entirely imaginary. His many drawings depict the districts, buildings, streets and monuments of a fantasy city called 'Urville'. In his recent book (Tréhin, 2006) the captions describe the buildings, their economic and cultural history, and famous people who lived there, often mixing real dates and names with fictitious ones.

One of the rarest and most puzzling savant talents is in languages. A young man called Daniel Tammet, who knows 11 languages, recently accepted a challenge to learn Icelandic in a week, and at the end of the week appeared on Icelandic television answering questions in this language.

Daniel has other outstanding skills, including calendrical calculation, and the ability to recite the decimal places of 'pi' to thousands of digits. He has strong synesthesia: for him Wednesday is a 'blue day', hence the title of his biography: *Born on a Blue Day: Inside the extraordinary mind of an autistic savant* (Tammet, 2006).

Figure 3.9   Jessica Park's picture of the Chrysler Building in New York. It is accurately depicted but enlivened by original use of colour. (Pure Vision Arts)

■   How does this profile of Daniel Tammet conflict with the usual definition of savant syndrome?

☐   Having skills in several different areas is unusual, and beyond the usual definition of savant syndrome.

Perhaps most important for a wider understanding of both savant syndrome and autism in general is Daniel's capacity to talk about his mental experience. As you have seen throughout this chapter, 'insider' accounts of autism, of which there are a growing number, add a rich dimension of insight to the scientific and clinical work of the experts. The challenge of reconciling special skills in autism with the many areas of difficulty outlined in this chapter is considerable. Chapter 4 considers the main theories that have been proposed to explain this complex and puzzling pattern.

3.6.3   Summary of Section 3.6

- Atypical sensory and perceptual processing in autism may include hyper- and/or hyposensitivity in each of the sensory modalities.
- Some individuals experience synesthesia or prosopagnosia.
- About 30% of people with autism spectrum conditions have areas of special skill or talent.
- Savant syndrome is defined as an isolated area of special skill, in the context of profound disability.

- Savant skills include splinter skills (the commonest form), talents and prodigious skills (the rarest form), the latter in domains including arithmetic, art, music and languages.
- Daniel Tammet has multiple savant skills and the capacity to reflect on his own experience.

3.7   Learning outcomes

3.1   Define and use, or recognise definitions and applications of, each of the terms printed in **bold** in the text.

3.2   Demonstrate knowledge of the psychological characteristics of the triad of impairments, and of other common characteristics beyond the triad.

3.3   Give examples of some of the ways these characteristics vary depending on the individual's stage of development and sub-group within the spectrum.

3.4   Demonstrate knowledge of the broad principles of intelligence tests, and their relevance to understanding autism.

3.5   Comment on the broad principles of the observational research method.

3.6   Comment on the principles involved in experiments on autism.

3.8   Self-assessment questions for Chapter 3

Question 3.1   (LO 3.2)

The following is a list of behaviours observed in Katya, a girl of 2 years, who is thought to be on the autism spectrum. Indicate which of the behaviours are consistent with: (a) communication difficulty; (b) difficulty in social interaction; (c) repetitive activities and interests; (d) sensory atypicalities; (e) special skills.

Katya:

1   rarely smiles
2   doesn't point to indicate objects of interests
3   can complete a jigsaw designed for 6 years and above
4   becomes very anxious if she cannot eat the same food every day
5   appears unresponsive when her mother calls her, but cannot bear the sound of the vacuum cleaner.

Question 3.2   (LO 3.2)

Which *two* of the following emotions are likely to be most difficult to recognise for a person on the autism spectrum? Give reasons for your answer.

(a) Happiness; (b) disappointment; (c) pride; (d) fear.

Question 3.3   (LO 3.3)

Which of the following communication difficulties are likely to occur in a person with Asperger syndrome?

(a) Restricted vocabulary; (b) incorrect use of grammar; (c) difficulty understanding irony and humour; (d) unusual tone of voice and use of gesture.

Question 3.4   (LO 3.4)

(a) What does it mean to say that a person has a verbal IQ of 110 and a non-verbal (performance) IQ of 90?
(b) Give three ways in which people on the autism spectrum may show a distinctive pattern of scores on IQ tests compared with the general population.

Question 3.5   (LOs 3.5 and 3.6)

Identify two similarities and two differences between the observational study in Box 3.3 and the experimental study in Box 3.4.

Chapter 4 Psychological explanations

Ilona Roth

4.1 Introduction

Chapter 3 described how the symptoms and characteristics in autism vary in their expression between individuals and groups and evolve with age. Explaining this complex and variable pattern is a challenging task, and this chapter considers some of the theories and models that have been proposed. A **theory** provides an account of a set of observed phenomena in terms of principles which explain how and why the phenomena occur. A **model** is also a form of theoretical explanation, often specifying mechanisms or processes depicted in visual form such as a chart. However, in psychological research on autism, the term model often means a broad approach or conceptualisation embracing several related theories.

Often scientific theories aim to identify the *cause* of the phenomena in question. When people talk about the causes of autism, they usually mean 'faults' in biological processes and mechanisms that ultimately lead to autism. So you may be wondering what role psychological theories play in explanation. Autism is almost certainly the end result of a complex *chain* of influences in which biological, psychological and perhaps even environmental factors all interact with one another. Psychological theories of autism try to identify the key psychological processes and mechanisms within this causal chain. Moreover, as pointed out in Section 3.1, psychological findings and theories often guide biological research, and also play a major role in the way both researchers and practitioners conceptualise and work with the problems of people on the autism spectrum.

It is important to consider the broad goals that psychological explanations of autism should achieve. For instance what phenomena should they take into account? What makes one explanation more convincing than another? Box 4.1 outlines some key criteria (see Boucher, 2009 and Pellicano, 2010 for analogous arguments).

> **Box 4.1 Criteria for evaluating psychological explanations of autism**
>
> Testability
>
> A theoretical explanation must be **testable**; that is, formulated so that it makes clear predictions about what outcomes should occur if it is correct. It must also be **falsifiable**, which means that it must be possible, in principle, to prove that the theory is incorrect. Theories that are very general or vague are not falsifiable, and therefore have no explanatory power. Testing the predictions of a theory about autism involves collecting empirical evidence, which may come from experiments (see Box 1.7), observational studies (Box 3.3) or a variety of other systematic methods.

Scope

It might seem essential that the scope of an explanation should accommodate as many as possible of the known characteristics of autism. Most of what Uta Frith has called 'the big ideas' about autism, which have emerged over the past 20 or so years, have tried to do just that. These approaches are known as **core deficit models**, because they assume that a single underlying problem accounts for the wide range of behavioural and psychological difficulties that are observed in autism. But it is also possible that separate influences, working alongside one another result in difficulties in communication, social interaction and inflexibility of thought and behaviour. Recently, many researchers have started to think more along these lines, adopting the approach of a **multiple factor model**. One consequence of this shift is that some of the 'big ideas', which were once considered mutually exclusive, because each competed to account for all the psychological characteristics of autism, may now be considered complementary, because each addresses different aspects.

Deficits and skills

Psychological explanations have traditionally focused on the difficulties in autism. But with increasing recognition that many individuals have specific areas of enhanced functioning, contemporary explanations often seek to capture both deficits and skills. One possibility is that the same underlying processes generate skills in some tasks and situations, and deficits in others.

Universal features of autism

To meet the criterion of **universality**, an explanation should identify something that affects all individuals on the spectrum, i.e. a universal factor or factors. Otherwise additional explanations will be needed for those not accounted for. However, as autism is quite a heterogeneous category, in some specific circumstances, an explanation applicable to a sub-group (such as individuals with Asperger syndrome) may be useful.

Problem specific to autism

The **specificity** criterion means that an explanation should identify a factor or influence which is specific to autism, rather than highlighting the overlap and similarities between autism and other psychological conditions. However, the boundaries of the autism spectrum are not completely clear-cut. For instance, there is some overlap of symptoms with **attention-deficit hyperactivity disorder (ADHD)**. An idea of key factors that are common to autism and to other conditions may be informative in some circumstances.

Developmental trajectory

The fact that autism unfolds over the course of development is important for theory. As you saw in earlier chapters, the early behaviours of typically developing children provide the building blocks for development throughout life. Similarly, the early problems in autism may set the child off on a different developmental trajectory, in which difficulties at one stage have knock-on effects for the next. Effective

ADHD is characterised by persistent and pronounced overactivity and difficulty in attending.

explanations cannot just deal with the behaviour that is the outcome of the developmental trajectory, but should explain *why* this pathway is initiated and how it unfolds over time.

4.1.1 Summary of Section 4.1

- Psychological explanations of autism seek to identify the psychological influences within a complex causal chain.

- Criteria for evaluating theories include the testability, scope, universality and specificity of the proposals, and whether they address the developmental trajectory.

4.2 The theory of mind approach

Since the mid-1980s, one psychological explanation of autism has been especially influential. Fundamental to this approach is the idea that our capacity to communicate and interact socially with other people depends on understanding what they think, feel and believe, that is their **mental states**. This is known as having a **theory of mind**, often abbreviated to ToM.

You may be wondering whether the 'theory' in ToM has anything to do with the concept of theory outlined in Section 4.1. According to the original formulation of ToM, our knowledge of other people's thoughts, feelings and intentions is a bit like a scientific theory of why they behave as they do. These days this theory analogy is considered less appropriate, but the label has stuck.

The philosopher Daniel Dennett (1978) was the first to suggest that if a person was unable to understand other people's thoughts, beliefs or intentions, much of social interaction and communication would be a mystery. Building on this claim, it was proposed that people on the autism spectrum have a diminished capacity to understand other people's mental states, and perhaps their own too. Indeed, it was argued that people with autism may be unaware that others have a 'mental life'. In both these ways they lack ToM. This idea has had a major impact on the way researchers and clinicians, as well as families and individuals, think about autism.

4.2.1 The false belief test

Dennett reasoned that the most stringent test of ToM was whether a person could understand that someone else's belief about a situation was different from their own, and from reality – the so-called **false belief test**. To grasp what this means, imagine the following scenario.

You and a friend, Kelly, drive to the shops in your car. You park your car in a particular street (Mount Street) and as you both have different shops to visit, you arrange to meet back at the car in an hour's time. Shortly after parting from your friend, you realise you have left your wallet at home, so you drive back home to fetch it. When you get back to where you parked before, it is full up, so you have to park in a different street (Park Street). You *know* that when Kelly goes to meet you, she will assume that the car is where you originally parked it. Unless you can find her first, she will go to meet you in Mount Street, not in Park Street. In this situation you understand that Kelly's belief about the location of the car is false, and that she will act on the basis of this false belief.

Developmental studies suggest that children typically develop an understanding of false belief at about the age of four. Simon Baron-Cohen (Figure 4.1), Uta Frith (Figure 4.2) and Alan Leslie (Baron-Cohen et al., 1985) conducted a pioneering experimental test of whether children with autism could understand false belief, called the 'Sally-Anne task'. The ToM theory *predicts* that children with autism will have difficulty in this false belief task. Hence the experiment is designed as a *test* of the ToM theory as an explanation of autism. This is described in Box 4.2.

Figure 4.1 Simon Baron-Cohen (b. 1958), Director of the Autism Research Centre, University of Cambridge, and a leading figure in the autism field since collaborating with Uta Frith in the 1980s. (Brian Harris)

Box 4.2   The Sally-Anne false belief task

Method

The child sits at a table on which two dolls (Sally and Anne) are positioned facing lidded containers (a basket and a square box). The experimenter names the dolls, and checks that the child knows which is which, before using them to enact the stages in the scenario shown in Figure 4.3.

After viewing the scenario the child is asked three questions:

1   'Where will Sally look for her marble?' (belief question: the correct answer is 'in the basket')

2   'Where is the marble really?' (reality question: the correct answer is 'in the box')

3   'Where was the marble in the beginning?' (memory question: the correct answer is 'in the basket').

Three groups of children were tested (one at a time) on the task – see Table 4.1.

Figure 4.2 Uta Frith (b. 1941), a leading pioneer in research on both autism and dyslexia since the 1970s, when she worked with Beate Hermelin and Neil O'Connor. (Robert Taylor)

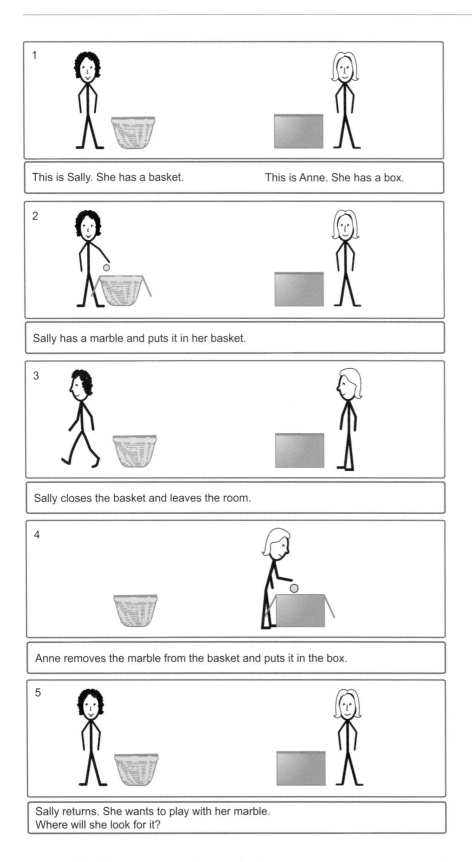

Figure 4.3 The sequence of events in the Sally-Anne false belief task. (Adapted from Frith, 1989)

Table 4.1   The Sally-Anne false belief task.

Participant groups	Participants	Mean chrono-logical age	Mean mental age (non-verbal)	Mean mental age (verbal)
Experimental group	20 children with autism	11 years 11 months	9 years 3 months	5 years 5 months
Control group 1	14 children with Down syndrome	10 years 11 months	5 years 11 months	2 years 11 months
Control group 2	27 typically developing children	4 years 5 months	Not tested	Not tested

- Why do you think the mental age (MA) of the typically developing children was not tested?

- In a typically developing group it is reasonable to assume that MA, on both verbal and non-verbal tests, will correspond to chronological age (CA).

- Why has the group with autism been chosen to have a higher MA than the other two groups?

- If the MA of the children with autism is higher, any differences between their performance on the task and that of the two control groups cannot arise simply because intellectual difficulties impair their understanding of the task.

Results

The children in all three groups answered the reality and memory questions correctly. 85% of the typically developing children and 86% of the children with Down syndrome also answered the belief question correctly. In contrast, 80% of the children with autism answered the belief question incorrectly. When asked 'Where will Sally look for her marble?' they pointed to the marble's current location rather than to where the marble had originally been placed.

- Why do you think the participants were asked reality and memory questions as well as the belief question?

☐ The experimenters needed to be sure that children had understood and recalled the basic set-up correctly. If they didn't remember where the marble was originally, or had not noticed where it was moved to, it wouldn't be possible to interpret their answers to the belief question.

The crucial issue is why most children with autism fail on the belief question in this experiment, while children in the two control groups mostly pass. One explanation is that since children with autism have difficulties with pretend play, the participants misunderstood the pretend 'drama' that the experimenter enacted using the dolls. But this was ruled out by later experiments that replicated the task with real people enacting the scenario. **Replication** means repeated with the same outcome. Baron-Cohen et al. argued that autistic children tend to fail on the belief question because, instead of 'putting themselves in Sally's shoes', they assume that her belief about where the marble is hidden is the same as their own knowledge of where the marble really is. In short, the study provides supportive evidence for the theory that children with autism lack the capacity for understanding another person's mental state (which, in this case, is different from their own). This basic finding has been replicated many times, employing numerous variants of the task (Figure 4.4).

Figure 4.4 Screenshot from a film of the Sally-Anne task, with Uta Frith (centre) enacting the scenario and Alan Leslie at right. (Taken from the BBC Series *Antenna*, 1988. © BBC)

Of course other people's thoughts and feelings will sometimes be similar to your own, rather than different. The broad principle which the theory of mind approach tries to capture is that you cannot assume that other people's mental states are just 'replicas' of your own. Understanding this is fundamental for interactions with other people – and that's what the false belief task tests. Information about what knowledge or beliefs another person can be reasonably expected to have, comes from their behaviour and the context in which it is occurring. Think back to the car parking example. Your judgement that your friend Kelly will go back to the original car parking place in Mount Street, rather than to the new parking place, is actually a well-informed 'guess' based on evidence from her behaviour. For instance, Kelly *saw* you parking the car and walked off *without* seeing you moving the car – so she cannot be expected to know that you have moved it. This illustrates a principle known as **'seeing leads to knowing'**, meaning that a person's belief or knowledge about a situation depends partly on what perceptual information has been available to them. Understanding this principle also emerges in typically developing children somewhere between 36 and 48 months (Baron-Cohen and Goodhart, 1994).

The following reminiscence, from a young person with Asperger syndrome, neatly illustrates how failing to understand that seeing leads to knowing may relate to ToM difficulties:

> One of the most recurrent problems throughout middle childhood was my constant failure to distinguish between my knowledge and that of others. Very often my parents would miss deadlines or appointments because I failed to tell them of these matters. For instance, my parents missed the school's Open House in my fifth grade and my mom asked me afterward 'why didn't you tell us about it?' 'I thought you knew it', I replied.
>
> *(Sarah in Sainsbury, 2000, p. 60)*

Notice that, despite her difficulties, Sarah has the capacity to reflect on them. The interesting issue of self-awareness will be revisited in Chapter 9.

4.2.2   Evaluating the theory of mind approach

Since the ToM approach was first formulated, there have been many studies proposing modifications or improvements to the original theory. This evaluation focuses on the core features of the theory – Section 4.3 considers some of the reinterpretations and extensions.

Testability?

The original false belief test provided an elegant and stringent test of the prediction that people on the autism spectrum will fail to grasp another person's beliefs about a situation. Notice, however, that the test focuses on one specific (albeit important) aspect of ToM. Our understanding of what people think, intend and feel is not confined to appreciating that their thoughts are different from our own. Some different ways of testing ToM impairments are discussed in Section 4.3.

Scope?

Children and adults on the autism spectrum have a wide range of difficulties that are consistent with a ToM deficit. You have already seen that a common communication difficulty, even in high-functioning individuals with good language skills, is with non-literal or ambiguous utterances and communications. Inability to understand what another person intends (i.e. their mental state) in the context is a likely reason for this. The reason that irony, metaphor and also deception are lost on people on the autism spectrum may well be that they fail to pick up the cues (especially the non-verbal and contextual ones) that suggest that what another person says is not necessarily the same as what they are thinking or feeling.

Children with autism also make relatively little use of mental state language (words like 'think', 'know', 'believe', 'feel') in their speech (Tager-Flusberg, 2000), suggesting that the whole activity of **mentalising** (another term for thinking about mental states) is alien to them.

The ToM approach can also help to explain difficulties in social interaction. To succeed in social interaction requires a subtle and complex understanding of the norms of what other people expect. For instance, to develop a friendship with a peer, a child needs to understand principles such as sharing and 'give and take'. A child who barges into games, pursuing their own interests without taking into account the expectations and needs of others (i.e. without appreciating their psychological point of view) is likely to be excluded. Over time, this means that the child will miss out on the learning experiences by which other children's interactions develop. Sadly, all too often this is what happens to children on the autism spectrum.

ToM seems less relevant to the third triad feature: why should difficulty in understanding other people's mental states impact on a person's capacity for flexible thought and behaviour? Baron-Cohen (1989) argued that it is the social character of most everyday events and activities that gives them their meaning and coherence. Since this will be lost on people without ToM, they will seek stimulation through repetitive activities and predictable interests which don't require social understanding. Interestingly this idea, which links the third triad area with the ToM approach, has received little follow-up.

Deficits and skills?

ToM was not formulated to address the characteristic skills in autism, though a later section will describe how elements of the approach have been adapted within a 'skills/deficits' framework.

Universality?

As you saw (Box 4.2), approximately 20% of children on the autism spectrum passed the Sally-Anne false belief test. In some studies an even higher percentage of participants, especially able individuals with better language skills, have been found to pass ToM tests. In addition, it is only possible to test participants who can understand task instructions, which means that the ToM capacities of 'low-functioning' individuals with little receptive language are not well understood. If some people pass ToM tests, while others cannot be tested, the theory does not have universal application. However, some autism researchers have suggested how the ToM framework might accommodate some of these variations in performance (see Section 4.3).

Specificity?

While ToM difficulties are especially prevalent in children and adults on the autism spectrum, they occur to some extent in other psychological conditions; for instance, in children with congenital blindness (Minter et al., 1998), and in old people with cognitive decline, or dementia (Gregory et al., 2002). A measure of overlap with these other conditions may draw attention to common and informative underlying factors, such as areas of the brain that are functioning atypically in both conditions. Nonetheless, to serve as an explanation specific to autism, the ToM difficulties in this condition should be distinctive.

Developmental trajectory?

One of the most serious drawbacks of this approach is that it does not identify *processes* of early development that might result in ToM problems. Chapter 3 discussed differences in behaviour that were emerging as early as 12 months of age (for instance the amount of social attention in the studies of home videos by Maestro et al. (2005, 2008) – Box 3.3), and which were clearly apparent by 18 months, such as pretence, protodeclarative pointing and joint attention. This is much earlier than the age (four years) at which typically developing children pass false belief tasks, and the link between the earlier and later difficulties is not clear.

As you have seen, many people on the autism spectrum do have impaired ToM skills, which could fundamentally affect their capacity to communicate and operate in social situations. But the original ToM theory did not explain how ToM difficulties could develop, or why some people on the autism spectrum pass ToM tests. The approach also adopted a relatively narrow conception of what it means to understand other people's thoughts and feelings. The next section considers some proposals that aimed to address these three difficulties.

4.2.3 Summary of Section 4.2

- The theory of mind (ToM) explanation of autism proposes an underlying psychological difficulty in understanding other people's thoughts, beliefs, intentions and emotions.
- Children on the autism spectrum typically fail the 'Sally-Anne' false belief task, designed as a test of ToM.
- The ToM approach is primarily relevant to explaining communication and social interaction difficulties.
- The ToM approach generates testable predictions in relation to deficits, but lacks universality and specificity.
- The ToM approach does not address the developmental origins of ToM failure, and offers a narrow conception of understanding other minds.

4.3 The theory of mind approach: modifications and extensions

When a scientific theory is challenged by the evidence, this does not necessarily or immediately lead to the theory being discarded. Rather, researchers will look at ways of revising the theory to accommodate the difficulties. This section looks at three theoretical extensions to the original ideas.

4.3.1 Developmental origins of theory of mind

One influential idea about the origins of ToM in early behaviour was proposed by Alan Leslie (1991). He suggested that understanding mental states such as false belief depends on a specialised mental system which enables the individual to disengage or 'decouple' (mentally speaking) from the truth of a situation in order to hold in mind an idea that differs from this reality. For instance, in the car parking example outlined in Section 4.2.1, in order to understand that your friend would have a false belief about where you parked the car, you needed to decouple your ideas from the reality – the car is now in Park Street – in order to hold in mind the proposition that 'Kelly thinks the car is in Mount Street'.

■ In the Sally-Anne false belief task, identify: (a) the true situation that the child watching the scenario must decouple from and (b) the proposition that the child must hold in mind about Sally's belief about the situation.

☐ (a) The marble is in the box;

(b) Sally thinks the marble is in the basket.

Leslie argued that typically developing children display a simple, early developing type of decoupling at around 18 months, when they start enacting pretend play. In his words, when a child puts a banana to his/her ear, pretending that it is a telephone, s/he is temporarily disengaging from the reality ('This object in my hand is a banana') in order to indulge in the pretence (I'll pretend that 'this object is a telephone'). In this way, Leslie argued, the 'simpler' decoupling skills involved in pretence act as developmental precursors for understanding that one's own or other people's thoughts can be hypothetical or different from reality.

There have been many critiques of Leslie's ideas. One key problem is that the decoupling system was conceived as a specialised 'on or off' mechanism, that is, one which worked in typical development, but was dysfunctional in autism. This does not fit with evidence from Jarrold (2003), cited in Chapter 3, that children with autism may understand pretence enacted by someone else, even when they cannot enact it themselves. A second problem is that the decoupling mechanism was considered to start functioning at the age of 18 months, when typically developing children start to pretend. However, studies like those by Maestro and colleagues (Chapter 3) suggest that atypical behaviour is apparent well before this stage.

Partly in response to this last point, Baron-Cohen (1995) outlined a developmental system comprising the early 'building blocks' for ToM skills in typical development. He suggested that from just a few months, infants are equipped with special perceptual mechanisms including an 'intention detector' which alerts them to the distinctive goal-directed movement of animate beings (humans, animals, etc.), and an 'eye direction detector' which tells them whether another human is looking at them or at something else. By 12 months of age, these detectors are passing information to a 'shared attention mechanism' which enables the child to look where someone else is looking or pointing. In this way, the child may begin to coordinate their own thinking processes with another person's from an early age. For instance, if a child looks to the same place that another person is looking, they can participate in the interest of what the person is looking at. If the child points to something, and the other person looks at it too, they have found a way to influence the other person's attention. The idea is that these are the early stages in 'reading the minds' of other people, which later develop into a fully functioning theory of mind.

There is certainly evidence that children give special attention to animate (particularly human) stimuli from early infancy, and that joint attention, including looking the same way, and protodeclarative pointing, develops at around 12 months (see Chapter 3). However, there is no conclusive evidence that these skills rely on the special mechanisms that Baron-Cohen proposed.

4.3.2 Explaining passes on theory of mind tests

Some researchers have suggested that the 20% or more of individuals on the autistic spectrum who consistently pass tests such as Sally-Anne have relied on 'problem-solving' strategies that avoid the need for genuine understanding of other people's mental states.

- ■ How do you think a person could learn to solve tasks such as Sally-Anne without understanding the mental state of false belief?

- □ The person could learn to invoke the rule that if someone leaves the room while something of theirs is moved, they will look for it in the place where they left it. This rule does not necessarily involve understanding the principle that seeing leads to knowing.

Many of the individuals who pass Sally-Anne fail more complex false belief tasks, in which participants have to show understanding of one character's false belief about a second character's belief about a situation. As an illustration, suppose that, in the car parking example, unbeknown to you, Kelly *saw* you *re-parking* the car in Park Street. You would then believe (falsely) that she believed that you were parked in Mount Street. In fact, your friend had had the opportunity to update her belief. Understanding this kind of situation involves understanding **second-order false belief**. Failures on such second-order false belief tasks suggest that most people on the autism spectrum have *some* degree of ToM difficulty.

On the other hand, some high-functioning individuals with autism pass these second-order tasks. The fact that these same individuals remain disabled in

Figure 4.5 Francesca Happé (b. 1967) is another influential autism researcher. (Andrew Atkinson)

everyday social situations questions whether the somewhat contrived experimental tests of ToM are really the best guide to everyday **mind-reading** skills. Happé (1994) (Figure 4.5) devised a more naturalistic and subtle probe for these skills, described in Box 4.3.

The term mind-reading is often used instead of ToM to emphasise that mental state understanding in everyday life involves more than formal skills such as false belief tasks.

Box 4.3 The 'Strange Stories' task (Happé, 1994)

Method

Participants were presented with stories like this one which contains an example of irony:

Ann's mother has spent a long time cooking Ann's favourite meal: fish and chips. But when she brings it in, Ann is watching TV, and she doesn't even look up or say thank you. Ann's mother is cross and says 'Well that's very nice isn't it! That's what I call politeness!'

The participants were asked:

Question 1: Is it true what Ann's mother says?

Question 2: Why does Ann's mother say this?

Figure 4.6   Ann and her mother. (Axel Scheffler)

Similar stories were presented testing understanding of other subtly ambiguous expressions, such as a white lie, a deliberate lie, persuasion.

Happé tested three groups of participants with autism:

- those failing 'first-order' ToM tasks
- those passing first-order ToM tasks
- those passing first-order and second-order ToM tasks.

Results

There were clear differences between the three groups in accuracy on Question 1 and in the justifications they gave on Question 2. The third, most able, group performed reasonably well, yet still less accurately than an appropriately matched control group. Their attributions of mental states to the story characters were often wrong. For example, one participant said that Ann's mother said what she said so as 'not to shock her daughter'.

Conclusion

High-functioning individuals, who are both intellectually able *and* skilled at *formal* ToM tasks, nonetheless have problems with these subtle tasks of everyday social understanding. Happé suggested that people in this sub-group have come by their social and mind-reading skills by a painstaking process of learning, outside of the normal developmental context. As a result, their skills remain formal and stilted, and do not serve them well in many real-life situations.

4.3.3 Mind-reading emotional states

Another everyday mind-reading skill is understanding other people's feelings. As you saw in Section 3.4.4, research on recognition of basic emotions such as happiness, sadness and fear, in children with autism, is inconclusive – some studies report difficulties while others do not. However, research into recognition of complex emotions, such as embarrassment or pride, provides consistent evidence of difficulties.

As suggested in Chapter 3, understanding complex emotions requires a complex integration of behaviours, such as a person's expression and tone of voice, with information about the context or situation in which the person's emotion occurs. Research by Golan, Baron-Cohen and colleagues (2006, 2008) highlights some of the difficulties that both children and adults on the autism spectrum have with this sort of task. Their method and some of their findings are described in Box 4.4.

Box 4.4 'Reading the mind in films' task

The aim of the studies was to test the capacity of adults and children on the autism spectrum to recognise complex emotions.

Method

The task materials consisted of short scenes taken from feature films, in which a main character portrayed a complex emotion within a particular situation or context.

Participants in one study (Golan et al., 2006) were 22 adults with Asperger syndrome or HFA (the experimental group) matched for age and verbal and non-verbal IQ with 22 adults without Asperger syndrome or HFA (the control group). Participants in the second study (Golan et al., 2008) were experimental and control groups of children with an average age of 10 years, and like the adults, matched for verbal and non-verbal IQ. The two studies used different materials as appropriate for the age group.

Participants had to view each of the scenes and decide on the emotion being portrayed from a list of four alternatives. The correct emotions had been established through pilot work in which panels of individuals without autism spectrum diagnoses decided what emotions were being portrayed in the film sequences, which were only included if there was an adequate level of agreement.

Figure 4.7 A still shot from a scene in the adult task (from Golan et al. (2006, p. 116, figure 2b)). In this scene a man is seen in a house looking for the owner. He walks into a room full of women and then says 'I seem to have picked the wrong time'. The choice of emotions is (1) ashamed, (2) unsure, (3) awkward and (4) annoyed. (ITN Archive, *Lost for Words*, 1999)

■ What do you think is the correct option to match the man's emotion in Figure 4.7?

☐ Option (3), awkward.

Notice that unlike the participants in the study, you only have a static facial expression and some background about the story to help you identify the emotion.

The researchers used film sequences because they are relatively 'naturalistic' or 'real-life'. Such stimuli are said to have **ecological validity**.

■ To what extent do you think film sequences are ecologically valid?

☐ Viewing dynamic (moving) rather than static (still) images is similar to how people observe emotions in everyday situations. Film sequences also provide multiple sources of information including speech; intonation, pitch and tone of voice; other non-verbal cues such as facial expression and gestures; and situation. The observer has to integrate this information to decide what is happening. However, the emotions are portrayed by actors, who may well employ exaggerated speech, expression and gestures to convey the feelings.

Results

Both children and adults in the autistic participant groups had significantly more difficulty than the controls in recognising the emotions portrayed in the film sequences. They also appeared to focus unduly on the verbal information, leading to some interesting errors. For instance, in one scene, a father kicks his son under the table to warn him not to tell his mother about something he has seen. The boy then recounts a 'made-up' story and the father acts as if it is very interesting. Many of the children on the autism spectrum did not spot this deception because they did not take non-verbal cues (such as the kick under the table, or the father's expression) into account.

These results confirm that individuals on the autism spectrum have difficulty in integrating all the types of cues that enable others to recognise the thoughts and feelings of those around them. Notice that difficulty in combining multiple sources of information into an overall interpretation may also reflect a more general bias in autism towards focus on details rather than the overall picture. This is taken up in Section 4.6.

Modifications to the ToM approach, as outlined in this section, improve its universality, scope and, arguably, its developmental relevance. However, the approach still doesn't cover difficulties such as inflexibility of thought and behaviour. Section 4.4 outlines an alternative theory specifically formulated with these non-social difficulties in mind. The ToM approach also implies that people understand each other emotionally and socially by *processing information*, including gestures, expressions, language and other behaviour, and drawing conclusions about what others are thinking and feeling. This emphasis on rational or 'considered' thinking underplays the role of direct, intuitive understanding in experiencing and recognising emotions. Section 4.5 considers a theory that approaches autism from the latter perspective. Finally, the ToM approach, and also those discussed in Sections 4.4 and 4.5 focus exclusively on deficits. Sections 4.6 and 4.7 look at theories that address both deficits and skills.

4.3.4 Summary of Section 4.3

- Suggestions for early developmental difficulties which could lead to theory of mind problems include lack of pretend play and impairments in joint attention and protodeclarative pointing.
- Individuals on the autism spectrum who pass first-order and second-order ToM tasks, have more difficulty in tasks such as Happé's, which test understanding of the subtle communications involved in irony, deception and persuasion.
- Even those who pass this test have difficulties in everyday social situations, suggesting that some mind-reading difficulties are present in all people with autism.

- Individuals with Asperger syndrome or HFA have difficulties in a relatively naturalistic mind-reading task involving recognition of complex emotions.

4.4 The executive function approach

> Children with Asperger's often end up perseverating, obsessively repeating a particular response even when it is no longer of use (repeating a question once it has been answered, for example, or repeating a strategy that has already failed to solve a problem). We are often unable to shift our attention away from the point at which we have become stuck, or generate new strategies to try.

> *(Sainsbury, 2000, p. 64)*

In this passage from her book, Claire Sainsbury touches on the inflexible thinking and behaviours which form the third area of the diagnostic triad. Section 3.5 described problems including repeated and stereotyped movements such as twirling or hand flapping, and rigid routines, such as always wearing the same clothes, or completing an action in exactly the same sequence. It was also suggested that narrowly focused interests and lack of imagination or pretence might reflect inflexibility of thought and action. The executive function approach prioritises explaining these difficulties.

4.4.1 Executive function and its components

Executive function (EF) is a collective term for four main types of cognitive capacity (Hill, 2008), which are listed below with some everyday examples:

- **planning:** organising activities to achieve a goal (e.g. assembling everything you need to go on a trip)
- **mental flexibility:** completing one task or activity and shifting one's attention readily to another quite different one
- **inhibition:** suppressing inappropriate responses (e.g. refraining from reading a newly arrived text message during a meeting at work)
- **generativity:** generating new activities and ideas (e.g. deciding on a new hobby, thinking up new ideas for meals).

Some people on the autism spectrum have considerable difficulties on experimental tests of these skills, and especially planning, mental flexibility and generativity (Hill, 2008). Box 4.5 describes some representative tests.

Box 4.5 Tests of executive function

Tower of Hanoi

This is a puzzle consisting of three pegs, A, B and C, and a set of rings that vary in size. At the start of the test, the rings are arranged in order of size on peg A (see Figure 4.8). The aim is to move all the rings, one at a time, and in as few moves as possible, to peg C, with the constraint that a larger ring can never be placed on top of a smaller ring. To be effective at this task, the participant must work out an overall strategy for transferring the rings – the secret is in the way all three pegs, including peg B, are used as 'staging posts'.

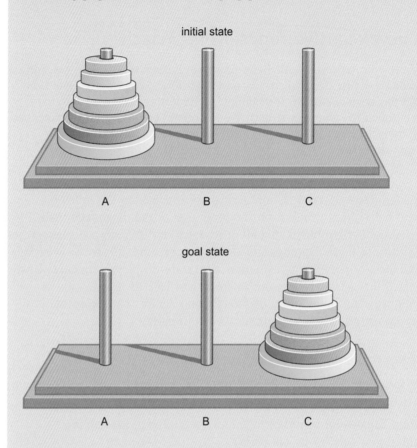

initial state

A   B   C

goal state

A   B   C

Figure 4.8   The Tower of Hanoi puzzle.

Wisconsin card sorting task (WCST)

This task involves four stimulus cards like the top four cards in Figure 4.9, and a further 128 response cards like the one at the bottom of the figure. The symbols on the cards vary in shape, number and colour. The participant is asked to sort the response cards, placing each successive card under one of the stimulus cards, matching them by whichever dimension they think is correct. For instance, if the participant thinks the basis for matching is colour, then the response card shown will be placed under card 1. The participant is not told the rule for matching, but must work it out by trial and error, based on the feedback received from the experimenter after each card is sorted. After 10 correct matches, the rule is arbitrarily changed (e.g. to shape) and the participant must continue sorting until the correct basis for sorting is detected again. To be effective at this task, the participant must relinquish the rule they have learned as soon as the feedback indicates that it is no longer valid, in order to work out the new sorting rule. Failure to do this is known as **perseveration**, which as Claire Sainsbury describes, means that the individual is stuck working with a rule or strategy that is no longer useful.

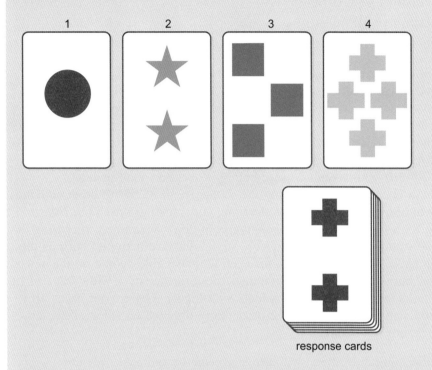

Figure 4.9 The Wisconsin card sorting task.

Windows task

This task, devised by James Russell and colleagues (Hughes and Russell, 1993) involves a game in which a child competes with an adult for a sweet or chocolate hidden in one of two small boxes. In the first phase of the experiment, the child is shown the principle that whenever he guides the adult to the *empty* box, he (the child) will receive the chocolate. This is reiterated over a series of trials. In the second phase of the experiment, the child can actually see where the reward is on each trial, but the adult cannot. To succeed at this task, the child has to suppress what probably seems the most natural response in the situation – to point to the box containing the chocolate.

Fluency tasks

Participants respond to a word or instruction with as many names, concepts or ideas as possible in a limited space of time (similar to the well-known creativity test, in which people are asked to think of as many uses as possible for a brick). Good examples of these tasks are described in Box 3.4, where children had to suggest ways of making a toy more interesting, or to suggest new uses for a piece of foam. Participants are scored on the quantity and quality of new ideas that they generate.

All these tasks, and other similar ones, have proved difficult for some individuals on the autism spectrum (Hill, 2004, 2008).

■ Each of the tasks described in Box 4.5 primarily tests a different aspect of executive function as outlined earlier. Can you identify which aspect is tested by each task?

☐ Tower of Hanoi tests planning; WCST tests flexibility; the windows task tests inhibition; fluency tasks test generativity.

Proponents of the EF theory have argued that impairments in the capacities illustrated would predispose the individual to repetitive behaviours, rigid routines and narrow interests, with profound implications for their scope to engage in typical everyday activities. Obviously, the different components of EF are not neatly segregated in daily life. Imagine, for instance, that you have decided to impress a friend you have invited for a meal, by preparing an exotic dish that you haven't cooked before. Your tasks may include: researching the recipe and planning the shopping; finishing off other activities in order to allow enough time for shopping and cooking; refraining from stopping for a coffee while out shopping (you don't have time); preparing the meal; and setting the table. Reasonably straightforward activities such as these can pose an impossible challenge for even the most able people on the autism spectrum. Turner (1999) looked at autistic performance on a wide range of EF fluency tasks and found that individuals with higher IQ were not necessarily more proficient; indeed some were particularly disabled on some of the tests. Ros Blackburn has commented:

> ...I am autistic (Kanner) with above average IQ and have very low functioning, e.g. I have 9 O levels but cannot make myself a sandwich!!!

> *(Blackburn, 2009, personal communication)*

Note that Ros interprets 'low-functioning' as difficulty with everyday skills, not, in contrast to the usual definition, as related to low IQ.

4.4.2 Evaluating the executive function theory

Many people on the autism spectrum and their families can relate to the kinds of difficulty identified by executive function tests. Yet as a core deficit explanation of autism, the theory has many limitations.

Testability?

The theory predicts difficulty on experimental tests of EF, and in this sense is testable. However, as Boucher (2009) has pointed out, just how difficulties highlighted in EF tests relate to stereotyped, repetitive behaviours, rigid routines and narrow interests is not well worked out. Lopez et al. (2005) devised a measure of behavioural inflexibility, which included 'low-level' repetitive behaviours such as hand-flapping movements, 'higher-level' repetitive behaviours, such as rigid pursuit of preferred activities, and the desire for sameness and narrow interests. Autistic individuals' scores on the WCST – a test of *mental* inflexibility – correlated with their scores on the researchers' behavioural measure. However, performance on planning and fluency tests did not correlate with the behavioural measure. These findings suggest that the relationship between EF impairments and the third triad area is far from straightforward.

Scope?

Since the theory does not directly address social interaction and communication, its scope seems narrower than ToM. However, several researchers have claimed that difficulties in both ToM and other areas of functioning could be *secondary* to problems with EF (Russell, 1997). For instance, rigid thinking might prevent a child from developing the capacity to imagine points of view other than their own. This could affect their ability to consider another person's mental perspective, and also restrict their capacity to 'step outside their own world' to generate ideas for pretence and fantasy (Currie and Ravenscroft, 2002). However, the EF skills needed for tasks like the tower of Hanoi and WCST develop much later than false belief and ToM-type skills. There is little evidence for early-developing EF skills which, if impaired, would lead to the wide range of problems in autism.

Deficits and skills?

Like ToM, EF was formulated specifically to address deficits in autism. However, focus and persistence, which are directly predicted by the EF approach, could be seen as autistic personality strengths.

Universality and specificity?

EF problems are not universal (i.e. experienced by all people on the autism spectrum). The proportion who score significantly lower than typically developing individuals may be no more than 50% in some tasks (Pellicano et al., 2006). Nor are EF problems specific to autism: they also occur in conditions such as ADHD and dementia. This overlap has usefully highlighted the possibility of a biological factor common to autism and other disorders. In one of the first accounts of EF problems in autism, Damasio and Maurer (1978) noted that autistic performance on tasks such as WCST is very similar to that of people with damage to the frontal lobes of the brain: both groups tend to get stuck with the wrong sorting rule. As you will see in the next chapter, biological studies now support the suggestion of atypical frontal lobe function in autism.

Developmental trajectory?

- Do you think the executive function explanation sheds any light on the developmental trajectory leading to the problems in autism?

- The explanation focuses on behaviour that develops quite late even in typically developing individuals. For instance, the capacity for planning and organisation is still developing in adolescence, as you will know if you have teenage children! The theory does not offer any clear account of how difficulties that are apparent from 18 months or earlier relate to EF difficulties. Consequently, some researchers have argued that EF difficulties are a *consequence*, rather than a cause of other symptoms in autism.

4.4.3   Summary of Section 4.4

- Executive function (EF) includes the mental activities of planning, flexibility, response inhibition and generativity.

- Some people on the autism spectrum have difficulties on EF tests, including the tower of Hanoi, the Wisconsin card sorting task, the windows task and tests of fluency.

- Difficulties in EF are likely to impact on many areas of everyday life.

- As a core deficit model, EF has limitations in terms of testability, scope, universality, specificity and developmental proposals.

4.5   A social developmental approach

Jane would allow herself to be cuddled, but only if I didn't look at her. She always resisted sitting on my lap unless she was facing away. And I could go to her with my arms out, just as I had a million times with my boys, but she would never reach out to me in return ... One day I found my husband smiling at her, with tears rolling down his face, begging her to smile back.

(From Randall and Parker, 1999, p. 107)

The age of the child referred to in this poignant extract is not known, but the description illustrates that parents typically expect to have close reciprocal interactions with their offspring from a very early age. You will recall from Section 1.3 that it was Kanner who first suggested that children with autism might lack the 'innate ability to form the usual biologically provided affective contact with people'.

4.5.1   Hobson's theory

Peter Hobson's theory of autism (1993; 2002) builds on Kanner's idea that most people are fundamentally social beings with a biological propensity to relate to others. Moreover, Hobson argues that rather than 'processing information' to derive conclusions about the thoughts and emotions of others (as in ToM approaches), typically developing individuals have an early-developing and **intuitive understanding** of other people's feelings involving empathy. This complex concept, first introduced in Chapter 3, features increasingly often in accounts of autism, but is defined differently by different researchers. In Hobson's account (see Hobson, 1993) empathy refers to a direct and intuitive capacity to feel 'for and with' other people. For instance, part of understanding that another person is feeling sad involves experiencing something like what they feel. This early emotional engagement forms the basis for both social and cognitive development.

Within this framework, Hobson contrasts how typically developing infants and those with autism engage with the world from birth onwards. Key points are outlined in Box 4.6.

Box 4.6 Features of Hobson's theory (Hobson, 1993; 2002)

Hobson argues that the following key features of typical development are impaired or missing in autism.

Human primacy

From birth onwards the infant engages emotionally and socially with humans in ways that are distinct from how he/she engages with the physical world. This engagement is referred to as **human primacy**.

Primary intersubjectivity

Primary intersubjectivity, derived from the pioneering work of Colwyn Trevarthen (1979), means that infants and their mothers are 'pre-programmed' to respond to each other's behaviour, triggering an ongoing cycle of reciprocal interaction in which the child's and mother's behaviour is closely attuned and synchronised. Trevarthen's extensive observational studies of mothers and their babies showed, from the first months of age, close coordination, reflected in mutual eye contact, smiling and baby-talk involving 'sing-song' use of voice as if in conversation. The child both imitates and is imitated by the mother. Hobson believes that emotional relatedness commences in these close interactions.

A fascinating observational study providing evidence for primary intersubjectivity was conducted by Tronick et al. (1978). Mothers of two-month-old infants were asked first to interact normally with their babies, then to remain expressionless and unresponsive for a couple of minutes, and then to resume normal interaction. The infant's response to the 'still face' episode was frequently to become uneasy and then unresponsive themselves. This confirms the fine synchronisation and interdependency of baby and mother's actions in typical development. See Figure 4.10.

(a)   (b)

Figure 4.10   These rather blurred video images are from (a) the first phase and (b) the second phase of Tronick's study. (Tronick, 2007)

- ■ What differences highlighted in the home video studies by Maestro and colleagues described in Chapter 3, support the claim that children with autism lack primary intersubjectivity?

- ☐ Between 0 and 6 months, the children later diagnosed with autism were showing fewer examples of social attention, such as looking and smiling at people and vocalising to people.

Secondary intersubjectivity

Secondary intersubjectivity is Trevarthen's term for the phase, during the second year of life, when typically developing infants not only coordinate one-to-one with a parent, but also start to join with the parent in attending to something or someone else.

- ■ These forms of joint attention also featured in Baron-Cohen's developmental system described in Section 4.3.1. Can you identify them?

- ☐ Protodeclarative pointing and looking where another person is looking.

In Hobson's account, through the sharing of experience in this phase of secondary intersubjectivity, the typically developing child begins to acquire knowledge of others as subjective beings with their own feelings, thoughts, intentions and beliefs. For instance, imagine that the child looks to where his/her mother is looking – at some chocolate. This shared attention enables the child to understand that his/her mother is interested in the chocolate. According to Hobson, this kind of shared experience is the origin of the child's understanding that another person has mental states that may be the same as (or different from) his own; in other words, a theory of mind.

Reflexivity

At some point, the child's intersubjective sharing of mental experience develops into an appreciation that his/her own mental experiences are distinct from other people's. In this way, through developing an awareness of others as beings with their own thoughts and feelings, the typically developing child acquires **reflexivity**. This means a reflexive understanding of self as a human individual distinct from others.

This account gives just a flavour of Hobson's complex ideas, which are described in more detail in his delightful book *The Cradle of Thought* (Hobson, 2002). The aim of his theory is not to challenge the claim that ToM difficulties are important in autism, but rather to provide a different explanation of how these difficulties first arise. This treats difficulty in emotional relatedness as the primary problem, which fundamentally disrupts both cognitive and social development. Some of the strengths and weaknesses of the approach will become clear through the evaluation process.

4.5.2   Evaluating Hobson's theory

Testability?

The approach generates predictions concerning:

- atypicalities in the earliest behaviour of children later diagnosed with autism
- emotional impairments in all individuals with autism
- difficulty in recognising self and others as distinct human 'subjects'.

The evidence from parents' retrospective reports, and from the home video studies described in Chapter 3, is at least consistent with the first prediction, while evidence of later difficulties in recognising and responding to the emotions is consistent with the second. However, other approaches make similar predictions. For instance, as you saw in Sections 4.3.1 and 4.3.3, early lack of protodeclarative pointing and joint attention, and later difficulties with emotional recognition, are consistent with the mind-reading approach. In support of the third prediction, Hobson (1993) cites pronominal reversal (see Chapters 1 and 3), interpreting confusion of 'I' and 'you' as evidence that the child does not distinguish himself from other subjects. However, atypical pronoun use could equally be part of wider pragmatic language difficulties, rather than reflecting specific problems of self-recognition.

As these examples show, it is quite difficult to derive *critical* tests that favour Hobson's approach over other interpretations.

Scope?

Hobson's theory aimed to link emotional, social and theory of mind deficits in autism. It also addresses problems in the development of self in autism. Like ToM, this theory seems less equipped to explain the non-social deficits such as repetitive activities and restricted interests. However, Hobson has recently updated his account with the aim of addressing difficulties in flexibility of thought and action (Hobson and Hobson, 2010).

Deficits and skills?

The theory deals primarily with the basis for difficulties in autism, and has little to say about skills.

Universality and specificity?

The theory focuses on aspects of early infant behaviour that are well documented in typically developing children. However, it is not clear that these same behaviours are universally absent in infants later diagnosed with autism. For instance, parents do not always report that the behaviour of their child with autism was atypically withdrawn or unresponsive from birth. In some cases, development seems to proceed quite normally, followed by a gradual decline. In a survey by Frith and Soares (1993), two-thirds of the mothers of children with autism had not been worried by their children's behaviour in the first year. Lack of social responsiveness is also not specific to autism, as it is observed in children with congenital visual or hearing problems. Later problems in recognising emotions should also be universal according to Hobson's theory, and this seems to be true for complex emotions. However, you have seen that recognition of basic emotions is not always affected. Since basic emotion recognition is more likely to rely on the spontaneous, intuitive processes favoured in Hobson's account, while complex emotions may require more 'considered' conscious processing of different cues, this finding poses some difficulties.

Developmental trajectory?

A key strength of Hobson's theory is that it considers development, drawing on well-documented evidence about what occurs early on in a typical trajectory. Hobson considers how autism might unfold developmentally, emphasising the direct, intuitive quality of much social and emotional understanding, and the fact that development involves both the infant and 'significant others' in his/her environment. Since the typical process involves a continuous cycle of interaction between infant and carer, a lack of responsiveness on the part of the child may lead to changes in the responsiveness of those around him/her, with profound consequences for the child's opportunities for emotional, social and intellectual development.

4.5.3   Summary of Section 4.5

- Hobson's social developmental theory echoes Kanner's claim that the innate capacity for emotional relatedness is central to autism.

- Drawing on evidence about early typical development, the theory identifies problems in human primacy, primary and secondary intersubjectivity and reflexive understanding of self.

- Evidence consistent with this theory includes early lack of joint attention and protodeclarative pointing, later problems with emotion recognition, and pronominal reversal.

- As a core deficit model, there are problems with testability, universality and specificity.

4.6   Weak central coherence

> I can actually remember lying awake in my cot, along with what my cot looked like. I can remember being very interested in the colours in a picture which had been stuck on to the end of my cot. Although I can still remember what this picture looked like, I never actually understood what it was portraying at the time.
>
> *(Therese Jolliffe with Richard Lansdown and Clive Robinson, 1992)*

Therese Jolliffe studied experimental psychology at university, and completed a PhD on autism with Simon Baron-Cohen. Personal accounts by high-functioning individuals provide a unique and valuable 'inside' view of what autism is like.

In this reminiscence about her early infancy, Therese Jolliffe highlights the common autistic trait of remarkable attention to detail, often at the expense of more global grasp of form or meaning.

4.6.1 Processing for detail

Uta Frith (1989) was one of the first to propose that a strong bias towards detail could constitute a core deficit in autism. She argued that when processing information from the environment, most people focus on overall form and meaning, rather than on the details. In recalling a picture, they are likely to remember more about its main theme and overall appearance, than the specific colours and shapes – for many purposes, the overall or global features of the scene carry more useful information. Similarly, if recounting the story of a film, people mostly concentrate on the overall gist and theme, not on the exact details of what individual characters said. Frith described this focus on global form and meaning as reflecting **central coherence**. In contrast, individuals on the autism spectrum are said to attend to detail at the expense of overall form and meaning. This processing style is described as showing **weak central coherence (WCC)**.

One of the goals of this theory was to bring together the characteristic skills and deficits in autism. Frith suggested that, depending on the task, WCC may be either beneficial or detrimental to an individual's performance. As you saw in Box 3.1, people with autism often perform especially well on tasks such as the block design sub-test of the IQ test.

■ If you look back at Figure 3.1a now, can you see why WCC and attention to detail might be of benefit in copying the pattern?

☐ Seeing the upper pattern as a diamond on a white background makes it difficult to 'segment' the pattern into components that will match with the designs on the blocks. People with autism complete this test rapidly because they can immediately focus on the individual components of the pattern.

For similar reasons, people on the autism spectrum often perform well in the **embedded figures test**, where the task is to find a shape such as a triangle within a picture – see Figure 4.11. Taking in the shape and pattern of the pram makes it more difficult to pick out the embedded element that matches the test triangle. People with autism find it easier to see the sub-components of the pattern.

Figure 4.11 Example of the embedded figures test.

Jolliffe and Baron-Cohen (2001) devised a visual task in which processing for detail puts people on the autism spectrum at a disadvantage. Participants with classic autism and Asperger syndrome were shown line drawings consisting of fragments of familiar objects, and asked to work out what the object was. The example in Figure 4.12 has three fragments which together make up a picture of a hinge.

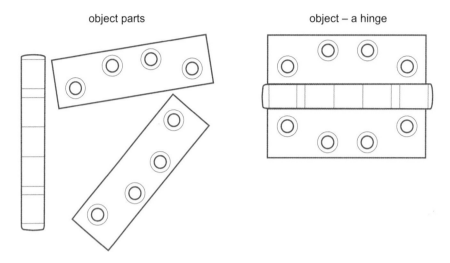

object parts   object – a hinge

Figure 4.12   Participants try to identify objects (a hinge in this case) from viewing their components. (Adapted from Jolliffe and Baron-Cohen, 2001, p. 215)

Compared with control non-autistic participants, matched for CA and IQ, the autism spectrum participants took longer, and were less accurate at identifying what objects the fragments formed. Since this task tests the capacity to identify a whole from its parts, poor performance is consistent with the WCC theory.

These visual tasks highlight local processing as a perceptual phenomenon. Happé (1997) devised a task which showed an effect of local processing on understanding language. Participants were asked to read out aloud words such as 'tear' in the context of sentences suggesting either a 'tear' in the eye or a 'tear' in a piece of fabric. Participants with autism often chose the wrong pronunciation, suggesting that they had difficulty taking into account the overall meaning of the sentence in order to interpret the word appropriately. Similarly Jolliffe and Baron-Cohen (2000) showed that individuals with classic autism and Asperger syndrome found it difficult to arrange sets of sentences appropriately to form a coherent story, or to answer questions about what the story meant.

WCC relates most clearly to the third triad area. Repetitive activities and rigid adherence to the same routines might arise if a person has difficulty in interpreting information or events in terms of their overall meaning. If your usual bus is late some mornings, you are likely to interpret this within wider context – for instance, that the traffic is exceptionally heavy, or that the weather is bad. But for a person who is unable to do this, such fluctuations in routine may be intolerable and cause great anxiety. Rigid adherence to 'sameness', as first described by Kanner, may provide an alternative source of meaning and predictability. WCC may also be relevant to sensory difficulties. For instance, if a person has difficulty in integrating information coming from sight, sound, touch, and so on, they are likely to experience sensory stimuli as an overwhelming mass of fragmentary experiences – which is how some people on the autism spectrum describe them:

> Sometimes if there was too much commotion around me, either in movement of people or in noise, I would automatically tune out. In situations such as these, my senses would sometimes not be integrated and each individual sound would be heard crisply as a separate sound and each visual detail would clutter my line of sight.

> *(Sarah in Sainsbury, 2000, p. 102)*

4.6.2 Evaluating the weak central coherence theory

Testability?

The theory predicts that individuals with autism will perform well in tasks calling for detailed processing, and poorly in tasks calling for global processing, and this has been explored. However, ambiguity concerning the precise meaning of global and detailed processing restricts the theory's testability. The inability to integrate visual or auditory information into perceptual wholes, such as patterns and forms, may reflect atypical functioning of basic perceptual mechanisms, while the inability to take context into account in interpreting the meaning of words or sentences suggests atypical functioning of 'higher-level' cognitive processes. The theory implies that there is a common problem underlying these different difficulties, but does not explain what it is. A second ambiguity relates to whether the focus on detail in autism indicates an *impairment* in global processing or just a *preference* for local processing. This is discussed further in considering scope.

Scope?

The WCC theory was originally formulated as a core deficit explanation, accounting not only for sensory difficulties and repetitive behaviour, but also social and communication difficulties. Frith (1989) suggested that people with autism have a fundamental and general difficulty in using contextual information to integrate different types of information into coherent, meaningful interpretations. She pointed out that for most people, coherence and meaning often come from understanding what other people are thinking and feeling within particular contexts – that is, theory of mind. Failure to integrate information about other people's mental states would result in just the kinds of social and cultural misunderstandings that are typical of individuals on the autism spectrum. Autistic performance on false belief tasks, and in many everyday mind-reading situations, could be interpreted this way.

- Can you think of some examples from this chapter where failing to integrate sources of information would lead to inappropriate interpretations?

- In both Happé's 'Strange Stories' task, and Golan's study of complex emotion recognition, participants could be seen as failing to integrate the

The Autism Spectrum in the 21st Century: Exploring Psychology, Biology and Practice

behaviour they saw with the context, and with the most likely intentions or feelings of the protagonists.

However, it has been found that people with autism do not always focus on detail, and can, in some circumstances, take global form and context into account.

Figure 4.13 illustrates a test of global processing devised by Navon (1977). Participants are shown a series of such letters and asked either to identify the large letters, ignoring the smaller component letters, or to identify the small component letters, ignoring the large letters. In Figure 4.13a, the large and small components are compatible, while in Figure 4.13b they are incompatible. A participant who attends to global information, filtering out local detail, should have no difficulty when asked to identify the large letters. Identifying the small letters in Figure 4.13a should also be easy, as the small and large letters match. But the presence of the large conflicting symbol in Figure 4.13b should interfere with identifying the small letters.

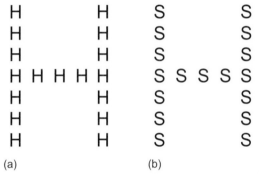

(a)   (b)

Figure 4.13 (a) A capital H made up of Hs; (b) a capital H made up of Ss. (Navon, 1977)

■ According to WCC, how should participants with autism perform on Figure 4.13b?

□ They should find it easy to ignore the large H when responding to the small Ss, but difficult to ignore the small Ss when responding to the large letter H.

In practice, there is little consistency in how people with autism perform on this task: in some studies, participants demonstrate a 'local advantage', while in others, they show the typical global interference effect. Another study, of musical (auditory) abilities in a person with autism, showed the capacity for global processing (Heaton, 2003). In further tasks, it has been found that people with autism can adjust their processing from 'local' to global' when instructed to do so.

If people with autism have fundamental difficulty with processing information globally, as proposed in Frith and Happé's first formulation of WCC, they should not be able to override this difficulty in some tasks and situations. Happé and Frith (2006) therefore revised their theory, proposing that processing information for detail is a **cognitive style** – in other words, a *preference* for processing the fine detail rather than the overall form or meaning of things, and not a *deficit* which prevents people with autism from processing in any other way.

Deficits and skills?

WCC was probably the first theory to consider skills alongside deficits, suggesting that they were the outcomes of the same set of underlying processes. This was an important step forward in the psychological explanation of autism, and is probably the theory's strongest feature. As you saw in Chapter 3, skills in autism are not confined to enhanced performance on tasks such as block design, and the embedded figures test. In some individuals, they extend to outstanding talent in fields such as art and music.

126

So does the idea of a detail-oriented processing style provide a useful insight into these savant skills?

■ The cover design for this book, and also Figures 3.8 and 3.9 are by artists on the autism spectrum. Do you think these images show a particular focus on detail?

☐ All of these artists display meticulous attention to detail, whether the subject matter is real (Figures 3.8 and 3.9 are drawn from actual buildings) or imaginary (the fish on the front cover). But these artists also show an excellent feel for the overall scene or object.

Moreover, the skills of savant artists have other special characteristics besides detail. For instance, both Stephen Wiltshire and Gilles Tréhin have an exceptional skill in depicting perspective in their city scenes. Explaining this is beyond the scope of the weak central coherence approach.

Another savant artist, Richard Wawro, paints in an impressionistic style which is not dominated by attention to detail (Wawro, 2009).

All in all, the WCC theory does not adequately explain the different and varied skills which are involved in this talented work. Mottron et al. (2006) has suggested that the common underlying feature is not so much attention to detail, but rather an enhanced processing of perceptual qualities, such as the shapes and colours in visual scenes, or qualities such as pitch in musical works.

Universality and specificity?

The suggestion that weak central coherence is a cognitive style is relatively recent, and it is not really clear how prevalent this is on the autism spectrum. It has been claimed, however, that this processing style is specific to autism.

Developmental trajectory?

A weakness of this approach is that there is no systematic evidence about how and when a style favouring detail or perceptual qualities might develop. The fact that savant artists often demonstrate a very early talent for drawing, and seem to bypass the stages that typically developing children pass through when they learn to draw is consistent with early emergence of a detailed processing style. This merits more work.

4.6.3 Summary of Section 4.6

• The weak central coherence theory first suggested that people on the autism spectrum focus on detail, and have difficulty in processing overall form or meaning.

• Evidence that people with autism do not invariably show a global processing deficit has led to a reformulation of this theory as a *cognitive style* explanation.

• The model addresses some aspects of skilled performance in autism, but does not account for all of the skills involved in savant art.

4.7   The empathising-systemising approach

I will remember how people feel when they get irritated. First the voice is loud and abrupt. But expression could be wrinkle face. Like frowning.

(Jessy, in her forties, in Claiborne Park, 2001, p. 153)

I like the idea of chain reactions – one thing happening which triggers off another, which triggers off another and so on and so on. I used to put string round a dozen objects and watch them all fall down at once. That's why I love slinkies (coiled springs) so much. When you wind one round loads of things and then let go, it pulls itself through all of them.

(Jackson, 2002, p. 52)

These two quotes illustrate two different facets of autism which are brought together in Baron-Cohen's **empathising-systemising (E-S) theory** (see, for instance, Baron-Cohen, 2008). Rather like WCC, E-S sees the psychological characteristics of autism as a cognitive profile, which combines deficits and strengths. The deficit in empathy has two suggested components:

cognitive: understanding what someone else is feeling, e.g. realising they are sad

affective: experiencing the appropriate emotional reaction, e.g. feeling sad yourself, or trying to comfort someone.

The cognitive component is essentially theory of mind, while the second is closer to Hobson's concept of empathy, discussed in Section 4.5.1. Baron-Cohen suggests that both aspects of empathy are impaired in autism.

■   Do you think the quote from Jessy above illustrates a problem with empathy?

☐   Understanding other people's feelings doesn't come naturally to Jessy. This quote suggests that she has worked hard to develop rules providing a cognitive understanding of emotions such as irritation. It is not clear whether she has any affective reaction to the emotion.

Empathising or empathy combines Baron-Cohen's early ToM approach (see Section 4.2) and subsequent work on emotional recognition (see Section 4.3.3). The more novel element of the approach is systemising, proposed as a specific and characteristic area of strength in autism.

4.7.1   What is systemising?

Baron-Cohen claims that people on the autism spectrum are highly prone to **systemising**, meaning that they are driven to 'analyse or construct systems'. A system is any domain that lends itself to a set of rules predicting or explaining how the domain works. The quote from Luke Jackson above provides a convincing example of systemising in a situation governed by physical laws. He describes his fascination with how one falling object of a set which are tied or linked together will inevitably pull the others down. The gravitational forces are such that Luke can predict, with certainty, that when one object falls it will set off a chain reaction. Evidence that some people on the autism spectrum have particular skill with such systems comes from a study of **intuitive physics**, that is everyday insight into the forces governing physical objects, described in Box 4.7.

Box 4.7 Understanding of intuitive physics in children with Asperger syndrome

Baron-Cohen et al. (2001) gave two groups of participants aged 12–13 years a set of 20 tests like those shown in Figure 4.14. The experimental group comprised children with a diagnosis of Asperger syndrome, all of whom had measured IQ in the normal range. In the control group of typically developing children, IQ was assumed to be in the normal range. The Asperger group was also compared with a younger control group on a 'mind-reading' test involving judging emotions from the expression in a person's eyes, as portrayed in photographs.

If the wheel rotates as shown, P will

(i) move to the right and stop
(ii) move to the left and stop
(iii) move to and fro
(iv) none of these

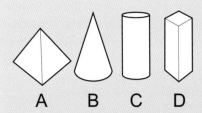

If each block weighs the same, which one will be the most difficult to push over?

(i) A (ii) B (iii) C (iv) D

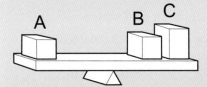

Which box is the heaviest?

(i) A (ii) B (iii) C (iv) all equal

Figure 4.14 Items from the intuitive physics test. (Adapted from Baron-Cohen et al., 2001)

■ Choose what you think is the right answer for each test in Figure 4.14.

☐ From top to bottom the answers are (iii), (i) and (i).

Participants with AS performed significantly better than controls on the intuitive physics tests, and significantly worse than the controls on the mind-reading test, even though the latter group was much younger.

These findings are consistent with the claim that individuals on the autism spectrum have good insights into physical systems. Parents often report that their children on the spectrum are fascinated by machines such as vacuum cleaners, hair dryers and so on, though it does not necessarily follow that they have particular mechanical skills. Another interesting finding, from a survey of the fathers and grandfathers of individuals on the autism spectrum (Baron-Cohen et al., 1997), suggested that more worked in engineering than in professions such as medicine.

■ How is this relevant to Baron-Cohen's theory?

☐ Genetic studies suggest the presence of autistic characteristics in some family members (see Section 1.6). If systemising is an autistic trait, evidence for enhanced systemising skills in relatives would be consistent with the theory.

The empathising-systemising theory extends this idea further to suggest that systemising and empathising are traits present to a greater or lesser extent across the whole population.

4.7.2 Autism as a continuum?

Just as human height is a continuous dimension or scale, on which every individual has a measurable position, similarly according to Baron-Cohen, everyone's position on scales of empathising and systemising can be measured. This is achieved using questionnaires, in which individuals respond to questions exploring empathising and systemising. Here are some illustrative questions from the **empathising quotient (EQ)** and the **systemising quotient (SQ)** (Autism Research Centre, 2009). People are asked whether they strongly agree, slightly agree, strongly disagree or slightly disagree with each question. Total EQ and SQ scores are calculated from the responses to individual questions.

Empathising quotient (EQ)

1 I can easily tell if someone wants to enter a conversation
2 I can pick up quickly if someone says one thing but means another
3 Seeing people cry doesn't really upset me

Systemising quotient

4 I am fascinated by how machines work
5 I rarely read articles or web pages about new technology
6 I am interested in knowing the path a river takes from its source to the sea

■ How do you think a person who was low on empathising and high on systemising might answer each of these questions?

☐ A person with these traits would probably:

1 Strongly disagree
2 Strongly disagree

3 Strongly agree
4 Strongly agree
5 Strongly disagree
6 Strongly agree

Baron-Cohen predicted that if the EQ and SQ scores of individuals across the population were plotted within a two-dimensional grid, the pattern would look something like Figure 4.15.

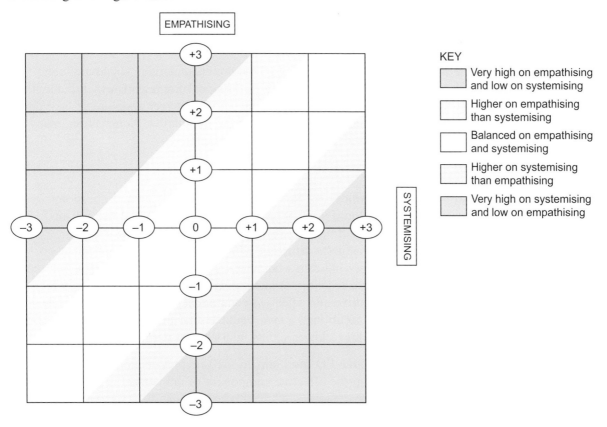

Figure 4.15   Predicted distribution of EQ and SQ scores in schematic form. (Adapted from Baron-Cohen et al., 2001)

The broad white band running diagonally across the figure suggests that most individuals should score about the same on EQ and SQ. The light green band above this indicates that some people should score a bit higher on EQ than SQ, while the darker green top left corner indicates people with scores much higher on EQ than SQ. Similarly, the light turquoise band below the white indicates that some individuals will score slightly higher on SQ than EQ, while the stronger turquoise triangle at the bottom right corner represents a minority who will score much more highly on SQ. Crucially, Baron-Cohen claims that most males should score towards the lower right of the grid (higher on systemising than empathising) and that people on the autism spectrum should tend to score in the extreme bottom right corner. This proposes a measurable basis for the stereotypical 'male' interest in machines and other systems, also linking this to why autism, which shows the extreme version of this profile, is more common in males. Hence this theory is sometimes known as the **extreme male brain theory** of autism.

Results of a questionnaire survey, in which participants completed both the EQ and SQ (Wheelwright et al., 2006), are broadly consistent with this pattern. 45% of females in a typical adult group had higher EQ than SQ scores; 62% of typical adult males had SQ scores higher than their EQ scores; 62% of participants (both male and female) with an autism spectrum diagnosis had the extreme version of the 'male' profile.

4.7.3 Evaluating the empathising-systemising theory

One merit of E-S theory is that it unites the characteristic social and non-social difficulties of autism within a dimensional framework which recognises that the expression of autistic symptoms varies between individuals, and may also 'shade into' traits within the rest of the population. Nonetheless, many consider this fairly recent approach very speculative.

Testability?

Baron-Cohen and colleagues have used both experiments and questionnaires to test whether the low-E/high-S profile is true of people on the autism spectrum. Impaired performance in emotion recognition tasks (see, for instance, Box 4.4) suggests difficulty with the cognitive component of empathy, but does not indicate whether the affective component (having the appropriate emotional reaction) is lacking. On the EQ questionnaire, which addresses both cognitive and affective components of empathy, studies such as Wheelwright et al., mentioned above, indicate that people on the autism spectrum tend to achieve lower scores than control participants.

■ Which of the three EQ questions in the previous section seems most likely to pick up the affective component of empathy?

☐ Strongly agreeing with item 3 (seeing people crying doesn't really upset me) might indicate the lack of an appropriate emotional response to other people's grief. Items 1 and 2 are more directly concerned with cognitive empathy, though emotional empathy may play a role, for instance, in realising that someone is not saying what they mean.

A possible difficulty with the EQ is that a person on the autism spectrum may not have the relevant self-knowledge to answer the questions. For instance, someone who does not notice how his behaviour affects other people might not be aware of whether others are interested or bored in what he is saying – one of the EQ questions. A parallel version of the EQ, designed for a parent to answer goes some way to address this difficulty.

Both experiments (such as the intuitive physics test) and a questionnaire measure (the SQ) have been used in testing systemising. However, one difficulty with systemising is its very broad definition. Baron-Cohen extends the idea beyond the more obvious physical and mechanical domains, to a whole range of characteristic autistic preoccupations, including:

• collecting objects or items on a list

- knowing a lot about an aspect of the natural world such as dinosaurs, trees or the weather
- numerical obsession e.g. with calendars or train timetables
- repetitive activities and routines, such as spinning, rocking, always eating the same foods or watching the same videos.

The suggested common element in these and many other domains is that they are governed by systematic rules or principles which the individual with autism is seeking to understand through an obsessive, repetitive focus. However, this claim has not been tested. Being familiar with lots of examples of trees, for instance, does not necessarily mean that the person has a good understanding of botanical science, or even that this is their goal. This very broad definition and application of systemising makes it more difficult to test critically the theory as a whole. As explained in Box 4.1, a theory which is not falsifiable in principle lacks explanatory power.

Scope?

The broad scope of the theory, encompassing a wide range of social and non-social characteristics and symptoms within the same two-factor framework, is a potential merit. However, the relevance of the theory to many of these areas is as yet untested.

Deficits and skills?

Like WCC, E-S theory seeks to explain both difficulties and strengths in autism. In some ways systemising is a quite similar idea to weak central coherence. Both approaches predict attention to detail in a range of situations. However, whereas WCC has difficulty explaining how individuals can bring detail together to form coherent patterns or meanings, E-S allows for this – the cover illustration of this book is a good example.

Universality?

It is by no means clear that the accentuated low-E, high-S pattern depicted in Figure 4.15 is universal across the autism spectrum. In the survey cited earlier 62% showed this pattern. These participants all had HFA or Asperger syndrome, and the prevalence of the pattern across the rest of the spectrum is not known.

Specificity?

As a dimensional approach, E-S theory recognises that some individuals who are not autistic may show the same pattern as those on the spectrum. This is the case in Wheelwright et al.'s survey, where a few typical individuals, both male and female, had scores in the lower right corner of the grid.

Developmental trajectory?

Baron-Cohen's proposals for early stages in the development of mind-reading in typical children (see Section 4.3.1) could help to explain how problems of empathy might develop in autism. But there is as yet little information about how the E-S profile might arise.

4.7.4   Summary of Section 4.7

- The empathising-systemising theory suggests that autism is characterised by poor empathising ability, combined with enhanced systemising.

- Empathising and systemising are seen as continuous dimensions on which all individuals within a population can be located by their scores.

- There is evidence that males tend to score more highly on systemising than empathising scales, with autism representing an extreme version of this pattern.

- While understanding physical forces and mechanisms are convincing examples of systemising, wider application of the concept is less well justified.

4.8   Conclusions

In this chapter, you have encountered the most prominent psychological explanations of autism to have emerged in the modern era. Each of these has some persuasive features, and the illustrative quotes from people on the spectrum indicate that each approach in some way echoes their own experience. But the framework used to compare and evaluate these approaches has also highlighted substantial shortcomings.

First of all, in relation to scope, if you consider the full range of symptoms and characteristics discussed in Chapter 3, you will realise that some of the phenomena are not clearly addressed by any theory. Notably, atypical sensory responses (Section 3.6.1) do not feature prominently in any approach. While sensory and perceptual characteristics remain outside the diagnostic triad, many individuals on the spectrum and their families, consider difficulties in these areas especially important and Geschwind (2009) estimates that they occur in as many as 90% of children with classic autism. The work of Mottron and his colleagues, mentioned briefly in Section 4.6.2, is likely to bring this area of functioning in autism into greater prominence. Another key area of difficulty which is not adequately integrated with the theories is language. While an approach such as ToM offers an interesting and plausible account of the pragmatic language difficulties of high-functioning individuals, the wider language difficulties in LFA (see Section 3.3.2) are not directly handled by the theories.

Since none of the existing theories satisfies all the evaluative criteria, it might seem logical to reject them and start again from scratch. However, since several theories provide useful, if partial, insights into autism, a combination of these explanations may be helpful. In this case approaches first conceived as 'core deficit models' in their own right would become part of a multiple factor explanation of autism. Evidence supporting a multiple factor model comes from work by Pellicano et al. (2006). A group of 40 children aged between 4 and 7 years, with diagnoses of classic autism or PDD-NOS, were compared with a matched control group on tests of theory of mind (first and second order false belief), executive function (planning, cognitive flexibility and inhibition) and weak central coherence (e.g. the embedded figures test). The results suggested a profile of difficulties in ToM and EF, together with strengths in tasks calling for local processing. Each of these areas of functioning seemed to constitute a separate factor differentiating the performance of the autistic and control groups.

What does a multiple factor explanation mean? Are several underlying psychological factors at work in all cases of autism, resulting in the wide range of social and non-social deficits and characteristic skills? Or do different underlying factors play a greater or lesser role in different cases of autism? The biological explanations considered in the next chapter shed further light on this interesting question.

4.9   Learning outcomes

4.1   Define and use, or recognise definitions and applications of, each of the terms printed in **bold** in the text.

4.2   Explain what is meant by a psychological explanation of autism and identify key criteria for evaluating explanations.

4.3   Identify key features of theory of mind/mind-reading, executive function, social developmental, weak central coherence and empathising-systemising accounts of autism.

4.4   Describe evidence (from experiments and other studies) for and against each of these explanations.

4.5   Comment on the evidence that suggests there are multiple underlying deficits in autism rather than one core deficit.

4.10   Self-assessment questions for Chapter 4

Question 4.1   (LO 4.2)

(a) What is the difference between an explanation that is universal to autism and an explanation that is specific to autism? What evidence is there that ToM difficulty may be neither of these?

(b) Why is it important for explanations of autism to consider developmental trajectory? Which approaches discussed in the chapter shed possible light on this?

Question 4.2   (LO 4.3)

(a) George, who is on the autism spectrum, has difficulty in understanding the plot of a thriller he is reading. How might this be explained by (i) the ToM approach and (ii) WCC theory?

(b) Section 4.4.1 described tasks involved in planning and preparing a special meal for a guest. Which aspects of EF might be involved at each stage?

Question 4.3   (LO 4.4)

(a) Which of the following statements fits better with the evidence for WCC?
   (i)   people on the autism spectrum cannot take in the overall form or meaning of things
   (ii) people on the autism spectrum prefer to focus on detail.

(b) In a recent survey of Cambridge mathematics undergraduates, there was found to be a much higher rate of autism spectrum conditions than in control groups of law, medicine and social sciences. Does this support the E-S theory?

Question 4.4   (LO 4.5)

If there are several psychological factors underlying autism, does this mean that explanations such as ToM or EF should be abandoned?

Chapter 5   Biological explanations

Rosa Hoekstra and Terry Whatson

5.1   Introduction and overview

You read in Chapter 2 that autism was diagnosed on the basis of behaviour exhibited by individuals, behaviour that was atypical and distinguishable from that of typically developing individuals. In Chapters 3 and 4 you read about characteristic difficulties with communication, social interaction and flexible behaviour, and underlying problems such as mind-reading and executive function. Such activities occur in the brain, and are accompanied by muscle actions, which in turn result in observed behaviour. It follows that an examination of the brain, a science called **neurobiology**, might provide clues as to how specific psychological difficulties and behaviours arise. The neurobiology of autism is still a relatively new field of research, yet already some important progress has been made; this is discussed in Sections 5.4 and 5.5. Scientists are beginning to understand how our genes (Section 5.3), nervous system and hormones (Section 5.4) interact with the anatomy and functioning of our brain (Section 5.5) to create the circumstances where autism is likely to develop. These studies have not identified a *single* biological cause for autism: there is no 'single gene for autism', there is no single hormonal explanation for autism, nor is there one area of the brain where autism 'resides'. Rather, it has become clear that there are multiple biological components underlying autism.

One of the earliest studies of biological factors underlying autism confirmed the clinical observation that epilepsy is very common in people with autism. In 1970 a study from Australia (Gubbay et al., 1970) found that in a group of 25 children with autism, approximately 30% had experienced seizures. The researchers also measured brain activity in these children using **electroencephalography (EEG)**. In EEG research several electrodes are attached to the scalp of the participant, and these electrodes measure the electrical activity that is produced by the neurons in the brain (see Section 5.4 for further discussion). Strikingly, the Australian study indicated that the EEGs of up to 80% of the children with autism could be classified as abnormal, suggesting that their brain activity is different from that of typically developing children, even in cases where epilepsy is not diagnosed.

■   How does this study support the notion that 'there are multiple components underlying autism'?

☐   Not all the people with autism had epilepsy, nor did they all have abnormal EEGs. If these were important contributory factors to the autism in some people, then there must be other contributory factors for other people with autism.

Another line of evidence for the biological influences on autism came from the observation that some developmental disorders with an established genetic basis are common in people with autism. For instance, about 25% of the

Tuberous sclerosis is a genetic disease that causes benign tumours to grow in the brain and also other organs (e.g. the kidneys, heart). It often affects the central nervous system, resulting in symptoms such as seizures, delayed development, and behavioural problems.

males and 6% of the females with a medical condition called fragile X syndrome (see Section 5.3.2) have autism. Tuberous sclerosis is another medical condition in which an autism spectrum diagnosis is common. Examining the faulty genes that are associated with these conditions, and the functions they typically perform, has helped in shaping the ideas of what biological mechanisms may underlie autism. It should be noted that, although autism is common in people with medical conditions such as fragile X syndrome and tuberous sclerosis, these patients only constitute a minority of the total number of people with an autism spectrum diagnosis. Rare medical syndromes and chromosomal abnormalities (see Section 5.3.2 for discussion) are associated with about 10–20% of autism diagnoses.

Autism is a complex cluster of conditions and the predisposing factors or **aetiology** remain largely unknown. It is now thought that multiple factors combine to influence the development, structure and functioning of the brain, eventually leading to the pattern of behavioural and psychological symptoms consistent with a clinical diagnosis of autism.

5.1.1 Summary of Section 5.1

- Autism is a behaviourally defined condition and in some cases it is the recognised end-point of medical conditions (such as fragile X) for which the aetiology is known. However, these cases account for only 10–20% of all cases diagnosed.
- For the majority of cases of autism, the aetiology remains unknown, but it is likely to be multifactorial involving genetic, developmental and neurobiological factors.

5.2 The MMR vaccine and autism

Before setting out to explore the biological basis of autism, you will first briefly examine a highly controversial topic that has been much publicised by the media, and that many parents have been concerned about over recent years – that is, the relationship between the measles, mumps and rubella (MMR) vaccine and autism. This topic was touched upon in Sections 1.1 and 2.6.

The MMR vaccine is a combination vaccine, originally licensed in 1971 (and first prescribed within the UK in 1988) to protect against three highly infectious diseases, measles, mumps and rubella (the latter also known as German measles), each of which is potentially life-threatening. MMR vaccination helps to limit the spread of these debilitating diseases. In order for the vaccine to be fully effective, two doses are usually administered: the first during early infancy (at 12–15 months of age); and the second – which is optional – during early childhood (four to six years of age). Given that pain at the site of injection, fever, mild rash and swollen glands (in the neck) are common side effects of vaccination, it is clearly advantageous to limit the number of injections administered to the child, and the combination vaccine appears to be an effective method of achieving this (there is no published scientific evidence to indicate any benefit in separating the MMR vaccine into three individual shots).

■ Based on the previous paragraph, can you identify one reason why some parents and families have been concerned that the vaccine may cause autism?

▢ One reason is that some of the first signs of autism tend to appear around 18 months of age, which is soon after the child receives the first dose of MMR vaccine (see also Section 3.4.2 on early signs of autism).

Concerned parents have reported that their child was 'normal' until they received the MMR vaccine, subsequent to which they began to show symptoms of autism (i.e. they underwent a form of **regression**).

A second reason why some people have linked the MMR vaccine and autism is their perception that the number of children diagnosed with autism has been rising from around the period the vaccine was introduced. However, just because the events happen to coincide does not necessarily mean that one caused the other (Box 5.1).

It is called regression because certain behaviours, most commonly language, stop developing and may indeed become less proficient and more like the behaviour that the child exhibited at an earlier age. (See also Section 3.4.1.)

Box 5.1 Cause and effect

In many circumstances there is a simple and neat relationship between a cause and an effect. Unexpectedly placing your hand on a pin will result in both pain and the immediate removal of your hand from the pin. The cause, or agent, of the pain and the movement can be easily identified as the pin. In addition the effect of the pin can also be easily identified: pain and movement of the hand away from the pin. In other circumstances the relationship between an event (the cause) and its effect may be less easy to establish. How, for example, do we determine whether we have suffered from food poisoning? The effects of eating a slightly contaminated meal (headache, nausea, sweating) may not be evident until several hours after the meal. In the intervening period the individual may have been exposed to other potential agents, such as drinking alcohol, or coming into contact with people carrying a stomach virus. Another complication in this example is that a companion who ate the same meal may report no ill effects. The example illustrates three separate components that diminish our confidence in determining cause and effect: delay, effect and susceptibility. (There is a fourth component, reliability, i.e. the likelihood that an agent will have the same effect on every application, but this need not concern you here.)

• The longer the delay between exposure to the agent and any effects, the harder it is to be sure that the agent has any effect. Other influences may occur in the intervening period.

• The less specific any effect, or the more varied the possible effect(s), the harder it is to be sure that the agent is responsible for the effect.

• The greater the range in susceptibility to the agent, or the fewer people who are susceptible, the harder it is to establish any effect.

Determining any MMR and autism relationship is complicated by each of the three issues introduced in Box 5.1:

1 Delay: consequences that might be due to the vaccine, e.g. regression, may not be observed or reported immediately, but weeks or months after vaccination.

2 Effect: any one (or combination) of the symptoms on the autistic spectrum may be included as an effect.

3 Susceptibility: most children exhibit no susceptibility to the MMR vaccine. Indeed, it remains unknown whether any children are susceptible to the MMR vaccine.

In the late 1990s, concerns over the MMR vaccine were augmented with the publication of a small study looking at bowel disease and autism in 12 children. The paper, by the gastroenterologist, Andrew Wakefield and his colleagues (1998), implied a possible link between the MMR vaccine and autism. The study, later retracted by most of the authors, did not actually provide scientific evidence for such a link, but led to considerable publicity, following which the rates of MMR vaccination fell considerably to just over 60% in England over the course of the next few years. This low rate of vaccination poses a health risk as it is not sufficient to contain the three diseases, and restrict their spread through the population.

By considering the relative numbers of those vaccinated and those receiving an autism spectrum diagnosis, it is possible to state categorically that MMR is not a primary cause of autism; there is no straightforward causal link between MMR and the autism spectrum.

■ How do the relative numbers of those vaccinated and those diagnosed with autism enable this categorical statement to be made?

☐ If MMR was a primary cause of autism, most of those vaccinated, i.e. most children, would be diagnosed with autism. But most children are not diagnosed with autism; hence there cannot be a straightforward causal relationship between MMR and autism.

However, even if there is no straightforward association between the MMR vaccine and the autism spectrum, it is possible that there might be a weak or indirect association and several studies have investigated this possibility. Three of those studies are considered here.

Taylor and colleagues (1999) looked at all children up to the age of five born from 1979 onwards within certain districts of London. From these children they identified those who had received an autism diagnosis, using the ICD-10 criteria for childhood (classic) autism, Asperger syndrome and atypical autism (see Chapter 2 for an explanation of these terms). They then grouped the children by year of birth and plotted a graph (the children with Asperger syndrome were left out of this graph because of their small numbers). The total number of children born in 1979 who received a diagnosis of autism at any time up to the age of five was plotted above their birth year of 1979. The total number of children born in 1980 who received a diagnosis of autism at any time up to the age of five was plotted above their birth year of 1980, and so on. The results are shown in Figure 5.1. Taylor et al. found that the number of children diagnosed with autism had increased steadily from 1979 until 1992.

■   Look carefully at Figure 5.1. The vaccine was introduced in 1988. If the vaccine caused autism, why might you expect to see a marked rise in the number of children born in 1987 diagnosed with autism, compared with those born before 1986? (*Note*: remember that children are vaccinated at 12–15 months of age.)

☐   Most children born in 1987 would receive their MMR vaccine in 1988. If the MMR vaccine causes autism, you would expect to see a large increase in the number of cases in this 1987 group, compared with those born before 1986 who were not vaccinated. In fact, the number of cases follows the steady upward trend of earlier years.

Some children born towards the end of 1986 would have been vaccinated in 1988, hence the use of those born before 1986 for comparison.

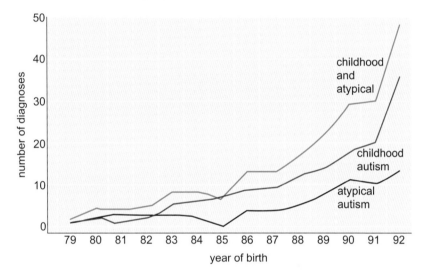

Figure 5.1   Number of children born between 1979 and 1992 in certain districts of London who were diagnosed with childhood (classic) autism or atypical autism. (Adapted from Taylor et al., 1999)

A more recent study by Honda et al. (2005) examined more than 31 000 children in the city of Yokohama in Japan. The study is telling, but complex. Honda et al. (2005) looked at the records of all the children born in the district of Yokohama between 1988 and 1996, and noted all children diagnosed with autism by the age of seven. They then grouped the children by year of birth and plotted a graph, in the same way that Taylor et al. did, as was described above. The total number of children born in 1988 who received a diagnosis of autism at any time up to the age of seven was plotted above their birth year of 1988, and so on. They distinguished between those children with autism with and without regression. The reason for looking separately at the sub-group with regressive symptoms is that since they are children in which an apparently typical developmental trajectory reverses during infancy, they have raised the greatest concerns amongst parents for an effect of vaccination (Figure 5.2a). In Japan, the vaccine was administered to children of one year of age. The vaccination was introduced in 1989, so the first

The particular type of mumps virus on which the Japanese MMR vaccine was based is no longer used.

children to be vaccinated were those born in 1988. Almost immediately after its introduction, the vaccine was phased out following reports that the anti-mumps component was causing meningitis (where the membrane coverings of the nervous system become swollen and damaged). The MMR vaccine was completely withdrawn in Japan by 1993. Honda et al. report that 70% of eligible children were vaccinated in 1989, but only 43% were vaccinated in 1990, and only 33% in 1991. The percentage of children vaccinated in each birth year cohort is shown by the bars above the year of birth (Figure 5.2b: note that the scale for percentage of vaccinations is on the right of the figure).

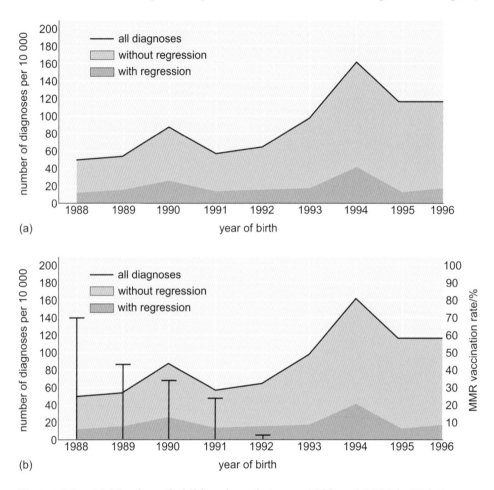

(a)

(b)

Figure 5.2 (a) Number of children born between 1988 and 1996 in Yokohama who were diagnosed with autism (including autism with regression) by age seven (per 10 000). (b) Number of children born between 1988 and 1996 in Yokohama who were diagnosed with autism (including autism with regression) by age seven (per 10 000) (left-hand axis). The percentage of eligible children in each birth year cohort who were vaccinated (right-hand axis) is shown by the T-shaped bars. (Adapted from Honda et al., 2005)

■ Children become eligible to be vaccinated in the year after they are born. What percentage of eligible children were vaccinated in 1992?

☐ About 24% of eligible children were vaccinated in 1992 (look at the bar above the birth year, 1991 in this case).

Figure 5.2b shows that diagnoses continued to rise, despite the complete withdrawal of the vaccine.

■ Children born in which year received the highest rate of autism diagnosis?

☐ 1994.

■ What percentage of children born in 1994 received the MMR vaccine?

☐ No children born in 1994 were vaccinated.

Note that the number of cases of autism follows a generally upward trend during the years after the vaccine was withdrawn. Moreover, the rate of the regressive form of autism hardly changed throughout this period. The conclusion from this study is that the MMR vaccine cannot have caused the rise in the prevalence of autism seen in children born in or after 1993.

The results of these studies are typical of all the many independent and carefully conducted studies that have investigated MMR and autism: there is no link between autism and the MMR vaccine. Neither has a link been established with other vaccines that contain thimerosal, which is the same preservative found within the MMR vaccine.

Thimerosal has been phased out of vaccine preparations in the USA over a number of years, being virtually eliminated by 2004. The change in prevalence of autism in California over the period when thimerosal was being withdrawn from vaccines is shown in Figure 5.3. Note that the graph uses a different scale along the bottom, the 'x', axis. Any three-, four- or five-year-old child who has a diagnosis of autism is included for each year. So a child diagnosed at three years of age will be included in three successive years, whilst a child diagnosed at five years of age will only be included once. Despite this confusion, any rise in the line on the graph represents an increase in prevalence and any fall in the line represents a decrease in prevalence.

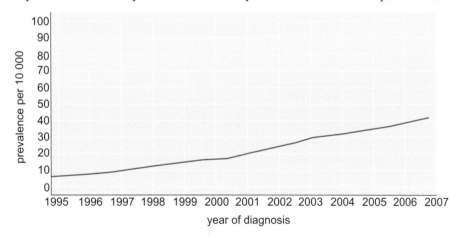

Figure 5.3 Prevalence of autism per 10 000 children aged three to five years in California over the years 1995 to 2007. (Adapted from Schechter and Grether, 2008)

■   What can you say about the prevalence of autism in California over the years 1995 to 2007?

☐   The prevalence of autism in California over this period has steadily increased.

No reduction in prevalence is evident since thimerosal was withdrawn. Indeed the prevalence has continued to increase.

A more plausible explanation to account for the rise in the number of children diagnosed with autism is that the diagnostic criteria (definitions) have broadened considerably from 1980 up to the modern-day (DSM-IV-TR in 2000), and that specialists are far better at detecting and diagnosing the condition now than they were two decades ago (see Chapter 2).

Whilst it remains possible that some individuals may be particularly susceptible to an environmental agent at some specific time in infancy, or before, what that agent might be or which individuals might be particularly susceptible are unknown.

5.2.1   Summary of Section 5.2

- The timing of MMR vaccination and emergence of the symptoms of autism are similar.
- The rise in the diagnosis of autism began before the MMR vaccine was introduced, and continued to rise in Japan after the vaccine was withdrawn there.
- No formal large-scale studies have established any causal link between the MMR vaccine and autism.
- Environmental factors may play a role in some individuals with autism. What these factors are and who are particularly susceptible is still unknown.

5.3   The genetic basis of autism

As soon as autism was recognised as a separate condition, researchers and clinicians began investigating its underlying causes. As described in Chapter 1, early theories suggesting that autism may be caused by 'refrigerator mothers' were largely dismissed after the findings of the first twin study into autism were published (Folstein and Rutter, 1977; see Box 1.9 in Chapter 1). This study, together with subsequent twin and family studies, suggest that autism has a large genetic component and thus can be inherited from parents by their child(ren), a propensity known as **heritability**. It is now thought that autism is one of the most heritable conditions in mental health (Rutter, 2005). You will now look at the evidence for this claim in a bit more detail.

The first twin study by Folstein and Rutter included only 21 twin pairs. In 1995, Bailey et al. re-contacted all participants, re-checked the diagnostic and medical assessments and augmented the overall sample, providing data on a total of 25 identical (or **monozygotic**, MZ) and 20 non-identical (or **dizygotic**, DZ) same-sex pairs. The findings confirmed and extended those of the original study. The overall MZ concordance rate for classic autism was 60%. However, the concordance rate rose to 92% when twins showing a broader spectrum of autistic-type symptoms were taken into account. The concordance rate for classic autism in DZ twins was 0%, but increased to 10% when the broader-spectrum symptoms were included.

- What does it mean to say that the concordance rate for classic autism in DZ twins was 0%?

□ A concordance rate of 0% means that in none of the DZ twin pairs were both siblings diagnosed with classic autism.

In Bailey et al.'s 1995 study, among three of the MZ pairs, the non-autistic twin met the ICD-10 criteria for PDD-unspecified (see Section 2.2.2). Given the evolution of diagnostic practices since 1995, it seems possible that the autistic-type symptoms of further MZ twins from the study might today be considered to meet criteria for an autism spectrum diagnosis. Several research groups are carrying out studies in a larger number of twin pairs that include all different autism spectrum diagnoses. These studies will shed a light on the concordance rate of MZ and DZ twins using contemporary diagnostic criteria.

The markedly raised concordance in MZ twins compared with DZ twins suggests that genetic influences are important in explaining the risk for the condition. Both MZ and DZ pairs grow up in the same family and consequently share certain environmental influences, for example their diet, pets and the neighbourhood. Both types of twins are also exposed to unique environmental influences that are not shared with their co-twin, such as being in different classes in school or having an illness or accident. The only aspect that is consistently different between MZ and DZ twin pairs is their genetic similarity: MZ twins share all their genetic material, whilst DZ twins on average share about 50% of their genes. Finding that the concordance rate for autism is much higher in MZ twins than in DZ twins (see Figure 5.4) thus suggests that genes play an important role in autism.

(a) (b)

Figure 5.4 Comparing (a) identical and (b) non-identical twins can give insight into the genetic and environmental influences on behaviour. (digitalskillet/iStockphoto; robh/iStockphoto)

■ What other explanatory factors might be considered when interpreting these twin studies?

□ You might have argued that the researcher checking the clinical diagnoses of participants would recognise the second twin of identical, MZ, pairs and be inclined to make the same diagnosis as they did for the previous twin, whereas they would not recognise the second twin of non-identical, DZ, twin pairs. Psychologists go to great lengths to prevent this sort of bias from occurring; using, for example, two clinicians who each independently diagnose each child in order to reduce experimenter bias. Alternatively, you may have suggested that MZ twins, being of very similar height, physique and attributes, might share the same interests; whereas DZ twins may be rather different from each other in height, physique and attributes and hence not share the same interests. The consequence would be that MZ twins would share a more similar environment for more of the time, than DZ twins.

Other evidence for the strong genetic influence on autism comes from non-twin family studies. These studies show that autism tends to 'run in families': relatives of individuals with autism are at increased risk of also being affected compared with the general population. The likelihood that a sibling of an individual with autism will also be affected (the **sibling recurrence risk**) is estimated at between 5% and 10%. As discussed in Chapter 2, the prevalence of autism spectrum diagnoses in the general population is estimated to be at least 0.6%, with more recent studies suggesting a prevalence of around 1%. Thus, the risk for autism in a sibling of an autistic individual is markedly higher than the general population risk, again suggesting a genetic predisposition for autism.

■ If autism has a genetic basis, why would you expect the sibling recurrence risk and the concordance rate for DZ twins to be similar?

□ Pairs of dizygotic twins share on average 50% of their genes. Pairs of non-twin siblings also share, on average, 50% of their genes. So the genetic predisposition for autism (concordance rate) in DZ twins ought to be the same as the genetic predisposition for autism (sibling recurrence risk) in siblings.

■ Are the values for sibling recurrence rate and DZ concordance rate similar?

□ Broadly they are similar: the concordance rate for DZ twins was 10% when broader spectrum symptoms were included. The sibling recurrence rate is estimated at between 5% and 10%.

Gillberg (1991) carried out a study in which he looked at the incidence of Asperger syndrome and the broader autism spectrum across three generations of certain families. One of the family patterns is shown in Figure 5.5.

Gillberg's study nicely illustrates how autism tends to run in families. It also illustrates that there seems to be a genetic risk for the full spectrum of autism, rather than for classic autism and Asperger syndrome as distinct conditions. The fact that classic autism and Asperger syndrome are present in the same

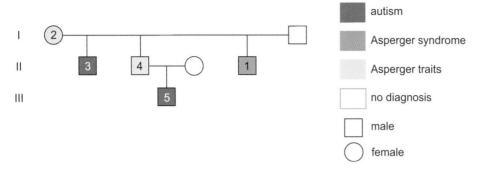

	autism
	Asperger syndrome
	Asperger traits
	no diagnosis
	male
	female

Figure 5.5 A family tree showing the distribution of autism across three generations, I, II and III. (1) was the original patient. He is an unmarried man of 33 with Asperger syndrome. He works as a lawyer. (2) is the mother of (1). She is described as highly intelligent and shows some Asperger traits. (3) is the eldest brother of (1). He was diagnosed with classic autism at the age of four and lives in a group home. (4) is the middle brother of (1). He has Asperger traits, including odd pedantic speech, and is married. (5) is the first-born son of (4), aged three. He is described as showing signs of classic autism. (Adapted from Gillberg, 1991)

family suggests that these sub-types of autism share a common genetic aetiology. Moreover, the mother of the family shown in Figure 5.5 had Asperger symptoms, not a full diagnosis. Hence any genetic predisposition leads to symptoms that are graded from affected through subtle expression of autistic features to unaffected. Similarly, many of the non-autistic twins in the twin studies described earlier showed a milder form of autistic-type difficulties. These milder manifestations of autistic symptoms in relatives of individuals with autism are often referred to as the **broader autism phenotype (BAP)**. Examples of expression of the BAP include mild social and communication difficulties, a preference for routine, or difficulty with change. Several studies have investigated this phenomenon. Importantly, some of these studies compared families with autism with clinical control families with other behavioural and/or intellectual difficulties.

■   Why is it important to include a clinical control group when studying the BAP in relatives of individuals with autism?

☐   It is conceivable that raising a child with autism, or growing up in a family with a child with autism, may induce the expression of atypical psychological traits. It is therefore important to include a clinical comparison group, to test whether the increased expression of the BAP is really due to genetic factors, and cannot be attributed to the psychological impact of living with a child with behavioural and/or learning difficulties.

Bolton and colleagues (1994) examined family history data in 99 individuals with autism and 36 individuals with Down syndrome. Both classic autism and more broadly defined pervasive developmental disorders (see also Section 2.2) were increased in siblings of individuals with autism (2.9%), but not in the siblings of individuals with Down syndrome (0%). Moreover, between 12.4% and 20.4% of the autism siblings showed subtle communication/social impairments or stereotypic behaviours; this rate was only 1.6% to 3.2% in the Down syndrome siblings. Similarly, Piven et al. (1997) found that parents of children with autism had higher rates of particular personality characteristics and language difficulties than parents of a child with Down syndrome. Parents of the children with autism were more often described as rigid, aloof, hypersensitive to criticism, or anxious than parents in the comparison group. Speech and pragmatic language deficits were also more frequent in the autism families. Moreover, 37% of parents of individuals with autism reported no friendships compared with only 4% of parents of Down syndrome individuals.

All in all, these findings from twin and family studies suggest a strong genetic predisposition for autism. The presence of milder manifestations of autistic-type difficulties in relatives of people with autism suggests a genetically based spectrum of autistic traits and is consistent with the idea of an autistic continuum. However, the twin studies also show that the concordance in MZ twins is not complete. A concordance rate of less than 100% implies that non-genetic effects also play a role. Also, even in MZ twin pairs, the expression of autistic symptoms and the severity of autism can differ markedly between twins. Since MZ twins are genetically identical, environmental influences, as yet unidentified, are likely to be important in explaining the differences in autistic features within these affected pairs.

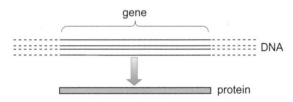

Figure 5.6 The relationship between a gene and the protein for which it codes. The DNA in our body contains tens of thousands of different genes. Each gene codes for a specific protein, and this protein in turn has a particular function in the body.

5.3.1 Genes and genetic variation

Overall, the results from twin and family studies suggest a strong genetic influence in autism, but this does not mean that there is a 'gene for autism'. The pattern of inheritance and range of symptoms indicate influences that are **polygenic**, i.e. due to the combined effects of multiple genes. Many different research groups have started to explore which genes may be involved in autism. In order to understand the methodology and the findings of these studies, it is important to understand some basic concepts of genetics.

Genes are commonly referred to as the 'blueprints' for life – what sets us apart in terms of, for example, eye colour or hair structure is down to our genetic make-up inherited from our parents. Genes are small sections of very long molecules of a substance called **deoxyribonucleic acid (DNA)**. DNA has a precise sequence of units, a section of these units together constitute a gene. Each gene encodes (i.e. contains the instructions for making) a specific protein (see Figure 5.6), which in turn instructs our cells and tissues how to interact or grow or respond to damage and diseases, and so forth. For example, there is a gene that codes for the protein hormone insulin, which has a role in regulating our blood sugar level.

Our genes are the basic units of heredity. Nearly all the hereditary information we carry within each of our cells (also referred to as the **human genome)** is organised into 23 distinctive pairs of structural units called **chromosomes** (see Figure 5.7). Of each pair of chromosomes, one is inherited from the mother and one is inherited from the father. The pairs numbered 1 to 22 are visually indistinguishable between males and females. The remaining pair of chromosomes shown in the figure is visually very different and constitutes the sex chromosomes, known as **X and Y chromosomes**. The body cells of human females typically possess two X chromosomes, whilst the cells of males have one X chromosome and one Y chromosome.

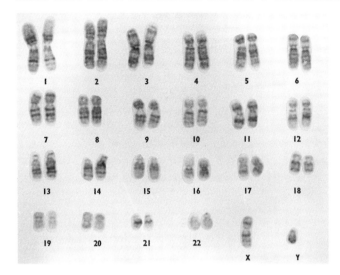

Figure 5.7 Photograph of the 23 pairs of chromosomes of a human male. The first 22 pairs of chromosomes are the same for men and women. The last pair are the sex chromosomes. The body cells of males have one copy of the X chromosome and one copy of the (much smaller) Y chromosome, while the cells of females typically have two X chromosomes. (This image was photographed through a light microscope and is magnified approximately 1000 times.) (Professor Ferguson Smith)

■ The transmission of the sex chromosome of which parent determines the sex of the child: the father or the mother?

□ The father; mothers can only transmit an X chromosome, so the sex chromosome passed on by the father (which can be either X or Y) determines the sex of the child. If the father transmits the Y chromosome, the child will be XY and will be male. If he transmits the X chromosome, the child will be XX and will thus be female.

In 2000, researchers, after many years of effort, made a historic announcement – they had catalogued and mapped the tens of thousands of genes that make up the human genome. This monumental work has paved the way for new scientific discoveries, based on a deeper understanding of how genes interact and respond in health and disease. Although we all share the same set of genes, variants of these genes can exist. These different forms of the same gene are commonly termed **alleles**. Allelic differences between people cause individual differences. Each allele codes for a slightly different version of the protein and can therefore result in a slight difference in functioning of the body. Such allelic differences can, for instance, account for why some people have blue eyes whilst others have brown eye colour. Gene variants can also explain why people differ in their susceptibility to different conditions, behaviours and psychological traits. Remember that the chromosomes and hence the genes they carry are paired. Normally, an individual inherits one variant of each gene from their mother and one variant from their father. The

A mutation is a change in the genetic material.

two variants of one particular gene can be the same, or a person can inherit two different variants of the gene from their two parents. Sometimes, a spontaneous **mutation (*de novo* mutation)** arises in the formation of eggs or sperm, resulting in a new gene variant in the offspring. In that case, one of the child's gene variants for a particular gene will be different from the gene variants found in either the mother or the father.

5.3.2 Searching for genes involved in autism

The finding that autism is strongly influenced by genetic factors prompted the quest to find exactly what genes, on which chromosomes, might be involved in autism. In this pursuit, a variety of methods, each with their own advantages and disadvantages, are used. The following paragraphs outline the different methods that are commonly used in genetic research and some of the findings.

A first glimpse of the role of genes in susceptibility for autism was given by studying chromosomal abnormalities. Gross chromosomal abnormalities are either **deletions**, where DNA has been lost, or **duplications**, where DNA has been added, and can be identified by observing chromosomes under the light microscope. Because the sequence of DNA which makes up the genes along chromosomes is critical in determining what characteristics are expressed, deletion or duplication of parts of this sequence can have serious consequences. Most deletions or duplications are lethal. If they are not lethal they may result in atypical physical, behavioural and psychological traits. In about 6–7% of people with autism, deletions are identified, and deletions are especially common in autistic people who also have physical abnormalities and intellectual disability. About 1% of individuals with autism have a deletion on chromosome 22. Duplications of a region on chromosome 15 occur in 1–2% of the autism diagnoses (Abrahams and Geschwind, 2008). Using the light microscope, only large regions (typically containing more than 50 genes) can be identified and such chromosomal abnormalities are not present in the majority of people with autism. Nevertheless, this type of research indicated that certain regions on particular chromosomes may be important in the aetiology of autism, prompting further, more detailed studies.

Abbreviated gene names are printed in italics to distinguish them from their protein products that often have the same abbreviated name, but are printed in normal type.

Similarly, research has been guided by other medical conditions in which autism is diagnosed. For instance, **fragile X syndrome** is a genetic syndrome in which part of a gene called *FMR1*, located on the X chromosome, has lost its function. Fragile X is associated with mild to severe intellectual disability and about a quarter of males with the syndrome have autism. The mutation in the *FMR1* gene causes a loss of (or significant reduction in) the function of the protein it codes for – the unfortunately named fragile X mental retardation protein, or FMRP. FMRP is thought to be of importance in establishing connections between cells in the brain (**neurons**) and in making existing connections more efficient. Many researchers now think that abnormalities in cell communication and in cell connections are important in explaining autism. Thus, although fragile X syndrome only accounts for about 1–2% of the cases on the autism spectrum, it provided researchers with important clues about the biological mechanisms that may underlie autism. The neurobiological systems involved in autism will be further explained in

Section 5.4. In most people with autism, the cause of their condition is unknown. To further our understanding of the more subtle genetic variants (not detectable using a microscope) that may be involved in these **idiopathic** cases, various research groups have conducted **linkage analysis** and **association studies**.

Idiopathic means of no known cause.

Chromosomes commonly break and reconnect during the formation of sperm or eggs, leading to the physical separation of previously associated genes. Linkage analysis relies on the tendency for genes to remain associated and be inherited together, if they are physically close together on the same chromosome. The same tendency applies to the non-coding sections of DNA that are found all over the chromosomes. The locations of some non-coding sections are well known and these are used as DNA markers, essentially landmarks in the DNA. If a certain DNA marker is more often found in affected members of the same family compared to unaffected family members, it is likely that a gene involved in this disease or condition is located close to the marker. The more frequently the DNA marker is present with the disease or condition, the nearer the DNA marker is to a gene or genes involved in the disease. The strongest linkage evidence implicates regions on chromosomes 2, 3, 6 and 17, and particularly chromosome 7 (Freitag, 2007).

Linkage analysis is a technique used to get a general idea of what region of which chromosomes may be involved in the risk for autism, but it does not identify the precise gene involved. To do that, association studies have been used to identify **candidate genes**. In such studies, the association between a certain genetic variant that prior evidence has suggested may be of importance, and the condition, is tested. The prior evidence can be from linkage studies, or it can be that the function of the gene suggests that it might play a role. For instance, if a gene is known to be involved in the development of language ability, then it might be a good gene to consider as a possible candidate gene for autism.

- Can you recall a candidate gene that was mentioned earlier?

□ The gene associated with fragile X syndrome, *FMR1*.

In candidate gene association studies, variants (alleles) of the candidate gene of individuals with autism (cases) are compared with the alleles of unaffected individuals (controls). If a certain allele is more frequent in cases compared to controls, this gene variant may constitute a risk factor for the condition. In contrast to linkage studies, association studies are also able to detect genes with a smaller effect.

In the past years, dozens of candidate genes for autism have been suggested in nearly 100 independent studies (Yang and Gill, 2007). For example, after finding that some individuals with autism have a duplication on chromosome 15, researchers started studying the particular area where the abnormality was observed in more detail. Within this region, several of the genes that encode the **GABA** receptor protein are located. As will be outlined in Section 5.4, GABA is a **neurotransmitter**, a chemical involved in carrying a signal from one neuron to another. Malfunctioning of any of the GABA receptor genes may impair early development of the brain and may harm the communication

GABA stands for gamma-aminobutyric acid.

between neurons. Some studies suggest that GABA levels are altered in autism. Some candidate gene studies in turn suggested that the GABA receptor genes may be associated with autism. However, the findings were inconclusive: some studies found significant association, but others failed to find a connection between any of these genes and autism (Freitag, 2007).

After linkage studies had suggested that chromosome 7 plays a role in autism aetiology, several candidate gene studies tried to identify exactly which genes on chromosome 7 may be involved. One of the genes on this chromosome, *EN2*, plays a role in the development of the brainstem and the cerebellum (an area at the back of the brain), and both these brain regions have been implicated in autism. Independent studies suggested that the *EN2* gene may be associated with the risk for autism (Abrahams and Geschwind, 2008). The role of different brain areas in autism, and how atypical functioning of these areas is thought to be related to the behavioural characteristics of autism, will be discussed further in Section 5.5.

Numerous linkage studies have suggested the involvement of many different chromosomal regions in autism. Even more plentiful candidate gene studies pointed to the possible role of different susceptibility genes for autism. Figure 5.8 gives an overview of all gene locations that had been linked to autism aetiology by 2008. A quick look at this figure reveals one thing: nearly all the chromosomes have been reported to be involved in the risk for autism in some individuals! Figure 5.8 illustrates again that there is not one single gene for autism. Rather, the available evidence converges towards many different genes affecting susceptibility. Some of the gene variants of these susceptibility genes are rare and only affect a limited number of people, but in these cases the effects can be quite pronounced. Other gene variants are much more common in the population, but it is likely that they have only a small effect on the overall risk for autism. Thus, autism is thought to be **genetically heterogeneous** (i.e. have multiple genetic causes). Different genes may be involved in different people with autism. Additionally, different genetic influences may underlie different autistic symptoms. For instance, the genes that underlie social difficulties may be different from those underlying repetitive behaviours.

5.3.3 Future directions of genetic studies of autism

The wide range of symptoms and the likely polygenic nature of autism has meant that there has been little replication of findings from genetic studies. Studies are more likely to yield consistent and reliable results if they include many well-characterised individuals. Large-scale studies (including the International Molecular Genetic Study of Autism Consortium (IMGSAC) led by Professor Tony Monaco at the Wellcome Trust Centre for Human Genetics in Oxford, and the Autism Genetic Resource Exchange (AGRE), the world's first gene bank for autism) have been collecting detailed information from families with individuals with autism (autism families). These large-scale international studies may in the near future provide important clues about the aetiology of autism, using a new methodology: **genome-wide association**.

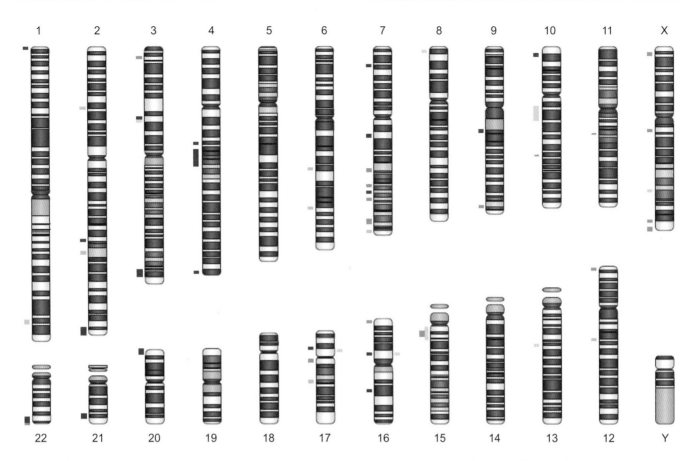

Figure 5.8 Gene locations implicated in autism by 2008. One chromosome of each pair and the X and Y chromosomes are shown. Red and yellow bars correspond to approximate locations on the chromosome where genetic losses (deletions) (red) and gains (duplications) (yellow) are observed in people diagnosed with autism but not in controls. Green bars represent promising (light green) or probable (dark green) candidate genes. Regions shaded in purple correspond to regions identified in linkage studies. The bands on the chromosome do not refer to individual genes. (Adapted from Abrahams and Geschwind, 2008)

Previously, it was costly to analyse each candidate gene of interest, and association studies would therefore only include a limited number of candidate genes. However, recently, the development of microarrays (chips the size of a postage stamp comprising microscopic spots of short DNA sequences) made it possible to analyse thousands of genes at once at much lower costs than previously. Some of these chips include up to half a million gene variants. Many participants are needed in order to reliably test the association of so many genes. International collaborations such as IMGSAC and AGRE make it possible to conduct these genome-wide association studies. This strategy has already yielded results. One recent study (Wang et al., 2009) that examined genome-wide association in more than 10 000 participants from both control and autism families identified association with two further genes, *CDH10* and *CDH9*, involved in the early development of the frontal lobe of the cerebral cortex (see Section 5.5).

In addition, within these large cohorts of people with autism, it becomes possible to select individuals with the same symptoms; for instance, those with no language delay, or with very strong repetitive behaviours. Such selectivity increases the likelihood that the aetiology of the autism in those being studied is similar.

Ultimately the integration of findings from large-scale linkage and association studies, together with findings from studies of individuals with autism *and* rare genetic abnormalities, will give us a better idea of what biological pathways are involved in the aetiology of autism. The next section of this chapter will further elaborate on this topic.

5.3.4 Summary of Section 5.3

- Twin and family studies indicate that autism is strongly heritable.
- These studies also show that the expression of the autistic symptoms and their severity are highly variable, even within families and twin pairs.
- Environmental factors probably also play some role in the risk for autism and in the variability of the expression of autistic symptoms. However, up until now, no single major environmental risk factor has been identified.
- The strong heritability of autism prompted the search for genes that are involved in autism. A large range of both linkage and association studies have identified several susceptibility genes for autism. However, none of these genes has a major effect in large numbers of people with autism. The identified genetic variants tend to be either common in the population but have only a small effect, or be a rare genetic variant with a larger effect.
- Different genes can affect the susceptibility for autism in different individuals. Within an individual, multiple genes may contribute to the development of autism.
- Atypical variants of the genes that affect the development of the frontal lobe of the cerebral cortex and communication between neurons have been found in people with autism.

5.4 The neurobiological basis of autism

In the previous section you learned about genetic variants that can affect the risk of developing autism. You also learned that genes code for proteins and these proteins in turn have a role in the functioning of the body. Various proteins have a role in the development and functioning of neurons and in communication between neurons. In this section you will find out more about the structure and function of neurons and how these cells communicate with each other. Some important notions of how this communication is thought to be different in people with autism will also be discussed.

5.4.1 Neurons and neuronal communication

Neurons are specialised cells that process information, both within the cell itself and between different cells. By processing information, they are directly involved in cognition and behaviour. For instance, enhanced communication between neurons is important in learning new skills or remembering new information. Communication between neurons enables functions such as inducing motor movements, or leads to the release of hormones (chemical messengers) which in turn can affect our behaviour. The network of all the neurons in the body is called the **nervous system**. Most neurons are in the brain, but they are also found throughout the body, particularly in the spinal cord (the column of neurons housed within the backbone).

As you can see in Figure 5.9, neurons can be of different shapes, but all have three specific features that allow them to perform their function in processing information. All neurons have a **cell body** which extends into a single axon at one location and an array of dendrites elsewhere. The **dendrites** of the neuron receive signals from other neurons (input) and the **axon** is the part of the cell by which the neuron sends information to other cells (output) some distance away. When a signal is being carried by an axon, the neuron is said to be **firing**. In Section 5.1 the technique of EEG was described as a way of measuring brain activity. But what is meant by brain activity?

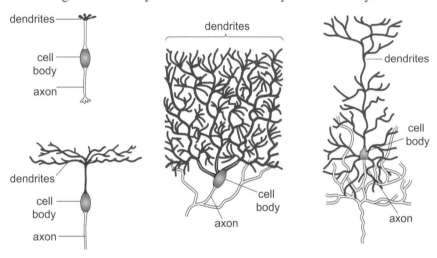

Figure 5.9 Neurons can have different forms and somewhat different functions, but all have three features in common: they all consist of a cell body, one thin axon and a tree of dendrites. (*Note*: the axon may branch beyond the cell body, but only one axon emerges from the cell body.) (Purves, 2001)

Every neuron is like a miniature battery with an electrical voltage between the inside and outside of the cell. When the neuron is inactive, this voltage stays constant. But when the dendrites and cell body of the neuron detect a signal, the electrical state of the neuron changes and, if the signal is sufficiently strong, a wave of electrical activity – a change in the voltage – is propagated along the axon. This sudden change from the resting state to an outburst of electrical activity and back to the resting state is called an **action potential**. The action potential travels from the point of initiation to the end of the axon. Once it has reached the end of the axon, it can instigate effects in other cells. It can for instance induce an action potential in a second neuron, and this neuron can in turn activate a third neuron of the type called a motor neuron, which can activate a muscle. This way, when a signal is sent from the brain, via intermediate neurons to a muscle, the muscle can be 'told' to contract. The action potentials take place against a background of slower fluctuations in the voltages within the neurons. Together they make up the electrical activity that can be measured to reveal underlying brain activity.

But how does activity in the one neuron influence another cell? The communication between neurons takes place at the **synapse**, the junction between two neurons. Figure 5.10 gives an impression of a synapse. The neuron on the left is the presynaptic neuron (the one before the synapse). When an action potential arrives at the end of the axon of this neuron, it cannot jump the gap (just as electric current cannot jump gaps in a wire). Instead the action potential causes the release of a chemical messenger called a neurotransmitter into the synaptic gap or cleft. The neurotransmitter molecules bind to appropriate receptors located on the surface of the adjacent postsynaptic neuron (the one after the synapse). When this occurs, the electrical state of the postsynaptic neuron is altered, enabling this neuron in turn to send a signal towards its axon and thus to send information through to subsequent cells (e.g. another neuron or a muscle cell).

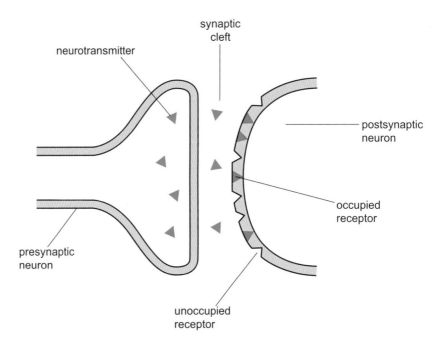

Figure 5.10 A schematic drawing of a synapse between two neurons. The ending of the presynaptic neuron is close to but not in contact with the postsynaptic neuron. In response to a signal in the presynaptic neuron, neurotransmitter molecules (shown here as triangles) are released from the presynaptic neuron into the synaptic cleft. The neurotransmitters bind to appropriate receptors on the surface of the postsynaptic neuron; this binding changes the electrical state of the postsynaptic neuron, a change in state that travels across the neuron towards its axon where it may initiate an action potential.

Neurons are specialised in the type of neurotransmitter they store and release. For example, a neuron that stores and releases the neurotransmitter serotonin is called 'serotonergic'. Imagine neuron 1 in Figure 5.11 to be a serotonergic cell. Neurons 1 and 2 will only be able to communicate with each other if neuron 2 has receptors for serotonin on its cell surface. If this is the case, then the synapse between neurons 1 and 2 is termed serotonergic.

The changes caused by neurotransmitters at the synapse can either be **excitatory** or **inhibitory**. When a neurotransmitter induces an action potential in the postsynaptic neuron or increases the existing activity of this neuron, the effect is said to be excitatory. When a neurotransmitter suppresses the activity in the postsynaptic neuron, its effect is inhibitory.

Figures 5.10 and 5.11 may give the impression that a synapse is a fixed structure, of a particular size and with a constant number of receptors on the postsynaptic membrane. That impression is incorrect: the synapse is dynamic, with the number of receptors and the length (more correctly, the area) of membrane on either side of the cleft subject to change, as is the number of synapses on a neuron. This dynamic feature of synapses is known as **neural plasticity**. Neural plasticity alters the efficiency of communication across the synapse and underlies important processes such as learning, memory and development.

Apart from neurotransmitters, **hormones** are another type of chemical that have a major role in transmitting signals around the body. Unlike neurotransmitters, which only move across the synapse, hormones typically travel further in the body through the bloodstream. One example of a hormone is insulin (discussed in Section 5.3.1), which by travelling through the bloodstream has a role in regulating our blood sugar level. Another example of a hormone is oxytocin. **Oxytocin** is produced in the brain of women after stimulation of the nipples by breastfeeding. The hormone is released into the bloodstream and after circulating round the body acts on any cells with the appropriate receptor, such as those in the mammary glands (the milk-producing glands) where it induces the release of further milk from the nipple. Thus, while neurotransmitters act locally, hormones can exert their effect over a larger distance and ensure that different types of tissue in the body can communicate with each other.

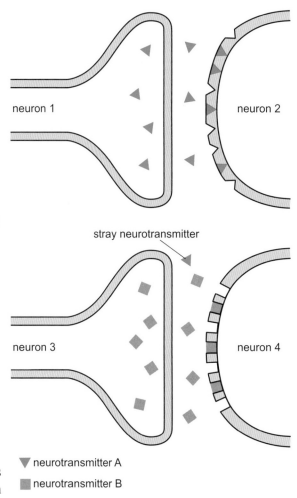

▼ neurotransmitter A

■ neurotransmitter B

Figure 5.11 Two synapses employing different neurotransmitters. Neuron 1 employs a neurotransmitter that fits receptors on neuron 2, but not on neuron 4. Neuron 3 employs a neurotransmitter that fits receptors on neuron 4, but not on neuron 2.

5.4.2 Synapses, neurotransmitters and hormones in autism

Synaptic structure and functioning

Many researchers think that the functioning of synapses may be impaired in autism. Evidence for this comes from different lines of research. The first clue is provided by research into fragile X syndrome. As discussed in Section 5.3.2, this syndrome is caused by a mutation in the *FMR1* gene which results in a loss of the function of the protein FMRP. Mice in which the *FMR1* gene was experimentally disrupted had altered synapses, both in their structure and operation. **Post-mortem studies** of the brain (examination of the brain after death; see Box 5.3) of people with fragile X syndrome revealed differences in the structure and number of dendrites. As mentioned earlier in this chapter, a significant number of people with fragile X syndrome also have autism. Some researchers now think that fragile X syndrome may serve as a biological model for autism, and that synaptic dysfunction may be important in both conditions (Pfeiffer and Huber, 2009).

Genetic studies also hint at abnormalities of the synapse in people with autism (Südhof, 2008). Different studies found that some people on the autism spectrum have mutations in the genes *NRXN1*, *NLGN3* or *NLGN4*. The gene variants or alleles that arise from these mutations may differ, but they all result in disruption of either of two proteins, called neurexin (NRXN) and neuroligin (NLGN). These proteins assist in holding the presynaptic and postsynaptic neurons together to form the synapse, a property known as adhesion. By doing so, both proteins are thought to mediate signalling across the synapse. Mutations in a gene called *SHANK3* have also been found in people with autism. SHANK3 is a protein that functions as a scaffolding molecule within the cell and it indirectly binds to neuroligins. Thus, the mutations of these different genes may lead to a common end-point: abnormalities in synaptic functioning.

Altogether, these gene studies suggest that synaptic dysfunction may be important in autism. However, the relationship between synaptic dysfunction and autistic behaviours is still unclear. Mutations in the neurexin and neuroligin genes are not specific to autism, but are also associated with other conditions, such as Tourette's syndrome, intellectual disability or schizophrenia (compare with discussion of specificity in Boxes 4.1 and 5.1). Moreover, many people on the autism spectrum have normal intelligence, and it is still unclear how synaptic dysfunction could result in specific behavioural impairments whilst intellectual abilities are spared. This is a good illustration of the complex problem of linking causal agents (in this case gene mutations) and effects (in this case autistic symptoms).

Apart from the structure and functioning of the synapse, several studies also suggest that abnormal amounts of neurotransmitters and hormones might play a role in autism. You will now learn about some of the neurotransmitters and hormones that are thought to be implicated in the aetiology of autism.

Serotonin

The neurotransmitter **serotonin** is synthesised by neurons in the Raphe nuclei in the brain (Figure 5.12). These neurons have long axons extending to other parts of the brain and down into the spinal cord. These connections are also collectively referred to as the serotonergic **pathway**. Because the serotonergic neurons connect to thousands of other neurons in the brain and spinal cord, the neurotransmitter has a great influence over complex brain processes, including the regulation of mood, emotions, aggression, sleep and body temperature.

Apart from its role as a messenger in the mature brain, serotonin is also important during brain development, particularly for the development of the cortex (see Section 5.5 for discussion of the cerebral cortex). Studies in rodents (see Box 5.2) have shown that when these animals are depleted of serotonin in early life, the development of their cortex is delayed and the

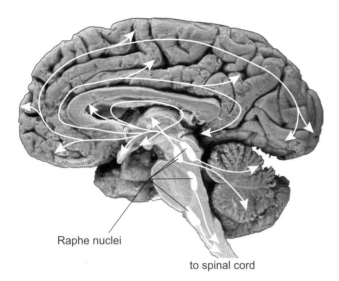

Raphe nuclei

to spinal cord

Figure 5.12   The serotonergic pathway in the brain. (Science Pictures Limited/ Science Photo Library)

synapses show abnormalities. It is thus thought that too little or too much serotonin can have detrimental effects on the development of the brain (Pardo and Eberhart, 2007).

In an early study in children with autism, Schain and Freedman (1961) found unusually high amounts of serotonin in the blood. Since then, many studies have replicated this finding. Taken together these studies do not suggest that serotonin levels are elevated in *all* people with autism, but rather that there is a sub-group who are characterised by very high blood serotonin levels, whilst others have normal serotonin levels. The effect of high serotonin levels in this sub-group and its role in the development of autism is still unclear. For instance, having high serotonin levels appears to be unrelated to the severity of autistic behaviours and to language development (Mulder et al., 2004).

■   Why might it seem odd to examine the amount of serotonin in the blood?

☐   Serotonin is a neurotransmitter that works locally within synapses; it is hormones that are transported in the blood. So you might consider it odd that serotonin is found in the blood. In fact many substances and their breakdown products are found in the blood as they are carried to the kidneys and liver before being removed from the body. The blood is an accessible source of biological material and hence a reasonable place to start looking.

Another line of research suggesting a role for serotonin in autism comes from pharmacological studies. Drugs that act on one of the several types of serotonin receptor seem to alleviate some behavioural difficulties, such as aggressive and stereotyped behaviours, and may improve social behaviour. However, the exact benefits of these drugs are still unclear. Finally, several genetic studies have suggested that people who have particular variants of genes that are important in the regulation of serotonin may be at greater risk for autism. How these different lines of evidence tie up and how exactly serotonin production is involved in the development of autism is still unknown.

Glutamate and GABA

Glutamate and GABA (gamma-aminobutyric acid in full) are both neurotransmitters that are found throughout the brain. Glutamate has an excitatory effect on the postsynaptic neuron and is thought to be crucial in neural plasticity and in cognitive functions such as learning and memory. Like serotonin, it is also thought to be important in the development of the cortex. GABA has the primary inhibitory effect in the brain. So-called GABAergic pathways also play an important role in early brain development. A balance between excitation and inhibition is crucial for normal development, so it is important that both the glutamate and GABAergic systems are well regulated.

Abnormalities in GABA and glutamate levels in the blood have been reported in autism. However, the results of these studies are mixed: some studies report elevated levels of both or one of the neurotransmitters, whilst other studies report reduced levels. As discussed in Section 5.3.2, several studies have suggested that genes coding for the GABA receptor may be associated with autism. Again, the findings were inconclusive: some studies found a significant association, others did not.

The glutamate and GABA systems have also been examined in post-mortem studies (see Box 5.3). These studies indicated that the number of GABA receptors in a measured amount of brain tissue, known as the density of GABA receptors, may be decreased in certain sections of the brain. They also suggested that various genes and proteins involved with glutamate and GABA functioning may be abnormal in autism.

Oxytocin

Apart from its involvement in breastfeeding mentioned in Section 5.4.1, the hormone oxytocin is thought to play a key role in social relationships. People who report that they are falling in love are found to have peak levels of oxytocin in their blood. Animal research (see Box 5.2) in prairie voles (small mouse-like creatures) showed that the release of oxytocin in the female vole during sexual activity promotes the formation of a monogamous pair bond with her partner. Ferguson et al. (2000) looked at the role of oxytocin in mice. In one group of mice, the gene coding for oxytocin was made dysfunctional, with the effect that these mice did not produce any oxytocin (these mice are referred to as 'oxytocin knockout mice'). The behaviour of these mice was compared to the behaviour of mice with a functional oxytocin gene, so-called wild-type mice. When a wild-type mouse meets another mouse it has not seen before, it will perform a kind of meet and greet ritual to investigate the newcomer. When the mice are introduced to each other again, after they have been separated for 30 minutes, the time spent meeting and greeting is about 70% shorter than during the initial meeting, suggesting that the mice recognise each other. However, when re-introduced, the oxytocin knockout mice spent just as long as the first time investigating each other (see Figure 5.13). Researchers have interpreted this finding as evidence for a role of oxytocin in social recognition. The oxytocin knockout mice were not impaired in non-

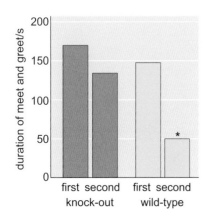

Figure 5.13 Time spent meeting and greeting a new mouse by oxytocin knockout mice compared with wild-type mice. The wild-type mice spend a lot less time investigating each other when they meet for the second time (right green bar) compared with when they meet for the first time (left green bar). This difference in time is statistically significant (denoted by the *). In contrast, the knockout mice spend as long investigating each other on the second encounter as on the first (red bars) (the difference in the height of the red bars is not statistically significant). (Adapted from Ferguson et al., 2000)

social memory tasks, so the difference between the two groups of mice seemed to be specific to social events. The amygdala, a region of the brain implicated in autism (see Section 5.5), has large numbers of oxytocin receptors. Further studies in mice showed that when oxytocin was injected into the amygdala of oxytocin knockout mice, the social recognition was reinstated.

Box 5.2 Animal studies

There are occasions when animal studies can provide considerable insight into factors underlying human conditions. These studies are performed as humanely as possible under a strict code of conduct, and are done in the knowledge that there are differences between human and non-human animals. These differences do not detract from the fact that the nervous system of certain non-human animals is sufficiently similar to the human nervous system to provide informative insights. Investigating how the nervous system responds to adverse events such as altered neurotransmitter or hormone levels, or the role of certain genes using knockout mice, has advanced understanding of how these neurotransmitters, hormones and genes are involved in numerous clinical conditions.

Studies in humans have shown that if a person's oxytocin levels are boosted (this can be done using a nasal spray of oxytocin), their ability to recognise emotional expressions in the faces of other people improves. People with boosted oxytocin levels are also better at remembering faces and show changes of activation in the amygdala. Children with autism are reported to have lower levels of oxytocin in their blood compared to typically developing children. There is some evidence that an artificial increase of oxytocin enhances the emotion recognition skills in people with autism, and may also result in reduced repetitive behaviours (McDougle et al., 2005).

All in all, these studies suggest that oxytocin is important in social relationships. Low oxytocin levels may play a role in the social difficulties that people with autism experience. However, a lot more research still needs to be done on this hormone and its effect on autistic behaviours. It is as yet unknown if oxytocin would work as a pharmacological treatment. Moreover, its long-term effects are still unexplored and it is not known if it has any side effects.

5.4.3 Summary of Section 5.4

- Neurons are cells throughout the body and the brain that are specialised in information processing. Neurons together form the nervous system.
- Neural signalling occurs through waves of electrical activity called action potentials.
- Communication between neurons takes place when chemical messengers called neurotransmitters cross synapses.

- Neurotransmitters are vital for communication between cells in close proximity, whilst hormones are essential for communication between cells that are not in close proximity.

- Several studies suggest that differences in the structure and functioning of the synapse may be important in the development of autism.

- The neurotransmitters serotonin, GABA and glutamate have been implicated in autism. These neurotransmitters all have a crucial role in the development of the nervous system, particularly in the development of the cerebral cortex.

- The hormone oxytocin plays an important role in social relationships and low levels of oxytocin may also be implicated in autism.

- Much is still unknown about the neurobiology of the autism spectrum. Research findings are often inconsistent and much more research needs to be done before the precise role of synaptic function and of different neurotransmitters and hormones in autism can be identified.

5.5   The neuroanatomical basis of autism

So far, the discussion of the biological influences on autism in this chapter has focused on the genetic, cellular and chemical aspects. In this section you will look at the brain as a whole. You will learn about the anatomical organisation of the brain (**neuroanatomy**) and how particular areas of the brain are thought to be involved in autism and in autistic behaviours. You will see that the development of various sophisticated **imaging** techniques has contributed to our current knowledge of the neuroanatomical basis of autism.

5.5.1   Anatomy of the brain

The brain is divided into two approximately symmetrical halves, referred to as the left and the right **cerebral hemispheres**. The hemispheres are named taking the perspective of the individual whose brain is being considered. Thus, when you look at a brain from the front (i.e. taking an anterior view), as in Figure 5.14, the left hemisphere is to your right. The outer layer of the brain is termed the **cerebral cortex**. The word cortex means bark (as in the bark of a tree), and in humans and higher mammals this part of the brain contains many convolutions (infoldings), making it look like a walnut. The foldings of the cortex that form grooves are referred to as sulci (singular term is **sulcus**); the smooth areas between foldings, which form crowns, are termed gyri (singular term is **gyrus**).

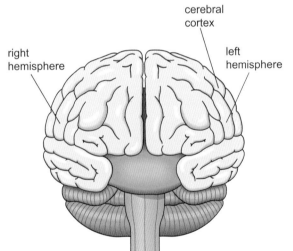

Figure 5.14   Anterior view of the human brain. Note sulci and gyri over the brain surface.

■   Why do you suppose the cortex has a creased structure?

☐   The folds of the human cortex make it possible to pack more cortical surface into the skull. If the human cortex was smooth, like that of a rat, humans would need very large heads to maintain enhanced brain capacity.

As shown in Figure 5.15, the cerebral cortex can be divided into different regions, termed lobes. Although the activities of the different brain lobes are interconnected and coordinated in many ways, each lobe is known to be involved in specific functions. One major source of evidence for this is that accidental brain damage tends to selectively affect different cognitive functions, depending on which brain areas are damaged. The **frontal lobe** is concerned with articulation of speech, movement, emotions, reasoning and problem solving. It is also important for executive functions such as planning and mental flexibility discussed in Chapter 4. The **parietal lobe** is concerned with the perception of stimuli related to touch, pressure, temperature and pain (also referred to as **somatosensory perception**). At the back of the brain, the **occipital lobe** is important for many aspects of visual perception and for the processing of spatial information. The **temporal lobe** is involved in memory and language functions and is concerned with perceiving and recognising auditory information. Within the temporal lobe lies the **fusiform gyrus**. This brain area is essential for recognising faces and for differentiating between different faces, objects and emotions. The **cerebellum** is located under the occipital lobe of the cortex. It plays an important role in the control of motor movements, posture and balance. It is particularly important in movements with a social function, such as gestures and expression.

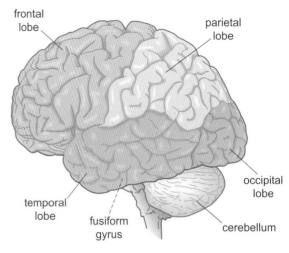

Figure 5.15 A view of the left hemisphere of the human brain. The dashed line indicates the position of the fusiform gyrus which is embedded within the temporal lobe.

Taking a look at the inside, different structures of the brain show up in slightly different colours (see Figure 5.16). The cortex mainly contains the cell bodies of neurons and their dendrites. Because the cortex has such a high density of cell bodies, it has a relatively dark colour. These areas are therefore also referred to as **grey matter**. The underlying regions of the brain are primarily composed of the axons of neurons. Because axons are encased in a fatty white substance called **myelin**, these brain areas look much paler. Researchers studying the anatomy of the brain refer to these areas as **white matter**.

Hidden from view under the cerebral hemispheres are many important structures, one of which is an almond-shaped structure, the **amygdala** (Figure 5.17). The amygdala has an important role in emotion and in regulating associated behavioural responses such as flushing, trembling or sweating when frightened. It is thought that the amygdala is concerned with evaluating the emotional significance of external events. In response to those events, the amygdala can induce the release of hormones or neurotransmitters, thereby modulating both cognitive processes in the cortex and the action of muscles.

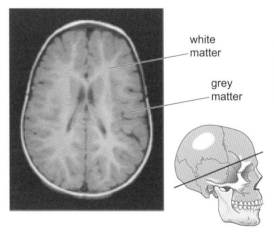

Figure 5.16 Horizontal section through the cerebral hemispheres at the level indicated at the right. Grey matter is primarily composed of the cell bodies and dendrites of neurons. White matter is composed of the neurons' axons. (Sweeney et al., 2000)

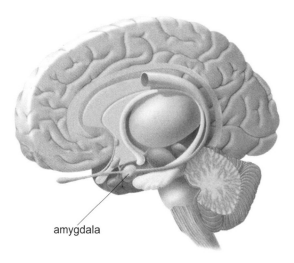

amygdala

Figure 5.17 Internal view of the brain showing the right hemisphere. The amygdala shown is located in the left temporal lobe; there is an equivalent structure embedded in the right temporal lobe.

There are a number of different ways of studying the anatomy and functioning of the brain. Some of the more prevalent techniques are discussed in Box 5.3.

Box 5.3 Post-mortem and imaging studies of the brain

The most widely used method of studying the individual cells and the connections between them in the human brain is the post-mortem study, the study of the brain after death. In post-mortem studies, very thin slices of brain can be examined under the microscope. Some people give consent for their brains to be used for scientific purposes after their death. Their brain tissue is preserved, to prevent decay and fixed, to prevent disintegration, then stored in a so-called brain bank until required. The basic procedure is to compare brain tissue from one or more people who had a diagnosis for a specific condition with similar brain tissue from people who did not have the condition (i.e. controls). In this way researchers can determine whether specific physical brain abnormalities are associated with the condition.

■ There are relatively few post-mortem studies of autism. Why do you think that is?

☐ There is a shortage of people who give consent for their brains to be donated to research after their death. Post-mortem studies of autism are therefore hampered by the limited availability of brains. So far, fewer than 100 cases have been studied, and most studies only include about five brains of people with autism. Since autism is such a diverse condition with multiple manifestations, it can be hard to draw firm conclusions from these small studies.

The last decades have seen important advances in the techniques used to form images of the brain. These techniques can study either the anatomical structure or the functionality of the brain in a harmless non-invasive way in live humans. The techniques all rely on detectors that are able to measure very small amounts of energy. The energy may be produced by small (and harmless) amounts of radioactive material injected into the brain, by influencing the way molecules in the brain spin, or by recording the activity of firing neurons. The detectors are located all around the skull and are linked to computers that convert the signals received by the detectors into images. Those areas of the brain that produce the same amount of energy will appear as the same colour or shade of grey. Those areas that produce different amounts of energy will appear as different colours or shades of grey.

Three important techniques are described briefly below.

Structural **magnetic resonance imaging (MRI)**. This is a readily available and widely used technique that reveals the anatomy of the brain (Figure 5.18).

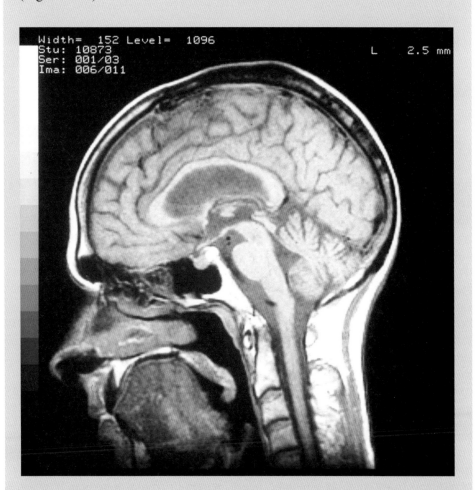

Figure 5.18 Example of a structural MRI scan. (Mira/Alamy)

Functional magnetic resonance imaging (fMRI) is a variant of MRI scanning that offers insight into the brain at work. Whilst the participant lies very still in the scanner, they can be presented with visual images, or with sounds or smell or touch stimuli. They can also be asked to perform certain tasks, such as pressing a button, or moving a joystick. fMRI maps the difference in the level of oxygen in the blood while such a task is, and is not, being performed. When the task is being performed, areas of the brain where the oxygen level is higher are more active and are thus considered to be involved in the task. fMRI can give very detailed information about the location of the brain activity, but is limited to changes that take place over about a second (quite slow in terms of the nervous system).

Magnetoencephalography (MEG) is a method that measures brain activity more directly. MEG exploits the fact that active neurons induce weak magnetic fields, so when a group of neurons is collectively active, they produce a signal that is strong enough to be measured. MEG detects the brain's electrical activity during a task directly (without much time delay). The disadvantage of MEG is that it is less precise (compared with fMRI studies) in determining the exact location of brain activity and it is less sensitive to activity deep in the brain (from areas beneath the cortex).

5.5.2   Brain structure and function in autism

One of the most prominent findings in neuroanatomical research is that children with autism on average have larger brains than typically developing children (Courchesne et al., 2007). Evidence comes from studies measuring head circumference (by using a tape measure) and from studies with more precise measures of brain volume using magnetic resonance imaging (MRI; see Box 5.3). Head circumference of children subsequently diagnosed with autism seems normal or somewhat small at birth. This is followed by rapid growth at about 12 months of age. The brain volumes of young children with autism are 5–10% enlarged compared to the brain volumes of typically developing children (Figure 5.19). The relatively large brain volume persists at least through early childhood, but the differential might disappear by the time the child reaches adolescence. In typically developing children the brain continues to develop and grow throughout childhood. MRI studies suggest that this slow continuous maturing of the brain might not happen in autism. Eventually, brain volumes of typically developing children become similar to the brain volumes of children with autism. Later in development, certain regions of the brain may even show a decline in volume in some people with autism (Figure 5.19).

Structural MRI scans can not only give a precise measure of the total brain volume, but can also distinguish different brain structures. The increase in brain volume has been most consistently reported for the frontal lobe. As you may recall from previous chapters, many important frontal lobe activities are compromised in autism, including speech articulation, aspects of emotion and executive function. Multiple MRI studies have also found enlargements of the temporal lobe, the cerebellum and the amygdala in children with autism compared to controls (Figure 5.20). A recent MRI study measured brain volume in three- to four-year-old children on the autism spectrum and

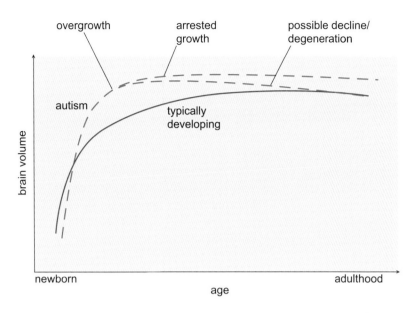

Figure 5.19 Stylised graph of relative brain growth in children with autism (blue lines) and age-matched typically developing children (red line). The figure shows an early rapid growth in children with autism, leading to an enlarged brain in early childhood, followed by an arrest in growth in later childhood and adolescence. In some individuals, the arrest in growth may be followed by a decline in brain size. (Adapted from Courchesne et al., 2007)

assessed their social and communication skills (Munson et al., 2006). Children with increased volume of the amygdala in the right hemisphere were found to have more severe social and communication impairments. The children with a large amygdala also had poorer social and communication abilities when they were assessed again at age six. This study is important because it links abnormal brain development to specific autistic behaviours. It implicates amygdala development in the social and communication difficulties characteristic for autism.

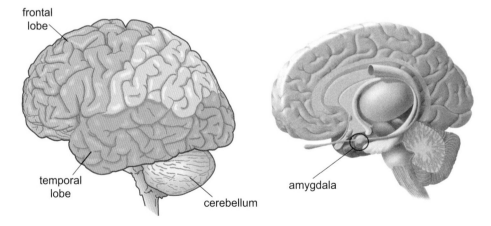

Figure 5.20 The regions of brain overgrowth in autism include the frontal and temporal lobes and the cerebellum (image on the left) and the amygdala (image on the right).

A post-mortem study including six cases of people with autism aged between nine and 29 years indicated that neurons in certain areas of the amygdala may be unusually small and more densely packed than in controls of the same age. Another post-mortem study did not find increased density or decreased size of the neurons, but rather found fewer neurons in the amygdala in the brains of people with autism compared to controls. You may find it puzzling that both smaller size and greater density of neurons has been associated with functional difficulties. Effective brain function arises from a very precisely regulated development of just the right numbers and sizes of neurons with just the right connections between them. Future post-mortem studies in larger samples will have to establish the exact amygdala abnormalities in autism. In the meantime, the variability of findings raises the problem of effect described in Box 5.1. Box 5.4 outlines further difficulties in studying the brain in autism.

Box 5.4   Methodological difficulties in studying the brain in autism

As you will have gathered throughout this book, there are large differences between people on the autism spectrum. People differ in the severity of autistic traits, in the type of autistic symptoms expressed and in their intellectual abilities. The development of children with autism through time and their symptoms as adults may also differ sharply. Consequently, the findings from studies can be variable, depending on the group of individuals with autism who participate in any particular study. The group of individuals who take part in a study is called a **sample**. The smaller the sample, the less likely it is to be representative of the population of people with autism.

Post-mortem research is hampered by small sample size – the small number of brains that are available for this type of research. Additionally, in most post-mortem studies the majority of brains under investigation were donated by the families of people with autism who also suffered from epilepsy or who had intellectual disability. This situation makes it hard to determine whether the observed brain atypicalities are truly associated with autism, or are primarily related to epilepsy or intellectual disability. Even if the atypical features are associated with autism, they cannot be seen as representative of the whole spectrum (see universality in Box 4.1).

Sometimes the very nature of the equipment excludes people with certain symptoms. In order to make an MRI or fMRI scan (Box 5.3), the participant has to lie down and remain motionless in a scanner for a considerable amount of time. So most research using MRI is done in high-functioning individuals who are free from seizures. The consequence is that the samples used in post-mortem research are different from the samples used in MRI research. Hence it is often difficult to compare findings from post-mortem and MRI studies.

Similarly, the small space and loud noise inside the MRI scanner make it difficult to study vulnerable groups of people, such as very young children. Consequently MRI imaging studies are usually conducted in older children and adults, making the study of the developmental process with this method dependent on small samples. MEG scanning (Box 5.3) has gone some way to solve these problems, as the participant does not need to lie down, and the machine is not as noisy as an MRI scanner.

Finally, most knowledge about the development of the brain comes from imaging studies that were conducted on several samples of different ages (**cross-sectional studies**), rather than in one sample in a succession of ages (**longitudinal studies**). Because there are individual differences in brain structure and function, cross-sectional studies will reveal differences just because they are using different samples. More reliable insights about the development of the brain have to come from future longitudinal studies.

Within these constraints, the development of functional imaging techniques such as fMRI and MEG has begun to provide valuable insights into brain function in people with autism. In the past decade, a wealth of studies has aimed to elucidate how the patterns of activity of the brain are different in people with autism. Functional imaging also makes it possible to investigate links between known psychological differences in people with autism and the activity of specific areas and circuits in the brain. Usually the investigations involve two groups of a dozen or so young people or adults: a group with a diagnosis of high-functioning autism or Asperger syndrome and a matched group of control participants without autism. The two groups are matched for characteristics such as age, IQ, educational level and handedness. While brain scanning is taking place, the participants are presented with stimuli such as pictures, video clips, samples of speech or other sounds, and asked to make appropriate responses. In this way, researchers have been able to study the brain activity accompanying psychological processes known to be atypical in autism, such as face recognition, responses to emotional stimuli, understanding of language, and so on.

For example, Schultz (2005) required participants to push a button if they recognised pictures of faces that they had seen before (a task that people with autism find harder than matched controls). People with autism, unlike controls, do not show activation of the fusiform gyrus (see Figure 5.21 and Section 5.5.1), a part of the brain in the temporal lobe, known to play a specialised role in processing information about human faces. Both groups performed equally well on a test where non-face objects had to be recognised. Moreover, no differences in brain activity were found between the two groups on this non-face task. These results suggest that the deficit is specific to the perception of faces and linked to a specific brain area: the fusiform gyrus.

However, what is becoming increasingly clear is that deficit interpretations, where one specific area of the brain 'underperforms' on a particular task, are too simplistic; the brain operates in a much more integrated way, and many imaging studies of autism are beginning to show complex patterns of atypicality involving the brain activity in several coordinated areas.

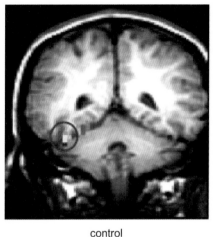
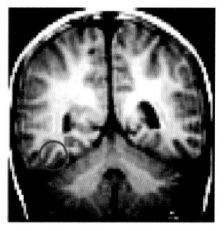

control   autism spectrum

Figure 5.21   Images of fMRI scans of an adolescent male on the autism spectrum (right) compared with an age- and IQ-matched typically developing control (left). These fMRI images show the right and left cerebral cortex above and the cerebellum below. The fusiform gyrus lies within the red circle. The red/yellow signal shows brain areas that are significantly more active during perception of faces; signals in blue show areas more active during perception of non-face objects. Note the lack of face activation in the boy with an autism spectrum diagnosis, but average levels of non-face object activation. (Schultz, 2005)

Ashwin et al. (2007) performed one such study looking at eight areas of the brain that are involved in different aspects of face processing. Human faces are complex stimuli which can be perceived in different ways; for instance, as a face rather than another type of 'object', or as a source of emotional cues about how the person is feeling. The difference between these two types of responses is that the first involves considering the face primarily as a neutral physical stimulus, while the second involves treating the face as a socially significant stimulus. Much of the time, people's responses to faces take in both physical and social aspects of faces simultaneously, and it seems that a complex configuration of different brain areas is involved.

Ashwin et al. wanted to see whether participants on the autism spectrum would differ from participants without autism in the configuration of brain areas activated when looking at faces. Brain imaging was carried out while participants with Asperger syndrome or HFA, and matched control participants, were presented with stimuli such as those in Figure 5.22. The task was simply to press a button with their finger as soon as a stimulus appeared on the screen. Some of the stimuli were neutral faces like the one in Figure 5.22a, while others, like the one in Figure 5.22b, expressed fear. The task was designed in this way so that participants could register emotional or neutral expressions, without having to explicitly identify what they were.

The key outcome from this study is that the autistic participants had decreased activity in some of the brain areas scanned during the study, notably the amygdala and the orbitofrontal cortex (the part of the frontal lobe just above the eyes) and increased activity in other areas, such as the superior temporal region (the top of the temporal lobe region). Their conclusion was that the

 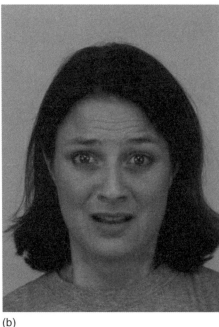

(a)   (b)

Figure 5.22 Examples of test stimuli used by Ashwin et al. (2007) portraying (a) neutral expression and (b) fearful expression. (Karolinska Institutet)

way information about faces is processed is different in people with autism. Essentially, the participants with autism responded to the faces as physical stimuli, much in the same way that they would recognise non-face objects. Their responses to the socially significant emotional aspects of the faces were substantially diminished.

- Do the findings from this study complement or contradict those from structural imaging studies showing changes in amygdala size?

□ They complement the structural imaging studies in that in both studies there are differences in the amygdala.

- In what way could the stimuli used in this study be made more naturalistic or true to life?

□ Using video clips of facial expressions, similar to those used in the 'Reading the mind in films' task (Box 4.4), would provide a more naturalistic task, as usually people don't 'read' emotional expressions from still photographs.

You may have noticed that the discussion has considered quite a range of brain areas that may be involved in autism. It is indeed thought that there is no single site in the brain that is primarily associated with the autism spectrum, but rather that several brain areas are involved. Different areas and circuits in the brain may also be linked to different characteristics of autism. Just as the amygdala and associated structures seem to be linked to deficits in recognising emotions and other forms of 'mind reading', other areas of the brain may be more important in communication or repetitive activities (Amaral et al., 2008). Figure 5.23 illustrates the areas of the brain that have been linked to the three diagnostic symptom clusters in autism (according to the DSM-IV-TR that you read about in Chapter 2).

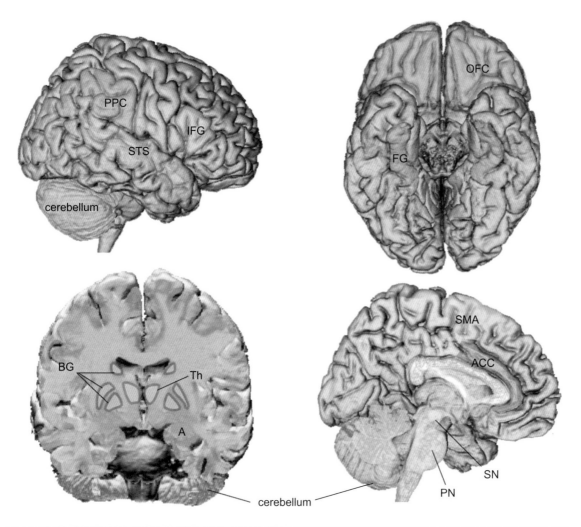

social interaction	communication	repetitive activities
OFC – orbitofrontal cortex	IFG – inferior frontal gyrus	OFC – orbitofrontal cortex
ACC – anterior cingulate cortex	STS – superior temporal sulcus	ACC – anterior cingulate cortex
FG – fusiform gyrus	SMA – supplementary motor area	BG – basal ganglia
STS – superior temporal sulcus	BG – basal ganglia	Th – thalamus
A – amygdala	SN – substantia nigra	
IFG – inferior frontal gyrus	Th – thalamus	
PPC – posterior parietal cortex	PN – pontine nuclei	
	cerebellum	

Figure 5.23 Illustration of the brain areas that have been implicated in the three diagnostic characteristics of autism: social interaction (in blue), communication (in yellow) and repetitive activities (in red). *Note*: the labels in this figure have been included for information only to give an indication of the different brain regions involved in characteristics of autism. You do not need to know or learn these terms. (Adapted from Amaral et al., 2008)

Moreover, it is thought that the **connectivity** between different brain areas (the connections between different parts of the brain and how well they communicate) may be impaired in autism. Functional imaging studies suggest that there is reduced long-range connectivity in autism (Müller, 2008); that is, reduced connectivity between the parts of the brain that are a bit further away from each other, especially in the cerebral regions. This notion fits in well with some of the evidence discussed in earlier sections. Abnormalities in neurotransmitter and hormone levels as well as the presence of particular gene variants may reduce the connectivity between brain regions. Moreover, disturbances in the neurotransmitter levels may prohibit normal brain development, which may ultimately result in connectivity problems.

5.5.3 Summary of Section 5.5

- The cerebral cortex of the brain consists of four regions: the frontal, parietal, temporal and occipital lobes. Under the occipital lobe, the cerebellum can be found.

- The amygdala, internal to the temporal lobe, is the prime area of the brain associated with emotion.

- The fusiform gyrus lies within the temporal lobe and is essential for perception and recognition of faces.

- Children with autism on average have larger brains than typically developing children of the same age. Later in development, the brain growth in children with autism is thought to arrest, while the brains of typically developing children steadily mature and grow further, eventually catching up with the brain volumes of children with autism.

- Both structural and functional imaging studies and post-mortem studies suggest the involvement of multiple areas of the brain in autism. The frontal lobes, the cerebellum, amygdala and fusiform gyrus are brain areas that are especially associated with different characteristics of autism.

- Impaired connectivity between the different brain areas is implicated in autism.

- Sampling consistency is a major difficulty in the study of autism.

5.6 Integrating all levels of biological explanation

In the previous sections you have read about the biological factors that are thought to be implicated in the development of autism. In Section 5.3 you read about the genetic influences on autism. Section 5.4 provided an overview of some of the neurobiological mechanisms that are thought to be implicated in autism, whilst Section 5.5 discussed which brain areas may be linked to autism. As you will have gathered whilst reading the chapter, these different explanations are not distinct from each other, but are neatly intertwined. Different alleles may result in increased or decreased concentrations of particular neurotransmitters or hormones, which may in turn affect brain development and the connectivity between different brain areas. Conversely, high or low levels of certain hormones may lead to the increased or decreased expression of certain genes.

Thus, a combination of genetic and environmental factors may influence the early development of the brain, and may thereby alter the typical trajectory of brain development (see Figure 5.24). The altered brain development is, in turn, likely to have behavioural consequences in early childhood and may lead to impairments in social interaction and communication and/or to repetitive behaviours. Ultimately, the aggregation and interaction of all these different factors may result in the clinical end-point: an autism diagnosis.

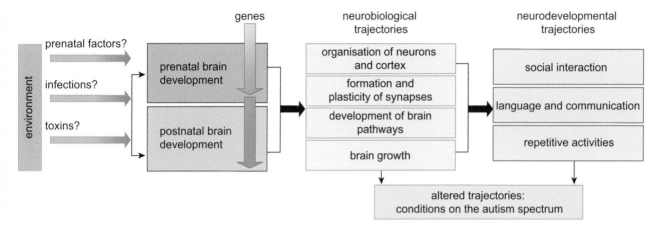

Figure 5.24 Genetic and environmental factors may influence brain development before and early after birth, thereby altering the neurobiological and neurodevelopmental trajectories that ultimately lead to the expression of the clinical characteristics of the autism spectrum. (Adapted from Pardo and Eberhart, 2007)

It is important to realise that none of these influences necessarily has its impact at one point in time. Throughout development, certain genes may be switched on or off and their effect may thus be different at different moments in time. Likewise, environmental influences may change over time. Moreover, genetic and environmental influences may interact with each other. Environmental influences may dampen the effect of genes, or instead may increase their effects.

It is also important to recognise that none of these influences results in a clear-cut outcome. All factors, whether environmental, genetic or neurobiological, may have different effects in different individuals. Thus, although the accumulation of different factors may greatly increase the risk for a child to develop autism, there will also be some individuals who somehow escape the altered trajectory and grow up to become typically functioning adults. Moreover, the neurobiological and neurodevelopmental trajectories may look different for different people on the autism spectrum. In some people the end of this trajectory may result in very severe autistic impairments, perhaps including intellectual disability. Others may have intellectual abilities in the normal or above-normal range and a somewhat milder form of social communication impairments and repetitive interests and activities.

The last few decades have brought us a wealth of knowledge about the biological influences on autism, but there are still a lot of unknowns. The large variability in the expression of autism and the likely heterogeneity in causes make it hard to advance our knowledge of the aetiology of autism.

Researchers from all over the world have now started to collaborate in large international studies. In these large-scale studies it may be possible to examine specific sub-groups of people with autism, who may share a more homogeneous neurodevelopmental trajectory, and thus a common aetiology. These studies are likely to contribute greatly to our understanding of autism in the near future. As you will see in the next chapter, the subtlety and complexity of these biological influences means that biologically based interventions for autism are still in their infancy.

5.6.1 Summary of Section 5.6

- Genetic, environmental, neurobiological and neuroanatomical explanations of autism are all closely intertwined. All these factors may contribute to an altered neurodevelopmental trajectory, ultimately resulting in the behavioural characteristics of autism.

- The biological influences, their interactions, and the neurodevelopmental trajectories may differ for different people on the autism spectrum, resulting in different outcomes.

5.7 Learning outcomes

5.1   Define and use, or recognise definitions and applications of, each of the terms printed in **bold** in the text.

5.2   Describe some of the main biological factors that may be involved in autism.

5.3   Explain the main techniques that are leading to an understanding of (i) the genetics of autism and (ii) the neuroanatomical basis of autism.

5.4   Describe some differences in the neurobiology of those with and those without autism.

5.5   Suggest reasons for caution when evaluating data for evidence of cause and effect.

5.8 Self-assessment questions for Chapter 5

Question 5.1   (LO 5.2)

(a) Name one hormone and one neurotransmitter. (b) Give one general similarity and one general difference between hormones and neurotransmitters.

Question 5.2   (LO 5.3)

Give two kinds of evidence that suggest there is an underlying genetic basis for autism.

Question 5.3   (LO 5.4)

You might expect a large amygdala to enhance the performance of those tasks in which the amygdala is involved. (a) Is this true for children with autism? (b) How might a knowledge of the action of the hormone oxytocin explain your answer to (a)? (*Hint*: consider how oxytocin levels might affect the amygdala: Section 5.4.2.)

Question 5.4 (LO 5.4)

Using your knowledge of synapses and the brain, explain why it might be 'still unclear how synaptic dysfunction could result in specific behavioural impairments, whilst intellectual abilities are spared' (Section 5.4.2).

Question 5.5 (LO 5.5)

In 1990 what percentage of children in Yokohama were vaccinated? (*Hint*: you may need to remind yourself of how long after birth Japanese children were vaccinated.)

Question 5.6 (LO 5.5)

(a) What is the peak prevalence shown in Figure 5.2b? (b) In what year should the group of children with the highest prevalence have been vaccinated? (c) What percentage of children were vaccinated in that year (i.e. the year given in answer to (b))?

Question 5.7 (LO 5.5)

Why should issues of sampling be considered when interpreting data from studies on the neurobiology of autism?

Chapter 6   Perspectives on intervention

Greg Pasco and Ilona Roth

6.1   Introduction

This chapter considers approaches to providing help and support for people on the autism spectrum. The chapter discusses a range of interventions which are targeted at different problems and different groups. It is often assumed that early intervention has most effect, and most of the interventions are designed for children, especially those with classic autism and some degree of intellectual disability. In one sense it is this group who most need support, but though individuals with high-functioning autism or Asperger syndrome have better language and intellectual skills, their difficulties in interacting, behaving flexibly and in other everyday skills may also be very disabling. Some approaches discussed in this chapter lend themselves well to supporting these more able groups, and also to the needs of adults. The chapter will also describe how interventions are evaluated, and consider the available evidence for the benefits of different approaches.

Most of the interventions discussed are **psychosocial interventions**. That is, they draw upon learning techniques such as those introduced in Section 1.7, and/or psychological processes such as those outlined in Chapters 3 and 4, to influence the behaviour, social and communication skills, and/or ways of thinking of the people receiving the intervention. The chapter also considers the use of drugs, medicines or dietary changes to alleviate the problems associated with autism. Some of these approaches draw broadly on biological principles, such as those discussed in Chapter 5, but the evidence that they work is as yet limited. Finally, the chapter touches on the other, often unconventional, approaches that are advocated from time to time.

But first, something must be said about the important difference between 'interventions' and 'cures' for autism.

6.1.1   The myth of miracle cures

■   What do you think it means for an illness, medical condition or disability to be 'cured'? Why do you think that claims for a cure for autism might be controversial?

▢   In general, 'curing' a condition means that the problem is no longer present, and perhaps that it has left no trace at all. One reason that this concept is controversial in relation to the autism spectrum, is that autism and its variants are developmental conditions, where key aspects of communication and social development have been disrupted from an early age, making a complete 'reversal' unlikely. Whilst an individual's profile of skills and behaviours might improve over time, the current consensus is that fundamental aspects of autism, such as difficulties in social understanding and social relationships will always be present to some degree or another.

The notion of 'cure' is controversial for a second reason. Many individuals on the autism spectrum and their families argue that autism is a difference rather than a disorder or disability, and as such, the notion of cure – or even that of intervention – is unacceptable and demeaning to the individual. The journalist Charlotte Moore, who has two children on the autism spectrum, wrote:

> I hope I was never looking for a cure; now, I'm sure I'm not. I want Sam to stop scattering his food and biting his hands, but I don't dream of a neurotypical Sam with the usual emotional and intellectual range of a boy of 11, because no such Sam could possibly exist.

(Moore, 2003a)

The term **neurotypical (NT)** was first coined within the autism community to denote people who are not on the autism spectrum. The implication is that their brain and mental functioning is typical rather than atypical, particularly in relation to communication and social interaction. The term avoids the problematic connotations of 'normal' (as opposed to 'abnormal'), has been quite widely adopted, and is recommended by the NAS.

Not all families share Charlotte Moore's perspective. The profound impact that autism can have on both families and individuals was illustrated by the case studies in Chapter 2, and will be further discussed in Chapter 8. Consequently approaches promising a cure have an understandable appeal to some parents, even if only on the principle of 'try anything if it might help'. This may leave parents vulnerable to exaggerated claims made by charismatic practitioners.

Interventions promising a cure often use unusual, extreme or untested methods, which are not based on accepted techniques or a widely shared theoretical understanding of autism. This was the case with Bettelheim's approach, described in Section 1.3. Another controversial approach, introduced in the 1980s, and known as 'holding therapy', was based on the unfounded claim that autism results from profound anxiety which prevents children from establishing emotional bonds with others.

The therapy aimed to overcome this anxiety by encouraging close and sustained physical contact between a child and his or her mother. Usually the child would sit on the mother's lap facing her, while the therapist instructed the mother to initiate and maintain the hold, and develop direct eye contact. As the child would typically find such close and prolonged contact disagreeable or frightening, considerable force was often needed to maintain it. See Figure 6.1.

Both parents and professionals began to cast serious doubt on the success claimed for this approach, and there were cases where it was actively harmful. One mother who tried the technique with her son over a three-year period later reflected:

> After I stopped the therapy, it took me a long time before I could see the whole experience in perspective and was appalled by some of the things we had done ... my son's response to our attempts to blast a way through his protective wall was to withdraw even further.

(Hocking, 1987, p. 15)

Even if an intervention is clearly demonstrated to be beneficial for people on the autism spectrum, this does not mean that the intervention is a cure, in the wide sense of the word discussed here. Most of the approaches described in this chapter are therefore considered as interventions. However, two of them – the Lovaas approach and the Son-Rise approach – make strong claims about

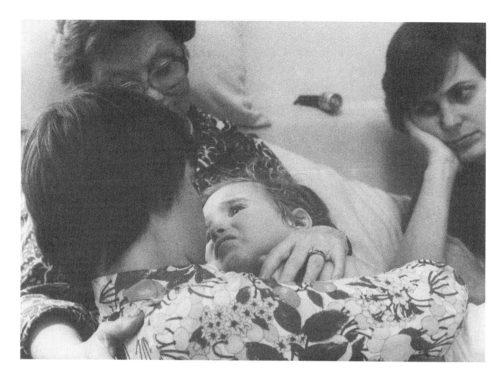

Figure 6.1 A holding therapy session. The child is held close by the mother, and in this session the mother is also supported by the grandmother. The therapist is at the right. From Tinbergen and Tinbergen (1985) *Autistic Children: New Hope for a Cure*.

recovery from autism. Given the serious ethical issues here, for *all* procedures to be used in helping a child on the autism spectrum, the starting point must be a clear set of guidelines for designing, applying and evaluating the approach. These are discussed next.

6.1.2 Summary of Section 6.1

- Approaches to helping people on the autism spectrum are best considered as interventions not cures.
- The idea of a cure for autism is controversial at present because it implies complete reversal of a process that develops from early infancy onwards.
- Many families reject the idea that their child on the autism spectrum needs curing.
- 'Miracle' cures such as holding therapy have been discredited.

6.2 Evidence-based practice

The guiding principles for all practical interventions should be: firstly, a sound grounding in theory and research about autism, though as you will see, the relationship between theory and intervention is more direct in some cases than in others; secondly, robust ethical procedures; and thirdly, well-supported claims about the benefits of the intervention.

Sir Michael Rutter observes, 'It has become generally accepted that all of us, as clinicians, need to base what we do on solid empirical research findings' (1999, p. 169). This approach, which is widely advocated in clinical psychology, is known as **evidence-based practice**.

Activity 6.1 invites you to consider the issues to be addressed in evaluating an intervention.

Activity 6.1 Evidence-based practice: evaluating interventions

Allow 20 minutes for this activity

Imagine that you are a practitioner seeking to evaluate the claims made for the success of a particular intervention. What would you want to know before you were prepared to accept these claims? Note down some ideas before comparing your points with those in Box 6.1.

The remainder of this section will help you to understand the processes involved in collecting evidence relating to the benefits or otherwise of interventions.

Deciding whether an intervention works might seem like a relatively straightforward process of applying the treatment to an appropriate recipient, and then seeing if the problems or difficulties experienced by the patient are reduced (or whether 'positive' aspects of behaviour improve). Unfortunately, evaluating interventions is never this simple or straightforward, particularly in relation to psychosocial interventions. The key issues to be addressed by any study attempting to measure the effectiveness of a treatment or intervention are listed in Box 6.1.

Box 6.1 Key issues for evaluating approaches to intervention

- What are the problems, behaviours or skills that are the target of the intervention? Do the observed outcomes actually relate to these target difficulties?
- Is the intervention informed by well-established theory and research concerning the explanation for the targeted difficulties?
- Are the procedures ethical, i.e. if you decided to use the intervention would you be confident that it safeguarded the well-being of participants?
- What are the criteria for 'success', i.e. how would you decide whether the targeted problem had reduced?
- Who are the participants taking part in the study? Can their diagnoses be verified?

- Are there sufficient participants? (A study involving say 40 participants merits more confidence than a study involving four.) Are these participants representative of the target population?

- Have the specific procedures in the intervention been clearly defined, and is it certain that they have been followed during the study?

- Is it clear that any improvements experienced by the participants occurred as a result of the intervention, rather than spontaneously, or as the result of some other factor?

- Were the researchers who conducted the study independent of the intervention, or are they involved with developing and promoting it?

- Would the intervention be effective if administered by non-professionals, e.g. parents or teachers?

- Would the beneficial effects of the intervention last, and would they generalise to 'real-life' settings that would be meaningful to the participants and their families?

Generalisation means the carrying over of a skill or response to a different situation or context, e.g. one that is more complex, more 'real-life' or involves interacting with different people.

There has been a dramatic improvement in the state of the **evidence base** (the quantity and quality of the available evidence) for autism-focused interventions over the past few years. Although the evidence base might still be considered extremely limited compared with that for medicines and other widely used conventional treatments, autism researchers now advocate applying medical standards of evidence to interventions for autism. Before these interventions are discussed, it is important to look at the framework of methods for evaluating them. These methods form a hierarchy, commencing with relatively limited or informal tests, and building up to more formal and wide-ranging evaluation. Each level in this hierarchy requires more rigorous standards of evidence to show that an intervention is effective.

6.2.1 Informal evaluation

After developing a set of procedures for an intervention, a practitioner first tests it on an individual for whom it is targeted (in this case a child or adult with autism). This type of preliminary evaluation is often known as a **pilot**. It may be that no data are collected at this stage, and the new intervention is therefore evaluated only informally. Nevertheless, it is important to find out whether any observed improvements relate to the specific aspect(s) of behaviour or skills that are targeted by the intervention. Since exposing a potentially vulnerable individual to what may be an essentially exploratory procedure raises ethical issues, practitioners must adhere strictly to the rules and practices outlined by their profession's governing body. The participants (or parents on participants' behalf) must also give their consent to being part of an intervention study.

6.2.2 Small-scale evaluation

Once a procedure has been shown to have a positive effect, the developer may carry out a more formal evaluation. This stage of evaluation, which is essential if the intervention is going to enter the public domain, may involve just one participant, or a small group of participants. There are established techniques for conducting such small-scale studies, a common method being a **multiple-baseline study**, which is carried out as follows.

Suppose that the intervention being tested aims to increase the number of times a child spontaneously asks for something that they like (such as bubbles or a piece of chocolate). The researcher recruits three children as participants, and observes the number of times each child makes spontaneous requests ('initiations') during a 10-minute interaction with an adult, repeating this observation once a week for 12 weeks. After the first three weeks the researcher starts the intervention with one child. For this child, these first three weeks comprise the **baseline period**. The number of spontaneous requests from the child during this period serves as a comparison for what happens after the intervention. After five weeks the second child starts to receive the intervention, and after seven weeks the third child starts to receive the intervention. If the number of initiations appears to increase for each child following the introduction of the intervention (i.e. after 'multiple baselines') this would provide some good preliminary evidence for the benefits of the intervention. The reason for starting the intervention at different points for each child is that it is easier to identify whether it is the intervention that leads to any observed differences, or whether some other factor, such as the introduction of a new teacher, the removal of a classmate with difficult behaviour, or even a sudden change in the weather, may have had an impact on the participants' behaviour. The chart in Figure 6.2 illustrates how the data from this (hypothetical) study might be presented.

- Do you think there is evidence that the intervention is effective in this small-scale evaluation?

- The study does seem to show evidence of effectiveness in the weeks following the start of the intervention, each child showing a marked increase in the frequency of initiations compared with their baseline. However, as this study involved only three children, these findings would provide only preliminary evidence of the potential benefits of this intervention.

6.2.3   Controlled studies

Controlled studies represent a more rigorous level of formal evaluation and typically involve two groups of participants on the autism spectrum. One group (the experimental group) receives the intervention, and the other (the control group) does not. The group receiving the intervention is most often known as the **intervention group**. Notice that in Hermelin and O'Connor's studies described in Section 1.5, the memory performance of children with autism (the experimental group) was compared with that of typically developing children (the control group). Both groups received the *same* test of their memory for a list of words, in order to see whether having autism affected their memory skills. In the present case both experimental/ intervention and control group will have an autism spectrum diagnosis. What varies between them is whether they receive the intervention or not. Ideally

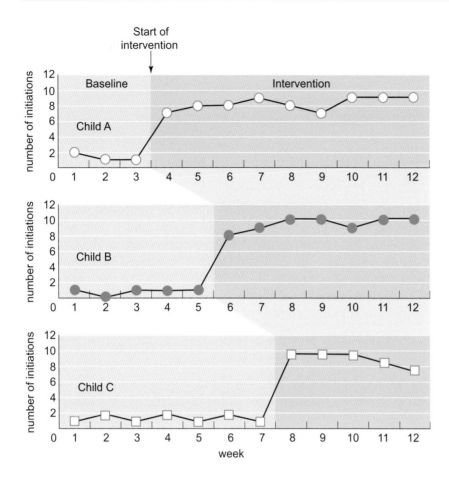

Figure 6.2 Data from a hypothetical multiple-baseline study of an intervention designed to increase the amount of child-initiated communication. For each child (A, B and C), the horizontal ('x') axis shows the passage of time, in weeks, and the vertical ('y') axis shows the number of initiations per weekly session. The baseline (pre-intervention) periods are 3, 5 and 7 weeks, respectively. Note that there is a marked increase in initiations for each child in the week following the start of the intervention, suggesting that the intervention has been effective.

the two groups should be matched on some criterion such as age, IQ or severity of symptoms, before the intervention begins.

■ What is the purpose of such matching?

☐ If the two groups are not comparable – for instance, if one group is high-functioning and the other group is low-functioning – then differences in the outcome of the intervention may be due to this factor (known as a **confounding factor**), and not to the intervention itself.

After the intervention period, the two groups are compared to see if there are differences between them. In order to make this comparison, there needs to be a specific measure related to the skills or behaviours targeted by the intervention; this is known as the **outcome measure** or **dependent variable**. For researchers to be reasonably sure that the findings are robust (i.e. that the intervention will work on more than just a few people), group studies generally involve at least 10 participants in each group. Controlled studies carried out by researchers who are independent from the developers of the intervention will have more credibility than those conducted by the creators themselves.

■ Why is this the case?

☐ Researchers who have developed the intervention are obviously committed to it working, and this may undermine the objectivity of their evaluation.

Figure 6.3 illustrates the data from another hypothetical controlled study, involving 10 children in intervention and control groups, and testing an intervention designed to increase spontaneous communication in children with autism. The figure takes the form of a **bar chart**. The vertical bars show the mean (average) number of initiations for each group, after the intervention phase of the study. The mean is calculated by dividing the total number of initiations for the group by the number of participants in the group.

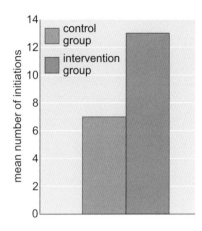

Figure 6.3 Data from a hypothetical intervention study. Each vertical bar shows the mean number of child initiations for the control and intervention groups following the intervention phase of the study.

■ Do you think this study provides evidence that the intervention might work?

☐ The data do show differences between the two groups following intervention. However, without information about the mean number of initiations *before* the intervention group received treatment, it is not possible to know whether these differences were due to the intervention or not.

Now consider the data presented in Figure 6.4. In this chart there are four bars, two for each of the two groups in the same study described above. The two left-hand bars represent the mean number of initiations during the baseline (i.e. pre-intervention) phase of the study, and the two right-hand bars represent the same data shown in Figure 6.3 for the post-intervention phase.

■ Do you think that this study provides evidence that the intervention might work?

☐ Now there is stronger evidence for the potential benefits of the intervention. Before the children in the intervention group received the intervention there was very little difference between the intervention and control groups. Following the intervention, the bar representing initiations for the intervention group suggests a definite increase.

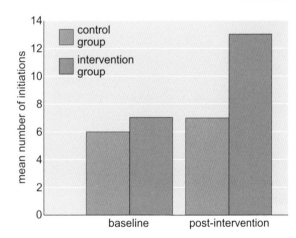

Figure 6.4 Data from a hypothetical intervention study. Each bar shows the mean number of child initiations before (baseline) and after (post-intervention) the intervention phase of the study for the control group and the intervention group.

Even so, these findings cannot be taken as definitive evidence in favour of the intervention. For instance, as in the experiment in Section 1.5, a statistical test is needed to establish whether this apparently striking difference could have occurred just by chance. In addition, the design and methodology of the study, and the basis for allocating children to their respective groups, must be carefully evaluated before drawing any conclusions.

6.2.4   Randomised control trials

Suppose that a researcher set out to evaluate an intervention that requires a significant degree of motivation and effort on the part of the participants (or their parents) and that those who volunteered for the intervention were assigned to the intervention group. It may be that the level of motivation, rather than the effects of the intervention itself, was responsible for any post-intervention differences between the groups. To avoid such biases, participants may be assigned randomly to treatment and non-treatment groups – much like drawing numbers out of a hat. This type of study is known as a **randomised control trial (RCT)**. RCTs are widely used to evaluate medical interventions, but to date there have been very few in the field of autism. One problem with RCTs is that parents will naturally be hoping that their child is going to receive the potential benefit of a new intervention. If they think that there is a chance that their child will be in the control group, they may be less motivated to participate.

6.2.5   Reviews

A review involves the evaluation of all the evidence relating to a particular intervention (or a range of interventions of a similar type). When the review is conducted with clearly defined criteria (for example, including only controlled studies carried out by independent researchers), this is known as a **systematic review**.

6.2.6   Ethical issues in formal evaluations

In all evaluation studies involving control groups, there will be some children on the autism spectrum who do not receive the new intervention. Moreover, from a scientific point of view, it is often ideal that control participants do not receive *any* kind of intervention.

■   Do you think it is ethically acceptable for some children or adults with autism to serve as control groups in formal evaluations?

☐   There is no easy answer to this: the ultimate goal of a new intervention is that it should benefit all of the population for whom it is designed, but children in the control group will miss out on this. On the other hand, without a formal evaluation, no benefits can be guaranteed for anyone.

One method that goes some way to addressing this ethical problem is to compare the effects of a new intervention with another established intervention, or to 'treatment as usual' (for example, speech and language therapy that is provided through the local health service). That way, the control group should derive some benefit from being in the study. Similarly, if the new intervention is claimed to be superior to other existing interventions, then the control group may be treated with one of these other interventions so that the effects can be compared.

There is another consideration too: the intervention under investigation may be completely unproven, and in fact turn out to be ineffective or have undesirable consequences for those who experience it. In this case, the evaluation process may have less desirable consequences for the intervention group and their families than the control group.

6.2.7 The use of the evidence base

Although it may seem ideal for an intervention to be evaluated through all of the evaluative stages outlined above before being pronounced effective, this rarely happens in practice. The findings of studies are ideally published in **peer-reviewed journals** after rigorous scrutiny and critique by fellow professionals, but the developer of an intervention may publicise it via websites, magazines or other sources, perhaps making ill-founded claims for the benefits of the approach. If the intervention can be accessed via training events, books or manuals, then it may become very popular in the absence of a more formal evidence base. This is often a cause for concern for organisations such as the National Autistic Society (NAS): as mentioned in Section 6.1.1, parents of children with autism may be highly vulnerable to any claims for 'cure' and 'recovery', and understandably, they also feel empowered by doing anything they can to help their child. Developers of new approaches, and the parents and professionals who support their intervention, may rightly claim that they cannot afford to wait for years, even decades, before independent researchers secure funding and ethical approval to conduct a large-scale evaluation study, implement the study and then publish the findings.

The UK charity **Research Autism** has a database that aims to provide accessible and impartial guidance for parents, practitioners and individuals with autism, who may not have access to the academic literature relating to the evidence base for interventions. Research Autism commissions research from independent researchers, as well as asking expert reviewers to evaluate the existing evidence base for the whole range of interventions that are used for people on the autism spectrum.

Activity 6.2 invites you to investigate evaluations of different interventions.

Activity 6.2   Exploring the evidence for interventions
Allow 30 minutes for this activity

The Research Autism website can be readily located via a search engine. From the list of evaluated interventions, find one that has been evaluated positively and one that has received a negative evaluation and consider the differences between the interventions.

The remainder of this chapter introduces a selection of interventions, explaining the underlying principles and considering their evidence base. The discussion of psychosocial interventions will begin with so-called **comprehensive** or **integrated approaches** which aim to support people on the autism spectrum across many aspects of functioning, including learning, behaviour, social and communication needs. Then interventions that focus on more specific areas of psychosocial development will be discussed.

6.2.8 Summary of Section 6.2

* Evidence-based practice refers to the need to ground proposed interventions in theory and research, a robust ethical framework and rigorous evaluation of the benefits.

* The evaluation of an intervention must address questions including how the targeted problem is defined and measured, the methodology for testing the approach, and the basis for drawing conclusions from the study.

* Evaluations of interventions proceed from informal and small-scale evaluations to formal evaluations, including controlled studies and RCTs.

* Interventions have often not been evaluated through all these stages: parents and professionals sometimes proceed without this background.

6.3 Psychosocial interventions: comprehensive or integrated approaches

This section illustrates approaches that support and foster individuals within a broad educational and therapeutic framework. Such approaches address key characteristics of autism discussed in earlier chapters, such as the need for structure and routine, and difficulty interpreting ambiguous social messages. These approaches often build on key skills of people on the autism spectrum such as precision, accuracy and tolerance of repetition, and many of them aim to address the specific needs and outlook of the individual. These approaches are called comprehensive approaches because they address a broad range of skills and deficits, and also because they may be used across different settings (at home, school, in respite services and other locations) as well as across the lifespan of an individual with autism. The main approaches considered here are **TEACCH (Treatment and Education of Autistic and related Communication-handicapped CHildren)**, the **Lovaas approach** and the **Son-Rise programme**.

6.3.1 TEACCH

TEACCH was originally developed in North Carolina in the early 1970s. Contemporary versions are widely used in many countries in both home and school settings, and it is one of several educational frameworks recommended by the NAS and the Autism Society of America (ASA) (see Box 6.2).

Box 6.2 Key principles of the TEACCH framework

1 Provision of structure, both in the person's environment and in the approach to teaching, which is typically one to one.

2 Emphasis on identifying and harnessing skills, particularly visual abilities, memory for factual information, attention to detail, accuracy and tolerance of repetition.

---

3   Evaluation of individual therapeutic needs on a regular basis, and the use of appropriate behavioural and socio-cognitive interventions to complement the approach.

4   Empowering parents by encouraging their full participation.

5   Emphasis on developing independence, and generalising from learning experiences in order to master a range of everyday situations.

6   Training for practitioners that emphasises a 'whole person' approach.

In implementing these principles, a key technique is the visual structuring of the person's environment and teaching. For instance, pictures, symbols or objects may be set out on a TEACCH board, to help the person in structuring space, concepts, tasks and activities. In some cases, the board is presented as a visual timetable providing descriptions of activities in the order in which they are to be carried out, together with small illustrations of the activities (Figure 6.5).

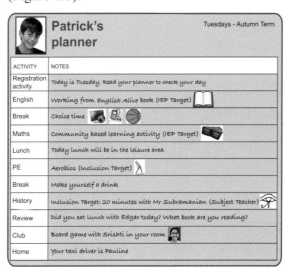

Figure 6.5   Picture of a visual timetable for a boy's day at school. You may like to check the larger version of this figure provided as Figure 7.5. (Based on source material provided by Gillian Roberts, Principal, Robert Ogden School, South Yorkshire, UK; Photos: PhotoEuphoria/iStockphoto; Vikram Raghuvananshi/ iStockphoto)

TEACCH can be equally useful in adult settings. The manager of a service for adults on the spectrum gave the following example of implementing a TEACCH-based programme:

A young woman living at home had become extremely anxious and nervous about changing her clothes, wanting to wear the same things all the time and seeming to find a security in doing so. Trying to encourage her to change had become a time of stress and tension for all concerned. TEACCH principles were applied as shown in Table 6.1.

Table 6.1 An example of TEACCH in an adult setting.

Establishing visual boundaries	Seven small coloured baskets were organised (one for each day of the week) and labelled.
How much?	One complete set of clothes was put into each of the daily baskets.
When have I finished?	Once she was dressed in the clothes each day, the empty basket was upturned onto the other empty baskets.
What next?	At the end of the day, the new basket of clothes was put out for the next day, and she put what she was wearing into the family laundry basket.

Once the system was understood this young woman took to it without problems, and nightly traumas about changing clothes faded away. Her independence was further developed by involving her in setting up the baskets at the beginning of each week.

(Robinson, 1997, pp. 8–10)

The TEACCH approach draws upon a number of important theoretical insights; for instance, that inappropriate behaviour and anxiety may reflect a fixation on details, or an inability to understand the effect of one's behaviour on other people (see Chapter 4 for a discussion of relevant theories). TEACCH principles also build on the finding that people on the autism spectrum respond positively to information that is presented visually and in a structured way. These principles can be successfully adapted for individuals with high-functioning autism or Asperger syndrome. For instance, an individual may be encouraged to structure daily activities using a diary, personal organiser or mobile device. A visual checklist may be helpful in preparing for a task at school or at work.

The evidence base for TEACCH

Despite its popularity, there have been no RCTs or large-scale controlled studies to provide strong evidence for the benefits of TEACCH. A very significant barrier to conducting such studies is the nature of TEACCH itself. It is designed as a 'whole life' approach tailored to the individual child or adult, and aiming to be beneficial across a wide range of difficulties. As such it is not easy to identify specific outcome measures that will be appropriate for all participants in a study.

One general drawback may be that children and adults who are exposed to TEACCH become too dependent upon its strong, externally imposed structure. They may regress in their behaviour and stress levels on moving away from a TEACCH-based system (Powell and Jordan, 1997), or fail to generalise their improved behaviour to situations other than those for which the TEACCH structures have been provided.

Nonetheless, Schopler et al. (1982) reported positive outcomes for over 600 students enrolled in TEACCH programmes. The more extensive a student's involvement, the better the outcomes across a number of measures, including whether they could manage without the support of specialist schools or adult services. However, while this study had an impressive number of participants, it lacked a control group and the researchers were not independent of the intervention – Eric Schopler was one of the originators of the TEACCH approach. In three additional follow-up studies, outcomes included substantial increases in participants' IQ scores. These gains were most pronounced in the very young children who were non-verbal prior to entering the TEACCH programme. Since the intervention actually targets social adaptation and everyday life skills rather than intellectual ability, these IQ gains may have been due to maturation rather than the intervention itself. Unfortunately these studies also lacked the control groups that would have provided an answer to this question.

Later studies incorporating control groups have demonstrated positive outcomes for children in TEACCH programmes but these have been relatively small in scale. Research Autism suggests that there are significant benefits for people with autism who use TEACCH, but that outcomes may be dependent upon the skill and expertise of the professionals who work with them, and concludes that there is a need for 'larger, systematic and controlled studies … in order to evaluate the immediate and long-term outcomes'.

■ From this outline of TEACCH, list some strengths and limitations of the evidence base. You may find it helpful to check the key issues for evaluations in Box 6.1 and the hierarchy of evaluation stages outlined in Section 6.2.

□ Strengths: informal – TEACCH is widely used and is recommended by the NAS; more formal – several evaluations involving large numbers of participants have reported improved outcomes including enhanced IQ scores and benefits for young non-verbal children; formal – some controlled studies have also reported evidence of benefits.

Limitations: some outcome measures (e.g. enhanced IQ) do not relate closely to target skills; large-scale studies did not have control groups and were carried out by the developers of TEACCH, not by independent researchers; studies involving control groups were small-scale; benefits may be dependent on expertise of professionals rather than the intervention itself.

6.3.2   The Lovaas approach

Ivar Lovaas and his colleagues developed a curriculum that focused on language development, social interaction and school integration skills, known as the University of California Los Angeles (UCLA) Young Autism Project. Section 1.7 provided a brief introduction to the underlying behaviour modification principles and these are further explained in Box 6.3.

Box 6.3 Key principles of the Lovaas approach

1   Controversially, the theoretical orientation of this approach is that the search for underlying causes of autism is theoretically misguided and irrelevant to developing effective therapy. This follows Skinner's claim that intervention should focus only on what can be observed directly and objectively, such as an individual's behaviour. Attempting to understand or change the way that an individual thinks is, according to Skinner, both subjective and ineffective. (See also discussion of Skinner in Box 1.10.)

2   Learning is seen as playing a central role in the failure of the child with autism to acquire 'desirable' behaviours (such as physical contact with others), and in the acquisition of 'undesirable' behaviours (e.g. repetitive behaviours that may be injurious or antisocial, such as head banging, destruction of objects, taking clothes off in public). Modifying such behaviours through learning is considered the appropriate technique for improving the child's general functioning.

3   Operant conditioning and reinforcement: according to Skinner 'the behaviour is followed by a consequence, and the nature of the consequence modifies the organism's tendency to repeat the behaviour in the future'. Implementing this learning process using reinforcement is known as **operant conditioning**. If the target behaviour is one that the adult wants to encourage, the reinforcement needs to be a positive outcome for the child. If the behaviour is something that the adult wants to discourage (disruptive activity or self-injury, for example), then withholding reinforcement (e.g. by ignoring the behaviour) should eventually result in the behaviour disappearing – known as extinction. (See Box 1.10 for examples.)

4   **Discrete trial procedures** involve analysing the child's behaviour into components that can be individually tackled. For instance, a child might be taught the single task of standing up when an adult tells them to. This behaviour will be rewarded in some way (perhaps with a favourite snack or a non-edible reward). When the child achieves the desired skill to an acceptable level (e.g. eight out of ten trials correct), the adult then targets another skill.

5   An important extension of this approach (introduced in the 1980s) is training parents to carry out the therapy themselves at home.

The first stages of the Lovaas programme focus on teaching self-help and receptive language skills (i.e. language understanding), non-verbal and verbal imitation, and the foundations of appropriate play. The second stage of the intervention emphasises the teaching of expressive language and interactive play with peers. Advanced stages, taught at home or school, involve the learning of early academic tasks, socialisation skills, cause–effect relationships and learning by observation. Aggressive and self-stimulatory behaviours are managed in several ways. For instance, the therapist or parent may ignore the behaviour or deliver a loud 'no'; they may remove the child from a context in which the 'undesirable' behaviour is being reinforced, known as 'time out'; and/or they may reinforce alternative behaviour as it approximates closer to the desired response, known as 'shaping'. Earlier forms of Lovaas therapy also employed aversive techniques (such as a slap on the child's thigh), but such practices would no longer be considered appropriate, and are not now part of the Lovaas repertoire. The approach has been delivered in a variety of settings and contexts, including clinic-based services provided by highly trained professionals, and home-based provision with graduate therapists and parents as the primary trainers, supported periodically by consultants. The intervention might seem particularly relevant for young children who are lacking basic communication skills and everyday capabilities. Yet evaluations have not considered the effects on low-functioning children with autism, so the most appropriate target group for this approach is unclear.

The evidence base for Lovaas

Evaluations of the Lovaas approach have been the focus of much interest, controversy and criticism. In particular, Lovaas's initial report (1987) provoked controversy because he claimed that some children in the intervention group recovered from autism. A follow-up study (McEachin et al., 1993) again claimed that some children achieved 'normal' functioning to the extent that they were indistinguishable from their neurotypical peers in mainstream educational settings. More recently, in an independent study (Sallows and Graupner, 2005), the autism diagnoses of some children were removed after intervention. It is possible, of course, that their initial autism diagnosis was erroneous.

Following the publicity surrounding Lovaas's initial claims of recovery from autism, many parents spent considerable amounts of money funding programmes for their children and devoted hundreds of hours of their time delivering home-based therapy. They also lobbied local authorities to provide Lovaas therapy, or pursued legal channels to force local services to fund programmes.

The methodology of the initial studies by Lovaas and his colleagues has been widely criticised. For instance, the assignment of children to treatment groups was non-random, children with low IQ scores were excluded, and different tests were used to assess cognitive skills before and after treatment.

■ Why do you think that these issues might be important when considering the findings of these studies?

☐ Non-random assignment to treatment and non-treatment groups means that there may have been a bias in terms of which children received the intervention. For example, allocation may have been based upon the motivation of parents or their willingness or ability to take time off from work or implement the programmes in their homes. The exclusion of low-functioning children means that the potential benefits for this group – who are arguably most in need of help – are unknown. Although two tests may appear to measure the same skill or aspect of development (e.g. IQ), in practice, different children, and particularly those with autism, may respond to one test more favourably than another. Therefore, it is not clear whether different scores on the tests used before and after intervention are due to the effects of the intervention, or due to the change in tests.

Finally, children in the original treatment group received 40 hours of intervention per week. This level of intervention is not really viable in most practical settings. For instance, parents who participated in the study were asked to take a year off work. Nonetheless, a number of independent single case studies and randomised trials have found that intensive early intervention approaches similar to Lovaas are beneficial for children on the autism spectrum. One RCT, described as having 'rigorous design methodology and a clear analytical approach' (Rogers and Vismara, 2008), evaluated a Lovaas-type programme involving 25 or fewer hours per week and reported positive outcomes following the treatment. Other studies have included children of various ages and levels of ability, mostly concluding that children with higher initial intellectual ability and less pronounced autism make most progress following early behavioural intervention.

Activity 6.3 invites you to think about the impact on a family of adopting the Lovaas approach.

Activity 6.3   Implementing the Lovaas approach: the impact on the family

Allow 15 minutes for this activity

Consider the impact on a family if the parents of a young child with autism decide to implement the Lovaas programme. Think about how this might affect the child's siblings, as well as how the parents might feel if the intervention is eventually deemed to be unsuccessful for the child. Comments are at the end of the book.

6.3.3   The Son-Rise programme

Like the Lovaas approach, the Son-Rise programme (Kaufman, 1994) – sometimes referred to as the Option approach – also makes strong claims for recovery from autism. It was developed by Barry and Samahria Kaufman to help their son Raun, who had been diagnosed with severe autism as a young child. In their book *Son-Rise*, published in 1976 they detailed Raun's progress, and claimed that he completely recovered from autism – he eventually graduated from university and became director at the Autism Treatment Center of America, where the programme is now based. Needless to say, many parents were determined to use this approach with their children, and many made sacrifices just like the parents who pursued Lovaas therapy.

Son-Rise differs significantly from the Lovaas approach in its philosophy. It is a **child-centred approach**, which advocates following the child's interests and motivation as a means of encouraging interaction and learning. The key features of the Son-Rise approach are detailed in Box 6.4.

Box 6.4   Key principles of the Son-Rise approach

1   Joining in a child's repetitive and ritualistic behaviours, for instance by copying them.
2   Utilising a child's own motivation to advance learning and build the foundation for education and skill acquisition.
3   Teaching through interactive play.
4   Using energy, excitement and enthusiasm to engage the child.
5   Adopting a non-judgemental and optimistic attitude.
6   Placing the parent as the child's most important and consistent teacher.

Parents using the Son-Rise programme are advised to create a safe, distraction-free area in their homes to optimise their child's learning opportunities.

The evidence base for Son-Rise

In addition to the claims of Raun Kaufman's recovery, there have been many anecdotal reports of significant improvements in the behaviour, social interaction and communication skills of children with autism who have been through the Son-Rise programme. However, the approach has never been formally evaluated and Research Autism calls for large-scale objective studies into its effectiveness.

6.3.4   The continuum of interventions

As you have seen, the Lovaas and Son-Rise approaches differ in their theoretical emphasis and philosophy, and this suggests a way of differentiating among other comprehensive and specifically focused psychosocial interventions for autism. At one end of a continuum, Lovaas and other **behavioural interventions** apply a general understanding of learning and behaviour to the therapeutic process. They typically avoid any theoretical explanation of the underlying causes of problematic behaviour, but use specific learning techniques to identify and reinforce or reward target behaviour and reduce or extinguish unwanted behaviour. The skills to be developed are decided by an adult, usually as part of a hierarchy of 'desirable' skills. Hence these approaches are termed **adult-directed**.

At the other end of the continuum are interventions such as Son-Rise that apply theoretical understanding of development in typically developing infants and young children to the treatment of children with autism and other developmental disabilities. These so-called **developmental–pragmatic** or **social pragmatic approaches** are often described as child-centred, because they emphasise that adults follow the child's interests and focus of attention, and therapists and parents are taught to respond to the child's spontaneous behaviour in order to encourage the child into an interaction. While Son-Rise is a comprehensive approach, many of these child-centred interventions focus more specifically on facilitating early social communication and interaction skills.

A third class of approaches lies between the adult-directed, behavioural and child-centred approaches, integrating aspects of both philosophies. Generally known as **naturalistic** or **milieu approaches**, these treatments incorporate certain behavioural techniques, but use them to support the development of target skills in a child's everyday environment or in naturally occurring situations. Two of the earliest proponents of the naturalistic approach, Betty Hart and Todd Risley, argued that 'instruction' should take place *following*, rather than *preceding*, a child's initiation of communication, thus expressing the essential difference between naturalistic approaches and their more conventional behavioural counterparts: the adults (whether professionals or parents) use recognisable behavioural techniques, but the target behaviours are based on the child's interests and preferred activities rather than being decided on in advance by the adult.

Table 6.2 illustrates the continuum from adult-directed to child-centred approaches. This table provides some of the alternative names for each general approach, as well as some examples of specific interventions that fall within each category, including some that are discussed in this chapter. You may wish to consult sources such as the Research Autism database or the NAS website, to find out more about these approaches, as well as those that are mentioned but not discussed in detail. Note that TEACCH is not included in this table. Though it seeks to target and modify behaviour, it borrows techniques from a wide range of approaches, and does not fit neatly within any specific part of this continuum model.

The notion of a continuum came up in Section 1.9 denoting the idea of continuity across the autism spectrum. In the present case, continuum means that the types of approach are not sharply differentiated, but are at different positions on a dimension from adult-directed to child-centred.

6.3.5 Summary of Section 6.3

- Comprehensive or integrated approaches to intervention address multiple areas of the individual's functioning, and may be adapted to a range of settings.

- TEACCH emphasises visual structuring of the individual's environment and learning. Evidence includes small-scale controlled studies.

- The Lovaas approach employs behaviour modification principles to teach elements of language and communication, and to help eradicate undesirable behaviours. Evidence is mixed but includes a recent RCT.

- Son-Rise emphasises building on the child's interests and motivation. Evidence is purely anecdotal.

- The contrasting adult-directed and child-centred approaches of Lovaas and Son-Rise represent extremes of a continuum.

Table 6.2 The continuum of psychosocial approaches for people with autism.

Category	Behavioural Adult-directed	Naturalistic	Developmental–pragmatic Child-centred
Also known as	Didactic Applied behaviour analysis (ABA) Discrete trial training (DTT)	Milieu	Social pragmatic
Interventions discussed in this chapter	Lovaas	Picture Exchange Communication System (PECS)	Son-Rise (Option) Developmental, Individual-difference, Relationship-based (DIR)/Floortime Relationship Development Intervention (RDI)
Other interventions	Early intensive behavioural intervention (EIBI) Rapid motor imitation (RMI)	Pivotal response training (PRT) Natural language paradigm (NLP)	More Than Words Social Communication Emotional Regulation Transactional Support (SCERTS)
	Verbal behaviour (VB)	Enhanced milieu teaching (EMT) Prelinguistic milieu teaching (PMT) Incidental teaching Minimal speech/ Proximal communication	

6.4 Psychosocial interventions for language and communication

6.4.1 Developmental–pragmatic approaches

As you learned in Chapter 3, most children are already good communicators before they learn to talk.

- Think of some of the non-verbal means by which babies and young children show other people what they want, what they are interested in and how they are feeling.

- Newborn babies signal their needs mainly by crying, but quickly learn to smile to communicate pleasure. Between six and 12 months, young typically developing children are able to focus on both objects and people and begin to share attention with adults. They start to use expressions, vocalising, babbling and some simple gestures (such as both palms raised to mean 'Where's it gone?'). By 18 months, typically developing children use and combine many different ways of communicating: these include pointing and gestures, eye contact and facial expression, vocalisations and some single words or two-word phrases.

However, in order to use these skills effectively the child has to be motivated to communicate and to understand something about what the other person thinks and knows. As you have seen in Chapters 3 and 4, both communication and the understanding of others' minds are particular difficulties for people on the autism spectrum.

Interventions designed to enhance the communication skills of children on the autism spectrum mostly aim to provide them with positive experiences of communicating and interacting with others. The majority of communication-focused interventions are child centred (see Table 6.2) and are aimed at young, often non-verbal children with classic autism. As parents are usually the main communication partners of preschool children, these approaches emphasise the support and training of parents to enhance and facilitate their child's emerging social communication skills. Experts and trainers may have limited direct contact with the child. The fundamental principles of these developmental–pragmatic approaches are described in Box 6.5.

> ### Box 6.5 Key principles of developmental–pragmatic approaches
>
> 1 Using the sequence of communicative development in typical children to decide what areas of difficulty to target.
>
> 2 Providing intensified opportunities for children with autism to engage in activities similar to those of their typically developing peers, in the belief that these are the most effective contexts for learning social and communication skills.
>
> 3 Exploiting learning opportunities that naturally arise during interactions, rather than setting out a 'curriculum' in advance.

4 Facilitating interactions, including pretend play, by: focusing on what the child is already interested in; acknowledging and responding to the child's intentions even if these are expressed unconventionally (e.g. using echolalia or stereotyped language); modelling ways to communicate about activities that the child chooses and is already engaged in; and expanding on communication that the child produces spontaneously.

5 Targeting functional goals for intervention, i.e. behaviours that are applicable to daily, meaningful activities in a variety of contexts apart from the one in which they were originally learned.

6 Acknowledging that non-verbal communication (including gestures, gaze, vocalisation and other non-verbal means) is a vital part in the development of language.

DIR/Floortime

Greenspan and Weider (1999) developed an intensely child-centred approach called **Developmental, Individual-difference, Relationship-based (DIR)**, also known as **Floortime**. Greenspan and Weider believe that the main problem for children on the autism spectrum is an inability to connect social and emotional knowledge to their developing motor and symbolic skills. In the DIR approach, the emphasis is on following and imitating the child's actions, using sensorimotor techniques, such as swinging the child or applying physical pressure, if this increases attention to the adult. Adults also present problem-solving activities to the children, and playfully obstruct any repetitive routines. For example, if a child enjoys sliding down a slide, the adult may put their arm across to block the slide, thus providing the child with an opportunity to interact communicatively – by looking at the adult, vocalising or making a gesture as a request. Adults also attempt to elicit communication by not responding to non-communicative actions. For instance, if the child reaches for a door handle to signal their desire to leave the room, instead of opening the door, the adult will wait for a more communicative behaviour, such as the child looking to the adult when standing near to the door.

Relationship Development Intervention programme

The **Relationship Development Intervention (RDI) programme** (Gutstein and Sheely, 2002) is one of several interventions that train parents to foster the social communication skills of their children with autism. Parents are trained to target deficits in their child's interpersonal interaction skills (such as joint attention, gaze direction and use of facial expression) through stimulating and fun activities. Parents are trained to use indirect prompts and 'invitations' rather than directive ways of interacting. The idea is that once children with autism have discovered the value of relationships through repeated positive experience of interpersonal activity, they will be motivated to learn the verbal and non-verbal skills required to sustain these relationships.

Evidence base for developmental–pragmatic approaches

Some recent evidence suggests that developmental–pragmatic approaches can benefit young children with autism. McConachie et al. (2005) compared intervention and control groups of children who already had some speech, and found that those in the intervention group showed a significant increase in their use of speech compared with the control group. Gutstein et al. (2007) report improvements in measures of autistic symptoms for children who participated in the RDI programme. However, this study had limitations: there was no control or comparison group; parents in the intervention group had volunteered for it; all participants attended just one clinic; and the research was carried out by the developer of RDI. There have been no independent published studies of DIR, though Greenspan (1998, p. 3) claims that he and his colleagues 'have worked with a number of children diagnosed with autism or PDD-NOS between the ages of 18 and 30 months who, now older, are fully communicative … creative, warm, loving and joyful'. (Autism in this quote means classic autism; see Section 2.2.2 for a definition of PDD-NOS.)

6.4.2 Naturalistic approaches

One of the first naturalistic approaches was **incidental teaching**, defined as 'the interaction between an adult and a single child, which arises naturally in an unstructured situation such as free play and which is used by the adult to transmit information or give the child practice in developing a skill' (Hart and Risley, 1975, p. 411). Although naturalistic treatments incorporate behavioural techniques, they have evolved away from traditional behavioural interventions to emphasise child-centred teaching activities and stimuli based upon children's interests and preferences. These approaches also take place in the context of natural communicative behaviours, where the teacher delivers prompts based on the child's initiations, rather than in relation to predefined, adult-selected activities. **Prompt fading** is a technique whereby the adult may initially need to physically move a child's hand to reach for an object, or to physically shape the child's hand in order to make a communicative sign. As the child becomes more familiar with the action, the adult progressively reduces ('fades') the degree of physical support given, maybe just touching the child's hand or elbow, for example, until eventually no physical prompting is required.

Picture Exchange Communication System

One of the best-known and most widely used naturalistic interventions is the Picture Exchange Communication System (PECS) devised by Bondy and Frost (1998). PECS was developed as a means of teaching functional communication skills to children with autism, and is especially suited to children with classic autism and little or no language. Each child who is introduced to PECS is individually assessed to identify objects and activities that he or she finds rewarding. The child is then taught to make spontaneous requests for these items. This initial process involves one adult as a *communication partner* and a second adult as a *physical prompter*. The physical prompter stays behind the child and waits for the child to reach for the desired object. The physical prompter then physically guides the child to pick up a picture of the object and release it into the communication partner's hand. The physical prompter fades the prompting as the child becomes more independent in carrying out the picture exchange.

Once spontaneous communicative exchange has been established, PECS intervention aims to strengthen this spontaneity and to enhance the child's ability to distinguish between pictures. Another important aim is generalisation (see Box 6.1). This means that the child should use his/her new-found communication skills in different settings and with different communication partners, produce more complex communications, and eventually make comments about things they can see rather than just make requests for things they want. The six phases of PECS are described in Box 6.6.

Box 6.6 PECS

Table 6.3 The six phases of PECS.

Phase	Description	Target skill
I	'How' to communicate	Upon seeing a 'highly preferred' item, the child will pick up a picture of the item, reach towards the communicative partner, and release the picture into the trainer's hand.
II	Distance and persistence	The child goes to his/her communication board, pulls the picture off, goes to the trainer, gets the trainer's attention and releases the picture into the trainer's hand.
III	Picture discrimination	The child requests desired items by going to a communication folder (see Figure 6.6), selecting the appropriate picture from an array, going to a communication partner and giving the picture.
IV	Sentence structure	The child requests items using a multi-word phrase by combining a picture/symbol of 'I want' with a picture of the desired item on a sentence strip and giving it to the communication partner. The child is expected to use 20 or more pictures and to communicate with a variety of partners.
V	Responding to 'What do you want?'	The child spontaneously requests a variety of items and answers the question, 'What do you want?'
VI	Commenting	The child answers 'What do you want/see/have/hear?' and 'What is it?' and spontaneously requests and comments.

The evidence base for PECS

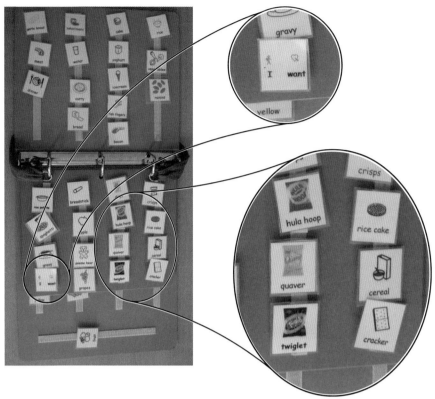

Figure 6.6 A PECS communication folder holding an array of small pictures of items about which the child might want to communicate. This page shows food items, and a page for colours is just visible underneath. As the child progresses to phase IV, he or she will combine phrases such as 'I want' (left-hand corner and pull-out) with the desired item, placing multi-word phrases onto the sentence strip at the bottom. Children are encouraged to carry their folders whenever possible. (Queensmill School)

PECS is one of the few autism-specific interventions to have been evaluated through all of the stages described earlier in this chapter. The developers of PECS presented initial findings based on a large number of children who had attended their own services, although these studies did not have a control group or use experimental methodology. A number of small-scale studies have reported positive findings for children following PECS intervention, including a study by Charlop-Christie et al. (2002). This multiple-baseline study involved three children who all made progress to phase VI and showed increases in their use of speech. Carr and Felce (2007) conducted a controlled trial involving 41 children with autism and reported improved communicative interaction and speech in the intervention group.

Yoder and Stone (2006a; 2006b) conducted an RCT involving 36 children comparing PECS with another naturalistic intervention (prelinguistic milieu teaching (PMT)). The children in the PECS group improved in their use of requesting behaviour and of spontaneous speech compared with those in the PMT group. In contrast, the children in the PMT group improved in their use of commenting and turn-taking skills compared with those in the PECS group. It is important to note that in this study the intervention was carried out under 'ideal' conditions, that is, by highly trained specialists. This is known as an **efficacy study**. Howlin et al. (2007) carried out an RCT involving 84 children and report that children in the PECS intervention group increased in their frequency of PECS use and spontaneous communication compared with children in the control group. This study was carried out in 'real-world' conditions using non-specialists. This is known as an **effectiveness study**.

■ Consider why this difference is important.

☐ There may be a big difference between the impact of an intervention when administered by professionals, and by parents, for instance. It is important to know if an intervention will work in a real-world setting.

■ What are the strengths and limitations of the evidence base (as it is presented above) relating to PECS?

☐ Strengths: informal – PECS is widely used; more formal – reports of positive evaluations involving large numbers of participants; apparent gains in young non-verbal children; formal – several small-scale studies reporting improvements in language and communication skills; one reasonably sized controlled study showing benefits from PECS use; two RCTs with fairly large numbers of participants showing positive outcomes, one of which had a control group that received an alternative intervention, rather than no intervention.

Limitations: initial studies did not have control groups and were carried out by the developers of PECS; one controlled study did not have random allocation.

Research Autism states that there is 'strong positive evidence' supporting PECS as a beneficial intervention. Even so, further well-conducted studies would help to clarify the profiles of children who would benefit most from using PECS; that is, whether success depends on such factors as the age, degree of intellectual disability and severity of autism.

6.4.3 Summary of Section 6.4

• Developmental–pragmatic interventions are child-centred approaches that seek to foster the language and communication skills of young children with autism and little or no language.

• DIR (Floortime) uses sensorimotor activities to foster the child's communication skills; RDI trains parents to foster their child's use of joint attention, gaze direction and facial expression.

• There is some limited evidence for RDI, but there are no independent published studies of DIR.

• PECS is a naturalistic approach which harnesses behavioural techniques to develop the child's spontaneous communications about objects that he/she finds interesting.

- PECS is picture-based and also aimed primarily at young children with classic autism and little or no language; there is a good evidence base for its beneficial effects.

6.5 Psychosocial interventions for socio-cognitive skills

Up to now most of the interventions have focused on behavioural and communication problems in autism, particularly those of children with poor language and communication skills. TEACCH was the approach that could be most readily adapted to a range of ages and ability groups. Recently there has been a focus on developing interventions suitable for slightly more able children, and also adults on the autism spectrum. These approaches seek to address core psychological difficulties in areas such as emotion recognition and other aspects of ToM or mind-reading, which were discussed in Chapter 4. *Mind Reading* is a computer-based intervention designed by Ofer Golan, Simon Baron-Cohen and colleagues to help people on the autism spectrum to recognise emotions and mental states (Golan and Baron-Cohen, 2006).

The approach capitalises on the interest that computers hold for many people who are on the autism spectrum, and also assumes that these individuals will learn well from highly systematised materials (see Section 4.7 for a discussion of the theoretical approach). The *Mind Reading* software comprises 412 emotions and mental states. These are organised into 24 groups and arranged for six different developmental levels from age four years to adult. For each emotion and mental state, there is a definition together with examples. These consist of silent video clips showing animated facial expressions, voice recordings of people expressing the emotion, and descriptions of situations in which it would be evoked. The software includes three different zones: an emotion 'library' in which information about a particular emotion can be looked up, a 'learning centre' providing lessons, quizzes and rewards related to learning about the emotions, and a 'game zone' in which the participant learns about emotions while playing a game. Figure 6.7 illustrates some of the materials and tasks from the *Mind Reading* software.

The approach is designed for individuals to interact with the software in their own time, using the materials to analyse and compare the qualities of the emotions depicted, so that they gradually learn how to identify them. The quizzes in the learning centre provide opportunities for the individual to test their knowledge, receive feedback and gain rewards for accurate learning. The goal of the intervention is to enhance an individual's ability to recognise emotions and mental states, generalising from the stimuli supplied within the software to more naturalistic or real-world situations.

- Think back to the continuum of approaches, from those in which the professional specifies the desired behaviour and tasks, to those that use the interests and motivations of the individual to develop skills. Where, if at all, do you think the *Mind Reading* approach fits on this continuum?

□   The approach has some adult-directed features in that the target skills are to recognise a pre-specified set of emotional expressions. However, it also has some individual-centred features in that it provides scope for the user to choose which emotions to learn about, and which learning methods to use. As the intervention is designed not just for children on the spectrum but for adults too, the scope for the individual to take control of their own learning is especially important.

The emotions library: an emotion page

6 out of the 24 Emotion groups

The learning centre: a quiz question

The game zone: 'Hidden face'

Figure 6.7 Examples of materials and tasks from the *Mind Reading* software. The images to top right depict six out of 24 groups of emotions. The participant can learn more about a selected emotion group in the emotions library (top left), where there is a definition of each emotion in the group together with visual, voice and situational examples. The participant can test their knowledge in the quiz centre (bottom left) or use it for games (bottom right). (Jessica Kingsley Publishers)

The evidence base for *Mind Reading*

This approach is fairly new and has received relatively little evaluation. However, Golan and colleagues have employed RCTs to evaluate the efficacy of the intervention for both adults and children (Golan and Baron-Cohen, 2006; 2008). For an adult group with high-functioning autism, the findings showed some improvement in the participants' ability to recognise emotions within the set presented in the software. However, there was little evidence of generalisation to more naturalistic emotion recognition situations beyond the software. More encouraging results were provisionally reported for a group of high-functioning children. In this case, the emotion recognition skills apparently generalised to novel stimuli; that is, the children were able to apply their newly learned skills to emotion examples they had not previously encountered.

■   Why is such generalisation so important?

☐   Each expression of an emotion is to some extent unique: a person's facial expression of happiness will vary from one situation and time to another; different individuals may express their happiness in different ways. The ability to recognise the common factor despite these variations is crucial if the intervention is to equip the individual with useful skills for everyday situations.

Activity 6.4 invites you to explore another interesting new intervention aimed at improving emotion recognition skills in young children – *The Transporters* DVD.

Activity 6.4   *The Transporters* DVD
Allow 20 minutes for this activity

Take some time to look up the website that demonstrates how this works. Make some notes on the elements of *The Transporters* that might make it a useful intervention for children on the autism spectrum. Comments are at the end of the book.

6.5.1   Summary of Section 6.5

* Interventions aimed at developing socio-cognitive skills are especially suitable for more able children on the autism spectrum, and in some cases for adults.
* *Mind Reading* is a recently developed computer-based intervention designed to teach emotion recognition.
* *Mind Reading* builds on the claim that people on the autism spectrum are interested in computers and prefer highly systematised materials.
* Some randomised control trials suggest improvement in recognising the emotions depicted on the *Mind Reading* software.

6.6   Biological interventions

Despite the promising evidence for many psychosocial approaches, there is a school of thought (among some parents and professionals) that such interventions are not really tackling the underlying causes of the problems in autism. Since the role of biological factors in causing autism is in little doubt, it might seem that the most effective interventions will be biologically based. This echoes the common belief that medical or pharmacological intervention is the best way of treating many illnesses, diseases or conditions. In practice, therapeutic approaches targeted at biological functioning raise many problematic issues. Genetic and neuropsychological influences in autism are not reversible, given the current state of knowledge of medical science. Though studies in the field of molecular genetics, such as those described in Section 5.3, have begun to offer some insights into which genes might be involved, there is no immediate prospect of interventions that could reverse these effects. In addition, it is widely acknowledged that influences at the biological level are only part of a complex causal and developmental process. An effective biological therapy would need to intervene in this process from a very early stage.

6.6.1   Pharmacological interventions

Despite the lack of interventions for core biological influences, there are some widely used **pharmacological interventions** (i.e. those involving medicines and drugs) which play a helpful role in tackling symptoms that often accompany autism. For example, excessive hyperactivity and repetitive behaviours such as head banging need to be managed to avoid self-injury, and there is evidence that certain drugs may help to reduce these behaviours. Whilst behavioural techniques such as Lovaas are generally preferable for such behaviours, it may be necessary to prescribe drug treatments that influence brain functioning directly.

The evidence base for pharmacological interventions

It is important to grasp that these are not interventions developed specifically for autism, but rather treatments developed in the context of other conditions, which have been 'borrowed' because they appear to tackle a relevant problem area. As medical treatments, the safety and efficacy of these drug treatments will have been evaluated in the contexts for which they were first intended. In this sense, there will be a sound evidence base for these treatments. But evaluating such treatments specifically as an intervention for the symptoms in autism is a more complex process, requiring collaboration between specialists in clinical medicine and pharmacology, as well as experts specialising in the psychology and biology of autism. In this sense, the evidence base is very limited. In the UK, there are no drugs that are specifically licensed to be used for people with autism, and in fact very few are specifically recommended for use with children or adolescents. Any beneficial effects that are observed must be weighed against the quite serious side effects that may occur.

Risperidone

A medication used to treat psychosis, risperidone has been used in low doses to alleviate aggression and self-injury in people with autism. A couple of studies have suggested some short-term benefits in reducing these negative behaviours in children, although the effects tended not to continue after the medication was ceased. Side effects associated with risperidone use include tiredness, increased appetite and weight gain. Some children have shown raised levels of prolactin, a hormone primarily involved in producing breast milk, following risperidone treatment, but it is not known whether this has any harmful consequences for children.

Methylphenidate

Methylphenidate, also known by the brand name Ritalin, is a stimulant that is widely used in the treatment of attention-deficit hyperactivity disorder (ADHD). Methylphenidate has been used with children with autism, including those with ADHD as a co-morbid condition (see Box 1.1). It has been found to have some positive effects in reducing hyperactivity and increasing attention. One pilot study of the short-term effects of methylphenidate on children's social communication skills found that it appeared to increase the frequency of joint attention in children with autism. Side effects include sleeping difficulties, reduced appetite, irritability, hypersensitivity, dermatitis and dizziness.

Melatonin

Melatonin is a naturally occurring hormone that is primarily involved in the regulation of the 'body clocks' of humans and animals. Melatonin is often prescribed as a means of treating insomnia and other sleep problems. Some research suggests that people with autism, as well as their parents, may have reduced levels of melatonin. Studies involving children with autism have shown some benefits in treating sleep problems, but further research is required in order to decide whether or not melatonin treatment should be recommended.

Antidepressants

One group of antidepressants, known as **selective serotonin re-uptake inhibitors (SSRIs)**, is believed to work by increasing the availability of the neurotransmitter serotonin, thought to be involved in mood regulation. The abnormal levels of serotonin sometimes detected in people with autism are also thought to play a role in hyperactivity and repetitive behaviours. There is some, though limited, evidence that the widely used SSRI fluoxetine (also known as Prozac) may help to alleviate these behaviours, but no evidence that it can reduce more specific autistic symptoms. Although the use of SSRIs may initially increase levels of serotonin, in the long term the effect is probably reversed, and early positive effects may eventually diminish. There are also great concerns about the range of side effects that accompany the use of these drugs, including weight gain, agitation, mood swings and liver damage.

Other biological interventions

In addition to drugs that are routinely used to treat psychiatric and mental health conditions, a number of other less well-established medical treatments have been used to treat children and adults with autism. Some of these have proved to be very controversial, possibly very hazardous and in some cases fatal. One such example is **chelation**, which involves injecting people with autism with agents that reduce the levels of certain heavy metals including lead and mercury. Other potentially dangerous biological treatments include testosterone regulation, immune globulin therapy and injection of secretin (a gastrointestinal hormone that stimulates digestion).

6.6.2 Diet-based intervention

Because of the high incidence of gastrointestinal problems in autism, diet-based interventions are very popular, particularly with the parents of children with autism. Dietary interventions may be additive, where individuals consume specific supplements such as minerals, vitamins, probiotics or essential fatty acids. Alternatively, diets may be restrictive, where certain substances, typically gluten (found in wheat-based products), casein (from cows'-milk-based products) and yeast, are avoided. Whilst some parents argue that dietary manipulation is extremely effective, systematic evaluations have tended to be inconclusive. One broad theoretical assumption informing these diets is that autism reflects the damaging effects of atypical metabolism (breakdown) of food substances on the brain. However, since such effects would occur early in development, they would not be readily reversed by a later change of diet.

6.6.3 Summary of Section 6.6

- There are currently no biologically based interventions that address 'core' difficulties in autism.

- Some pharmacological substances may be helpful in alleviating symptoms such as self-harming and repetitive behaviours and sleep problems.

- Evidence for the positive effects of such medications must be weighed against harmful side effects.

- Dietary interventions are popular with some parents, but evaluations are inconclusive.

6.7 Intervention in practice

Given that many different approaches appear to have some degree of evidence supporting their effectiveness, how do parents and professionals decide which particular intervention is most appropriate for an individual child or family member? As you will realise, the individual needs of people on the autism spectrum differ enormously, depending on the range and severity of their difficulties, age, intellectual ability, life situation, their own coping strategies and whether they have any co-morbid medical conditions. All of these factors play an important role in deciding what interventions, if any, should be used. Some high-functioning individuals and their families understandably reject the idea that intervention is necessary or appropriate. Other families will go to great lengths to secure the particular intervention that they think is best for their child, even when the evidence that it works is unclear. Especially in the case of dietary interventions, they may argue forcibly that the approach has benefits for their own child, even if it does not work for others. Some of the less conventional interventions that are enthusiastically promoted by some parents and certain professionals are:

- animal-assisted therapies (including those involving horses, dogs and dolphins)

- auditory integration training

- coloured filters

- facilitated communication
- light-wave stimulation
- restricted environmental stimulation therapy
- sensory integrative (integration) therapy.

Parents need to feel that they are doing everything that they can for their child, but they may place too much credence in the benefits of these unusual, and in some cases harmful, approaches. The best guideline remains that of practice grounded in a sound evidence base. Authoritative sources, such as the Research Autism database, indicate that the evidence base for these unconventional approaches is absent or unclear. Activity 6.5 invites you to find out what each approach involves.

Activity 6.5   Unconventional therapies: the evidence base

Allow 20 minutes for this activity

Use the Autism Research website to find out a little about each of these interventions. Are there any that you think merit further evaluation? Comments are at the end of the book.

For many families, decisions about interventions will be a matter of teamwork with the professionals, including teachers, speech and language therapists, psychologists and medical specialists. In these cases, there will be scope to consider a range of choices, and frequently to use several approaches in combination. A child may need a psychosocial intervention for behavioural problems, as well as medication to control epilepsy.

Most schools, units and classes attended by children with autism, as well as most services providing for adults with autism, could be described as having an **eclectic approach**. This means that they will base their practice on a range of different specific interventions and general approaches. For example, many classrooms in autism-specific schools have TEACCH boards, and non-verbal children in these classrooms may use PECS in order to communicate. When teaching some skills, such as sitting at the table, dressing or using the toilet independently, or dealing with unwanted behaviour, the teachers may use behavioural techniques, and during free play and unstructured activities a child-centred approach may be used. In these cases it is important that, as new teachers come into the school, they are trained on the approaches that are in place.

Finally, throughout this chapter, you will have noticed that intervention and education are closely intertwined. Given that autism and its variants are pervasive developmental conditions, it is inevitable that the problems that arise affect the individual at school just as much as other aspects of life. This theme is further developed in the next chapter.

6.7.1   Summary of Section 6.7

- People on the autism spectrum and their families vary enormously in terms of their needs, and in the type of intervention that might be most appropriate for them.

- Decisions about intervention depend on a range of factors, including personal choice and local availability.

- In many cases schools and other services use an eclectic approach, and many use approaches for which there is no formal evidence base.

6.8   Learning outcomes

6.1   Define and use, or recognise definitions and applications of, each of the terms printed in **bold** in the text.

6.2   Outline the broad principles of evidence-based practice.

6.3   Describe the basic principles of a range of psychosocial interventions, including both comprehensive and specifically focused approaches.

6.4   Explain the concept of the continuum of psychosocial approaches from adult-directed behavioural to child-centred developmental–pragmatic interventions.

6.5   Comment on some of the issues involved in the use of pharmacological and other biological treatments for children and adults with autism.

6.6   Comment on the evidence base for each of the approaches discussed.

6.9   Self-assessment questions for Chapter 6

Question 6.1   (LOs 6.2, 6.3 and 6.6)

Briefly describe three of the most widely used interventions other than Lovaas for children or adults who are on the autism spectrum. To what degree have these interventions been demonstrated to be effective?

Question 6.2   (LO 6.4)

What are the main differences between adult-directed approaches and child-centred approaches?

Question 6.3   (LO 6.5 and 6.6)

To what extent can pharmacological interventions be considered effective in the treatment of people on the autism spectrum?

Chapter 7   Education

Chris Barson

The author expresses grateful thanks to the National Autistic Society for use of background material for this chapter, and to Ilona Roth for all her help in structuring and elucidating the ideas in this chapter.

7.1   Introduction

Education is an area of daily life where children on the autism spectrum often face profound difficulties. This chapter deals with the kinds of challenges that autism poses, and how these may be addressed. Section 7.2 outlines the implications of the main psychological features of autism for education, and some of the strategies that may be employed to overcome them in the classroom. Section 7.3 considers what educational provision is available for people on the autism spectrum, the framework of legislation in which this is set, and the choices (and sometimes lack of choices) that this offers individuals and their parents. This section also discusses what is meant by inclusion in education, and provides an example of how this has been implemented in a particular educational setting. Finally, Section 7.4 discusses the features of two 'whole school' approaches to educating children on the autism spectrum.

The key issues highlighted by this chapter are generic, but the specific details of educational provision are based on the example of the UK educational system. Educational provision for children with autism elsewhere in the world varies very widely. The range of educational provision and options in the USA and in some European countries is comparable to that in the UK, though shaped by the specific system of schooling in the country concerned. However, in many parts of the world, there is little or no autism-specific educational provision. This is taken up again in Chapter 9.

7.2   Educational implications of autism

Earlier chapters discussed a range of difficulties experienced by children and young people on the autism spectrum which, in varying degrees, are likely to influence learning and intellectual development. First-hand accounts like these below confirm the difficulties that the person with autism may experience at school. The first extract comes from the autobiography of the writer and artist Donna Williams (see Figure 7.1).

> At primary school my teachers found me unable to stay in my seat, constantly chatting to myself, singing or fiddling with something.
>
> *(Williams, 2003, p. 52)*

Figure 7.1   Donna Williams as a child. (Donna Williams)

> I hate it when people point something out to me that they think I will find interesting … I can never see it. But I can see the really boring things straight away.
>
> *(Young person on the autism spectrum,* A is for Autism, *Channel 4, 1992)*

This section looks further at some of the main areas of difficulty experienced by children on the spectrum at school. However, it would be inappropriate to focus solely on the difficulties. Autism brings with it its own set of preferences, interests and strengths. This chapter will also take a look at how teachers might harness these characteristic features of autism to support and enhance learning.

7.2.1 The physical and sensory environment and autism

When you look at a photograph of a typical classroom (Figure 7.2), you probably see a busy, colourful, information-rich learning environment, but for children with autism, sometimes these are the very things that prove to be barriers to learning.

Figure 7.2 A typical primary classroom. (Peter Titmuss/Alamy)

■ Given the difficulties discussed in Chapter 3, can you think of visual and auditory features of a typical classroom that might be distracting or disturbing for a child on the spectrum?

☐ Visual problems: brightly coloured objects and decor; bright lighting; the movement of other students. Auditory problems: the noise of students talking and moving about; the whirring or buzzing of electronic systems; sounds from adjacent rooms/activities.

The normal use of colour in the classroom to attract or excite a child's attention might have an overpowering effect for visually hypersensitive children on the autism spectrum. The presence of patterned flooring or walls might also be a visual 'stimulator' for some children, which will compete for their attention. See Figure 7.3.

> A patterned carpet or wallpaper floods my senses and shuts down a lot of my ability to understand … I felt like my connection to my body was being wiped out by the overload.

> *(Williams, 2006, p. 97)*

Figure 7.3 The carpet and decorated shelf ends in this school library might both act as sources of distraction or overstimulation for a child with autism. (Purestock/ Alamy)

It is common practice to decorate the classroom with examples of students' work from previous projects. This can be problematic for children on the autism spectrum at two levels. Besides the sensory overload created by too much colour, they may also find it hard to discriminate between the words or images that are part of the current lesson and those that are remaining displays of past work. The same thing happens with whiteboards, which often show the remnants of words from a previous session. Most typically developing children and young people know these are not part of what is being taught here and now. Many children with autism are unable to screen out irrelevant and competing data like this.

- ■ Which of the psychological theories discussed in Chapter 4 has most relevance to these problems?

□   Difficulty in deciding which elements belong to the current topic may reflect weak central coherence (see Section 4.6).

The movement of other students in a busy classroom, or at break times, can be hard for children with autism to process (Blake et al., 2003). People with autism often say that they see other people's movement as quite random or without meaning. It could even scare very sensitive young children. If you have difficulty interpreting other people's gestures and movement, dynamic places like the average primary classroom could be very confusing or even frightening.

Evidence suggests that noise levels in classrooms are often far in excess of the optimal conditions for understanding speech. Poor acoustics and 'noisy' activities could make for very difficult conditions for both hearing-impaired children and those with hypersensitive hearing. People with Asperger syndrome or high-functioning autism may have a specific problem hearing speech sounds against a background of other speech sounds (Alcantara, 2004). Specific sounds, quite imperceptible to most people (e.g. the ticking of a radiator, the 'buzz' of fluorescent lighting), might cause distraction or discomfort to children and young people on the spectrum. Touch sensitivity can make some fairly ordinary classroom experiences, such as sitting with other children on the carpet, intolerable for children on the spectrum (Figure 7.4). The texture of the carpet or the proximity of other children during a simple 'story time' session may be too much to bear.

Figure 7.4   The feel of the carpet, and the physical proximity of other children, as in this class session, may be upsetting or intolerable for a child on the spectrum. (Stock Connection Blue/Alamy)

Not being able to take part in these group activities might emphasise the aloneness or 'oddness' of a child on the spectrum. Teachers and other staff need to be aware that putting too much pressure on the young person to conform or join in, may result in sensory overload and panic in that person.

> Rowan loves art but he hates wearing a shirt to protect his clothing – the feeling of the fabric against his skin causes him distress. We have agreed with his school that he can wear a loose-fitting apron instead.

> *(A parent, NAS, 2009)*

Exploring materials and their properties in art, science and food technology lessons might also be hampered by sensory difficulties. Sometimes just the idea of touching something when the child can't predict what it will feel like can induce panic. For children who are hypersensitive to smell, their senses can be overwhelmed by 'school smells' such as those of cleaning materials, food preparation, science materials or even the smell of other children.

It is easy for neurotypical people to assume that children will get used to these sensory experiences given enough time and exposure, but for many children on the autism spectrum this doesn't happen. In the DVD *Sensory Challenges and Answers* (2000), Temple Grandin described an incredibly slow adjustment and habituation to sensory stimuli, which she experienced as painful.

7.2.2   The curricular environment

A child's level of intellectual disability will determine how much the curriculum needs to be differentiated and adapted to their individual needs. It will also inform the way the child is assessed and the setting of appropriate goals and attainment levels.

Children on the autism spectrum may find it very hard to engage with, or be motivated by, aspects of the curriculum that do not match their special interests. A child who loves science topics and is vocal and engaged in those classes might be very hard to manage in other subject classes and present with behaviour problems and poor attention.

The focus on attainment and competition within academic and sporting activities sometimes isolates children on the spectrum. If you have very little sense of competition or of out-scoring your fellow students, this aspect of school experience is hard to make sense of. Some children on the spectrum don't know what 'top of the class' means or why you would want to be there. Others can have problems because they desire to achieve 100% in activities or tests and react angrily or get excessively disappointed when they don't achieve this. This can make even simple tasks such as colouring a picture hard to complete – a child's need for perfection may prevent them from starting or completing the task in case, for instance, they go over the lines with their pencil or crayon.

The more abstract areas of the curriculum (as opposed to fact-based ones) may prove especially challenging for the student on the autism spectrum. For instance, several of the psychological difficulties in autism may have an impact on tasks and assignments such as creating an original piece of writing.

- ■ What difficulties might (a) executive function impairment, (b) theory of mind impairment and (c) lack of imagination create for writing a story?

- ☐ (a) Executive functioning difficulties make planning such a piece of writing difficult (e.g. when, where, who, what happens, how it ends). (b) Impaired theory of mind might mean that the student doesn't see the point of telling the reader or teacher something if they 'know it already', or might have difficulty constructing a fictional narrative involving human characters. (c) Lack of imagination would make it difficult to generate original or novel ideas.

Other tasks that require the student to organise materials independently, follow a sequence and produce an end-product can also be hampered by executive functioning difficulties.

- ■ What aspects of such tasks are likely to cause difficulties?

- ☐ Planning ahead, setting aside the right amount of time, knowing what materials or resources are needed, where to start and how to decide when the task is completed.

Executive function difficulties may also affect everyday skills such as getting ready for school, navigating around a large school campus, and getting to class on time. Even practical projects in craft or design and technology lessons – for instance, making a simple wooden bird-box – involve complex planning for a child on the autism spectrum:

> When do I sand the wood, after I have cut it or when it's all pieced together?

> I won't be able to work on some aspects of the project until *after* the glue is dry. This could take a whole day. What could I do while I'm waiting?

> Sealing the inside of the bird-box will be impossible once it is all fixed together.

Students on the spectrum also get very anxious about even small changes to their routine or where a lesson or learning activity takes place. Inflexible thinking may make it difficult to cope with change and transitions, and lack of imagination may make preparing for a new experience very challenging for the young person. Even able students may need a specialised approach to help them organise tasks, work to completion, pick up new tasks and work independently. The structured teaching and structured communication approaches collectively known as TEACCH (and described in Section 6.3.1) are aimed at precisely these problems. Figure 7.5 is an example of a student's individual timetable designed to support a student with curricular and school activities. It's an example of a real planner from the Robert Ogden School, a large National Autistic Society (NAS) school and children's home for children and young people with autism spectrum diagnoses. Notice that the planner specifies IEP targets. An **IEP** or **Individual Education Plan** specifies short-term targets and strategies, tailored to the educational needs of an individual child.

ACTIVITY	NOTES
Patrick's planner	*Tuesdays - Autumn Term*
Registration activity	Today is Tuesday. Read your planner to check your day
English	Working from *English Alive* book (IEP Target) 
Break	Choice time 
Maths	Community based learning activity (IEP Target) 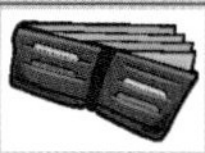
Lunch	Today lunch will be in the leisure area
PE	Aerobics (Inclusion Target) 
Break	Make yourself a drink
History	Inclusion Target: 20 minutes with Mr Subramanian (Subject Teacher) 
Review	Did you eat lunch with Edgar today? What book are you reading?
Club	Board game with Srishti in your room 
Home	Your taxi driver is Pauline

Figure 7.5 A child's individual planner. (Based on source material provided by Gillian Roberts, Principal, Robert Ogden School, South Yorkshire, UK; Photos: PhotoEuphoria/iStockphoto; Vikram Raghuvananshi/iStockphoto)

- In what ways does the planner provide support for the special difficulties in autism?

☐ It provides *specific* details of the activities that will take place, including small visual illustrations for clarity; for some activities locations and people are specified.

Besides educational and curricular targets, it specifies 'social' targets about mixing with other children, or developing life skills such as the use of money (signified by the wallet against Maths).

It schedules time in which the child does difficult tasks such as working with less familiar students and teachers, or reflecting on what he/she has done (see 'Review').

It includes a session where the child must make a choice between activities.

Some change is scheduled in (the lunch session is not *always* in the same place), though the details are sufficiently specific for the child to act on them.

■   Some elements of the programme are deliberately not as specific as others. Why do you think this is?

☐   It's important that the child learns to cope with activities where not every piece of information is available beforehand. For example, the planner says 'make a drink', but not what *kind* of drink. So the student has to make a choice. For a less confident student, it might offer a specific choice.

Exams are stressful for all children and young people (Figure 7.6). With a bit of preparation, typically developing children can understand what the exam will be like, and how to give of their best. Students on the autism spectrum might have huge difficulties coping with pre-exam anxieties, since the outcome is uncertain. In the exam hall itself, they may take considerable time to adjust to the size, scale and unfamiliarity of the environment. Understanding the rubric for the test, imagining what the examiner wants you to write and knowing where your strengths and weaknesses lie, are all prerequisites for exam success. In all of these areas, students with autism face more of a challenge.

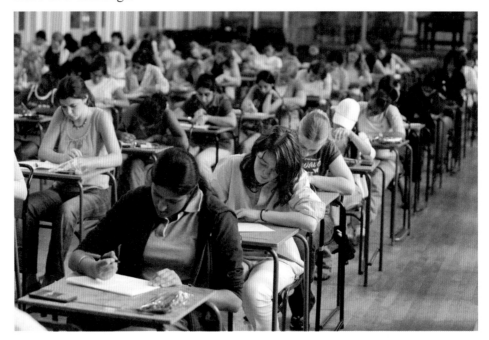

Figure 7.6   A typical exam hall. (Andrew Fox/Alamy)

In Box 7.1 a teacher describes in her own words how she helped a student with Asperger syndrome prepare for his exams (adapted from NAS, 2009 – advice on education).

Box 7.1 Supporting a student with Asperger syndrome

I have been teaching a student with Asperger syndrome for an AS (advanced level qualification) in Information and Communication Technology. When the student started, I noted that as soon as he came across a question on an exam paper that he couldn't answer he would clam up and get very frustrated, making him unable to answer the rest of the questions on the paper. I explained to him that the order was not important and although he accepted this point, he said he couldn't ignore order in an exam.

With his support tutor we cut up the exam paper and allowed him to sort the questions into three piles CAN DO, THINK and NO. The result was a significant improvement in his achievement, but the exam board would not allow us to do this. I spent ages racking my brains for another solution; colour coding with pens, using a traffic light system. Green for CAN DO, then orange for THINK and red for NO. He would then answer all the questions marked green first, then the orange and then the red. The effect of this method was that he was actually able to answer some of the red questions as well. This had a considerable effect on achievement and gave him confidence in exams; instead of going in worried, he was calm and composed. I developed other strategies for helping him deal with answering questions since he found the questions vague (however, they were expecting him to apply knowledge and he has difficulty in doing this).

7.2.3   The social environment

Teaching methods in schools increasingly make use of group work, discussion and team activities. These pedagogic styles place children with autism at a particular disadvantage. A more traditional 'chalk and talk' approach may work better for children on the autism spectrum. Memorising a list of presented facts and reproducing them may be easier than researching a topic and presenting the results.

Life skills, including understanding relationships and sexuality, physical, emotional and sexual health, are part of the modern curriculum of the 21st century.

■   Difficulties in theory of mind and imagination may make these topics particularly difficult for the young person on the autism spectrum, calling for a different teaching style and adaptation of the materials and presentation. How should the teacher go about this?

☐ The materials should be adapted to be more 'concrete' and explicit, providing specific examples of scenarios and detailed illustrations of outcomes so that the young person understands the implications and consequences.

School not only prepares young people for qualifications, employment and a career, it also develops independence and promotes friendship and social development. Chapter 4 discussed how a lack of theory of mind can undermine the development of skills necessary for social interaction. Some children on the autism spectrum would like to have friends and to participate in joint activities but find it difficult to grasp the rules of interaction or play. Friendships seem to them to be something that other children acquire and maintain by some invisible process. Other children on the spectrum have little or no social motivation, either because they don't understand or value the possibilities that other people represent, or because of negative experiences in the past.

> What really seems to throw people is that they can't seem to understand that a six-year-old boy who knows all the planets in the solar system and who can already subtract five from three may not yet have worked out that it is inappropriate to climb in the dust-bins during play time.

> *(Marc Segar,* The Battles of the Autistic Thinker*)*

Unstructured periods such as breaks and mealtimes are often dreaded by students with autism because of their difficulty in imagining things they could do, and lack of social awareness distances them from the games and conversations of others. Unusual behaviours and social naivety can earn them the tag of 'weird' or 'strange'. Unfortunately, the more anxious a young person gets, the more their social awkwardness may increase. Ritualistic and stereotyped behaviour may be a way of coping with anxiety and stress, yet tends to attract more attention and ridicule.

> I knew I was odd, I knew I was different. I had an odd way of flapping my hands when I was tensed up … and kids don't like kids that are different.

> *(Young man on the autism spectrum, in* A is for Autism*, 1992)*

The problems may heighten during adolescence. At this time the need to blend in, and be 'cool' may come to a head. Whether it is wearing the 'right kind' of trainers, liking the 'right kind' of pop music or knowing who is 'in' or 'out' of the gang are socially desirable skills for many teenagers. Unfortunately, young men and women with autism find this aspect of teenage life almost impossible, should they have the desire to play along in the first place. Moreover, sensory problems can make loud music, noisy school social activities and the physical/contact aspects of activities such as sports and drama too much to bear.

Recent research has shown that **bullying** is a major problem in schools and particularly for children on the autism spectrum. Bullying can take on many forms, including name-calling, physical violence or social isolation. According to a survey by the NAS, two in five children across the whole autism spectrum have been bullied (Batten et al., 2006). The rate for Asperger syndrome or high-functioning autism considered alone is even higher, with nearly three in five parents reporting that their children have been bullied at school. This may be an underestimate: a previous study had found that over 90% of parents of children with Asperger syndrome reported that their child has been the target of bullying in the past year (Little, 2002).

The negative effects of bullying may include low self-esteem, mental health problems, and poor performance academically (Figure 7.7). 83% of parents whose child was bullied reported that their child's self-esteem was damaged, and three-quarters reported that bullying affected their child's development of social skills and relationships. 56% of parents said that it has caused their child to miss school or even change schools.

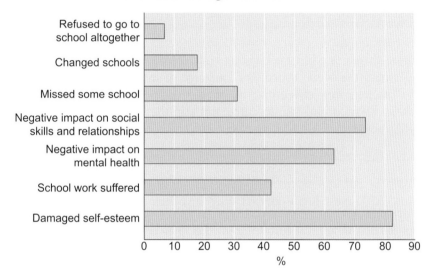

Figure 7.7 Bar chart illustrating the impact of bullying on children with autism. Each horizontal bar represents the percentage of parents reporting a specific negative effect of bullying on their child. (Reid and Batten, 2006)

7.2.4   The communication and language environment

■ From the material in Section 3.3, what aspects of difficulty in language and communication have implications for learning in school?

☐ For the child with severely impaired language, even understanding simple instructions may be a challenge. For more high-functioning children with better language skills, the main difficulties will lie in:

- interpreting non-literal instructions
- matching expressive language to the context, setting or topic
- understanding sarcasm, irony and jokes
- understanding non-verbal communication such as facial expression, eye contact and gesture.

Box 7.2 (overleaf) illustrates some of the language and communication difficulties that can occur.

> **Box 7.2 Juan**
>
> Juan is a nine-year-old student in a mainstream primary school. He has a lot of difficulties with staff because he often appears cheeky or rude. This is unintentional as he doesn't really understand the social context of language or the impact of what he says on other people. When things get too much for him, Juan will often run away. Recently, a teacher who was giving chase appealed to him, 'Stop running Juan, I'm too old to keep chasing you!' To which he replied, 'Well you should retire then'. When, after a short break from school, he was asked in a cheery way, 'Hello again Juan, what have you been up to?', he replied, 'Spitting'.

As this example shows, a child may appear rude or cheeky because he or she does not understand the social aspects of language or interprets what is said very literally. Teachers may exacerbate things by hiding instructions within a question such as: 'Would you like to come and join the group?' or 'Do you think that [your behaviour] is a good idea?'

■   Why might this create difficulty for a child on the autism spectrum?

☐   The child may not understand that this is really an instruction rather than a question. An honest literal answer may lead them into further trouble!

One intervention that is helpful for children like Juan is **Social Stories**. Each Social Story provides a description of a social situation written in the first person (as if from the perspective of the child), and in a concrete style and format. The story includes sufficient detail for the child to recognise the situation when it actually occurs, and examples of the appropriate kind of response to make. Other information might include details of how the child might feel in the situation, and how his/her response might affect others. The idea is that the child rehearses the story ahead of time, with an adult. When a comparable situation occurs, the child can then use the story to help guide his or her behaviour.

This approach might be very useful for explaining in a concrete way what phrases such as 'I'm getting too old for this' might mean in the context in which they were used, i.e. 'I'm not angry with you Juan, I just want you to stop – I want to help'.

■   What other techniques might a teacher use to help children like Juan?

☐   The teacher might do some teaching around the different meanings a phrase can have, perhaps asking children to match picture or word cards to a phrase written on the whiteboard or on a worksheet.

Pragmatic understanding of instructions in typically developing children is aided by the inflexion, tone of voice and facial expression that the speaker uses. Again, these are aspects of non-verbal communication from which children with autism may take little meaning. Their own language style, word choice or tone can also be unusual and this can be the source of teasing by other students. It is quite common for children with autism to assume odd accents or to adopt the language style of a favourite TV show or film. Some high-functioning children have a pedantic or very formal way of speaking which may mask some fundamental gaps in their understanding. As you saw in Section 3.3, complex sentence structures do not necessarily imply that a child has a full grasp of meaning.

When teachers rely predominantly on spoken language to give instructions or provide feedback on a child's work or behaviour, the risk is that the child misses much of the information. This might result in poor performance of a task or the failure to correct something the teacher has drawn attention to. Children and young people with autism, including more able students, respond far better when verbal communication is supported by pictorial, symbolic or written forms of communication such as PECS, described in Section 6.4.2.

7.2.5 The impact of medical difficulties

As you have seen, certain medical conditions, though not part of the diagnostic criteria, frequently accompany autism as co-morbid features. Epilepsy affects at least a third of children with classic autism by the time they reach adolescence (see Section 5.1 for relevant studies). Some types of seizure result in unusual behaviours such as smacking lips, wandering off or removing items of clothing. If teaching staff are unaware of the source of these behaviours, they may respond inappropriately. In generalised seizures (involving all parts of the brain), there will be a deeper loss of consciousness ranging from short 'absences' through to complete loss of consciousness, falling to the ground, muscular contractions and jerking. If a child is incontinent or sick during this seizure, they will need time out of class to deal with it. It's not unusual to need sleep after a seizure and it might be a while before someone who has experienced a seizure can rejoin the class. Other children might view the child as odd or even frightening and this might affect social development or lead to bullying. A school may feel that the child needs placement outside the mainstream as a result of their medical needs. Medication to control seizures may also lead to tiredness, loss of concentration, weight gain and changes to physical appearance. Other co-morbid difficulties include gastrointestinal problems and poor bowel or bladder control. Teachers will need to adapt and differentiate their teaching for these specific difficulties, and to be vigilant for bullying.

7.2.6 Assessing children's educational needs

Identification and diagnosis in preschool children is improving. However, a substantial number of children on the autism spectrum arrive at primary school with no diagnosis and, because of its more subtle presentation, Asperger syndrome may not be identified until adolescence. Diagnosis is useful provided it also gives access to educational resources and support. Diagnostic assessment must therefore be followed by a more practical assessment of the individual child's educational support needs in terms of speech, language and communication, behaviour, intellectual ability and any medical problems.

Often a child or young person's difficulties will not be immediately obvious to a teacher. If teaching staff are not sufficiently aware of the core features of autism, they may not recognise the true reasons for a child's behaviour:

> The fact that I am well-spoken, and my condition isn't obvious worked against me being understood, when my behaviour may have been put down to obstinacy, deviancy, pure eccentricity, or by school peers as being 'mental'.

(From Beardon and Edmonds, 2007, p. 50)

Without appropriate assessment and 'signposting', teaching staff will not always know the best way to approach a child's difficulties. Also children with autism often have a very uneven profile of skills and abilities. An uninitiated teacher may find it baffling that a child or young person can memorise the whole of the bus, tram and train timetable for a large city but can't make a simple sandwich or get dressed in the morning.

It is often felt by parents and young people themselves that if the exact nature of their difficulties had been recognised earlier, then it might have led to better outcomes:

By 'statemented' the authors mean a Statement of Special Educational Needs (see Case Study 2.1 and Section 7.3.3).

> I had been statemented at the age of 5 years for speech and language difficulties, communication problems and irrational fears but the doctors did not want to label me so it was not until the new special needs head at school was appointed that steps were taken to seek a diagnosis. If a diagnosis was made earlier I may have received more help at school.

(From Beardon and Edmonds, 2007, p. 25)

- Do you think that early assessment, identification and intervention necessarily lead to better outcomes in school?

- The 'labelling' that comes with diagnosis and assessment might lower people's expectations of a child, which could damage his or her progress. Having a diagnosis also increases the risk of teasing and bullying, with the possible result that the child finds school even more difficult.

Ofsted is the body that inspects standards in schools in England. Comparable inspection bodies with different names operate in Wales, Scotland and Northern Ireland.

In 2006, **Ofsted** reported that despite formal assessment of the type of interventions children or young people needed, there was inadequate evaluation of the progress and outcomes following intervention. So the beneficial impact of these interventions was less than it should have been (Ofsted, 2006).

7.2.7 Working with the positives

As you saw in Sections 4.6 and 4.7, a number of autism experts now see the psychological characteristics of autism as a cognitive profile involving strengths as well as weaknesses.

- Can you think of some areas of strength that may be advantageous for the child in educational settings?

☐ The child or young person:

- is likely to persevere, even where the topic may seem tedious to others
- is accurate and sees things in detail
- has powerful, detailed memories (often for things that other people have forgotten)
- likes patterns, systems, lists or sequences of things
- likes collecting.

The implication of this 'difference not deficit' view of autism is that there is no such thing as a 'wrong' learning style – just methods of teaching that are either well-matched to that style or not.

7.2.8 The autism-friendly school

An increasing number of authors refer to an **autism-friendly school** – an educational environment that works with and around the special difficulties in autism and their implications for schooling. Definitions of an 'autism-friendly school' and indeed an 'autism-friendly Local Education Authority' are set out for England in guidelines for good practice (DfES, 2002).

Box 7.3 summarises some key characteristics of an autism-friendly school.

Comparable guidelines in other parts of the UK include 'The Autism Toolbox', a resource commissioned by the Scottish government to provide guidance for schools and local authorities.

Box 7.3 Recommended features of an autism-friendly school

- An explicit and regularly updated policy on working with the autism spectrum
- Regular training and briefing for staff concerning their knowledge about and responsibilities for autism spectrum difficulties, and the needs of individual children
- A specialised staff member to provide leadership and guidance, and a point of contact for children who need help and support
- Liaison and close collaboration with parents and families
- Effective communication with local health, education and social services regarding individual children and changes in policy and practice
- A regularly updated database about the autism spectrum for staff and families
- Curriculum adapted to the needs and strengths of individual children
- Adaptations to the physical environment of the school
- Measures to ensure smooth transition for children moving on (e.g. to different schools or post-school situations).

Notice that these are general guidelines applicable to all the different settings in which children on the autism spectrum may be educated. The next section looks at the range of educational provision that is available, the need for children's educational experience to be as inclusive as possible, and the degree of choice that is available to parents.

7.2.9 Summary of Section 7.2
- The educational difficulties faced by a child on the autism spectrum can be considered in terms of four environments: physical and sensory; curricular; social; language and communication.
- To address each individual child's specific difficulties requires a thorough assessment of their support needs and monitoring of how well these are implemented.
- Working with the positive attributes of autism and promoting 'autism-friendly' schools are increasingly common responses to education for children on the autism spectrum.

7.3 The profile of provision, inclusion and parental choice

If you went to school with someone on the autism spectrum, or are on the spectrum yourself, you may recall that fitting in and being accepted was a challenge. If you are over 50 your memories will probably be different. Before the concept of special educational needs (see Case Study 2.1) was embodied in UK law, many children with autism didn't attend regular schools, and some children were put in long-stay hospitals.

With a spectrum such as autism a 'one size fits all' approach to education provision is not feasible. Thus in most parts of the UK, a range of education solutions have evolved to try to meet the specific learning needs of children and young people across the autism spectrum. For instance, in England, provision covers a spectrum from mainstream schools, to units or special classes within mainstream schools, to special schools. Moreover, a sizeable number of children with autism in both the UK and the USA are home-educated.

The profile of provision to be described here has many UK-wide features. But there are also differences among the different UK countries. Scotland, for instance, has a different system of education from England, which has an impact on the way educational provision for autism is organised.

7.3.1 What types of school are available?
Box 7.4 describes the different types of school available to children on the autism spectrum in the UK, but note that in a given area, not all of these will necessarily be on offer.

Box 7.4 Types of school available to children on the autism spectrum (adapted from NAS, 2009 – see choosing a school)

Mainstream primary and secondary schools: some children do all their learning within regular classes; for others this is supplemented by extra support in the school for a set number of hours per week. Children on the autism spectrum are regularly educated in mainstream schools, although there are some children who need a more specialised approach and environment.

A base or unit within a mainstream school: some mainstream primary and secondary schools have separate classes for students on the autism spectrum within them. The students join classes in mainstream school when appropriate and are educated in the base or unit for the rest of the time.

Special schools: these are schools specifically for children and young people with special educational needs. Some are exclusively for students on the autism spectrum, while others cater for a range of special needs, including learning difficulties, physical difficulties, or a mixture of the two. Special schools typically provide for children with significant needs in relation to their autism, and for children with severe intellectual impairments and autism. Some children attend a special school part of the time and a mainstream school for the remainder. Others may move on to the mainstream after spending several years in a special school.

Residential schools: students stay overnight and have a 24-hour curriculum – meaning there is support available 24 hours a day. Some have a 52-week placement; others go home at weekends or during the holidays. Some residential schools specialise in the education and care of children on the autism spectrum right up to the age of 23 years. Like special schools, children placed in these schools will have significant care needs in relation to their autism.

Independent or non-maintained schools: these schools can be mainstream, special or residential, but are not funded by the local authority. Parents can choose to place their child at their own expense or to make representations to their local authority for a placement at an independent or non-maintained school. The National Autistic Society's schools would be a good example; these have charitable status and cater for children right across the autism spectrum.

Activity 7.1   Exploring educational provision for autism

Allow 30 minutes for this activity

Use the internet to try and find out about educational provision for children with autism in an area near you. In the UK this information is available via the Autism Services Directory. This is a directory of services and events for people on the autism spectrum, their families and people who work with them. It is hosted by the National Autistic Society and can be accessed from their website.

Within the different educational settings described in Box 7.4, children with autism will receive a variety of help and support including quite specialised interventions such as structured teaching (TEACCH – Section 6.3.1 and PECS – Section 6.4.2), Social Stories (Section 7.2.4) and behaviour modification following Lovaas-type principles (Section 6.3.2). They may also be allocated extra resources such as one-to-one support from a **Learning Support Assistant** or **Teaching Assistant**. These are support staff who work alongside teachers in the classroom, helping students to progress in their learning.

7.3.2   The concept of inclusion

Inclusion is a term that has two different but related meanings. In one sense, it expresses the ethical aspiration that no child should be discriminated against in terms of their educational opportunities: children with a disability should have exactly the same rights and be valued in the same way as other children. More specifically, inclusion often refers to the right of a child to be educated in their own community and alongside children of that community. In this sense, inclusion is often used as a synonym for the mainstream.

■   Take a few minutes to reflect on these different meanings of inclusion. Are there other features of inclusion which should be added?

☐   Inclusion must mean being involved in the whole life of the school, whether it is a mainstream or specialised setting.

As a result of changes in English law in 2001, the **Department for Education and Skills (DfES)** strengthened the rights of students to mainstream placement:

> Schools supported by local education authorities and others should actively seek to remove the barriers to learning and participation that can hinder or exclude pupils with special educational needs.
>
> *(DfES, 2001, paragraph 7)*

Similarly, in Scotland, since the passing of the Standards in Scotland's Schools Act in 2000, there has been a presumption of mainstream education for all.

However, being in a mainstream school does not automatically mean that a child feels 'included'. If the term inclusion implies the opportunity to make friends and achieve academic or vocational potential, then a mainstream setting will not necessarily achieve inclusion for a child on the autism spectrum. A truly inclusive school is one where typically developing children learn from those with disabilities as well as vice versa. Simone Aspis, who describes herself as 'a special school survivor', offers the following definition:

> Inclusive education should create opportunities for all learners to work together. This requires recognition that learning is enhanced when individuals of different abilities, skills and aspirations can work together in a joint enterprise.

(Aspis, 2004, p. 129)

For those children for whom the mainstream setting does not deliver these broader goals of inclusion, education in a specialised setting may well provide a more inclusive experience. Decisions about a child's school and about how much support and help they will get are determined by a number of factors, which are discussed next.

7.3.3 Special needs and parent choice

As you have seen, the support needs of children with autism vary widely, depending on the nature and severity of their symptoms. In education, the needs of the individual child will depend on factors such as whether they have an intellectual disability, the severity of their communication difficulties, and the way their autism affects their learning and behaviour. Considering the range of educational options outlined in Box 7.3, it might seem that the more able children with high-functioning autism or Asperger syndrome will need less individual support, and therefore be more likely to study alongside typically developing children in the mainstream. In practice, some children with Asperger syndrome have as much need for special support as children with low-functioning autism.

When the special needs of a student are above those that a mainstream school can support within its normal framework, the local authority issues a Statement of Special Educational Needs. (In Scotland this type of statement has been superseded by Collaborative Support Plans or CSPs.) A Statement of SEN is a legally binding document which outlines a child's needs and how their local authority is going to meet them. A Statement may mean that the child receives extra help and support within the mainstream setting, or within a separate unit within the mainstream school. Alternatively, it may be decided that the child's needs are best met within a special school.

Some children with autism have a Statement of SEN before they start school. Others will go through the statementing process once they're in school and some do not have, or need, a Statement at all.

The Education Act of 1996 stipulated that, wherever possible, students should be educated in accordance with their parents' wishes. Decisions about the kind of education a child on the autism spectrum receives should ideally be made by a partnership of local authority, school and parents. However, the actuality will depend on factors such as whether the child has a Statement, and what options are locally available. When deciding which school to send their child to, parents may:

> *express a preference* for a maintained mainstream or special school
>
> *make a representation* for an independent or non-maintained mainstream or special school.

The difference is that if parents express a preference for a maintained school and it is refused, their local authority is required to prove that there is a valid reason for not sending a child to this type of school. In contrast, if the parents make a representation for an independent or non-maintained school that is refused, it is the parents who must prove that there is a strong case for their child attending that particular school, or type of school.

Surveys of parents suggest that there is sometimes insufficient choice and the Local Education Authority determines what is best. There is also lack of specialist placements for children with autism in their local area, both in special schools and in mainstream schools. In a recent survey by the NAS, parents who describe their children as being 'more able' or as having Asperger syndrome, were especially likely to feel that they had no say over what type of school their son or daughter attends:

> There were no special schools or units to meet the needs of such able yet disabled children. There were no meaningful choices, yet we are never away from the mainstream school with one issue or another.

> There is no suitable specialist provision for high-functioning autistic/ Asperger's children either within or anywhere near our borough. To try and get my son into such a provision further afield would mean a battle with the local authority to get funding and if we succeeded approximately two to three hours travelling a day.

> *(From Batten et al., 2006, p. 8)*

Other reports illustrate similar problems:

> [he was] simply informed at age 7 that he would have to attend a special school and that he could not be taught in a 'normal' junior school.

> *(From Beardon and Edmonds, 2007, p. 59)*

7.3.4 Exclusion

Children on the autism spectrum, and especially those with special educational needs, frequently have behavioural difficulties and other problems, which makes it difficult to accommodate their needs within the school setting that has been chosen for them. Recent estimates suggest that one in five children with autism experience **exclusion** from school, and a recent report by the NAS revealed that, of the children with autism who had been excluded, over two-thirds had been excluded more than once, and nearly one in four had been excluded permanently. 71% of parents said their local authority failed to put any support in place for their child whilst they were excluded.

Some of these problems are illustrated in Box 7.5.

Box 7.5   An experience of exclusion

What follows is part of the transcript of an interview with Sam who is 12 years old and has Asperger syndrome (Batten et al., 2006, p. 8). There are no specialist places for children with Asperger syndrome in Sam's local authority, and he is currently out of school.

Q   Why did you leave your last school?

Sam   Because they did not want to keep me ... Because I was too much trouble ... No the bullies were too much trouble. Going to other schools didn't work ... Because it was arranged quite quickly and it didn't work ... I feel that they should just get on with it ... I just want to go to a school, actually! The LEA [Local Education Authority] won't let me go into a mainstream school ... my theory is because we have failed at one mainstream school. On the other hand we have already failed at two specialist schools.

Q   How does it feel being out of school for a whole term?

Sam   I'm very frustrated. Well actually it is a bit more than a term. If you can call three lessons a day in the learning support room ... well I don't think it is actually an education.

Q   Would you like a school where there is more staff, maybe where the classes are smaller?

Sam   I dunno, I just want to go to a school.

Q   Would you like a school, where there are others like you?

Sam   Yes probably, but as I said, I just want to go to a school.

Q   If you could choose, what then?

Sam   Whichever one I could go to quicker!

Mum   It's a shocker isn't it, Sam?

Sam   Yes.

Mum   We will sort it out.

- What kind of effects might exclusion have on children on the autism spectrum?

- Being out of school might affect overall academic achievement, feelings of self-worth or the development of social skills. Parents of excluded children might not be able to put adequate supervision in place for them while they are out of school. It might place children on the autism spectrum at risk, e.g. getting involved in crime or antisocial behaviour.

7.3.5 Parent satisfaction

Factors such as how well staff are trained, and whether they are willing and able to understand children with autism, are obviously important in how satisfied parents are with placements. Whitaker (2007) conducted an extensive and thorough examination of parental satisfaction with mainstream provision. Parents who felt that school staff understood and empathised with their children's difficulties, and thought that the schools' responses to the children's needs were flexible, were much more likely to be satisfied with their child's school. 61% of parents reported themselves satisfied with the provision being made for their children. Those parents and carers who were dissatisfied (almost 40%) constitute a substantial minority with very real and often urgent concerns about the quality of provision being offered to their children.

Other factors such as poor communication between school and home, lack of flexibility in school rules, poorly differentiated curricular activities and bullying, are also cited by parents as influencing how satisfied they feel with a child's school.

7.3.6 Making inclusion work

In Box 7.6, Viv East, the coordinator for Special Educational Needs and Disabilities in Wolverhampton, gives her views on how to overcome the barriers to effective education for children on the autism spectrum, and make inclusion work.

Box 7.6 Educational provision for the autism spectrum in Wolverhampton (Viv East)

The feeling that you are part of a school, the feeling that you belong, is what is meant by inclusion.

(Warnock Report, 1978)

The City of Wolverhampton maintains a number of special schools, specialist units within mainstream schools and mainstream admissions. As in many authorities, the numbers of those diagnosed with autistic spectrum disorders doubled from 1992 to 2002, but now seems to be leveling off allowing for some strategic planning based on more reliable and robust data. This evidence, from research conducted by one of our local community paediatricians, has led us to rebuild, relocate and redesignate one of our special schools as a school specifically catering for the needs of children on the autism spectrum.

Our main aim is to meet the needs of the children and young people on the autism spectrum who are currently educated outside the city. We tend to be speaking here about the more challenging young people who do not fit comfortably into the mainstream, but who also may be considered 'too bright' for the traditional special school. Parents have made it clear that they would like their child(ren) to attend an autism-specific school

---

where the staff are experienced and/or qualified in dealing with the autism spectrum. The newly designated special school will be located alongside a mainstream secondary school that also has strong ties with a nearby primary school where we have opened a small resource base for children on the autism spectrum. This triangle of schools will open up options for the children and young people so that their individual needs can more readily be met in a variety of settings. In line with Removing Barriers to Achievement (DfES, 2004), the local authority has made best use of the expertise in the special schools to provide outreach services. The special school soon to be redesignated for children on the autism spectrum has already supported many schools across the city in developing understanding, knowledge and skills. This is part of the city's outreach strategy to ensure consistency in expectations, provision of support, recording of outcomes, and so on.

A familiar problem for anyone involved in special needs education is what to do about those schools that struggle to take on board the advice and support offered. Numerous studies indicate that one of the most important factors in ensuring all children feel included and that they belong to the school is the ethos. This is the human factor driven by personal experiences, motivation and feelings. To me this is one of the biggest challenges in making inclusion work for children with autism. Staff within a school must really value diversity rather than seeing it as a problem to address. Those of us at the strategic level can help by setting the example we expect to be set by our Heads and their senior management teams. Leadership is crucial at all levels not least by the local authority.

In Wolverhampton not everything has been fully achieved but there have been significant improvements in meeting the challenges to making inclusion work for children with autism. Besides the plans for schools and outreach services just outlined, our strategy includes a comprehensive training package, and accredited course for staff, a youth club and residential facilities for students, so that their families can have short breaks from caring for them.

■   How does this strategy seek to balance appropriate educational support for children on the spectrum with the need for inclusion?

☐   The provision of both a special school, and an autism resource base in the primary school, together with staff who are appropriately trained and motivated, ensures that children have the specialist support they need in a setting which embraces other children with similar needs. Physical proximity of the specialist and mainstream secondary schools should allow for some interaction between the children at each school, thus promoting a wider sense of inclusion.

7.3.7 Home education

So far this section has described the range of school settings for children on the autism spectrum, the measure of choice offered to parents, and the efforts that are being made to ensure a sense of inclusion. Yet a growing number of parents, in both the UK and the USA, opt to educate their children on the autism spectrum either partly or completely at home (Figure 7.8). For some parents this is a personal choice. However, other families highlight a lack of adequate provision for their child in the local area. Most are concerned that the school system can be inflexible, and struggles to respond to the individual needs of children with autism:

> My daughter became very distressed at school and her behaviour was appalling at home. After three years at school she still had no communication. Now, after four years of home education, she can talk in sentences, communicate and she is doing well academically.
>
> At the moment we don't home educate, but it is something we are seriously considering for next year (secondary) because there are no suitable placements in our county for high-functioning children with autism.
>
> *(From Batten et al., 2006, p. 11)*

■ Suggest some advantages of home education for children on the autism spectrum.

☐ Education at home can help relieve anxiety and stress and make learning much more effective, particularly given difficulties with social interaction and social communication, and the need for strong structure and routine in the day and environment. It also allows for control over the sensory environment.

Figure 7.8   Home education. For some parents this is the preferred option. Others may feel that they have no other choice. (AJ Photo/Science Photo Library)

One parent described home education as a 'life saver' and others refer to reduced anxiety and stress for them, their child and their siblings, improvements in their child's learning, behaviour, communication, and even mental health, when they begin educating at home. Parents may feel that they have no other choice and make the decision to home educate after much battling to get their child an appropriate education within the school system. It can be a costly decision for parents, who may give up paid employment and experience reduced circumstances and social contact as a result.

Dowty and Cowlishaw (2002) examined the experiences of parents in the UK who are educating their children on the autism spectrum at home. It had been possible in many cases to adjust the home teaching environment more closely to the needs of the child than would have been possible in school. One of the key differences the parents felt was the depth of knowledge and understanding of their child and the difference that can make to their teaching and learning experiences.

■ Outline the arguments *against* home education. What are the risks?

☐   Local authorities (UK) are required to safeguard children, but in fact they have very few powers to monitor home education. Safeguarding the welfare of children who do not go to school is more difficult than for those who do. Local authorities have limited scope to determine if the education is suitable.

Home education is unlikely to provide for a sufficiently wide social curriculum (e.g. opportunities to socialise with peers). In this sense it is unlikely to be inclusive.

Providing parents with support, guidance, teaching materials and other resources is difficult for local authorities (although charities do exist to help with home education).

7.3.8   Summary of Section 7.3

- A range of educational provision has developed to meet the different needs of children on the autism spectrum.
- Inclusion means firstly that all children, including those with disabilities, should have access to equal educational opportunities, and secondly that children have the right to be educated with others in their own community.
- For a child on the autism spectrum, mainstream education will not necessarily provide the most inclusive experience.
- A Statement of Special Educational Needs is a legally binding document stating a child's special needs and how their local authority is going to meet them.
- Parents have some rights when it comes to choosing education for their child, but are often dissatisfied with the provision, whether mainstream or special school.
- It is common for children on the autism spectrum to experience exclusion from school.
- Home education is the choice for a number of families.

7.4   Specific developments in autism education

As you have seen, children on the autism spectrum may be educated in a variety of settings ranging from the mainstream to special schools. In all settings that are geared to educating children on the spectrum, a range of interventions, tools and technologies may be employed, including some of the approaches that you read about in Chapter 6, as well as Social Stories, and other techniques discussed in this Chapter.

This section discusses two 'whole school' developments in the education of children with autism. A **whole school approach** is a collection of interventions, strategies and therapies which are embedded within the organisation and culture of the school, forming a framework for educating and supporting children on the autism spectrum. (See also Case Study 2.2.) The two approaches considered here are:

- **SPELL**: This is the National Autistic Society framework for intervention, and is widely used in NAS schools.
- **Daily Life Therapy** as practised at Higashi schools.

These approaches differ from each other in that SPELL is predominately 'ecological' in ethos and Daily Life Therapy is more 'behavioural' in style. Ecological approaches seek to support learning and positive behaviour by manipulating what happens *around* the child. This means the environment (see Section 7.2 for a description of the key environments in relation to autism), staff behaviour, organisation of the school, and its relationships with other partners (e.g. parents, specialists and social workers). Behavioural approaches work at an *individual* level, or in the case of Higashi schools at a *group* level, to support learning and positive behaviour. In practice, both SPELL and Daily Life Therapy combine some ecological and behavioural features.

Daily Life Therapy is limited to three schools: in Boston (USA), Tokyo (Japan) and Staffordshire (England). The approach is a highly specialised one and perhaps is more difficult to implement in mainstream settings than SPELL.

7.4.1 SPELL: the National Autistic Society framework for intervention

SPELL stands for Structure, Positive (approaches and expectations), Empathy, Low arousal, Links. The framework is used in identifying underlying issues; in reducing the disabling effects of the condition; and in providing a solid foundation for communication. It also forms the basis of all autism-specific staff training and an ethical basis for intervention.

Structure

The SPELL approach uses structure to make the environment of the child with autism feel more predictable, accessible and safe. Structure can aid personal autonomy and independence by reducing the child's dependence on others (similar to TEACCH where much of the focus is on getting the child to work independently). The environment is modified to ensure that each individual knows what is going to happen and what is expected of them. Structure plays to the child's sense of order and preference for visual organisation, which are strengths commonly associated with the autism spectrum.

In terms of the *curricular environment* this would include well-structured visual schedules, plans and routines providing:

- advance warning of what is about to happen
- help with staying on task during activities (e.g. visual reminders and reinforcers)
- visual support alongside spoken instructions (perhaps using devices such as PECS symbols – see Section 6.4.2)
- isolation of the central idea or key information

- clear, concrete expectations (again illustrated visually, e.g. with photographs of what the finished task should look like).

Visual timetables (Figure 7.9) are used to let the child know:

- What is expected of me?
- Where do I start?
- How long will this take?
- How will I know when it's finished?
- What will I be doing next?

Figure 7.9 An example of part of a visual timetable using pictures, words, and photographs illustrating objects of reference. (Queensmill School)

In terms of the *physical and sensory environment*, structure might take the form of well-defined spaces used for a designated purpose. Teachers and staff might use symbols, photographs and pictures to show exactly what is happening in a space or where something is kept (see Figure 7.10).

Figure 7.10   A well-organised and clearly labelled workspace. (Queensmill School)

Well-spaced-out hooks for a child's coat labelled clearly with their name or a photo might be used to make a communal area less cluttered and crowded. Sensory intrusion is kept to a minimum so that, as far as possible, only sensory experiences that are part of the activity or lesson are available.

In terms of the communication and language environment, students are supported using an **Augmentative and Alternative Communication (AAC)** system such as PECS (Figure 7.11) or **Blissymbols**. Systems such as these simplify the vocabulary, have a clear structure and can be used with more consistency than speech.

Blissymbols are a system of pictorial symbols. Each symbol represents a concept and can be combined with others to represent other concepts.

The *social environment* might be given more structure by use of interventions such as Social Stories (Section 7.2.4) or by enhancing social learning through 'concrete teaching' (see Figure 7.12).

Figure 7.11 A PECS sentence. (Macsnap/iStockphoto)

Social skill: how to do small talk

Definition: small talk is chatting with other people about everyday things
When: when I talk to people I know
Where: at home, on the playground, at school
With whom: my friends, my family and other people I know
What to say and do:

1 listen to what the other person says
2 talk about the same topic so we both talk for one minute about it
3 ask the other person questions about the topic
4 I can change the topic after we have talked about the topic for one minute
5 I can talk about any of the small talk topics
6 I need to remember not to talk just about my favourite topics

Reasoning: I do this because other people will learn something about me
and I will learn something about them. They will learn that I am friendly too.

Figure 7.12 An example of concrete teaching. The teacher provides the child with a definition of a particular activity ('small talk' in this case) with explicit details of the relevant context and rules for action. (Mackenzie, 2008)

Positive (approaches and expectations)

Schools using the SPELL 'framework' work *positively* with a child's autism and their learning style (see also Section 7.2.7 on working with positives). This might take the form of embedding aspects of a child's special interest within a target learning activity, or using access to their special interest as a reward for trying something new. Teachers might for instance be working on helping a child to travel independently, using the bus and handling money – both potentially anxiety-provoking activities for a child with autism. In an activity like this, the SPELL approach would be to ensure that the bus journey takes the child somewhere they are really motivated to go (perhaps connected to their special interest). SPELL is also positive in that it precludes the use of punishments or removal of privileges, etc.

Many children and young people with autism may avoid new or potentially difficult experiences. Through the medium of structure and positive, sensitive, supportive rehearsal they can reduce their level of anxiety, learn to tolerate and accept such experiences and develop new horizons and skills.

Empathy

This aspect of the SPELL framework focuses on staff attitudes to, and knowledge of, autism and how it uniquely affects each child or young person on the autism spectrum. You have read earlier in this chapter how the ability of school staff to understand autism is a key factor in parents' satisfaction with the placement of their child. Interventions in this area of the framework would include: staff induction and ongoing training, assessment of individual needs in relation to autism (e.g. audit of environments and sensory profiling) and regular reviews of a child's experiences and performance.

Low arousal

This aspect of SPELL relates to measures taken to reduce anxiety and aid concentration. Distractions are minimised as far as possible. As you saw in Section 7.2, some individuals have difficulty in processing sensory information, especially if it is auditory. Steps are taken to remove potentially aversive or distracting stimuli by attention to factors such as noise levels, colour schemes, odours, lighting and clutter.

This aspect of SPELL would also relate to how staff respond to and manage difficult behaviour; for instance, managing incidents and aggression with calmness and a positive disposition.

Links

This aspect of the SPELL framework relates to communication between school staff and also between parents and teachers. The objective of this component of SPELL is to ensure a holistic approach, thus reducing the possibility of unhelpful misunderstanding or confusion or the adoption of fragmented, piecemeal strategies. Children with autism can be easily confused or made angry by inconsistencies, even minor ones. Interventions might include regular staff meetings, formalised handover of information between staff teams or departments, and regular meetings with parents and peripatetic staff such as therapists and psychology professionals.

7.4.2 Evidence base for SPELL

To date, there is no research evidence for the SPELL framework as a comprehensive whole-environment approach to autism. SPELL combines elements of several approaches such as TEACCH and PECS, which have been evaluated individually, but not when combined as in SPELL. By its very nature, the principles underpinning SPELL are applied in a very individual way depending on the setting and the child. The evidence for the effectiveness of SPELL therefore remains at the level of the local context (the effects seen on specific targets in a school), clinical or practitioner experiences, and feedback from parents and children with autism.

- Why might it be difficult to evaluate the SPELL framework more systematically?

- Researchers seeking to evaluate SPELL would have difficulty identifying outcome measures (see Section 6.2.3). For instance, it is likely that SPELL improves expressive and receptive language, academic achievement, social learning and **challenging behaviours**, but to different degrees in different children.

Providing suitable control situations would also be difficult. It would be hard to find a naturalistic setting (a mainstream or special school) that didn't incorporate some of the elements of SPELL in relation to children with autism or without.

Challenging behaviours are behaviours of such intensity, frequency or duration that the physical safety of the person or others is placed in serious jeopardy, and/or access to and use of ordinary community facilities is impeded.

7.4.3 Daily Life Therapy

Daily Life Therapy is an educational methodology used in three schools, in Japan, the USA and the UK, and is based upon a methodology developed by the late Dr Kiyo Kitahara of Tokyo, Japan. Dr Kitahara believed that in order to create a stable emotional state, or 'kimochi', children and young people need to learn how to be independent. Proponents of Daily Life Therapy assert that it is not a 'treatment method', but more a cultural approach to education with an emphasis on teacher–student bonding and group participation.

The goal of this educational approach is for the children and young people to:

- develop independence in daily life skills such as washing, dressing and toileting
- improve body and behaviour awareness through extensive physical exercise
- participate in a group-focused, broad curriculum of activities.

Art, music and academic activities are used to facilitate the development of communication and daily living skills and to promote social independence. In particular, children and young people participate in a vigorous programme of physical activity such as running, dance and physical education.

The Boston Higashi School in the USA supports the day programme with a residential programme designed to teach daily living and social skills so that students can generalise their learning from one setting to another. The aim is to enable students to be involved in the wider community after they leave the programme. Parents are an integral part of the process with home versions of school programmes, regular meetings and school events.

In terms of social skills, Daily Life Therapy is group-orientated rather than a one-to-one approach. Building on the fact that children and young people with autism tend to be socially isolated, Dr Kitahara reasoned that they would benefit from the social interactions that arise within group therapy. Daily Life Therapy encourages and facilitates children and young people with autism to learn not only from the teacher but also from the other students.

In terms of communication, the schools take what they refer to as a 'multi-modal' approach. Students are encouraged to communicate using whatever means they can use most effectively (e.g. gaze shifting, signing, picture exchange or pointing) as well as spoken language. The schools also emphasise that by providing a context in which a child knows what's happening around them and what people expect of them, they are less anxious and can communicate more easily.

7.4.4   Evidence base for Daily Life Therapy

There has been little systematic research seeking to evaluate Daily Life Therapy. A report on the effectiveness of this approach with three children with autism (Larkin and Gurry, 1998) looked at progress in three areas: *attending behaviour, inappropriate responses* and *appropriate responses*. The researchers observed the children for six weeks in 1990 and again for the same period in 1998. Improvements were found in two target areas: firstly the children were better at attending in class; secondly inappropriate, stereotyped behaviours were reduced and they were able to cope well in groups of up to ten students.

However, the researchers raised concerns about the effectiveness of the approach in developing appropriate behaviours and the ability to understand instructions. At times, it was not at all clear what the children were learning. They were well-behaved, but learning in areas outside of participation in art, dance and music was uncertain.

In a report on a visit to the Boston Higashi School (Gould et al., 1991), the effectiveness of the approach in successfully eradicating 'adverse' behaviours was noted and improvements in self-esteem and confidence were also reported. The lack of a broader curriculum was a concern, as in the Larkin and Gurry study.

■   SPELL and Daily Life Therapy have some things in common. What are they?

☐   The common features are:
  •   establishing good links with parents

- understanding how the physical environment and social environment help communication
- a focus on developing independence (also a core component of the TEACCH approach)
- their effectiveness has not been researched extensively.

7.4.5 Summary of Section 7.4

- SPELL and Daily Life Therapy are whole school approaches rather than specific interventions.
- They share some features but also have some key differences.
- The evidence base for their effectiveness is very limited.

7.5 Conclusion

Educating children on the autism spectrum poses many challenges. The problems and skills of this group vary widely, and fitting them into any one school system is problematic. Specific problems in social skills and social understanding, speech, language and communication, and flexible thinking create individual educational needs in addition to the statutory curriculum or academic aspects of learning.

There is little reliable research evidence about which approaches, systems and interventions actually improve learning and support positive behaviour. Positive educational experiences for children with autism are likely to depend on qualities that are hard to achieve, such as consistency in the child's experience across the school, attitudes and awareness of staff, and their ability to empathise with children on the spectrum.

The education of children with autism – in terms of where this takes place and how success is measured – is bound up with debates about what inclusion actually means, and with issues relating to the rights of all children with disabilities, including children with special educational needs and/or who are at risk of marginalisation. The experiences of children and their parents are often far from the ideal. Children with autism are teased and bullied, and many parents are dissatisfied with the level of choice they have regarding educational placements, and lack confidence in the service provided at their child's school.

Some things seem to work. Although there is nowhere near enough research in this area, some individual approaches do have a positive effect. Working with and 'around' a person's autism and establishing an autism-friendly, whole school approach is becoming increasingly accepted as a quality standard in education provision. When a child's special educational needs are identified, acknowledged and used to inform the style of education environment and the range of learning technologies employed, then the lives of children and young people on the autism spectrum can be enriched.

7.6   Learning outcomes

7.1   Define and use, or recognise definitions and applications of, each of the terms printed in **bold** in the text.

7.2   Comment on how the psychological characteristics of autism affect education.

7.3   Describe the educational options for a child or young person on the autism spectrum.

7.4   Comment on the profile of provision, the issue of inclusion and parent satisfaction in relation to the education of children with autism.

7.5   Outline some examples of whole school educational approaches and the principles that underpin them.

7.7   Self-assessment questions for Chapter 7

Question 7.1   (LO 7.2)

Why might a child on the autism spectrum have difficulties with exams? Answer with reference to the four environments discussed in Sections 7.2.1 to 7.2.4.

Question 7.2   (LO 7.2)

Figure 7.5 shows an example of a child's individual planner from The Robert Ogden School. What might be the challenges of implementing an individual timetable like this for children with autism in a mainstream school?

Question 7.3   (LOs 7.3 and 7.4)

Do you think a mainstream school is necessarily a more inclusive setting for a child on the autism spectrum than a special school? Give reasons for your answer.

Question 7.4   (LO 7.5)

What is meant by a whole school approach? Illustrate your answer with reference to SPELL.

Chapter 8   Family perspectives

Chris Barson

The author expresses grateful thanks to the National Autistic Society for use of background material for this chapter, and to Rosa Hoekstra and Ilona Roth for all their help in structuring and elucidating the ideas in this chapter.

8.1   Introduction

When a person finds out that they are going to become a parent, they cannot help but start to imagine a life picture for this new person: will it be a boy or a girl? What will they look like? What will they be when they are older? They imagine them growing up, going to school, making friends and finding their independence. They imagine a quality of relationship with this new person that they see being part of their life into old age.

When, at the start of this new life, there are unusual behaviours, a lack of affective contact, developmental delay and communication difficulties, the picture formed starts to be challenged. When their child is diagnosed with autism, the picture may become even more fragmented and unclear, and it is hard for parents to know what the future will be. This complex condition undoubtedly will change the future but in the early years it is almost impossible to foresee what family life will be like, what this person will be capable of, how much help they will need and for how long.

How might brothers and sisters be affected by their sibling's autism? Between typically developing siblings, relationships can swing from cooperation and comradeship to squabbling and argument. Does autism change the picture significantly and, if so, is that change positive, negative or a bit of both?

The majority of children with autism remain living at home. The picture does not change much in adulthood, when most adults with autism (e.g. 70% in the UK) still live at home with their parents as the main carers. Growing up and learning to be an adult is tough on any young person – and tough on the rest of the family! The social and biological changes that hit young people when they reach adolescence can have a serious impact on them as individuals in terms of their feelings and behaviour, and have a compound effect on family life. Is it the same for families affected by autism, or different?

This chapter will build a picture of family life for the thousands of families affected by autism. The chapter will describe reactions to diagnosis, the effects of delay in diagnosis, and how living with a person with a diagnosis affects parents and the wider family. It will consider issues relating to the complex inheritance of autism and examine what life is like for **multiplex autism families**, where two or more members are on the autism spectrum. Through first-hand accounts, it illustrates how high-functioning individuals on the autism spectrum themselves perceive family life. This chapter will discuss the evidence relating to outcomes and resilience in families, and finally the different services and support that are available will come under the spotlight.

8.2   First encounters with the autism spectrum

The appearance of autism within a family is the start of a highly individual and often challenging journey, as you have seen in earlier chapters. First concerns often focus on delays in speech and language development, unusual social responses, or sleeping and eating difficulties. For those families whose child appeared to be developing in the ordinary way, it can be particularly difficult when the child starts to develop unusual behaviours, temper tantrums, or stops talking.

There is good evidence that parents may spot differences associated with autism in their child before the age of two (see Section 2.1 and Sections 3.4 to 3.6 on early signs of autism). In one recent study (Chawarska et al., 2007), the average age of first reported concerns was 14.7 months. These early concerns are sometimes not given the attention they should by health care professionals, and parents are left with an anxious wait for their child to 'catch up'.

When the delays and differences prove to be far from short-lived, parents are left wondering who to turn to and who will listen. As you saw in Chapter 2, there is often a long wait for diagnosis and early diagnosis is still relatively rare, particularly in children with high-functioning autism. For parents, diagnosis starts to explain why this child's behaviour is so different from that of his or her peers. Diagnosis may trigger help and support and provide access to information. Diagnosis can also be the first step towards a family recognising that they are not alone, that other families also experience the ups and downs of this condition.

Parents have said that the experience of having to pursue and even fight for a diagnosis has negatively influenced how they feel about autism and their child in those difficult early years. Howlin (2000) points out that a good experience of the diagnostic process has a positive impact on families. However, experiences may also be disappointing after the diagnosis is made, if parents do not get the level of help and support they hoped for. Moreover, parents still find it hard to get timely, accessible information. The World Wide Web has brought access to some excellent resources, but the explosion of material on the internet can also confuse parents. The diversity of 'voices' proffering causes, cures, diets and drugs can be baffling.

Activity 8.1   Autism on the internet

Allow 15 minutes for this activity

Try typing the words 'autism', 'Asperger syndrome' or 'ASD' into an internet search engine. If you were a parent doing this for the first time, what sort of impression would you form about the autism spectrum? Comments are at the end of the book.

8.2.1   Summary of Section 8.2

- The pathway towards a formal autism spectrum diagnosis can be lengthy; there is often a substantial gap between the time when the parents first become concerned and the actual diagnosis.

- Diagnosis can help parents to better understand their child's behaviour and may facilitate access to help and support.

- Sometimes parents do not get the good-quality information they need after diagnosis.

8.3   Reactions to diagnosis

■   What do you think might be the reaction of parents to the news that their son or daughter has an autism spectrum diagnosis? (Maybe you have experience of this yourself or a relative does – what was your/their reaction?)

☐   Reaction to an autism spectrum diagnosis varies very much from family to family. Sometimes diagnosis is felt as a relief: parents no longer feel that the problems they face are their fault and they have an explanation for themselves and others as to why their child is different. However, parents may also react with grief, surprise, devastation or helplessness; and they are likely to want additional information about autism.

Some parents may not believe the diagnosis and some may become angry or question the professional's ability. A study by Nissenbaum et al. (2002) indicated that many parents also worry about how other close relatives and friends would react to the diagnosis. Those who had suspected autism were less likely to be shocked. Many parents and professionals who were surveyed in this study said family members went through a grieving process after hearing the diagnosis. Regardless of their reaction, families did not feel that an autism spectrum diagnosis influenced their interactions with their child. However, Gray (2003) found that mothers, in particular, experienced considerable guilt and depression about their child's disability. The diagnosis also meant they experienced a number of additional stresses – such as issues relating to interventions, and the problems of access to appropriate education. The search for autism-friendly preschool provision, nurseries and play facilities can be challenging.

The UK National Initiative for Autism: Screening and Assessment (NIASA) report (2003) stressed the need to provide information and to involve families throughout the assessment process. Support from local parent groups, education and training for parents and information about support services are all seen as important.

To help parents come to terms with the autism spectrum diagnosis of their child, various parent education programmes have been developed. These programmes, such as **Hanen** in Canada and EarlyBird in the UK, teach parents or other care-givers how best to promote their child's social communicative behaviour and adaptation in the everyday life setting. More details of the EarlyBird programme and its efficacy can be found in Box 8.1.

The Hanen Centre, a charitable organisation based in Canada, has developed training programmes in which parents learn how to foster their child's communication and language development during everyday routines and activities.

Box 8.1   The NAS EarlyBird programme

The NAS **EarlyBird** programme is a three-month programme that combines group training sessions for parents with individual home visits, in which video feedback is used to help parents apply what they learn, whilst working with their child (Figure 8.1). During the three-month programme, parents have a weekly commitment to a two-and-a-half hour training session or a home visit, and to ongoing work with their child at home.

Figure 8.1   Photos of an EarlyBird session each featuring parent and child with an EarlyBird trainer who is recording the session. (National Autistic Society)

The NAS EarlyBird programme aims to:

- support parents in the period between diagnosis and school placement
- empower parents and help them facilitate their child's social communication and appropriate behaviour within the child's natural environment
- help parents establish good practice in handling their child at an early age so as to pre-empt the development of inappropriate behaviours.

Evaluation of the EarlyBird programme showed evidence of reduced stress and modified communication style in participating parents. The parents also showed more positive perceptions of their children. These effects were still present at follow-up, six months after the completion of the programme. The positive impact of the programme might have something to do with its naturalistic setting. The parents try out communication and behaviour strategies in the home, at nursery, when visiting relatives – in other words, in everyday settings. The children don't go somewhere special to learn how to communicate and behave, so the learning happens all the time.

Since January 2000, the EarlyBird Centre has regularly trained teams of professionals from across the UK and abroad to run the programme in their local areas. In June 2008, there were over 250 licensed teams, comprising over 1300 individual licensed users, who had run the programme with more than 6000 families.

- Most people feel that early intervention (via programmes such as EarlyBird or the Hanen programme) is desirable. Think of an advantage and a disadvantage of EarlyBird.

☐ Programmes such as EarlyBird differ from other early intervention programmes (see Chapter 6) because they focus on effecting change through raising parental knowledge, confidence and skills rather than focusing on the child. They work by equipping parents and carers with problem-solving skills and the confidence to use them. Participants benefit from what they learn from the EarlyBird practitioners, but also from the contact with other parents and carers. The programmes often engender informal or even formal groups of parents and carers who go on to support each other and even provide information to the wider community. Disadvantages or limitations centre on the availability of programme schemes. Given that autism may affect 1 child in 100, the 250 or so EarlyBird practitioner teams are insufficient for it to be a real option for most families. The three-month duration is both an advantage and a barrier – it allows time for participants to apply what they have learned and see progress, but it also requires a big commitment from the families.

Most parents feel a need to know what the **prognosis** (i.e. the likely outcome in the longer term) is for their child. Unfortunately, it is often really difficult to see how a child's autism will affect them in the future. Some people with autism will need a high level of care and support into adulthood and some will always be dependent on others for their daily living needs. A study by Howlin and colleagues (2004) examined the adult outcome of a group of 68 individuals who received autism spectrum diagnoses in childhood. Overall, only 12% were rated as having a 'very good' outcome, 10% were rated as 'good' and 19% as 'fair'. The majority was rated as having a 'poor' (46%) or 'very poor' (12%) outcome. Individuals without intellectual disability in childhood had a significantly better outcome than those with markedly impaired intelligence. However, even within the group of individuals with normal intellectual functioning, the outcome was very variable.

As exemplified by the figures from Howlin et al.'s study, some people on the autism spectrum do learn sufficient social, communication and thinking skills to achieve independence despite the fact that in early childhood they struggled with even the most basic tasks. Parents can be comforted too by the number of self-help 'survival' guides written by people on the spectrum who have 'found their way' in the world, such as those by Genevieve Edmonds (Edmonds and Worton, 2005) and Marc Segar (Segar, 1997). Autism spectrum conditions can thus become easier to live with, both for individuals and for their families. Parents and carers may take some comfort from this but, in reality, the long-term future for their son or daughter is difficult to predict.

8.3.1   Summary of Section 8.3

- Parents react in different ways to the autism diagnosis of their child and experience a range of feelings.

- Parent education programmes such as EarlyBird and Hanen have a role in helping parents come to terms with their child's diagnosis.

- Lifespan development in autism is not uniform so it is difficult to give parents a prognosis for their child.

8.4 Effects of delays in diagnosis

A median is a type of statistical average, but slightly different from a mean (Box 1.7). The median is the middle value of a range of values which have been ordered from smallest to largest.

Gray (2003) studied the impact on parents of having a child with Asperger syndrome or high-functioning autism. He found the **median** age of diagnosis to be nine years. This meant an exceptionally long referral process, involving contacts with a large number of professionals, as parents struggled to find an accurate diagnosis of their child's disability. As you saw in Chapter 2, children whose symptoms match the criteria for classic autism typically receive a diagnosis at a younger age but, even so, unwarranted delays can and do occur.

Self-injurious means behaviour such as head banging, scratching, biting or eye gouging, which is self-harming.

The absence of an accurate diagnosis can expose parents to accusations of parental incompetence by friends, relatives and health care professionals. The young child whose behaviour is difficult in nursery, who demands a lot of attention or is **self-injurious**, will attract critical comments from staff and other parents. Other children will notice these behaviours too and are likely to find it difficult to understand them without a label which provides an explanation.

Parents describe the process of having to repeat family history and retell their child's story to one professional after another as exhausting and frustrating. The fact that in many areas there is no clear, well-communicated diagnostic pathway compounds this problem, and leads to delay in diagnosis.

Services and help are hard to access without diagnosis. A diagnostic 'label' is often the key that unlocks services, resources, benefits and of course understanding. Without the label it is difficult to get help and support. But if parents seem to be pushing too hard for a diagnosis, they are often accused of having another agenda or of '**pathologising**' their child (i.e. attributing any problems to medical or psychological abnormality).

It can be harrowing for parents to talk about the extent of their child's behavioural problems, and feelings of guilt and failure are common. Parents can become distressed because they are recounting the story of the child they have 'lost'. For health professionals it can be all too easy to focus on the distressed, tearful parent and incorrectly attribute the source of the child's difficulties to the parent:

> The paediatrician started asking me all sorts of personal questions. At the same time I was given the diagnosis I was told I needed to go on a parenting skills programme.

> *(Parent comment from workshop, 2009)*

8.4.1 Summary of Section 8.4

- Diagnosis is often late, especially for children with high-functioning autism or Asperger syndrome.

- A late diagnosis may lead to additional stress both for the child concerned and for their parents.

- A diagnosis is often crucial in getting access to support, services and financial help.

8.5   Family life with a person on the autism spectrum

8.5.1   Parents

The accommodations that parents have to make and the extra things they have to do for their child with autism often have an enormous impact on them. In some cases, the child's problems lead to direct confrontations between the parents and may threaten their relationship. The findings of studies of divorce and family breakdown in families affected by disability are variable. Some research seems to suggest a slightly higher divorce rate in such families but other research suggests the opposite. A large survey of members of the National Autistic Society with over 600 respondents (Broach et al., 2003) showed a lone parent rate of 17% among parents of children on the autism spectrum, compared with a 10% national average for the UK.

There is evidence that mothers experience greater personal impact than fathers. Gray (2003) found that although most fathers acknowledged the severe difficulties that their child's autism presented for their families, they usually claimed that their child's condition did not have a significant effect on them personally. For fathers, the most serious effect of their child's autism was through the stress experienced by their partners.

The relatively less severe impact of the child's autism on most of the fathers may be partially due to their different gender roles. In a few cases in Gray's study (2003), fathers acknowledged that their child's autism might have encouraged a greater commitment to work. However, this does not mean that they were not emotionally distressed by their child's condition. They also had considerable concern about their child's future.

■   Why do you think that having a child diagnosed with autism may have less effect on fathers than mothers?

☐   If the father is the breadwinner, then his work will give him respite from constant reminders of the difficulties of his child. He might also play a less active role in the stressful process of child-rearing.

Gray (2003) found that mothers were much more likely to claim that their child's autism had severely affected their emotional well-being. Indeed, many mothers had experienced enough distress to require psychotherapy and/or medication. A study by Bromley et al. (2004) found that over 50% of mothers suffered from significant psychological distress and this was associated with low levels of family support and with bringing up a child with severely challenging behaviour (Section 7.4.2). Tomanik et al. (2004) estimated an even higher incidence of maternal stress, with significantly elevated stress levels being experienced by two-thirds of mothers.

- What features of autism do you think would cause particular distress for a parent?

☐ Examples of characteristics of autism that cause great distress for parents are:

- repetitive behaviours
- impulsiveness
- not appreciating or 'seeing' dangers
- speech, language and communication difficulties
- lack of emotional contact.

Mothers and fathers also cope differently with emotional distress, with fathers typically suppressing their feelings (Gray, 2003). Mothers tend to vent their feelings and have a wider range of emotional responses, expressing grief and sadness in addition to anger. They rely on talking to friends and family as a way of dealing with their emotions, particularly other mothers with a child with autism. Mothers were likely to feel more stigmatised by their child's condition. Stigma was exacerbated among parents with children who were more severely disabled by autism or who were under the age of 12.

Gray (2003) found that bringing up a child with autism also had a significant effect on careers. It's easy to imagine how a parent's career might be disrupted when they have to cope with their child's sleeplessness, behaviour problems, eating difficulties and the education system – on top of the responsibilities that are just part of typical family life. Those who do manage to work are often forced to miss days, perform below their normal level or drop back to part-time status.

Fathers are more likely to be employed full-time than mothers. Rodrigue et al. (1992) compared fathers of children with autism and fathers of Down syndrome children and found few significant differences. Both groups reported more use of wish-fulfilling fantasy (e.g. dreaming of 'escape' or a lottery win) and 'information seeking' (pouring frustrations into knowing as much about the diagnosis as possible) as coping strategies, than did the control group of fathers with typically developing children. Fathers of children with autism or Down syndrome also felt a greater financial impact and disruption of family activities than did the typically developing control group.

8.5.2 Siblings

Children pick up from an early age that their brother or sister is different, even if they do not understand the cause. They also notice other people's reactions to their sibling, especially those of their parents and grandparents. They may have many queries as well as secret fears (e.g. that they too will 'catch' autism) but be afraid to question their parents for fear of upsetting them. These questions and worries will change as the child becomes older. For instance, an older child may fear that their own offspring will have autism. Whilst they may have a deep love for their sibling, they may also harbour feelings of resentment at the amount of time their parents are spending with him or her, and feel that they are being treated unfairly. Feelings of anger, embarrassment and guilt can also be a feature.

The early years might be particularly difficult. In cases of a sibling of a young preschool child with disabilities, the parents themselves are likely to be in the initial stages of adjustment to the reality of the child's condition, resulting in fewer quality interactions with the sibling than usual. Consequently, these children may be particularly vulnerable to feelings of confusion, frustration or isolation. When a family is affected by other factors that are indirectly linked to the presence of a child or children with autism, such as low income or restricted leisure opportunities, or where there is a stress on the relationship of the parents, this may compound the difficulties for siblings.

Of course, not all feelings are negative. Indeed, as Howlin and Yates (1990) describe, there is some evidence that having a sibling with autism promotes positive self-concept, and interpersonal and care-giving skills (Figure 8.2). Also, and especially for sisters, who are more likely to assume a maternal role than brothers, this extra responsibility does not appear to contribute to poorer adjustment.

Figure 8.2 Two boys playing a board game. (National Autistic Society)

Research into the psychosocial adjustment of siblings of children with autism has produced mixed results. Some studies show decreased levels of social competence, high levels of loneliness and problems with peers (Bågenholm and Gillberg, 1991), while others reported few loneliness problems (Kaminsky and Dewey, 2002). In conclusion, the findings from studies exploring how siblings are affected by living with a brother or sister on the autism spectrum are complex and variable – it is difficult to draw general conclusions, as the impact will vary from family to family.

There is a growing number of 'sibling clubs' or groups where siblings get together and share their experiences of having a brother or sister on the autism spectrum. Helping the siblings understand the problems faced by someone on the spectrum helps too. There are a number of books and guides written for siblings (see, for example, Figure 8.3).

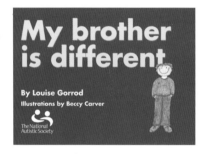

Figure 8.3 Front cover of *My Brother is Different*, written by Louise Gorrod and illustrated by Beccy Carver, a National Autistic Society publication (1997).

8.5.3 Multiplex autism families

The strong genetic influences on autism (see Chapters 1 and 5) mean that there are many families where more than one person is affected by autism, so-called multiplex autism families. In Section 6.1.1 you were introduced to journalist Charlotte Moore, who has two children on the autism spectrum (Figure 8.4). She describes with wit how life can be chaotic in a multiplex autism family, as in this excerpt from her newspaper column:

> I keep a lot of things under lock and key – most foodstuffs, cleaning materials, the hamster. I would love to leave a bowl of fruit out on the table – a humble ambition, you might think, but Sam takes one bite from each of the fruit and then throws it away. It is only recently that I have been able to

Figure 8.4 Charlotte Moore and family. (Linda Nylind/Guardian News & Media Ltd 2009)

> reintroduce vases of flowers. There was a time when George would strip the flowers off and use the stalks as flappers, and Sam would drink the water.

(Moore, 2003b)

Jacqui Jackson is the mother of seven children (Figure 8.5), of whom two boys, Luke and Ben, are on the autism spectrum. Additionally, her son Joe has ADHD. An extract from Jacqui Jackson's book *Multicoloured Mayhem* about her family life is reproduced below:

> When I meet people for the first time I often silently mouth to myself their next few sentences … 'Goodness how do you cope?' This is usually followed by questions about how I stay so slim when I have had seven children, closely followed by a 'joke' about whether or not I had a television or if I have found out what causes it yet … Yes I do know what causes it. Yes I did have a television. If you met Joe and Ben you would know exactly why I stay so slim, and I cope, not only because I have no choice in the matter, but mostly because we have fun. It may be different to the 'norm' but most definitely just as much, if not more, fun.

(Jackson, 2003)

Multiplex families are in some ways very different from the 'norm' but different isn't necessarily synonymous with worse. The extract from Jacqui Jackson's book indicates that her family is actually enriched by its diversity or unusualness. No one would pretend that life for families with multiple children on the autism spectrum (and in the case of the Jackson family, other conditions too) feels enriched all of the time. Holding a family together and managing the family dynamics can be tough even where autism isn't present. Autism make for a harder challenge at times, but, as Jacqui points out, it can also enhance the rewards for the hard work.

■ What areas of life might be more difficult for a multiplex autism family?

□ There might be difficulty in:
- going out together (where brothers and sisters have very fixed ideas about what is 'fun' or 'interesting')
- having friends to stay – not everyone is prepared for how children with autism behave
- getting homework done (especially if brothers and sisters don't understand how their behaviour impacts on others).

■ In what ways might having several children on the spectrum make family bonds stronger and life more fun?

□ The diversity of special interests could be enriching for everyone. There's also less opportunity to feel isolated when you have brothers and sisters who are also on the autism spectrum.

Figure 8.5 Jacqui Jackson and her seven children. The first boy on the left is Luke Jackson who wrote his own guide to Asperger syndrome. (Jacqui Jackson)

Luke Jackson, who at the age of 13 wrote his own guide to Asperger syndrome, describes his family life like this:

> I am very interested in commonly used expressions that seem to make little sense. They are called idioms. Ones that spring to mind in relation to my family are 'Too many cooks spoil the broth' and 'Many hands make light work'.

(Jackson, 2002, p. 18)

8.5.4   Partners

Although differences in social understanding, social skills and social motivation affect the likelihood of people on the autism spectrum forming relationships and partnerships, there are both undiagnosed and diagnosed individuals who have partners and children. Some may manage such a partnership and family life very well, whereas others may have great difficulties. Partners may find living with a person with autism very difficult because of the nature of the disability.

■ What aspects of autism would make it hard to live with a person on the spectrum?

□ It may be hard to live with some of the behaviours that are an integral part of the condition. Partners with autism may find social situations like parties or occasions when families join together for activities very difficult. They may come across as odd or rude in social settings, which may lead to feelings of awkwardness in their partner. Moreover, people with autism may find it very hard to effectively deal with the usual conflicts and disagreements that crop up in a relationship. The social communication difficulties may serve as an obstacle to resolving even small problems and may do more damage to the relationship than they should. A partner who can't anticipate what their loved one is thinking, enjoys/dislikes, or is motivated by may feel bemused or even annoyed by their actions.

Little research has been carried out to date in this area, but there are books on the subject written by partners. The following quote comes from the wife of Chris Slater-Walker, who has Asperger syndrome:

> Occasionally things do go wrong. Having explained carefully, calmly and rationally why I feel upset, I will check that Chris has understood and when he replies 'Not really', there is the old temptation to find something expendable in the kitchen.

(Slater-Walker and Slater-Walker, 2002, p. 72)

Some individuals with autism, like Temple Grandin, as described by Oliver Sacks, have deliberately avoided sexual or intimate relationships:

> She was celibate. Nor had she ever dated. She found such interactions completely baffling, and too complex to deal with. 'Have you cared for somebody else?' I asked her. She hesitated for a moment before answering, 'I think lots of times there are things that are missing from my life'.

(Sacks, 1993, p. 122)

8.5.5 First-hand accounts of family life

Not only parents, siblings and partners, but also people on the autism spectrum themselves have their views on family life. Sean Barron recalls how he needed order and rules in his early life, and how this could be difficult for his family:

> In sixth, seventh and eighth grade I had a fixation with school buses and would watch them line up at the end of the day in the school's back parking lot. I noted which ones arrived early and late and loved to see the angle at which they parked. Soon I invented a card game I called 'Buses', in which I would move the cards across a rug I had in my bedroom that represented the rectangular-shaped parking lot and simulate the movement of the buses from arrival to departure. I picked about twenty cards – the number that corresponded to the number of school buses – and had them slanted on the rug at the exact angle of the stationary school buses. After about ten minutes, I would have most of the cards 'leave' the rug before one or two others 'arrived' – the same situation that played out in the school's parking lot.
>
> In time, I added a variation to my game. Instead of simply using a deck of cards to represent the school buses, I chose to use, to the extent possible, people – specifically, myself, my two parents and my sister, Meg. Each weekday morning before Meg and I left for school and my parents left for work, we gathered for breakfast at the kitchen table. Eventually, I saw this

daily gathering as another means by which to satisfy my insatiable fixation on school buses. I 'assigned' each person to a seat at the table, as well as an approximate time and exact order in which I expected them to come downstairs. I was to be first, my parents second and third and my sister last. I remember many mornings in the kitchen actually listening for stirring upstairs and becoming worried if I heard what I thought was Meg getting up before it was her time to come down. Sometimes I would wolf down my food and try to finish and leave the table before her kitchen arrival – in the same manner that some school buses exited the school.

Everything went smoothly in the morning unless someone violated this precious family rule. When that happened – and it did more often than not – I became agitated and my morning would be ruined. If Meg came down early, sat in someone else's seat or both, I often left for school in a foul mood that sometimes took hours to diminish. My family knew I was unreasonably angry because of my rule being broken. They just didn't know how to break through those feelings, nor did I have the ability to explain why the violation led to such strong fury. I wasn't yet able to link my need to control the situation (and those in it) with my feelings of being powerless over the world around me. At that point in my life, the ends justified the means. I was functioning at a simpler level of response, based on action–reaction. If each person arrived in the kitchen and conformed to my desperate need for order, I felt empowered: if, on the other hand it was violated, I left the house feeling powerless, angry and helpless.

(Sean Barron in Grandin et al., 2005, p. 159)

Despite these difficulties in childhood, Sean Barron writes that he highly appreciates the 'extraordinary' relationship he has with his family, which affects him in positive ways. Three high-functioning individuals interviewed in a study by Hurlbutt and Chalmers (2002) also mention the importance of their family. They believe that the positive involvement and support of their family has helped them to develop the skills necessary to be successful as adults. A similar sentiment is noted by Temple Grandin:

They [my mother and father] worked hard to reach me through the hazy, fuzzy world I lived in and to make the 'impossible' possible. And I give my family as much credit as I give myself for creating the conditions that allowed me to come out.

(Temple Grandin in Grandin et al., 2005, p. 60)

8.5.6   Summary of Section 8.5

- Autism has a range of effects on parents. Mothers and fathers might differ in their feelings and reactions to their child's autism.

- Siblings are often very supportive towards their brother or sister with autism, despite the challenges they present.

- The psychosocial impact of having a sibling on the autism spectrum varies strongly. Sibling support groups can be of benefit to brothers and sisters of the affected child.

- Family life in multiplex families, where there is more than one family member on the autism spectrum, is complex, but can also be rewarding.

- Some people on the autism spectrum do have intimate relationships and/or long-term partnerships; however, these might be very difficult to maintain at times.

- Accounts from high-functioning people on the autism spectrum stress the value and importance for development of their family life.

8.6   Different life stages and the family

Families face a whole range of stressful influences, and these vary depending on the age and level of disability of the person with autism. The particular difficulties that families encounter may differ depending on the stage of life of the person with autism. Childhood, adolescence and adulthood in a person on the autism spectrum are likely to pose different problems for the family. This section will discuss the particular difficulties that families encounter in these different phases of life.

Childhood

Children with autism frequently engage in behaviours that are potentially disruptive to family life such as aggression, self-injury, impulsivity, hyperactivity, temper tantrums and obsessional, ritualistic behaviour. Parents report that they are sometimes stretched beyond their limits. The degree to which they have to prepare and structure even the most straightforward activities for their child can become exhausting. It precludes spontaneous and frivolous activities that for most typical families are undertaken relatively easily. On top of that come the difficulties that parents face in the process of getting a diagnosis for their child, and in coming to terms with this diagnosis (as described in Sections 8.2 to 8.4).

The financial impact of having a child with autism can be a significant burden to families. There is often a shortfall between the costs of bringing up a child with severe disabilities and the benefits received, and caring for a person on the spectrum frequently impacts on the parent's or carer's ability to work. Many families of children on the spectrum are reliant on benefits, having given up their employment due to the demands of caring for their child. A study of a small number of individuals with autism (Järbrink et al., 2003) estimated that the societal cost of a child with autism was around £689 per week and 50% of this figure was borne by parents.

Adolescence

When children on the autism spectrum reach adolescence, families may have to come to terms with the fact that their child's level of functioning or capacity for independence is not likely to change dramatically in the years ahead. Indeed, whereas for other families adolescence is a time of increased independence and autonomy, for parents of adolescents with autism, family relationships may deteriorate because children remain so dependent (Seltzer et al., 2001).

The onset of puberty comes with changes in appearance such as increased body hair, the development of breasts, the onset of acne, etc. Dealing with changes such as these is hard for all adolescents but particularly so for those affected by autism. Mood changes are common in puberty, and for young people with autism, who often have difficulty recognising and dealing with sensations and emotions, they can lead to very problematic behaviour.

Compared with typically developing young people, those with Asperger syndrome or HFA are more vulnerable to mental health problems, particularly depressive and anxiety-related disorders (Howlin et al., 2004). Depression in young people with Asperger syndrome or HFA may be related to a growing awareness of their disability or a sense of being different from their peer group. Their inability to form relationships or take part in social activities successfully may also be a source of suffering.

Personal accounts by young people with Asperger syndrome frequently refer to the hazards of attempting to make friends. People with Asperger syndrome are often highly socially motivated but have difficulties understanding how to 'fit in'. Matching the right behaviour to the social context or setting can be a major challenge. The social world around them seems impenetrable, and it is all too easy to make social gaffes and blunders.

> When I got to secondary school, I wasn't actively bullied anymore; I was just continually aware that no-one liked me, that whenever we were told to pair up in lessons, for example, I was always the one left over. Even if there were even numbers in the class, the teacher would still have to order someone else to form a pair with me. It wasn't until I was about 16 that I made any friends at all and even then I couldn't name someone whose 'best friend' I was. I could only conclude that I was basically unlikable.
>
> *(Sainsbury, 2000, p. 77)*

Adolescence is also a time of awakening sexuality and increased sexual drive, and young people will start to experiment and have their first sexual experiences and early relationships. Understanding sexuality, boundaries and relationships is difficult for young people with autism. Indeed, some people have even been accused of harassment in their attempts to socialise, something that may add to their depression and anxiety.

The isolating effect of Asperger syndrome can be hard to deal with for parents and siblings. Parents can't help but be acutely aware of how the social horizons of their children differ. Siblings commonly feel guilty that they are able to enjoy friendships, a social life and romantic relationships, whereas their affected brother or sister rarely or never has these experiences. Adolescents can be volatile and a bit selfish; showing patience and understanding towards a demanding sibling might be too much at times.

Adulthood

There is very little research into the impact of lifelong caring for a person with autism. Reasons for this include the fact that autism did not begin to be fully recognised until the 1960s and the first group of children to be diagnosed were those with the severest form of autism, many of whom went into residential care. Other children who may have had autism were given different diagnostic labels and therefore were not identified for follow-up studies.

The challenges of parenting an adult on the spectrum are stressful in ways that are different from those that parents confront when their son or daughter is a young child or adolescent. Anecdotally, parents of adults with autism who may have the additional caring role for their own ageing parents, experience considerable stress.

■   What support needs might parents have when their child becomes an adult?

☐   Support needs might include:

- good 'transition' planning from adolescence to adulthood and particularly planning for life after school (most adults on the autism spectrum are unemployed)
- reassurances about the long-term accommodation of their son or daughter
- financial support
- a break from caring
- the support of other parents.

Since many of the problems associated with autism are long term, autism-specific intervention and support remain important in adulthood. Many parents feel that there is a lack of such adult-focused services for people on the spectrum, and this seems to have a bearing on carer well-being. A study in Manchester, UK, found a strong association between emotional distress in parents of an adult with autism and unmet needs (such as getting a break from caring, planning for future care needs and social/health care in an emergency) (Hare et al., 2004). On the other hand, some research suggests that, after decades of care-giving, mothers of adults with autism became used to the caring process, resulting in reduced social and psychological stress (Seltzer et al., 2001).

8.6.1   Summary of Section 8.6

- The experiences for families change as children with autism grow older.
- In childhood, families need both psychological and financial support to help them to cope with living with a child with autism.
- In adolescence, social isolation and increased awareness of social disability may be compounded by the appearance of mental health problems such as anxiety and depression, especially in young people with HFA and Asperger syndrome.
- Many individuals with autism remain dependent on others as adults, so lifelong support is needed, both for the individuals themselves and for their care-givers.

8.7 Family resilience

Zoe Wood is the mother of a child with autism (Figure 8.6). Her description of family life illustrates that, although her family is faced with many challenges, they also perceive life as extremely wonderful:

> Life has never been the same since Matthew made his appearance in 2000. Everyday activities that people take for granted, are a challenge in my house. For instance Matthew's hair has probably been trimmed more times than it has been washed, because he says it hurts, and even the gentlest touch irritates him. He is still in nappies; I believe that one day, something will click and he will suddenly announce he doesn't want to wear nappies anymore.
>
> Sleeping is another issue! The whole household has had rude awakenings in the middle of the night by performances such as playing the French National Anthem. Furthermore, if someone fails to lock one of the many safety gates then Matthew will seize the opportunity to illuminate the house, literally, be it lights, hob or oven! Trips out can be complicated. For instance, on visits to the supermarket the assault on Matthew's senses can make him hyper- or hyposensitive. He may go around smelling the food or crawling around on his knees inspecting the fan systems. If this causes problems with the public, we have now come to believe that it's their problem and not ours or Matthew's. Holidays have never proved to be a problem: Matthew has been travelling abroad since he was 8 months old, by sea and air and land.
>
> Despite the pressure put onto us as a family, this has now become a way of life and we know no different. We feel that ignorance lies with other people and until they re-educate themselves into accepting diversity then life for us will remain quite a challenge! Life with Matthew is wonderful and marvellous!

(Zoe Wood)

Figure 8.6 Zoe Wood's son, Matthew, who has an autism spectrum diagnosis. (Zoe Wood)

There is evidence that some families benefit from the experience of caring for a child (or children) with autism and have even become stronger as a result of disability in the family. This quality is sometimes referred to in this context as **resilience**. Walsh (1998) defines this as the ability to withstand hardship and to rebound from adversity, becoming stronger and more resourceful.

In a study of families with a child with a disability such as autism (Walsh, 2003), families described having become closer as a consequence. Working together led to more understanding and stronger relationships among family members. The families were also reported to have developed heightened patience, compassion and respect for other people. Similar experiences are expressed by a parent of a son with autism, quoted in a study by Bayat (2007):

> My son's autism has made our life together, emotionally and financially. Each member has to devote additional time and effort to help him, and to learn how to live peacefully in such an environment. Through working together, we all learned how to help my son together. In some sense, this

also makes our family closer, because an individual cannot handle the toughness alone.

So what are the 'ingredients' that determine whether this strengthening effect takes place? It seems that flexibility and good communication are what underpin resilience (Bayat, 2007). Family members need to be flexible enough to accommodate the changes necessary in caring for a child with autism, and in order to adjust and adapt to the new demands on the family, they need to communicate well with each other.

Of course all families, including the ones studied by Walsh and Bayat, travel a very unique journey. You have explored in earlier chapters just how variable autistic conditions can be, and how they seem to engender some unique individual family experiences. Seeing progress, even in small steps, can provide motivation to carry on trying even in the toughest of times. Resilience is often shown in the way families make positive meaning out of adversity and develop a greater awareness and compassion towards individual differences.

There are a multitude of parent support groups, local autism societies and other examples of parents coming together to share experiences, offer help and indeed campaign for improvements in local and national services.

■ You have read about the time and energy that families have to invest in their children with autism and the kind of restrictions placed on them. Why do you think that parents also find the motivation to run, or contribute to, parent support groups?

☐ Often parents are motivated by the desire to protect new parents from going through what they had to. They often feel that they have had to become 'quasi-professionals' in order to understand the condition and fight the 'system', and they want to pass some of this knowledge on. They often state that they get their strength from their child with autism and a keen belief in their special qualities. Parents are often motivated by a desire to reassure, and let new parents know that things do get better. Some of their determination, single-mindedness and perfectionism may reflect autistic traits. Parents can sometimes be highly motivated to achieve political change and better provision for future children.

Bayat (2007) counsels professionals and practitioners to not only focus on the problems and needs of families, but to also acknowledge their strengths and help them recognise their own capacities for resilience. This echoes the trend in autism research towards considering strengths and positives as well as deficits (see Chapter 4).

8.7.1 Summary of Section 8.7

• Families affected by autism often show high levels of resilience. Positive experiences described include becoming more united and closer as a family, and developing greater compassion and respect for others.

- Flexibility and good communication between the family members are important factors contributing to resilience.

8.8   Services and support for children and families

Parents need a variety of information and support services, needs that continue and change over time as the child with autism moves through adolescence and into adulthood. The need for support may even start before life: as understanding of the genetic aspects of autism increases, there will be increasing demand from families with an affected member for advice regarding their risk of having further children with autism. Research evidence currently available makes it possible to give families some idea of the risk for any future children. It is important that this advice is given by **genetic counsellors** who understand the complex pattern of inheritance in autism and the variability in the way it is expressed. There is a need to give information regarding the likelihood of passing on autistic traits to their children, not only for those on the autism spectrum but also for individuals expressing the broader autism phenotype (see Box 8.2).

Box 8.2   The broader autism phenotype in parents

An important implication of the strong genetic influences on autism is that parents, and particularly fathers, sometimes fall within the broader autism phenotype, which you read about in Section 5.3. In other words, they share some of the traits associated with autism, but not so many that they would warrant diagnosis.

- If your work involved supporting families and individuals with autism, you would sometimes encounter parents with some of the difficulties (albeit in a minor form) associated with autism. What traits might it be necessary to allow for?

  - Examples might include: inflexibility in thinking, obsessive and perseverant behaviour and difficulties with non-verbal communication.

Relatively minor things, like a practitioner being late for an appointment, or not returning a phone message promptly may be met with a severe reaction by a parent. Parents may interpret something a social worker has said, such as 'we'll get this sorted out quickly', very differently to how the practitioner meant it. Parents with the characteristics associated with autism are often able to bring a great deal of determination and focus to getting help or services for their child. This can make them seem excessively 'pushy' or even lead practitioners to question their motives. Parents can become almost excessively knowledgeable in their quest to find answers to autism, and this can threaten professionals who feel their competence is on trial.

As you have read earlier in this chapter and in Chapter 2, the early signs of autism are often reliably detected by parents (although they usually don't appreciate the link between the behaviour and autism until the process of diagnosis gets underway). It is important for parents that their early concerns are heard. In the UK, several services, such as Health Visitors, Child and Adolescent Mental Health Services and Child Health clinics have a role in the early identification of children on the autism spectrum. However, professionals sometimes downplay early parental concerns or, as in the case study of Anton (Case Study 2.1), take a considerable time to evaluate them, resulting in a lengthy diagnostic process.

Early identification and diagnosis make intervention programmes such as EarlyBird (which you read about in Section 8.3) and other programmes (see Chapter 6) accessible to families. Early intervention programmes consist of specialised and/or inclusive preschool programmes designed to build social and communication skills. Many offer standard therapies, such as speech and language therapy, occupational therapy, social skills therapy, behavioural interventions, family therapy and applied behaviour analysis. There is a consensus that early intervention is helpful and that early intervention and support can have a significant impact on the quality of life for individuals and their families (Jordan, 2004). However, whether early intervention ultimately results in a better long-term prognosis is still unclear. The idea that investments in early provision might lessen the public cost of autism is not proven.

Once a child is of school age, this presents parents with both the opportunity for appropriate support for learning, and a break from the day-to-day work of caring. Chapter 7 explored issues relating to educational provision. You will have read that a large number of parents in the UK are satisfied with the learning provisions made for their child, but a significant number of parents also have very deep worries about the provision their child receives (see Section 7.3.5). It seems that school or placement has the potential to provide reassurance or extreme stress for parents. A school placement that is autism friendly (see Section 7.2.8), and is able to offer appropriate accommodations and adaptations to meet the needs of children and young people on the spectrum, ranks very highly in parents' list of concerns.

Like appropriate education, getting a short break from the hard work of caring is a high priority for parents and this is true of parents of children and adults with autism. In a study of families with an adult with autism, 89% of the parents/carers of the person with autism rated the need for a break as top of their list of needs (Hare et al., 2004). Box 8.3 provides an overview of the different types of short break service available.

Where short break services are available, flexible and autism friendly, families really value them. However, the lack of suitable **respite care** (i.e. a short break away from the family with support for the child with autism), adds to the stress of being a family affected by autism. Barson (1998) found that a third of families surveyed did not have any respite support at all, and of those who did, 28% were not satisfied with it. Parents felt there was a lack of choice in the style of support available, and that autism-specific/friendly provision was in short supply. Tarleton and Macaulay (2003) found almost a third of children on waiting lists for short breaks in the UK have a diagnosis on the autism spectrum. Obtaining respite care during school holidays is

Box 8.3   Types of short break service

- Befriending schemes: volunteer befrienders spend a few hours each week with a person with autism or their family; volunteers are matched to families and individuals who have something in common.

- Domiciliary support: help with the day-to-day caring and support for the child.

- Family-based short breaks (link families or shared care): children with disabilities including autism spend time with another family, either in that family's home or away on an activity.

- Holidays (usually in association with a charity) where help is provided for children with autism (Figure 8.7).

- Own home respite: a service provider (either professional or volunteer) takes on the caring role in the family home – from a few hours up to a day each week or a couple of weeks for a holiday.

- Play schemes: organised play activities during school vacations; sometimes specialist but most commonly integrated schemes.

- Residential care: a residential service which accommodates the child for short periods. (In the UK there are limits to how long a child can be looked after in this kind of provision, and parents also bear part of the cost.)

Figure 8.7   Group activity at a short break holiday provided by the Dutch charity SOVA. (Stichting Opvang & Vakantie Autisten)

particularly difficult, with autism-specific respite services being uncommon (Loynes, 2001). This is unfortunate as respite care provides a much needed break that has demonstrated a positive effect on parental stress levels (Chan and Sigafoos, 2000).

Another important source of support is advice services. Families need help accessing services, advice on benefits and assistance with making sense of the plethora of interventions and treatments on offer. As discussed earlier, the internet can help but parents also need professional advice services to enable them to make evidence-based decisions about the care for their child.

One of the most valued sources of support comes from other parents. Parent-led support groups have grown up all over the world since the early beginnings of the National Autistic Society in London (UK) in 1962 (see Section 1.4). Parents meet together to offer mutual support, run information and toy libraries, campaign for better local services and support families who are new to the world of autism. The larger parent bodies put pressure on governments to change laws relating to the health, social and educational services relevant to children and adults across the autism spectrum. The groups are of different sizes and complexions. Some campaign around particular issues or represent a sub-group within the autism movement. Groups and societies have also come together to contribute to wider organisations such as Autism Europe.

8.8.1   Summary of Section 8.8

- Families need support; this may come from statutory, voluntary or informal sources.
- Parents' concerns about educational placements are significant.
- Parents and carers need a break from caring, but breaks are not always available or right for their child.
- Parents have started initiatives to help other autism families through support groups and are the driving force behind bodies lobbying for law changes and for improved provisions and services for families with children with autism.

8.9   Conclusion

Finding out that your child is on the autism spectrum is the start of an uncertain journey for all families. At whatever age diagnosis occurs, it triggers a range of feelings in parents. Receiving a diagnosis can be a reassurance or something of a relief; however, it can also come as a great shock, and it can take a while to accept. After diagnosis, families often have to cope with a condition they know nothing about, and may have no idea of what to do and where to go next.

Diagnosis is followed by a need for explanation and information. Despite living in the 'information age', parents still find it hard to get timely, relevant high-quality information. A range of help and support is needed to help families survive and enjoy ordinary family experiences. These include help with the financial costs that come with a child with autism, getting a break from caring, support for siblings, and consideration of the family's needs once the child is an adult. Unfortunately some services have limited access or have long waiting lists.

All in all, caring for a child with autism can be hard for all family members. However, despite the hard work and difficulties that are regularly part of bringing up a child with autism, many families are actually quite resilient and highly value their life situation.

8.10   Learning outcomes

8.1   Define and use, or recognise definitions and applications of, each of the terms printed in **bold** in the text.

8.2   Discuss some of the effects of diagnosis on families.

8.3   Outline research into how autism impacts on families, including the effects on parents, siblings, partners and individuals with autism themselves.

8.4   Discuss the way problems and needs change at different life stages.

8.5   Identify support needs of families affected by autism, and evaluate services addressing these needs.

8.11   Self-assessment questions for Chapter 8

Question 8.1   (LOs 8.2 and 8.3)

In what ways may receiving an autism spectrum diagnosis impact on parents? Identify two positive and two less positive aspects.

Question 8.2   (LO 8.3)

List ways in which life might be (a) more difficult and (b) more rewarding in a family with autism compared with families without autism.

Question 8.3   (LOs 8.1 and 8.3)

Define what is meant by the term 'resilience' in families. Identify, with reference to research, the factors that contribute to resilience.

Question 8.4   (LO 8.4)

In what ways do the problems of childhood, adolescence and adulthood impact on families of individuals on the autism spectrum?

Question 8.5   (LO 8.5)

List the kinds of short break services available for families and state some of the problems in accessing these.

Chapter 9   Challenging issues

Ilona Roth

9.1   Introduction

In Chapter 1 you encountered key milestones between Kanner's first description of autism and the concept of the autism spectrum which emerged in the 1980s. Chapters 2 to 8 highlighted aspects of definition and diagnosis, theory and practice, education and family life, which contribute to a 21st century understanding of the autism spectrum. This last chapter reflects on some key themes and issues, and also looks forward to where the next main developments and challenges are likely to lie. Before reading on, Activity 9.1 invites you to note down your own reflections.

Activity 9.1   Reflecting on key themes, issues and challenges
Allow 30 minutes for this activity

Note down what *you* consider to be (i) the most important themes covered by this book, (ii) key issues that have emerged in discussion and (iii) challenges that remain in the autism field. The following discussion is inevitably selective, and you may well make some different choices.

9.2   Routes to understanding the autism spectrum

Today's sources for understanding autism are much richer and more varied than when Kanner and Asperger started out in the 1940s. To grasp the transformation that has occurred since those early days, consider the wide range of contemporary methods and approaches to autism that you have encountered in this book. The psychology of autism – the substantial current knowledge about symptoms and underlying processes – is extensively informed by clinical observations and case studies, and by research using well-established methods, including experiments, observational studies, questionnaires and surveys. **Psychometric techniques** provide ways of measuring intelligence, language skills and other cognitive capacities, and help to ensure appropriate sampling and matching in research studies, so that conclusions can be drawn with some confidence. The biology of autism draws upon the latest advances in scientific techniques. For instance, genetic insights have unfolded hand in hand with developments in molecular genetics and the mapping of the human genome. Today's brain imaging techniques, including MRI, fMRI and MEG, provide visual maps of the structure and functioning of the live brain that would have been undreamed of in earlier years. In the fields of clinical practice and education, well-specified interventions and robust techniques for evaluating their efficacy serve to guide and inform the work of practitioners. They can judge with some confidence which techniques will have a beneficial effect, and can help families and individuals to avoid bogus or risky interventions.

All of these developments in science and practice have enhanced 'outside' insights into autism; that is, insights from the perspective of the observer, whether scientist, practitioner, student or member of the public. But an equally significant development in this recent period has been the growth of 'inside' or 'first-hand' accounts of experience, and other contributions to the field, by people who are themselves on the autism spectrum.

9.2.1 First-hand contributions to understanding autism

When I had been gifted this mind of mine

I recall his voice very clearly

To you I have given this mind

And you shall be the only kind

No one ever will like you be

And I name you the mind tree

I can't see or talk

Yet I can imagine

I can hope and I can expect

I am able to feel pain but I cannot cry

So I just be and wait for the pain to subside

(From 'The mind tree', a poem by Tito Rajarshi Mukhopadhyay, 2000, p. 104)

At one time, it would have seemed inconceivable for a person on the autism spectrum to write this, or indeed any of the other personal testimonies that have illustrated this book. The prototype of the person with autism for many years was that of a profoundly disabled individual, with very limited powers of communication. Tito Mukhopadhyay fits this prototype in some ways – for instance, he has little spoken communication – and yet he is capable of expressing himself most eloquently through writing poetry.

Despite this striking achievement, there is still considerable scepticism about whether people on the spectrum have sufficient **awareness of self** to accurately describe their own experiences. To explain why this is so, the concept of self-awareness needs further elaboration.

Broadly speaking, awareness of self, or self-awareness, can be defined as the capacity to be aware of one's own inner states, experiences and characteristic ways of engaging with the world (Roth, 2007a). This covers many different levels, which include awareness of one's own:

- sensations and perceptions
- agency, i.e. capacity to act in ways that affect one's own environment
- mental states – thoughts, desires and emotions

- enduring qualities, such as personality and identity
- relationship to others.

Several researchers have suggested that awareness of one's own mental states (the third of the levels above) is a form of theory of mind, relying on the same or similar processes as awareness of other people's mental states. For instance, realising that you are feeling angry or sad and realising that another person is angry or sad may both require the capacity to 'reflect on thoughts'. On this view a person with ToM difficulties may also be expected to have difficulty in reflecting on the self. Frith and Happé (1999, p. 7) commented that people on the autism spectrum 'may know as little about their own minds as about the minds of other people'.

To test this claim, they asked three young men on the autism spectrum to write down what they were thinking at random intervals over a period of time. All three men found the task very difficult and unfamiliar, and their reports described visual images which they experienced as 'pictures in the mind'. The young man with the best ToM skills produced more complex reflections, including references to mental states, while the young man with the poorest ToM skills was completely unable to report his mental experience.

■ How does this research method differ from experimental methods you have encountered elsewhere in this book?

□ There was a very small sample (just three participants) and no control condition; the participants' responses were not measured.

This approach is an example of the **qualitative method**, typically used to gather rich descriptive information which is difficult to quantify or measure – in this case, the young men's first-hand accounts of their experiences.

Qualitative methods often provide very valuable initial insights into a topic. While they do not permit the more robust conclusions that can be derived from experiments and other types of **quantitative method**, they may highlight the questions that need to be further addressed with more systematic methodology.

The case study method (Box 1.2) is a qualitative method since it provides rich descriptive material about single individuals. Observational methods may be either quantitative (see Box 3.3 for an example) or qualitative.

More systematic research on self-awareness has produced mixed findings, especially when the self-awareness concerns an individual's memory for things that have happened to them. Neurotypical people are said to remember more about their own actions and experiences than about other people's, known as the **self-reference effect**. Lombardo et al. (2007) asked participants with HFA or Asperger syndrome to judge how well adjectives such as 'friendly' or 'intelligent' described themselves, a close friend, and a 'dissimilar other' (in this case Harry Potter). After an interval, participants were asked to recognise the previously used adjectives from a larger set that included 'distractors'. Participants on the autism spectrum showed a self-reference effect, i.e. they remembered more of the adjectives that they had applied to themselves than to others. However, this self-reference effect was smaller than in a control group.

Crane et al. (2009) compared the self-defining and autobiographical memories of people on the autism spectrum with those of a control group. Systematic analyses of content and themes suggested that memories in the group on the autism spectrum had fewer specific details than did the controls, and that they made less use of personal memories to update their concept of self.

While these studies suggest that aspects of self-awareness are affected in autism, they do not preclude that able individuals can provide useful insights into autism based upon their own experiences. This is especially so if the person is able to reflect in their own way and their own time, rather than following the exacting requirements of an experimental task. Box 9.1 provides a brief overview of first-hand contributions to the field.

Figure 9.1 Temple Grandin (b. 1947) is an Associate Professor of Animal Science at Colorado State University. She is an expert on animal science and animal welfare, and plays a leading role in advocacy for people on the autism spectrum. (Temple Grandin)

Figure 9.2 Michelle Dawson (b. 1961) collaborates on psychological studies of autism with colleagues at the University of Montreal. She has campaigned on many issues relating to autism, including rights in Canada. (Michelle Dawson)

Box 9.1   First-hand contributions to the autism field

Probably the first of many fascinating and valuable first-hand accounts of autism was the autobiography by the American academic Temple Grandin (Grandin and Scariano, 1986) (Figure 9.1). Grandin described her visual thinking style, and likened her intense anxiety to the fear experienced by livestock going to be branded, sheared or to the slaughterhouse. Inspired by the machines used to steady animals during such operations, she designed a human 'squeeze machine' which she herself found to be very soothing to sit in. Similar devices have since been adopted in schools for children with autism in both the USA and the UK. Grandin has built a very successful career in the field of livestock handling, and the design of more humane methods for slaughtering animals for the meat trade. Moreover, she has used the example of her own success and public standing to show how more could be done to both nurture and harness the talents of others with HFA and Asperger syndrome (Grandin and Duffy, 2004).

Another academic on the autism spectrum is Therese Jolliffe whose reminiscence of her childhood, and experimental work on weak central coherence featured in Section 4.6. Jolliffe's ability to channel her personal insights into the design of scientific tests of theory makes a special contribution to the field. Michelle Dawson (Figure 9.2), also an academic, collaborates on autism research with colleagues at the University of Montreal, and is active in promoting the interests of people on the autism spectrum through her regular blog on topical issues.

Luke Jackson (Figure 9.3), a member of the Jackson family discussed in Section 8.5.3, wrote his own guide to Asperger syndrome for teenagers when he was 13 (Jackson, 2002). His book, which is full of humour and insight, ranges widely across situations that many adolescents find challenging, such as sleep, bullying and dating. But his personal reminiscences and advice on topics such as 'fascinations and fixations', 'sense and sense abilities' and use of language provide a unique form of support for young people on the spectrum, as well as an invaluable resource for parents and teachers. Here is Jackson's sound response to television programmes that give the impression that everyone on the autism spectrum is an eccentric genius:

> Parents please don't expect your autistic or AS kid to suddenly burst forth with such talent. They just may not have any phenomenal

talents but that makes them no less a person than a 'savant'. We are all amazing in our own way.

(Jackson, 2002, p. 189)

Talented individuals like Daniel Tammet (Figure 9.4), who featured in Section 3.6.2, have the self-possession to deal with the difficulties presented by media attention. When Tammett read his autobiography on BBC Radio 4, he provided cogent insights into what it feels like to have an autistic condition.

The capacity for self-expression by people with autism is perhaps most surprising in literary fields such as poetry. After all, poetry usually requires flair in using language figuratively (i.e. with metaphors, similes and other non-literal expressions), as well as deep insights into 'the human condition'. As you saw in Chapters 3 and 4, these are both areas where people on the spectrum might be expected to have difficulties. Roth (2007b) conducted a systematic analysis of samples of poetry by five writers on the autism spectrum, and showed, nonetheless, that the poets with autism employed a range of imaginative language in their works. Thematically, their work often focused on the self, and spoke poignantly of the difficulties of autism, as in this extract from a poem by Craig Romkema:

Figure 9.3 Luke Jackson (b. 1988) wrote an award-winning guide to Asperger syndrome for adolescents, drawing extensively on his own experience, and life in a multiplex family.
(Jacqui Jackson)

From the beginnings of my differentness, I remember

doctors, students, therapists

measuring my head,

the tightness of my muscles,

the tracking of my eyes,

the dysfunctions of my stomach.

Some were stiff and cold,

others blessedly kind,

others not acknowledging I understood every word

they said,

so freely did they label me retarded,

or some other variant,

equally untrue.

(From 'Perspectives', a poem by Craig Romkema, 2002, p. 23)

Figure 9.4 Daniel Tammet (b. 1979) has provided, through books and media appearances, unique insights into his own prodigious talents, and the experience of growing up with synesthesia, epilepsy and Asperger syndrome.
(Jerome Tabet)

First-hand accounts both enrich and qualify insights from research and clinical practice, and enable people on the spectrum to voice their own feelings, opinions and preferences, rather than have others speak for them. However, there is no certain way of knowing whether the experiences and perspectives of those who can talk or write about themselves are representative. For instance, Temple Grandin's account of her visual thinking style is sometimes taken to indicate that all people on the autism spectrum think 'visually'. Yet

Figure 9.5 Wendy Lawson (b. 1952) studied psychology with The Open University and has gained a PhD from Deakin University, Victoria, Australia. She is a poet, writer and educator and has brought up four children. (Wendy Lawson)

other writers such as Wendy Lawson (Figure 9.5) have expressed a particular affinity with words, including poetry (Lawson, 2006).

One challenge for the future, therefore, is to empower as many individuals as possible across the autism spectrum to communicate about their experiences, feelings and attitudes. Section 6.5 described a range of interventions which focus on enhancing communication. Notice that they often employ communicative channels other than spoken language, which some find very difficult. One current campaign argues that computers should be widely available to people on the autism spectrum, as an autism-friendly form of communication which helps to overcome the social and educational barriers created by difficulties in producing and making sense of spoken language (Murray and Lawson, 2007). Murray (2008) has also made the important point that enhanced communication is a two-way process: neurotypical individuals need to adjust their communicative strategies when interacting with those on the autism spectrum, as well as the other way round.

9.2.2 Summary of Section 9.2

- Routes to understanding autism have increased substantially in scope and variety in recent years.

- Despite limitations in some self-awareness tasks, people on the autism spectrum can enhance understanding of autism through first-hand accounts of their experiences and other contributions to the field.

9.3 The autism spectrum: ongoing evolution of a concept

As Section 1.9 explained, autism specialists have often operated with both a sub-type and a continuum interpretation of the spectrum, depending upon which was more useful for specific purposes (recall the analogy to the spectrum of visible light in Figure 1.8). The sub-type interpretation, illustrated in Chapter 2, Figure 2.3, assumes overlapping but distinguishable diagnostic entities, each with its own slightly different set of criteria. Diagnosis following DSM-IV-TR and ICD-10 criteria embodies this sub-type approach.

Within the continuum approach *all* individuals in a population can be located along a scale or dimension, according to how they score on measurable autistic traits. Thus all individuals can be scored on Baron-Cohen's empathising and systemising quotients (EQ and SQ – see Section 4.7), only those with a markedly low EQ/high SQ pattern being considered as falling within the autism range. Baron-Cohen and colleagues have also developed an overall autism measure, the **autism-spectrum quotient (AQ)**, which combines some questions about empathising and systemising with others covering a range of characteristic autistic traits. Continuum approaches like this treat differences in communication, and other psychological characteristics that vary across the autism spectrum as differences of degree, not kind. Continuum approaches can also allow for a fuzzy or indistinct boundary between the autism spectrum and 'normality'. Thus on measures such as the EQ, SQ and AQ, there is no sharp cut-off between those with and those without autism diagnoses. The fact that parents and siblings of individuals on the autism spectrum sometimes have obvious or subtle autistic traits (the broader autism phenotype or BAP) is consistent with this graduated difference between those with autism and the neurotypical population.

While the sub-type and continuum approaches have coexisted up to now, they may become less compatible in the future, raising some challenging issues for both those working on autism, and those on the spectrum themselves. Two topical issues are highlighted here.

9.3.1 Diagnostic criteria of the future: DSM-V

At the time of completing this book (2009), the current version of the DSM criteria are due for replacement in a few years. The Neurodevelopmental Disorders Work Group is the panel that has been considering revisions to the diagnostic criteria for pervasive developmental disorders (see Sections 2.2.1 to 2.2.3). *No definitive decisions have been made*, but an interim Work Group report (Swedo, 2009) published as an online bulletin of the American Psychiatric Association, indicates a potential move away from sub-types towards a continuum approach. *Currently*, the revisions under discussion include:

- replacing the umbrella term 'pervasive developmental disorders' with the term 'autism spectrum disorders' (ASD)
- treating ASD as a single (albeit variable) diagnostic entity, diagnosed with a single set of criteria
- removing the sub-types (autistic disorder, Asperger's disorder and PDD-NOS) from the diagnostic criteria
- reflecting the wide differences in the expression of symptoms across the spectrum with a severity measure, to yield severe, moderately severe and less severe ASD diagnoses, together with a borderline range corresponding to the BAP, and a range reflecting autistic traits in the 'normal' population
- amalgamating the social interaction and communication aspects of the diagnostic triad into one social communication symptom group.

The Work Group's proposals are designed to address what are seen as significant shortcomings of the current DSM-IV-TR criteria. Some professionals now believe that relatively clear-cut distinctions between the symptoms of classic autism, Asperger syndrome and PDD-NOS are not supported by the evidence, making diagnostic separation of these sub-types unreliable and inconsistent. It has been suggested that in some cases the same child may receive different sub-type diagnoses, depending on the clinician and/or the area in which he or she lives. The proposed severity scale aims to address these anomalies by representing inter-individual variation both across and beyond the spectrum as points on a continuous scale.

- If you think back to Chapter 2, what aspects of the discussion suggest that diagnostic sub-types may be difficult to differentiate?

☐ Section 2.2.4 described instances in which symptoms meet more than one set of diagnostic criteria (e.g. for both classic autism and Asperger syndrome). In this case, diagnostic specialists may take a pragmatic or practical decision about which diagnosis to adopt.

While the Work Group proposals have attracted substantial support, they have also stimulated considerable debate among experts, individuals on the spectrum and their families (see, for instance, Dawson, 2009). One concern is that there is, as yet, no generally agreed criterion of what counts as more or less severe. For instance, if one child engages in more spinning or hand flapping than another, this might seem an obvious example of a more severe symptom. But more hand flapping does not invariably mean that the first child is more disabled or more severely autistic than the second. For some children, such behaviours may act as coping strategies enabling them to focus effectively in other respects. Estimating severity correctly might also prove difficult if a child has an uneven profile of skills and difficulties, which is frequently the case in autism. For instance, if a child has an exceptional knowledge of vocabulary and poor social interaction skills, a severity score based on an average of these two symptoms would give no indication of the child's enhanced ability in one area and difficulties in another.

A further implication of the new proposals is likely to be that the labels autistic disorder, Asperger syndrome and PDD-NOS will lose their current formal status. This too excites strong feelings among the autistic community and their families. As you saw in Chapter 2, diagnostic sub-types may have important practical consequences in terms of the support, education and services that the individual and his or her family will receive. Those parents who feel that a diagnosis of autistic disorder has helped them to access the appropriate special support and educational services for their child are likely to look unfavourably on the loss of this label. On the other hand, those parents who have found a diagnosis of Asperger syndrome, which some consider a non-disabling condition, an impediment to accessing necessary support, may welcome the more individually focused evaluation which a severity-based diagnosis of autism spectrum disorder would bring.

The identity offered by a specific diagnostic label is also important to some. Those with a current diagnosis of Asperger syndrome may feel that if this label loses its formal status, their identity will be eroded. They may fear an increased sense of stigma at being 'just' part of the autism spectrum, rather than a member of a separate, even elite group. On the other hand, some with a diagnosis of classic autism may see the severity continuum as less discriminatory: it avoids sharp divisions both between groups on the spectrum, and between the spectrum and the neurotypical population.

There are two further points to note about the Work Group proposals. Firstly, the final proposal in the list above is to merge communication and social interaction difficulties into one diagnostic symptom group.

■ What do you think is the reason for this?

☐ The two types of difficulty are closely interrelated. For instance, a child who lacks language and other communication skills is very likely to have difficulties in interacting socially; a child who lacks the motivation or skill for social interaction may fail to enhance his/her communication skills. Some symptoms, such as unusual eye gaze can be seen as both a social interaction and a communication difficulty.

Finally, notice that the DSM-V proposals outlined above do not include a formal role for sensory and perceptual atypicalities in the diagnostic criteria, though the Work Group is known to have discussed this at certain stages. The importance of these symptoms for many parents and individuals, and the strikingly high estimate of their prevalence cited in a recent paper (Geschwind, 2009) suggest that this should remain on the agenda. As indicated earlier, the 2009 version of the DSM-V proposals is provisional, and it remains to be seen how problems like those outlined will be addressed.

9.3.2 Autism: disorder or difference?

Regardless of how DSM-V finally turns out, the question of the relationship between the autism spectrum and the rest of the population is one with important social and ethical implications. Traditionally, autism has been viewed as akin to a medical problem like diabetes. This **medical model** of autism sees it as a disorder – a disabling condition that reflects a departure from 'normal' functioning, and calls for clinical diagnosis and treatment, with the aim of rendering the individual as near to 'normality' as possible. A number of able people on the spectrum are vociferous in rejecting this conception of autism, arguing that it should be viewed as a valid alternative to neurotypicality – as a difference, not a disordered, and by implication inferior, state.

You encountered versions of the 'disorder or difference' debate in Sections 6.1.1 and 7.2.7. In each of these contexts the concept of 'difference' is contrasted with those of 'disorder', 'disability' and 'deficit', with broadly similar implications. Related considerations have informed ongoing debates about autism terminology, such as the preferability of autism spectrum condition (ASC), autism spectrum disorder (ASD) or neither term (see Box 1.1).

An aspect of the difference perspective is illustrated in a research study by Hurlbutt and Chalmers (2002). They conducted interviews with three high-functioning individuals over a period of nine months and then used a qualitative method to analyse the material for key themes that recurred throughout. One such theme was the participants' strong disinclination to become like neurotypicals (i.e. like non-autistic members of the population). One participant commented:

> Now I don't want to be like anyone else, period. I don't necessarily see the idea of NT [neurotypical] as perfection. Hey, regular people do stupid, mean, and often evil things that people with autism would never do. I am supposed to look up to that?

> *(Joe in Hurlbutt and Chalmers, 2002, p. 106)*

The writer and poet Wendy Lawson (Figure 9.5) expresses related views in a recent book entitled *Concepts of Normality: The autistic and typical spectrum*

(Lawson, 2008). As the title implies, she rejects the idea of a single 'normality' from which the autism spectrum is a departure. Rather, she argues, what is normal for one individual or group may not be normal for another.

Those in the 'difference not disorder' lobby are making a very valuable contribution to changing perceptions of people with autism. However, their views are not universally shared. Some parents, in particular, feel that the 'difference' view may be appropriate for high-functioning individuals who are leading relatively fulfilled and independent lives, but does not accurately reflect the distress, suffering and disability that many experience as a result of their autism.

A challenge for the future will be to try and find some middle ground between these differing views. As this brief discussion has tried to show, the issues are complex and controversial, with no easy solutions. Indeed, the difference perspective is not a unified view, but lends itself to different interpretations.

■   Do you think people who view autism as a difference will favour the concept of the autism spectrum as a continuum?

☐   By locating all individuals along the same dimension, rather than placing them in distinct categories, the continuum approach supports the view that people with autism are part of the same population as neurotypicals, and not sharply differentiated from them as a disordered group. This non-categorical perspective seems less discriminatory. However, some people on the autism spectrum prefer the idea that they are *distinctively* different rather than being just at a different point on a scale with neurotypical people.

If you work with autism, have friends or family who are on the spectrum, or are on the spectrum yourself, you will no doubt have your own views. Regardless of the label, there is surely unanimous agreement on the right of people with autism to be treated with dignity, respect and without discrimination.

9.3.3   Summary of Section 9.3

*   Sub-type and continuum concepts of the autism spectrum are both in current use, each with different roles.
*   Provisional proposals for DSM-V, publicised in 2009, include withdrawing the main diagnostic sub-types and adopting a single scale to differentiate severity of symptoms in different individuals.
*   The question of autism as difference, rather than disorder or disability, is a complex issue which attracts different views.

9.4   Prevalence variations

Section 2.6 considered reasons for the increasing numbers of autism spectrum diagnoses compared with earlier years. As you saw, the most likely cause of this increase is the impact of constantly improving understanding of the autism spectrum on diagnostic criteria and diagnostic practices, though the possibility of an increase in the numbers of individuals actually affected by autism has not been conclusively ruled out.

Section 2.6 also considered the way estimates of autism prevalence vary worldwide. A review of research by Dyches et al. (2004) indicates that prevalence estimates also differ between ethnic groups within a population. For instance, in the USA, lower prevalence estimates have been reported in Hispanic and Native American groups. Here again, it is likely that some of these disparities reflect differences in awareness and attitudes between ethnic groups, together with differential access to diagnosis. But as Dyches et al. suggest, the possibility of factors that render some ethnic groups more susceptible to the risk of autism than others requires further investigation.

One of the most striking and reliable disparities in prevalence for the autism spectrum is that between males and females. There is currently a renewed interest in this difference, which is considered next.

9.4.1   The male/female difference in autism prevalence

The ratio of males to females with autism spectrum diagnoses is usually quoted as 4 : 1, and this rises to around 10 : 1 for those with a diagnosis of Asperger syndrome. The broader autism phenotype (BAP) is also more commonly found among male relatives than female relatives (Goin-Kochel et al., 2007). These differences have generally been attributed to biological differences in susceptibility.

The most obvious basis for greater autism prevalence in males might seem to be genetic. In certain inherited conditions which affect more males than females, the characteristics that confer susceptibility are **sex-linked**, meaning that the genes that code for these characteristics are located on the X chromosome. As you saw in Section 5.3.1, females have two X chromosomes while males have one X and one Y chromosome. In females, the effects of a mutation on the X chromosome inherited from one parent may be masked or neutralised if the X chromosome inherited from the other parent does not carry this gene variant. In contrast, since males have only one X chromosome, the effects of such a mutation are more likely to be expressed in the person's **phenotype**.

Phenotype means the sum of an individual's characteristics, as determined by the interaction of their genetic make-up with environmental influences. Phenotype includes physical features such as eye colour and height, together with biochemical, physiological and behavioural attributes.

There is some evidence to suggest a *small* association between genetic atypicalities on the X chromosome and autism.

■   Can you suggest two sources of evidence that were highlighted in Chapter 5?

☐   Autism occurs in about 25% of cases of Fragile X syndrome, which results from a mutation in the *FMR1* gene on the X chromosome. Figure 5.8 indicates four regions on the X chromosome in which promising candidate genes for autism have been found.

However, scientists currently believe that genes located on the X chromosomes are unlikely to play the major role in causing autism. As emphasised in Chapter 5, candidate genes for autism are located on many different chromosomes; the relative importance of the different candidate genes in autism and the biological mechanisms by which they have their impact are as yet unclear.

Another theory about the male/female disparity in autism focuses on hormonal rather than genetic influences. According to Baron-Cohen and colleagues (see, for instance, Auyeung et al., 2009), raised levels of the hormone testosterone, to which the fetus is exposed before birth, may predispose the child to autistic traits. Testosterone, which is present in high concentrations in males, and much lower concentrations in females, is responsible for the development of male sexual characteristics, such as penis, testes and facial hair, and is also thought to influence brain development in ways that result in 'typically masculine' psychological traits. Baron-Cohen and colleagues suggest that unusually high fetal levels of this hormone may lead to development of the 'extreme male brain' type characterised by skill at systemising and difficulties in empathising (see Section 4.7). This profile could occur in either a male or a female child, but is much more likely to occur in males, because their baseline levels of testosterone are much higher. So far, however, there is no direct evidence linking high levels of fetal testosterone to the development of autism in infancy.

The research outlined here offers a selective and critical snapshot of biological influences that might contribute to the higher prevalence of autism in males. Recently another quite different possibility has been highlighted. Anecdotal reports from clinicians, and from women on the spectrum themselves, suggest that autism spectrum diagnoses, especially those of Asperger syndrome, are more likely to be missed in girls than in boys.

- How might such under-diagnosis affect the strikingly higher estimated ratio of males to females for Asperger syndrome (10:1) than for the autism spectrum as a whole (4:1)?

□ It could be that some or all of this greater male/female disparity for Asperger syndrome is due to under-diagnosis in females.

Clinical experts such as Tony Attwood (Attwood et al., 2006) have suggested that under-diagnosis occurs because the symptoms of autism in women do not necessarily conform to the stereotype of obsessive interest in machines and other physical systems, coupled with emotional and social withdrawal. Girls on the autism spectrum may have more 'typically female' interests, such as dolls or fiction, with the result that an unusually obsessive focus in these areas may be overlooked. Through an interest in other people's behaviour, and/or a desire to conform, they may make a great effort to appear sociable, emulating the behaviour of their peers. This is well illustrated in this extract from the autobiography of Liane Holliday Willey:

> My mother tells me I was very good at capturing the essence and persona of people. At times I literally copied someone's looks and their actions. I was uncanny in my ability to copy accents, vocal inflections, facial expressions, hand movements, gaits and tiny gestures. It was as if I became the person I was emulating.

(Willey, 1999, p. 22)

In summary, disparities between the behaviour of girls on the spectrum and the usual expectations for autism may mean that difficulties, especially in intellectually able girls, are overlooked by parents, teachers and professionals. These girls may struggle with years of isolation and difference, and only in adulthood come to understand the source of their problems, sometimes through receiving help for a co-morbid condition such as depression. Nonetheless under-diagnosis alone is unlikely to explain all of the marked excess of males over females on the autism spectrum, and the challenge for future research will be to explore all sources of this difference, and how they relate to each other. The wider issue of integrating biological and psychological explanations with practice is considered next.

9.4.2 Summary of Section 9.4

- Disparities in prevalence rates across time and across cultural groups most probably reflect differences in awareness and diagnostic practices; the possibility of actual differences in the numbers affected merits further exploration.

- The markedly higher prevalence of autism in males is likely to reflect biological influences, though their precise nature remains unclear.

- More subtle expression of autism in females, together with male-oriented expectations about autistic behaviour, may also lead to under-diagnosis in females, especially in those with Asperger syndrome.

9.5 Psychology, biology and practice: integrating perspectives

Chapters 3 to 5 of this book presented a wealth of evidence concerning the psychology and biology of autism. Chapter 6 considered current techniques of intervention, and Chapter 7 covered further techniques which are used in educational settings. This section considers common threads between these approaches, but also indicates that they do not as yet constitute a unified framework.

9.5.1 Integrating psychological characteristics and psychological theories

Chapters 3 and 4 dealt in turn with the observable symptoms and characteristics of autism, and the psychological theories which seek to explain them. To a reasonable extent, the theories map onto the psychological characteristics: each theory identified a psychological process or processes (for instance, theory of mind, executive function) as the key influence underlying one or more observable symptoms and characteristics of autism (communication, repetitive activities and interests, etc.).

One important conclusion from Chapter 4 was that none of the theoretical approaches could account for all the observable symptoms and characteristics of autism; rather, several processes may operate together to produce these outcomes. However, this multiple factor model (see Box 4.1 and Section 4.8) begs several questions. For one thing, it is still not clear which processes *are* the crucial ones: it may be that intersubjectivity (a core process in Hobson's social developmental theory) or empathising difficulties play a more fundamental role in social and communication difficulties than theory of mind, or that systemising, rather than weak central coherence or executive function, is responsible for repetitive activities. A further question is whether these psychological processes operate entirely independently, or interact such that, for instance, difficulties in theory of mind and weak central coherence potentiate each other in the course of development. The study by Pellicano et al. described in Section 4.8 suggested independent effects of theory of mind, executive function and weak central coherence on autism. However, if other psychological processes are involved, their effects may be interactive.

Chapter 4 also emphasised the importance of considering how processes fit into a developmental framework. For instance, primary and secondary intersubjectivity operate at an early stage in development, with potential consequences for theory of mind. This is likely to involve two-way interactions between processes and behaviour: a problem with primary intersubjectivity may reduce a child's scope for social interaction and communication, which in turn affects their opportunities to develop theory of mind.

Some of these points are illustrated schematically in Figure 9.6. This figure is *provisional* and suggests one possible way of extending Figure 5.24 to incorporate psychological processes. For simplicity, the role of genetic, environmental and prenatal effects depicted at the left of Figure 5.24 are not shown in Figure 9.6 but are nonetheless assumed. *You do not need to understand all the details of Figure 9.6, but rather grasp some key points.*

Figure 9.6 interpolates psychological processes (central lilac-coloured boxes), between biological functions such as the organisation of neurons and cortex (green boxes at left) and observable characteristics of autism (blue boxes at right). Notice that these observable characteristics include not just the three diagnostic symptom groups shown in Figure 5.24, but also two other areas of functioning that are beginning to feature in psychological theories of autism.

■   Which two boxes in the right-hand column represent non-diagnostic characteristics?

☐   Sensory and perceptual atypicalities (third box down) and attention to detail/other special skills (fourth box down).

For now, consider just the central and right-hand columns of boxes: the next section will discuss how psychological processes integrate with biological understanding. Five of the boxes within the middle column represent psychological processes implicated in autism by the different theories outlined in Chapter 4. Further research may eliminate some of these processes and/or add others, the details of which are as yet unknown (see fourth box down labelled 'other process(es)'. One candidate for this box might be altered sensory processing strategies, which may produce both the atypical reactivity to sound, taste and other stimuli, and the attention to detail observed in autism. The arrows linking psychological processes to the symptoms and characteristics on the right also mirror the discussion in Chapter 4, and are

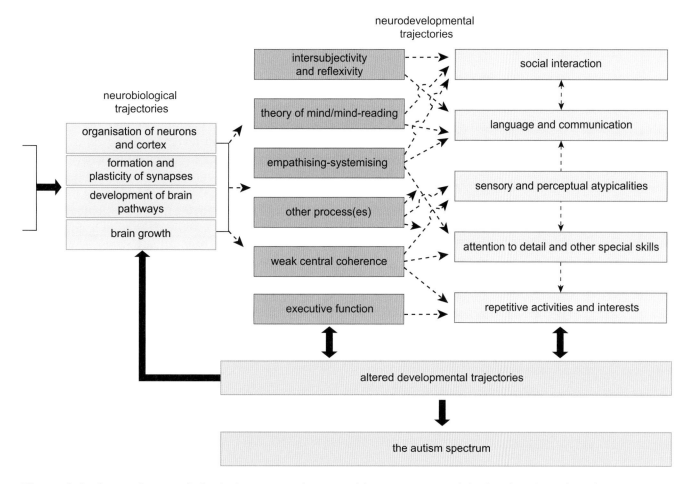

Figure 9.6 Integrating psychological processes into a multi-component model of autism (see also Figure 5.24).

dotted to indicate the provisional status of the links. Research evidence links the top two central boxes more closely to difficulties in social interaction and communication, while the bottom two boxes link most readily to characteristics such as attention to detail, special skills and repetitive activities. The E-S theory combines two processes – empathising, linking to social characteristics, and systemising, linking to 'non-social' characteristics, while for the box labelled 'other processes' links are as yet speculative.

Upwards and downward links between the right-hand blue group of boxes suggest some possible interactions at this level. Sensory and perceptual atypicalities may well affect the development of language, communication and social interaction. For instance, a child who does not pick up subtle cues, such as gestures, facial expressions and tones of voice, is likely to have difficulty in developing his own communication skills. As already suggested in Section 9.3.1, communication and social interaction are closely interrelated. Equally, sensory and perceptual atypicalities may promote attention to detail, and may also result in a narrow repetitive focus on specific objects and activities. Finally, notice the way both psychological processes and behavioural outcomes may influence and be influenced by the developmental trajectory (long yellow box towards the bottom of the figure). Difficulties emerging early in development are likely to have cumulative consequences over the course of later development.

9.5.2 Integrating psychology and biology

You may wonder why the psychological processes incorporated in Figure 9.6 did not feature in the earlier model depicted in Figure 5.24. One reason is that Figure 5.24 focused specifically on the different levels of biological evidence discussed in that chapter. In addition, Figure 5.24 illustrated the key importance that biological scientists place on working with observables, whether these are gene sequences along chromosomes, brain images or behavioural outcomes such as patterns of repetitive activity. Psychological theories represent a different level of analysis, and are derived in a different way from biological explanations. For instance, executive function is not an observable entity, but is a **theoretical construct** concerning cognitive activity – a concise theoretical summary, derived from observations of how individuals perform in tasks such as the Tower of Hanoi or the Wisconsin card sorting tasks.

Despite this less tangible status of psychological processes, there are reasons for including them as potential links in the causal chain leading to autism. For instance, there is growing evidence that alterations in the structure and functioning of the cortex have psychological consequences that are explicable as deficits in theory of mind, executive function and so on. This is depicted in Figure 9.6 as the dotted arrows from the green boxes at left to the central lilac-coloured boxes.

- ■ Can you think of evidence cited in Chapter 5 which links brain structures to some of the psychological processes shown in Figure 9.6?

- ☐ Section 5.5.2 linked frontal lobe atypicalities to executive function difficulties. This is further supported by the evidence (Section 4.4.2) that people with autism have similar difficulties in executive function tasks to people with frontal lobe damage. Section 5.5.2 linked atypical structure and function of the amygdala and associated brain regions to difficulties in recognising emotional expressions, a form of mind-reading.

Brain imaging carried out during tasks involving emotion recognition, empathising and executive function is helping to build a picture of how atypical brain functioning may underpin these processes. However, as Chapter 5 emphasised, there is no simple mapping between specific psychological processes and specific brain regions. For instance, emotion recognition and other forms of mind-reading have been shown to involve a complex configuration of structures linked into circuits across the brain, and including the amygdala, orbitofrontal cortex, superior temporal sulcus, fusiform gyrus and other structures. On a more speculative note, it has been suggested that weak central coherence, which promotes attention to detail at the expense of a more meaningful view of things, may stem from differences in connectivity, or the way in which different parts of the brain communicate via neurons (see Section 5.5.2).

Finally, notice from Figure 9.6 the arrows linking both psychological processes and behavioural outcomes, via altered developmental trajectories, to the neurobiological level. This is designed to show that atypicalities in psychological processes (intersubjectivity, theory of mind, executive function, etc.) are likely to affect the way the brain develops over time. In particular, the growth and development of synapses (neural plasticity – see Section 5.4.1) depends on the inputs to neurons, which in turn depends on how the individual interacts with the environment. A bias in the types of information the individual processes affects the type of information transmitted to neurons, and over time may alter the capacity of the nervous system to handle information in a more effective fashion.

9.5.3 Integrating psychology, biology and practice

Though the integration of theories about autism is important, for those who experience autism at close hand, it is more crucial to harness this knowledge to improve interventions. As you saw in Chapters 6 and 7, the best evaluated and most effective interventions to date employ psychosocial techniques and target the psychological characteristics of autism. Many of these psychosocial approaches are extensively informed by broad psychological principles relevant to autism, such as the importance of structure, and the value of visual means of communication. The increasing trend for interventions to draw specifically on psychological theory is also encouraging, since such interventions are likely to target core problems such as theory of mind and empathy difficulties. Examples include the *Mind Reading* and *Transporters* software-based interventions in Chapter 6, which seek to develop recognition of emotions and other mind-reading skills. Another interesting intervention, the 'CAT-Kit' developed by Dr Tony Attwood, uses a range of visual aids to help children and young people on the autism spectrum enhance their awareness of their *own* feelings and behaviour. One tool in the kit is a large picture of a thermometer, on which the child can place stickers of facial expressions to signify the strength of a feeling they are currently experiencing. Interventions drawing directly on theory reflect a promising trend, but require further evaluation of their effectiveness.

While knowledge of the biological bases of autism has increased dramatically over the last few years, this does not, for the moment, offer the prospect of a biological intervention which would target core difficulties in autism. Pharmacological interventions (Section 6.6.1) do not tackle core difficulties in autism, and the clear role of genetic factors in autism highlights how difficult it will be to develop biological interventions. Nonetheless, biological insights have implications for psychological interventions. It seems clear that alterations in the way neurons grow and connect to one another during early development plays a role in autism. As you saw in Section 5.4.1, these connections, which are made via synapses, are not immutable. Neural plasticity means that synaptic connections change, depending on the types of activation the synapse receives. This in turn depends on the way an individual interacts with his/her environment, and the types of information their brain receives via sensory, perceptual and cognitive processes. It follows from this that early identification of autism, followed by early intervention, are highly desirable as this offers potential scope to influence a child's neurodevelopmental trajectory. The challenges, then, are to improve the quality of early screening tools (see Section 2.5), so that autism can be reliably picked up at an early age, and to identify which interventions are most worth employing, taking into account that autism also creates different intervention needs in different children.

9.5.4 Summary of Section 9.5

- Theories about the key psychological processes in autism, and their role in the observable symptoms and characteristics of autism are likely to be further revised in the light of research.

- Key psychological processes can be provisionally included in an account of the causal sequence leading to autism. This sequence includes extensive interaction and feedback between psychological and biological levels, which impact on the developmental trajectory involved in autism.

- Insights into the psychological and biological influences in autism highlight the need for early identification and early intervention.

9.6 Autism and society

This book has legitimately presented a positive picture of advances in autism research, theory and practice, and both the UK and the USA have played a major role in this progress. Unfortunately, there is a long way to go in ensuring that the benefits of this knowledge and practice are experienced throughout the world, and indeed among different cultural and age-groups within countries such as the UK. This last section looks at some of the challenges in this area.

9.6.1 Global issues

The following extract is from an account posted by Martha Afriyie on the website of the organisation 'Autism Speaks':

> My name is Martha and I am a mother of a two (almost three) year old who has autism. I started noticing the signs when she was about a year old but it wasn't until she was two that we finally had a diagnosis of ASD. The delay in diagnosis was partly due to the fact that in our part of the world (I am in Ghana), autism is a fairly unknown condition even to the medical practitioners.
>
> [...]
>
> Getting the diagnosis didn't make matters easy. It meant my worst fear had been confirmed and I felt that I was just having a bad dream. There were moments of anger, frustration and disappointment. I had so many questions that I couldn't find answers to, and to make matters worse, my family didn't understand the full implications of the diagnosis.
>
> [...]
>
> I was introduced to a woman who has set up a school for children who have autism, here in Ghana. Her name is Mrs Serwaa Quainoo. She has a son

with autism; he is the inspiration behind the establishment of the school. The school is such a wonderful place and the passion and dedication of the staff is just amazing. Autism Awareness, Care and Training Centre is the only known institution for children who have autism in the whole West African sub-region and this school has transformed my daughter's life. I am forever grateful to the teachers, caregivers and staff of this school.

(Afriyie, 2009)

This extract epitomises the obstacles that many parents in non-Western countries confront, when they have a child with autism. Roy Grinker, an American anthropologist with a daughter with autism, has documented the kinds of problems Martha highlights (and more), in countries including Korea, India and South Africa (Grinker, 2009). Moreover, as he points out, the situation is little better in certain European countries.

- From the extract, can you identify three factors that make the situation in Ghana particularly difficult for parents like Martha?

- Martha mentions difficulty in accessing specialist diagnosis; lack of understanding within her family; limited availability of schools and other specialist services.

In many countries, difficulty accessing specialist diagnosis will be mainly due to a lack of medical or psychiatric practitioners with the relevant knowledge and training. However, in certain societies this difficulty may be compounded by cultural pressures to deny the existence of autism or to interpret autistic symptoms differently. As Grinker recounts, in South Korea children with autistic symptoms have typically been diagnosed with **reactive attachment disorder or RAD**. This label implies that the child's difficulties with communication and social interaction reflect emotional attachment problems arising from a lack of nurturing by the mother. It may seem surprising that this 'refrigerator mother' view of autism (see Section 1.3) persists anywhere in the world, especially given internet access to alternative perspectives, but the pressures for Korean parents to accept such a diagnosis are complex and subtle. For instance, while the label carries the stigma of blame for the mother, it also alleviates the family of the stigma of a genetic 'taint' which might compromise marriage opportunities for other offspring.

The second problem that Martha mentions, lack of awareness and understanding of autism within the family, may have several consequences. If parents accept the diagnosis and grandparents do not, this may cause family rupture. Grinker talks of a South African couple who, having understood their son's diagnosis, had to move far away from his grandparents, because their insistence on seeking traditional cures for their grandson caused such conflict, and undermined the parents' attempts to get more conventional help for their son. In the situation where no-one in a family has heard of autism, parents may not seek help at all, but rather try to contain, or hide their child's symptoms. In some traditional societies, families may believe that odd behaviour or epileptic fits show that a child is possessed by a spirit. They may seek the help of a shaman or traditional healer to cast out the spirit, with potentially terrifying and damaging consequences for the child.

Religious and cultural beliefs may impact in different ways on how a child with autism is treated. For instance, in Israel, where services for children on the autism spectrum are comparatively well informed and well resourced, it is nonetheless reported that certain orthodox religious groups treat children with autism as oracles or mediums – individuals imbued with divine powers to pronounce on the sins of the world (Lehmann and Siebzehner, 2006; Grinker, 2009). Inevitably there is the risk that these vulnerable children may be exploited as a means of influencing others. In India, where cults have grown up around eccentric individuals with unusual ways of relating to the world, children with autism may sometimes be considered as pure or close to God by analogy. In Native American and Native Hawaiian cultures, children with disabilities are not considered 'abnormal': they are valued and assimilated into the life of the family (Dyches et al., 2004). This last example serves to emphasise that cultural beliefs must be sensitively considered, and if possible harnessed, when dealing with autism in different societies.

Finally, Martha counts herself as very fortunate to have a place for her daughter at the Autism Awareness, Care and Training Centre, but also describes this as the only centre in the West African sub-region. Such scarcity is common. For instance, in India, schools and other support services for all children with autism remain totally inadequate. Grinker describes pioneering work by individual parents to set up schools, which is very reminiscent of how parents founded the NAS in the UK in the 1960s (see Section 1.4).

9.6.2 Ethnic minorities

It may seem that lack of knowledge and services is exclusively a problem of developing countries, while the UK and other developed European countries, as well as the USA, offer ideal models of how to deal with autism. But this would be inaccurate. For instance, while the provision of specialist diagnostic services, education and support for parents is incomparably better in the UK than in many developing countries, a report for the NAS (Corbett and Perepa, 2007) offers evidence that some ethnic minority groups in the UK are disadvantaged in their access to these services. For one thing – as in some traditional societies – in some ethnic minority groups, families may be reluctant to recognise or disclose disability, believing that it brings shame or even a curse on the family. Language and translation difficulties may mean that parents do not understand questions about their child, or are unable to describe his/her atypical behaviour clearly for others. Moreover, some of the early developmental milestones, which feature in diagnostic assessment tools such as the Autism Diagnostic Observation Schedule or ADOS, may be culturally specific, meaning that an ethnic minority family would not recognise the absence of these behaviours as a problem.

- Can you think of any symptoms of autism that might not have the same significance in different ethnic groups?

- ☐ If a child in a western society persistently avoids the gaze of adults, this may be considered impolite or unusual, whereas in many Asian societies making eye contact with an older person is considered inappropriate or disrespectful.

If ethnic minority families are less willing or less able to access diagnostic services, then autism is likely to be under-diagnosed in these communities. The results of a study carried out in the Netherlands were consistent with this prediction (Begeer et al., 2009). Among a group of 712 children referred to diagnostic assessment centres in the Netherlands, the referral rates for Turkish and Moroccan ethnic groups were significantly lower than would be expected by their percentage presence in the general population of that country. The researchers also showed that when paediatricians were presented with fictitious case studies of children from Turkish or Moroccan backgrounds with autistic symptoms, they showed a small bias against identifying autism in these groups. However, prevalence estimates are not invariably lower in ethnic minority groups, and as mentioned earlier, Dyches et al. (2004) do not rule out differences in susceptibility to autism between ethnic groups.

Finally, Corbett and Perepa (2007) considered the educational choices and experiences available to ethnic minority children with autism. They concluded that these children tended to be particularly disadvantaged in terms of the educational support available to them, and especially likely to be bullied. As one child put it:

> Sometimes I feel doubly discriminated, firstly, because of the disability and then because of our skin colour.

> *(Corbett and Perepa, 2007, p. 6)*

The lack of adequate provision for autism worldwide and the unequal access to provision within countries such as the UK present huge challenges for society as a whole. However, there are some encouraging indications. The worldwide accessibility of the internet has enabled many parents to inform themselves about their child's condition, even when local specialist knowledge is limited. Grinker recounts stories of parents who have set up support groups and even schools to help address local needs. Moreover, change takes place more rapidly than it did when parents started campaigning in the UK. In Korea, a film called *Malaton* (meaning 'running boy'), based on the life of an athletic young man with autism, had a massive impact on public awareness and insight when first screened in 2005. Soon afterwards Korean parents started to feel more comfortable about taking their autistic children into public places, universities started to train psychologists and psychiatrists in diagnosis, and the Korean government began to fund facilities and schools.

This chapter concludes by considering another issue of global concern – the situation of adults on the autism spectrum.

9.6.3   Autism in adults

Will Hadcroft, an adult with Asperger syndrome, writes this about his experiences of work:

> I'm happy to be working again after a four-year period of unemployment, and I can't believe that I'm working in an office as opposed to a factory. Six pounds an hour rather than the minimum wage. It's what I've been dreaming of for such a long time: a job I actually like that pays reasonably well.

Blended in with these positive emotions are other feelings, uneasy disturbing feelings, with which I have been doing battle for as long as I can remember.

As I get dressed and eat my breakfast I think about the day ahead: the eyes burning into the back of my skull, the uncertain looks on the faces of my peers as I say or do something not in keeping with the job or conversation. I feel nervous and apprehensive.

(Hadcroft, 2005, p. 9)

Will Hadcroft may seem relatively lucky. He is married, living independently of parents or carers, and has a job. An outcome like this for a person on the autism spectrum is counted as good. Yet Will's wages are small, his job is not commensurate with his evident abilities, and he is constantly anxious about making mistakes or social gaffes in the workplace.

As outlined in Sections 8.3 and 8.6, the outcome for many adults on the autism spectrum is nothing like this positive. One interesting feature of Howlin's follow-up study (Howlin et al., 2004) was that children with above-average IQ (i.e. 100 or higher) did not necessarily achieve better outcomes than those with IQs in the range 70–99. One reason for this was the disruptive influence of stereotyped or repetitive behaviours on life for some adults. One man with a childhood IQ of 114 had to live in a highly supported specialist accommodation, because of crippling anxiety about unpredictable surroundings. Another who had postgraduate qualifications had difficulty working independently because of the amount of time he spent obsessively checking things. The researchers suggested that outcome might have as much to do with the quality of family or other support, as with cognitive and other abilities.

The difficulties experienced by adults, and the crucial importance of adequate support in determining outcome, were confirmed by a major survey of autism in adults published by the NAS as the 'I Exist' report in 2008. The NAS analysed information from 1412 adults with autism and their parents or carers in England. Comparable surveys were conducted in Scotland and Wales. Box 9.2 presents a summary of findings from this survey drawn from the NAS website (NAS, 2008).

Box 9.2   Findings from the NAS 'I Exist' report (2008)

- Nearly two-thirds (63%) of adults with autism do not have enough support to meet their needs.
- 92% of parents are worried about their son's or daughter's future when they are no longer able to care for them.
- 61% of adults with autism rely on their family financially and 40% live with their parents.
- 60% of parents believed that a lack of support has led to higher support needs later on.
- At least one in three adults with autism are experiencing mental health difficulties due to a lack of support.

- 67% of local authorities do not keep a record of how many adults with autism there are in their area and 65% do not even know how many adults with autism they actually support.

It would be sad to conclude this book on the negative note evoked by the statistics in Box 9.2. Happily, however, the campaigning work of the NAS, in collaboration with other autism pressure groups and charities throughout the UK, has triggered some very positive developments designed to enhance services and support for adults. At the time of writing (2009), a piece of draft legislation, **The Autism Bill**, has passed through several stages of the English parliamentary scrutiny process. If it becomes law, both national and regional government will be obliged, by law, to address the serious needs outlined in Box 9.2. Alongside this legislation, the Government has launched a consultation process, inviting all individuals on the autism spectrum to contribute their views to the development of the **National Adult Autism Strategy** for England, due to be announced in 2010. The strategy will identify ways in which the difficulties outlined in Box 9.2 should be met.

Comparable initiatives are underway in Scotland.

Activity 9.2 invites you to reflect on what the priorities might be.

Activity 9.2   Suggested actions for the National Adult Autism Strategy

Allow 15 minutes for this activity

Considering the difficulties for adults on the autism spectrum outlined in this section, suggest some forms of action that you think the National Adult Autism Strategy should include. Comments are at the end of the book.

One of the most positive strategies for supporting adults on the autism spectrum is to support them in finding work. It has been estimated that the annual UK economic cost incurred by autism in adults is £25 billion (Knapp et al., 2009) and the fact that a majority of adults are out of work and dependent on their parents makes an important contribution to this figure. Yet a very successful Danish project demonstrates that many people on the spectrum are eminently employable, given the right kind of job and working environment. Having encountered the difficulties of people on the autism spectrum after the diagnosis of his own son, Lars Sonne started the company Specialisterne. This employs 60 people on the autism spectrum in jobs involving the careful checking of information systems, databases and other tasks requiring good numerical skills and memory, attention to detail and persistence. His company has been a resounding success with major IT companies, because of the accuracy and reliability of his employees' work, and the honesty and commitment of his workforce.

- Many of Sonne's employees work successfully at the premises of his clients. What measures do you think client companies need to take to create a suitable working environment?

- The environment should be quiet, calm, uncluttered and as stress-free as possible. The working day should be well structured and expectations made explicit.

With at least one branch of Specialisterne opening in the UK, it is to be hoped that this model for enhancing the lives of adults on the spectrum will be widely emulated.

9.7 Conclusion

This chapter has considered a range of complex issues that arise from the themes of earlier chapters, and has highlighted some of the challenges that lie ahead in the autism field. Understanding has come far from the days of Kanner and Asperger to this first phase of the 21st century, yet there is still much work to be done to explain autism, and to improve life for those on the spectrum.

9.8 Learning outcomes

9.1 Define and use, or recognise definitions and applications of, each of the terms printed in **bold** in the text.

9.2 Comment on the way first-hand accounts complement and extend other routes to understanding the autism spectrum.

9.3 Identify the main assumptions and implications of sub-type and continuum interpretations of the spectrum.

9.4 Comment on the issue of difference or disorder as it relates to the autism spectrum.

9.5 Outline possible explanations for the greater prevalence of autism in males.

9.6 Show that you appreciate the scope for integrating psychological and biological approaches and practice.

9.7 Comment on the challenge of autism in relation to global and cross-cultural context and adulthood.

9.9 Self-assessment questions for Chapter 9

Question 9.1 (LO 9.2)

(a) List three different ways in which the personal perspectives of people on the autism spectrum can contribute to the autism field.

(b) What difficulties may arise in interpreting first-hand accounts of autism?

Question 9.2   (LO 9.3)

Which of statements (a) to (d) apply most clearly to (i) the sub-type approach and (ii) the continuum approach?

(a) The autism spectrum comprises separable diagnostic groupings.
(b) The autism spectrum consists of a dimension on which all individuals with a diagnosis can be located.
(c) There is no clear cut-off between the characteristics of autism and the rest of the population.
(d) Asperger syndrome has qualitatively different characteristics from classic autism.

Question 9.3   (LO 9.4)

(a) Explain why many people prefer to view autism as a difference not a disorder or disability.
(b) Explain why some parents and individuals with autism have reservations about this view.

Question 9.4   (LO 9.5)

(a) Why might it be more difficult to detect autism in females than in males?
(b) What other influences may possibly contribute to the greater prevalence of autism in males?

Question 9.5   (LO 9.6)

Explain the importance of early intervention in relation to psychological and biological influences in autism.

Question 9.6   (LO 9.7)

(a) List three factors that may contribute to variations in autism prevalence estimates between different ethnic minorities.
(b) List three factors that are likely to contribute to the high costs of adult autism.

Answers and comments

Answers to self-assessment questions

Question 1.1

A syndrome is the term used in medicine and psychiatry for a specific disorder or condition, clearly defined by a characteristic set of symptoms. The term spectrum has more recent currency within psychiatry. While it also denotes a disorder or condition associated with characteristic symptoms, the expression and severity of these symptoms varies across a range. The spectrum may be seen as including identifiable sub-types of the disorder, or as a continuous scale of variation between individuals. Both interpretations of the spectrum exist in relation to autism.

Question 1.2

(a) The triad of impairments means the three main areas of difficulty which characterise autism – communication, social interaction, and repetitiveness and inflexibility in activities and interests.

(b) The boy's behaviour is consistent with the first and third of these. Note however, that this child's behaviour would need professional assessment, and would not necessarily lead to a diagnosis of autism. This is further discussed in Chapter 2.

(c) Diagnostic criteria constitute the formally agreed definition of a disorder, condition or spectrum, which are used in diagnosis by clinicians and researchers. Diagnostic criteria identify a pattern of symptoms which must be present for a diagnosis to be made, sometimes accompanied by symptoms or characteristics which must not be present.

Question 1.3

(a) Experimental group: children with autism; control group: typically developing children.

(b) Using the same story helps to ensure that the only variable differentiating the two groups is whether they have autism or not. If the groups were read different stories, other variables, such as the complexity and familiarity of the language, might make one story easier to remember than the other.

(c) When people remember stories, they usually focus on the meaning and narrative sequence, but don't seek to recall the sentences word for word. Asking participants with autism to perform this task is likely to highlight a tendency to recall word for word, with less attention to the overall meaning of the story.

Question 1.4

(a) Using the broader criterion, nine out of the twelve pairs of identical twins are concordant. The percentage concordance is $9/12 \times 100 = 75\%$.

(b) Folstein and Rutter's study, and others since, suggest that concordance for classic autism in the non-identical twins will be much lower (and also concordance for autism with language and social difficulties). Higher identical twin concordance is consistent with genetic influences in autism.

Question 1.5

(a) The prevalence for the US study is calculated as $1/150 \times 10\ 000$. This gives a prevalence of 67 per 10 000.

(b) The difference between the UK and US estimates does not necessarily mean that there are more children on the autism spectrum in the UK. Differences in the numbers of diagnosed cases (on which prevalence estimates are based) could reflect differences in public awareness, differences in the way diagnostic criteria are applied, and other factors which have nothing to do with the numbers of individuals actually affected by autism in the two countries.

Question 1.6

(a) This does not conclusively support a biological explanation of autism. However, the severity of the impairments in language, for instance, is difficult to explain purely by reference to social/environmental influences. Even in emotionally deprived settings most children learn to talk and to communicate.

(b) Epilepsy is associated with atypical brain activity. Its occurrence with autism is therefore consistent with a biological explanation, though not all individuals on the spectrum have epilepsy.

(c) The fact that autism occurs in more males than in females almost certainly reflects genetic and other biological influences. However, part of this male/female difference may possibly occur because autism diagnoses are more frequently missed in girls than in boys.

(d) A genetic factor in autism is an integral part of a biological explanation (see Chapter 5).

Question 2.1

(a) Similarities:

   (i)   Both boys exhibited restricted interests and repetitive behaviours in their early development, e.g. Anton showed repetitive use of plastic bricks; Oliver showed preoccupation with the video player controls. Both of these interests were troublesome for their parents and other family members.

   (ii) Both boys were referred for multidisciplinary assessment. Anton was seen by a paediatrician, a clinical psychologist, a speech and language therapist and a social worker; Oliver was seen by two psychologists and a psychiatrist.

   (iii) Both assessments used the ADOS and interviewed parents in detail about early development.

   (iv) Diagnosis brought benefits for both families. Anton's parents started to attend a local support group, and eventually decided that Anton should attend a special school for children with autism. Oliver's father eventually accepted that the diagnosis helped to explain some of Oliver's atypical thinking and behaviour. Although the support and understanding that Oliver received at school varied, the diagnosis did help the various professionals working with him to understand his needs more clearly.

(b) Differences:

    (i)   Anton's development gave rise to concern before he was two years old and he was referred for a specialist assessment before he was three years of age – although the actual diagnosis was after a further 10-month wait. Although Oliver's development raised some issues before he attended school, he was not referred for a specialist assessment until he was seven years old.

    (ii) Anton now attends an autism-specific school, and his parents hope that this will continue when he reaches secondary school age. Oliver has always attended mainstream schools, although with some difficulties, such as coping with the relative lack of structure at secondary school and being bullied by other students.

(c) Age differences in both the emergence of initial concerns and eventual diagnosis highlight the essential differences between 'classic' autism and Asperger syndrome: Anton had a clear delay in developing spoken language, a degree of intellectual disability, and behaviours suggestive of autism, such as his narrow, repetitive play and lack of interest in playing and sharing with other toddlers. This combination of factors would be sufficient to highlight developmental problems by the age of two or three years old. With hindsight, Anton's mother also recalled other, more subtle difficulties, such as a lack of smiling, pointing and bringing things to show her when he was a year or so in age. In contrast, Oliver appeared to be very precocious in his early development. His language was advanced for his age, he seemed to have taught himself to read and he learned how to use technical equipment. In his first year at school he also stood out as being very helpful and well behaved. Such positive aspects of development often 'mask' difficulties, such as an inability to engage in reciprocal conversation or understand the needs of others. It is quite typical for children with Asperger syndrome to be diagnosed after they have started school, as their difficulties may only become obvious as the social demands and expectations relating to 'normal' behaviour increase with age.

Question 2.2

(a) These categories mean that people can be identified as on the autism spectrum even if they don't meet all the criteria for classic autism. This highlights how understanding of the spectrum has expanded over the past few decades.

(b) The terms PDD-NOS and atypical autism are used more or less interchangeably in DSM-IV-TR, to accommodate cases meeting most but not all of the criteria for classic autism. In ICD-10 the category PDD-unspecified covers situations where there are indications of a pervasive developmental disorder, but insufficient or conflicting information makes this impossible to confirm, e.g. the parents are not available to provide a developmental history, or their account contradicts what the professionals have observed. In ICD-10 the term atypical autism refers specifically to cases which are atypical in terms of late onset or symptomatology.

Question 2.3

(a) In clinical practice diagnostic assessment instruments are used to provide evidence for (or against) a particular diagnosis. An interactive assessment such as the ADOS allows for observation of behaviour in a structured context, and diagnostic interviews are used in order to obtain a clear history of an individual's early development and current skills. In clinical practice the information gathered should be combined with other sources of information, such as the results of standardised test of language and other skills and reports from teachers or other professionals who know the individual, in order for the diagnostic professional or team to make an informed clinical opinion about the most appropriate diagnostic outcome for the person.

(b) In research, instruments such as the ADOS and the ADI are used to confirm that the study participants meet the diagnostic criteria required for the study. Individuals with a clinical diagnosis of autism may not always meet the research criteria for autism. These tend to be more conservative and are much less affected by the element of subjective judgement, or the practical considerations, which may go into clinical diagnosis.

In the ADOS modules 1 and 2 children are assessed to see how they request things that they want, and whether requests and other aspects of social communication involve non-verbal communication skills such as eye contact and smiling. Particular early social communication skills, such as initiating and responding to joint attention, responding to name calls and social smiling are also observed. In a module 2 assessment the child's use of expressive language is also assessed.

Question 2.4

One problem is that though the screening tool is identifying quite a number of children at risk of autism (34 in all), it is also picking up quite a number who are not (26). So the tool is not sufficiently specific. A second problem is that the tool is failing to pick up quite a few children who later prove to have an autism spectrum diagnosis (20). So the tool is not sufficiently sensitive.

Question 2.5

Two main factors besides the 'actual' number of individuals affected by autism may influence prevalence estimates in a given country. These are:

(a) Knowledge about autism, together with the availability of diagnostic services; for example, in a country where public and professional knowledge of the autism spectrum is relatively limited, and/or where few professionals have the skills and experience to make diagnoses, estimates of prevalence based on clinically diagnosed individuals are likely to be low.

(b) The criteria used in diagnosis. If these are not up to date, for instance they specify that all individuals should meet strict formal criteria for 'classic' autism, then prevalence estimates for this study will be lower than for a study where the criteria are more inclusive.

Question 3.1

1   Rarely smiling indicates a communication difficulty, though it also affects social interaction.

2   Failure to point to objects of interest reflects a difficulty in social interaction, though it is also, of course, a communication failure.

3   Precocity in completing a jigsaw indicates an area of special skill.

4   Insistence on eating the same food every day reflects repetitive activities and interests. Notice, however, that this may stem from sensory aversion to the tastes of other foods.

5   Lack of responsiveness to being called, coupled with aversion to the sound of the vacuum cleaner, may indicate sensory hypo- and hypersensitivity.

Question 3.2

Disappointment (b) and pride (c) are likely to be more difficult: recognition of these emotions is likely to require understanding of the context in which they occur; happiness and fear are 'basic' emotions which can be recognised from expression alone.

Question 3.3

Difficulty in understanding irony and humour (c) and unusual tone of voice and use of gesture (d) are more likely to occur in people with Asperger syndrome. Grammar and vocabulary are not usually affected.

Question 3.4

(a) A verbal IQ score of 110 means that the person scores 10 points above the mean for people of the same age on verbal tests, whereas the non-verbal (performance) score of 90 means that he scores 10 points below the mean for his age group on non-verbal (performance) tests. His full-scale IQ score – the mean of these two scores – is 100, or exactly average for his age.

(b) People on the autism spectrum often show a substantial discrepancy between their scores on the verbal and non-verbal tests, and an unusual profile of scores on the sub-tests. A greater than normal proportion of individuals will have scores in the 'disabled' range below 70.

Question 3.5

Similarities: any two of the following:

Both studies involve:

- systematic analysis of behaviour
- evaluation of behaviour/responses using a 'blind rating' procedure
- measurement or scoring of responses
- comparison of autism group with one or more control groups.

Differences: any two of the following:

- the experimental study involves specially devised tests, while the observational study involves observation of freely occurring behaviour
- the experimental study tested the children at one time point, while the observational study considered two time ranges
- the experimental study scored both quantity and quality in the children's responses, while the observational study only scored quantity.

Question 4.1

(a) A universal explanation is one which applies to all individuals with autism, while a specific explanation applies only to individuals with autism. Universal ToM difficulty is questionable: a proportion of individuals with autism pass tests such as false belief, though more subtle mind-reading difficulties may possibly be universal. ToM difficulty is not specific to autism: it also occurs in conditions such as congenital blindness and dementia.

(b) Since difficulties associated with autism probably commence in early development, it is important to consider their cumulative effect over the years in which psychological capacities are unfolding. Hobson's theory emphasises the importance of early developmental stages.

Question 4.2

(a) (i) ToM suggests two main problems for George: difficulty understanding the motives and actions of story characters, and also with non-literal language, such as metaphors would both interfere with his grasp of the plot.

(ii) WCC theory suggests that George will focus on the details of the story, failing to grasp the overall gist or meaning.

(b) Researching the recipe may involve generativity; planning the shopping, preparing the meal and setting the table all involve planning. These activities may also involve flexibility and inhibition, as does finishing off other activities; refraining from a coffee involves inhibition.

Question 4.3

(a) The second statement fits better with the evidence that WCC is a preferred cognitive style.

(b) Mathematics can be seen as a highly systematic subject, so this finding is consistent with E-S. Subjects such as medicine require good systemising skills too (e.g. to understand metabolism or the circulation of blood), but these must be coupled with empathy for patients.

Question 4.4

A multiple deficits account of autism does not rule out a role for difficulties in ToM, EF and so on, but as contributory factors, rather than as the single core deficit.

Question 5.1

(a) You may have named any of GABA, serotonin and glutamate as neurotransmitters and oxytocin and insulin as hormones.

(b) General similarities are that they function as chemical communicators and require specific receptors. General differences are that hormones travel to distant targets in the blood whereas neurotransmitters operate locally in synapses.

Question 5.2

You may have suggested: (i) the concordance rate for autism is much higher in identical twin pairs than in non-identical twin pairs; (ii) autism spectrum conditions tend to run in families, and mild autistic features are common in relatives of autistic individuals; (iii) some medical conditions that are genetically diagnosed (including fragile X syndrome) also have autism as a behavioural outcome.

Question 5.3

(a) No, it is not true of children with autism. Generally they have an enlarged amygdala, but emotional recognition, one of the functions of the amygdala, is impaired.

(b) The amygdala requires oxytocin to perform its function of emotional recognition properly. So low levels of oxytocin or a reduced number of oxytocin receptors in the amygdala might reduce the performance of even an enlarged amygdala.

Question 5.4

Synapses occur between *all* neurons, so synaptic dysfunction, like that described in Section 5.4, would affect all neurons. It follows that general synaptic dysfunction is likely to have an effect on all cognition and all behaviour. However, a less general effect could occur if specific neurotransmitters are selectively involved in autism; then there could be a selective effect on those cognitive functions and behaviours that involve synapses receptive to these neurotransmitters.

Question 5.5

The children vaccinated in 1990 were born in 1989. The bar above the year 1989 shows that 43% of the children born in Yokohama in that year were vaccinated.

Question 5.6

(a) The peak prevalence shown in Figure 5.2b is about 160 per 10 000.

(b) 1995. The cohort of children with the highest prevalence were born in 1994 and should have been vaccinated one year later, in 1995.

(c) 0%. None of the children born in 1994 were vaccinated; the vaccine had been withdrawn in Japan by 1993.

Question 5.7

Certain studies may use participants from different points on the autism spectrum. Imaging studies tend to use those from the high-functioning end of the spectrum, for example, so it remains unknown whether the results are relevant to those at other points on the spectrum.

Question 6.1

1   TEACCH (Treatment and Education of Autistic and related Communication-handicapped CHildren) is a comprehensive approach that was developed in the 1970s and is widely used in the UK and USA. TEACCH uses a structured visual approach to teaching skills, including attention to the way in which the individual's environment and schedule are structured. Pictures and symbols are often used to explain what is required, as well as how and where an activity needs to be carried out.

    TEACCH is recommended by many autism-specific organisations, and there have been a number of studies with many participants investigating the efficacy of TEACCH. However, these studies have generally lacked control groups, and have mostly been carried out by researchers associated with the TEACCH organisation.

2   PECS (Picture Exchange Communication System) is a naturalistic approach that draws on behavioural techniques. PECS is designed for children with autism who have non-existent or very limited speech, who are trained to exchange symbols for motivating rewards. There are six phases of PECS, which range from simple exchange of a single symbol, through to building up sentences using several symbols to enable the child to express their wants.

    PECS has been evaluated to a relatively high degree compared to many other psychosocial interventions for children on the autism spectrum. Studies include two randomised control trials demonstrating a number of benefits for PECS, including increases in spontaneity in communication, requesting behaviour and speech.

3   Son-Rise (also known as the Option approach) is a comprehensive child-centred approach where parents are encouraged to follow the interests of the child in order to engage in activities that are meaningful for the child.

Son-Rise has provoked controversy as its founders have claimed that it can cure autism.

There have been no systematic studies investigating the benefits of Son-Rise, and the evidence consists of anecdotal reports from parents whose children have experienced the programme. Most notably, the founders of the approach have written extensively about how their son recovered fully from autism to become a very competent and independent adult.

Question 6.2

Adult-directed approaches tend to incorporate behavioural techniques, such as reinforcement and prompt fading, and generally focus on teaching specific skills, often in a hierarchical format. Although individual programmes will be tailored to the level of the specific child or adult, targets will be set by the therapist (parent or professional) and success measured in relation to these predefined targets.

Child-centred approaches are broadly based on a developmental interpretation of the way in which skills, particularly language and communication skills, emerge in typically developing young children. This view emphasises that language and communication skills need to be facilitated and nurtured rather than taught, and that the most efficient way of engaging with young children with autism is by following their own interests and motivation. Child-centred approaches often involve parents as the main deliverers of the intervention, although other adults, including nursery workers and teachers, are also sometimes involved.

Question 6.3

No pharmacological interventions have been found to be effective at treating the core difficulties associated with autism, and certainly none can be claimed to be a 'cure' for autism. However, certain drug treatments are known to reduce some of the symptoms associated with autism, including hyperactivity, self-injury and sleep problems. In some cases the side effects of drug treatments may outweigh the potential benefits.

Question 7.1

Sensory difficulties might arise because of the large space, unfamiliar arrangement of desks and proximity of other students. Slight noises made by other students may be distracting. Equally, remaining quiet, not fidgeting or moving around might be harder for some students who have attention difficulties.

Executive function difficulties may make it difficult for the student to plan and organise revision, in order to be appropriately prepared for the questions. Equally, this may interfere with allocation of time to questions and planning of answers. Theory of mind difficulties may make it hard for the student to understand what the examiner requires of them.

Social difficulties may make it difficult for the student to understand what will happen in the exam and what the rules of the exam will be (e.g. you don't confer with other students or look at what they are writing).

The language used in questions or instructions might not be 'concrete' enough for students with autism.

Question 7.2

One-to-one teaching time might not be possible where additional resources are not made available. Supervising a student during unstructured activities such as breaks may not be possible.

The individual nature of the student's programme might isolate them from fellow students or even create negative feelings towards them. They may see it as special treatment and feel that it is unfair. It could also stigmatise the young person with autism – other children might see them as lacking independence and ability.

Question 7.3

For children to feel that they fit in with neurotypical young people, it may in some cases be best to expose them to the culturally normative environment of the mainstream school. It is certainly more likely that they will be educated alongside children from their own community at a local mainstream school. However, the degree to which a particular mainstream environment can adopt autism-friendly qualities, and the ability of the school to adapt the four environments (physical/sensory, curricular, social and communication) to the needs of the individual child will contribute substantially to whether the child can participate fully in the life of the mainstream school.

In some cases, the child's sensory, intellectual and social difficulties may be too difficult to accommodate in the mainstream in such a way that the child experiences true inclusion. Children with autism don't necessarily learn just by being in the company of neurotypical children. They may have more chance of learning (both academically and socially) where they are taught within a special environment.

Bullying can also have a profoundly detrimental effect, though this does not necessarily happen only in mainstream schools.

Question 7.4

A whole school approach is one where the culture, the teaching, the environment and the policies of the school are coordinated around a vision of what the needs of students are and what the school is trying to achieve for its individual students. Examples of how SPELL meets these requirements are:

- the emphasis on good communication and consistency between staff (links)
- the fact that all staff share the same positive view of autism and focus on strengths and abilities (positive approaches and positive expectations)
- the focus on structure, empathy and low arousal within the sensory, curricular, social and communication environments.

Question 8.1

Positive aspects might include:

- a sense of relief at finally having an answer

- having a name for the child's condition so that parents can access information and, when needed, apply for support

- realising they are not on their own and that other parents are going through the same process

- changing the way they see the child – realising that the child's behaviour is not 'naughtiness' or anything to do with their skills as parents.

Less positive aspects might include:

- feeling overawed by the diagnosis, a sense of not knowing enough about the condition

- experiencing feelings of guilt

- fears for the future – autism is a lifelong condition. Many parents worry about who will look after their son or daughter when they themselves can no longer do so.

Question 8.2

(a) Life might be more difficult because of:

- financial hardship
- reduced social and leisure opportunities
- lack of understanding in the wider family or community
- the child's rigidity and insistence on sameness reducing choices
- increased responsibility for siblings.

(b) Life might be more rewarding because:

- having a person with autism in the family brings a different perspective – people with autism have unique qualities that can teach us something about learning, communicating and caring
- autism can create a connection to other people – many families feel a sense of kinship with other similarly affected families and often work hard to support them
- for siblings, caring for their brother or sister can be very rewarding
- the hard work is sometimes outweighed by the sense of reward and fun (see Section 8.5.3, in which Jacqui Jackson makes this point in the extract from her book *Multicoloured Mayhem*).

Question 8.3

Resilience could be defined as the ability to withstand hardship and to rebound from adversity, becoming stronger and more resourceful. The key factors that contribute to resilience, as found by Bayat (2007), were flexibility and good communication.

Question 8.4

Problems of childhood might include getting over the shock of diagnosis, finding a way to deal with communication and behaviour difficulties and problems with feeding and toileting. There may be great difficulties finding the right preschool and school placements. Additionally the family may face financial difficulties due to the cost of bringing up a child with a disability. Problems for siblings might include jealousy or feelings of anger at how much time their parents need to devote to the young child with autism.

Problems of adolescence might include increased moodiness and social difficulties in the affected young person. Depression and anxiety disorder are common, especially in Asperger syndrome and HFA. Both parents and siblings may find it hard to deal with the isolating effect of autism.

Problems with adulthood might include the difficulties of accommodating an adult with autism at home, financial difficulties and unemployment (most adults with autism do not have a job). Parents of adults with autism may also have to care for their own ageing parents, which may lead to additional stress.

Question 8.5

Different types of short breaks include:

- befriending schemes
- domiciliary support
- family-based short breaks
- holidays for children with autism
- own home respite care
- play schemes during school vacations
- short term residential care.

Parents sometimes report that there is a lack of choice in terms of the style of support available, and that autism-specific/friendly provision is in short supply (Barson, 1998). Most families get very few breaks and respite care during school holidays is particularly difficult to find.

Question 9.1

(a) Any three of the following:

- ○ Autobiographical accounts provide insight into how the individual thinks, feels and experiences the world.
- ○ Poetry can offer similar insights to autobiography, but also demonstrates capacity for imagination.
- ○ Self-help books (e.g. Luke Jackson's) provide support and guidance for others on the spectrum.
- ○ Commentaries (e.g. books by Wendy Lawson and Temple Grandin, and Michelle Dawson's blog) provide forums in which the social needs and human rights of people on the spectrum are highlighted.
- ○ Contributions to scientific research (e.g. by Therese Jolliffe and Michelle Dawson) help to inform research questions and design.

(b) The main difficulty in using first-hand accounts is that they are contributed by a minority of high-functioning individuals and cannot be assumed to be representative. In addition, atypicalities of self-awareness may have implications for self-knowledge and recall of experiences.

Question 9.2

(i) Sub-type approach: statements (a) and (d).

(ii) Continuum approach: statements (b) and (c).

Question 9.3

(a) Important arguments for seeing autism as a difference are that this contradicts the view that people with autism need to be 'normalised', reduces the risk of discrimination, and highlights the skills, and in some cases autonomy, of people on the spectrum.

(b) Many parents and individuals with autism do experience it as a disorder or disability which affects the quality of their lives. They fear that by labelling autism purely as a difference, their access to help and support may be reduced, thus in practice increasing the discrimination against them.

Question 9.4

(a) The expression of autistic traits in females may not conform to standard assumptions about autistic behaviour: for example, interest in mechanical devices or computers may be less common. Females may also make more effort to emulate neurotypical behaviour.

(b) Biological factors are likely to contribute to the greater prevalence in males. The role of genetic influences is currently unclear; a suggested hormonal influence is the impact of fetal testosterone in promoting the development of 'male brain' characteristics.

Question 9.5

The information transmitted to a child's brain depends on the way the child interacts with their physical and social environment, influencing the activation of neurons, the growth of synapses, and the laying down of connections between different parts of the brain. The right kind of early intervention may enhance the child's interactions, with beneficial consequences in terms of altering the developmental trajectory which leads to autism.

Question 9.6

(a) Any three of the following: lack of awareness about autism within some ethnic minority groups; shame or fear at disclosing a disability; difficulty in understanding questions from professionals; difficulty in describing problems to professionals; different cultural norms leading to accommodation of disability.

(b) Typical costs include accommodation (either at home or in a sheltered setting); hospital and day services; education; specialist interventions for autism; respite care for parents; lost employment by the individual and his or her parents.

Comments on activities

Activity 1.1

Statement 1 is true: autistic conditions are at least four times as common in males as in females. The male : female ratio for Asperger syndrome is even higher at around 10 : 1. Note that an excess of males over females is also found in other developmental conditions such as dyslexia and attention-deficit hyperactivity disorder.

Statement 2 is false: despite claims made in the 1960s by Bettelheim, there is no evidence to support this suggestion, and much evidence that biological influences play the major role in autism (see this chapter and Chapter 5). One study of infants abandoned in Romanian orphanages (Rutter et al., 1999) identified an 'autistic-like' condition in some of the children, but these children showed substantial recovery when placed in a more nurturing environment.

Statement 3 is false: just a small minority of people on the autism spectrum have exceptional talent in areas such as numerical calculation, visual art and music, while a larger number have specific areas of special skill. Some people with autism have intellectual or learning difficulties. (See response to statement 12 and also Chapter 3.)

Statement 4 is uncertain: there has certainly been an increase in the numbers of children receiving autism spectrum diagnoses, but this does not necessarily mean that autism is on the increase; these changes could, for instance, be due to changes in diagnostic practice. (See Chapter 2.)

Statement 5 is uncertain: estimates of 'prevalence' vary from one country to another, but as for statement 4 this may be due to factors such as differences in diagnostic practices. (See Chapter 2.)

Statement 6 is uncertain: by the age of 18 months the failure of some children to pass typical development milestones, such as following a parent's gaze, places them in the 'at risk' category. But these early signs are not conclusive. To date, autism cannot be reliably diagnosed before the age of 2 years, but improved 'screening tools' for infants may change this situation. (See Chapter 2.)

Statement 7 is true: probably the most well-documented research finding from recent decades is that people on the autism spectrum typically have difficulty in understanding another person's point of view and feelings. (See Chapter 4.)

Statement 8 is true: in some families autistic conditions may affect more than one individual, though this is by no means always true. Parents and siblings of children on the autism spectrum may also show mild autistic traits, without actually meeting the criteria for an autism spectrum diagnosis. These facts point strongly to a genetic factor in autism. (See Chapter 5.)

Statement 9 is false: unlike conditions such as cystic fibrosis, where a defect in a specific gene is known to cause the condition, no single gene is implicated in autism. Autism almost certainly involves the combined impact of several genes, and different genes may be involved in autism in different families. (See Chapter 5 on genetics.)

Statement 10 is false: extensive scientific tests have produced absolutely no evidence for the claim that the MMR vaccine is influential in causing autistic conditions. Note, however, that it is not possible to prove conclusively a negative in science. (See Chapter 5.)

Statement 11 is false: despite some claims, there is no good evidence that children diagnosed with autism can become completely free of it as adults. However, in some cases the pattern and severity of symptoms changes radically. The adult may become much less affected by certain symptoms, though social difficulties are likely to persist. (See Chapter 3.)

Statement 12 is false: while some children and adults on the autism spectrum have mild to severe intellectual impairments, the intellectual functioning of many others is within, and in some cases above, the normal range. Children on the autism spectrum often attend mainstream schools. Note, however, that they may still have difficulties in coping with everyday situations, and may not achieve what they are capable of for this reason. (See Chapter 7.)

Statement 13 is false: people on the autism spectrum would often like to make friends and have the company of others, though they may also have difficulties in making this happen. (See Chapter 8.)

Activity 1.2

Each of the three autism societies (NAS, ASA and SSA) offers a wide range of information and services for people on the autism spectrum and their families. Five of the main areas of support are listed below. In the USA the availability of some services is likely to vary on a state by state basis. Some autism societies other than the three mentioned here may not yet cover the range outlined.

- Information and advice for families and individuals, e.g. helpline, resource database, and advisory and consultancy services.
- Support for families, e.g. workshops, seminars and intervention training for parents; family respite; access to a service co-ordinator and financial assistance (ASA).
- Education. Both the NAS and SSA run autism-specific schools and training programmes, while the ASA provides links to such services through its databases.
- Support for children, e.g. out of school clubs, vocational projects and outreach services (NAS and SSA) and access to camps and specialist practitioners (ASA).
- Support for adults, e.g. residential and day provision, supported living and social clubs (NAS and SSA), career centre and financial advice and support (ASA).

Activity 2.1

(a) It is not clear whether the health visitor realised that Anton had autism, although she may have suspected this because she confirmed that there was probably nothing wrong with his hearing. It is likely that the first SLT thought that he might have autism, because she referred him to the Social Communication Clinic, a type of clinic where children suspected of having autism are often referred for diagnosis. Even if the SLT knew that Anton probably had autism, it was not appropriate for her to say this to his parents at that time. As described in the chapter, the process of diagnostic decision-making is one that involves a range of professionals and careful consideration of the degree to which a child meets the criteria for autism.

(b) Anton's parents were probably upset upon receiving confirmation of his diagnosis because, having read about autism on the internet and talked to other parents of children with autism, they realised the impact that this would have on the rest of their lives. To some extent this initial reaction is a form of grieving for the child that they had expected to have.

(c) First there were several long delays before appointments with specialist professionals – the GP initially suggested that they wait for a while before seeking help; they then waited four months for the initial speech and language therapy appointment; and then a further 10 months for the appointment at the Social Communication Clinic at the CDC. Although the SLT did not mention the possibility of autism, Anton's parents discovered this following a slightly careless remark by the manager of his nursery.

(d) Following the diagnosis, and the statement of special educational needs that was subsequently agreed with the local education authority, Anton was able to attend a special school where his needs were understood, and where appropriate support, including respite care, was provided.

Activity 2.2

The key features of Anton's behaviour related to the criteria for autism include:

- the initial failure to develop language beyond single words
- a lack of response to being called by name – despite having no difficulties with hearing
- an obsession with repetitive, non-functional routines (playing with plastic bricks)
- failure to engage with peers (i.e. at nursery)
- not liking being cuddled as an infant
- limited social smiling
- no interest in sharing his interest with others (e.g. by showing or pointing).

From the information provided, it seems highly likely that the diagnosis of autism was appropriate. *Remember though, that diagnosis can only be made by a professional, who would never base his/her decision exclusively on such a small range of information.*

Activity 2.3

(a) ◦ Oliver met the criterion of achieving typical speech milestones.

◦ He had a strong, perhaps obsessive, interest in using the TV, video player and other technical equipment.

◦ He also demonstrated difficulties in relationships with peers.

◦ His language use, though accurate, was repetitive and stereotyped.

◦ There was a failure to understand social rules, both in his behaviour at school, and his response to the death of his grandfather.

◦ He certainly had an IQ within the normal range, or above.

It is unlikely, but not impossible, that he would meet the criteria for classic autism, particularly as he met the speech milestones requirement for Asperger syndrome. It is more likely, however, that he may have met the criteria for PDD-NOS. *Remember again, that diagnosis can only be made by a professional, who would never rely exclusively on such a small range of information.*

(b) When Oliver was young, most people who knew him believed that he was extremely precocious, especially because of his excellent vocabulary. It was only once he had started school, and particularly following the incident when he touched the girl inappropriately, that the concerns about his development and behaviour resulted in a referral to specialist professionals.

(c) Daniel may have resisted the idea that Oliver had a problem for several reasons. He may have believed that any difficulties Oliver had were a response to his parents' marriage breakdown. Alternatively, he may just have believed that Oliver's characteristics were essentially positive, especially given Daniel's own interest in technology.

(d) Following the diagnosis, Oliver started to attend a Communication Group at the school, where he found some friends with whom he shared some common interests. Eventually discovering the truth about his diagnosis helped him to understand why he had always struggled to get on with the majority of his peers, and diagnosis may also have helped the rest of the family to understand why he was sometimes difficult to get along with. It is also likely that clarification of his diagnostic status helped his teachers to anticipate Oliver's needs, and to provide him with the most appropriate level of support.

Activity 6.3

Clearly many families would struggle if implementing an intervention that required such intensive input. There may be a heavy financial burden if one parent is required to give up a job, exacerbated by the costs of employing the consultants and assistants needed to run the programme. The family dynamic may be affected, with siblings feeling that their parents' time and attention is completely devoted to the child with autism. If the parents were dissatisfied with their child's improvement, despite their intense efforts, then they might feel that they had not done enough for their child, or that they had failed to implement the intervention appropriately. This sense of failure could be exacerbated by the promoters' dramatic claims about effectiveness of the intervention, as well as by the incredible sacrifice made by the family.

Nonetheless many parents, and siblings feel empowered by being actively involved in the treatment of a child with autism and, whatever the outcome, they may feel that they have done everything they possibly could for the child.

Activity 6.4

1   Many children with autism seem to be drawn to vehicles – cars and trains for example – so they may be more interested in looking at the *Transporters* characters than if they were human. As the faces are superimposed on the front of the vehicles, a child with autism, who may tend to avoid looking at faces, might be more inclined to look at them. Also, whilst the faces do move, they do not talk, in order to portray each facial expression very clearly.

2   The range of emotions portrayed by the characters begins with simple or basic emotions, such as happy, sad and angry, before moving on to more complex emotions such as proud, jealous and ashamed. Each emotion, along with the precursors and responses to each emotional situation, is explained clearly within the episode, with a certain degree of repetition, in order to give the child the best possible opportunity to understand the emotion.

3   The episodes are structured, in order to enable the child to learn about the causes of the different emotions, and the context in which they occurred, rather than simply recognising and labelling each emotion.

4   Correct answers in the interactive quiz are rewarded with images that may be motivating to a child with autism – Barney's wheels moving, for example. This may help to reinforce the lessons learned.

Activity 6.5

Animal-assisted therapies

Dolphin therapies involve encouraging children to swim and interact with dolphins. Research Autism (RA) reports a lack of reliable evidence for this therapy and potential hazards.

Help Dogs are dogs specially trained to help a person with autism. While there is as yet little scientific evidence for this approach, RA regards it as worthy of further evaluation.

Auditory integration training

A person with autism listens to music modified by removing certain frequencies and controlling volume. The aim is to lessen sensitivity to previously disturbing sounds. RA indicates strong evidence that this intervention does not improve symptoms of autism.

Coloured filters

This involves the person with autism wearing spectacles with coloured filters. The aim is to reduce visual confusion and distortion, making it easier to read and to react to the visual environment. RA reports limited evidence that coloured filters may enhance reading, but no clear evidence that they reduce autistic symptoms.

Facilitated communication

To assist a person with limited communication in developing communicative skills, a helper physically supports the individual's arm so that the individual can select letters, symbols or words to indicate what they want. RA reports very strong evidence that this is ineffective and evidence that it may cause harm.

Light-wave stimulation

The individual views coloured light produced by a special machine. The aim is to enhance the transmission of information in the visual pathways, and to regulate bodily functions. RA reports no evidence that this is beneficial.

Restricted environmental stimulation therapy

The individual is placed for extended periods in an environment with minimal sensory inputs (e.g. a dimly lit room). The aim is to reduce distracting stimulation and encourage deep relaxation. RA is currently (2009) evaluating this intervention.

Sensory integrative (integration) therapy

This provides the person with autism with a range of sensory experiences to enhance the way sensory information is processed and integrated. For instance, the aim may be to reduce auditory hypersensitivity, or to increase the capacity to discriminate sounds. RA points out that not all people on the spectrum have sensory problems. While the evidence is as yet unclear, RA implies that further evaluation is worthwhile.

Activity 8.1

A web search at the time of writing (summer 2009) returned over 15 million hits, with information from the National Autistic Society, as well as links to discussions about MMR, promises of therapies 'that work', 'naturopathic' clinics, videos on YouTube, education law advisers, 'health conditions', and information from training companies specialising in challenging behaviour. The massive amount of information can be overwhelming for parents, and they may find it difficult to identify which information comes from reliable, reputable sources. Depending on the links you follow, you may encounter claims that the MMR vaccine is a major cause of autism, or that autism can be 'cured' by some miracle treatment. On the other hand, the web presence of organisations such as the National Autistic Society, Scottish Society for Autism and Autism Speaks provide useful sources of reliable information, for instance on the latest developments in autism research or on autism support groups.

Activity 9.2

Within the consultation process that has taken place in 2009, five main areas have been addressed as priorities for action within the National Adult Autism Strategy. These are:

- Social inclusion – adults on the autism spectrum should be able to enjoy the same rights and freedoms as others. This calls for the provision of more options in living arrangements and social relationships – for instance, the means for individuals on the spectrum to live independently of parents if they wish to.

- Health – many individuals on the spectrum have specific co-morbid health problems, such as depression, for which they receive little care. Access to treatment and support needs enhancement.

- Choice and control – the particular goals and needs of people on the spectrum are often not taken into account. There is a need for strategies that help people on the spectrum to assert their own choices about how they lead their lives.

- Awareness raising and training – the lack of understanding of autism, not only among the general public, but also among health and social care professionals, needs to be addressed. Local authorities need to be aware of the adults with autism in their area, and to train staff appropriately to support them.

- Access to training and employment – much could be done to improve access to education, training schemes and employment. This would in turn reduce financial hardship and reliance on parents.

References

A is for Autism (1992) Channel 4 TV programme, directed by Tim Webb, distributed by BFI.

Abrahams, B. S. and Geschwind, D. H. (2008) 'Advances in autism genetics: on the threshold of a new neurobiology', *Nature Reviews Genetics*, vol. 9, no. 5, pp. 341–55.

Afriyie, M. (2009) 'Autism in Ghana – I want my child to be happy', *Autism Speaks*. Available at: http://www.autismspeaks.org/community/ownwords/ intheirownwords_afriyie.php (Accessed 4 October 2009).

Alcantara, J. I. (2004) 'Speech-in-noise perception in high-functioning individuals with autism and Asperger syndrome', *Journal of Child Psychology and Psychiatry*, vol. 45, no. 6, pp. 1107–14.

Amaral, D. G., Schumann, C. M. and Nordahl, C. W. (2008) 'Neuroanatomy of autism', *Trends in Neurosciences*, vol. 31, pp. 137–45.

American Psychiatric Association (2000) Diagnostic and Statistical Manual of Mental Disorders DSM-IV-TR Fourth Edition (Text Revision).

Ashwin, C., Baron-Cohen, S., Wheelwright, S., O'Riordan, M. and Bullmore, E. T. (2007) 'Differential activation of the amygdala and the 'social brain' during fearful face-processing in Asperger syndrome', *Neuropsychologia*, vol. 45, pp. 2–14.

Asperger, A. (1944) 'Die 'Autistischen Psychopathen' in Kindersalter', *Archive für Psychiatrie und Nervenkrankheiten*, vol. 117, pp. 76–136. Published in translation in Frith, U. (1991) (ed.) *Autism and Asperger Syndrome*, Cambridge, Cambridge University Press.

Aspis, S. (2004) 'Why exams and tests do not help disabled and non-disabled children learn in the same school' [online], http://www.inclusion-boltondata.org.uk/ FrontPage/data14.htm (Accessed 13 June 2009).

Attwood, T., Grandin, T., Bolick, T., Faherty, C., Iland, L., McIlwee Myers, J., Snyder, R., Wagner, S. and Wrobel, M. (2006) *Asperger's and Girls*, Arlington, Future Horizons.

Autism Research Centre (2009) [online] Available at: http://www.autismresearchcentre.com/tests/default.asp (Accessed August 2009)

Auyeung, B., Baron-Cohen, S., Ashwin, A., Knickmeyer, R., Taylor, K. and Hackett, G. (2009) 'Foetal testosterone and autistic traits', *British Journal of Psychology*, vol. 100, pp. 1–22.

Bågenholm, A. and Gillberg, C. (1991) 'Psychosocial effects on siblings of children with autism and mental retardation', *Journal of Mental Deficiency Research*, vol. 35, pp. 291–307.

Bailey, A., Le Couteur, A., Gottesman, I., Bolton, P., Simonoff, E., Yuzda, E. and Rutter, M. (1995) 'Autism as a strongly genetic disorder: evidence from a British twin study', *Psychological Medicine*, vol. 25, no. 1, pp. 63–77.

Baird, G., Simonoff, E., Pickles, A., Chandler, S., Loucas, T., Meldrum, D., Charman, T. (2006) 'Prevalence of disorders of the autism spectrum in a population cohort of children in South Thames: the Special Needs and Autism Project (SNAP)', *Lancet*, vol. 368, pp. 210–15.

Baron-Cohen, S. (1987) 'Autism and symbolic play', *British Journal of Developmental Psychology*, vol. 5, pp. 139–48.

Baron-Cohen, S. (1989) 'Do autistic children have obsessions and compulsions?' *British Journal of Clinical Psychology*, vol. 28, pp. 193–200.

Baron-Cohen, S. (1995) *Mindblindness: An essay on autism and theory of mind*, Cambridge, MA, MIT Press.

Baron-Cohen, S. (2003) *The Essential Difference*, London, Allen Lane.

Baron-Cohen, S. (2008) *Autism and Asperger Syndrome: The facts*, Oxford, Oxford University Press.

Baron-Cohen, S. and Goodhart, F. (1994) 'The "seeing leads to knowing" deficit in autism: the Pratt and Bryant probe, *British Journal of Developmental Psychology*, vol. 12, pp. 397–402.

Baron-Cohen, S., Leslie, A. M. and Frith, U. (1985) 'Does the autistic child have a 'theory of mind'?' *Cognition*, vol. 21, pp. 37–46.

Baron-Cohen, S., Cox, A., Baird, G., Swettenham, J., Nightingale, N., Morgan, K., Drew, A. and Charman, T. (1996) 'Psychological markers in the detection of autism in infancy in a large population', *British Journal of Psychiatry*, vol. 168, pp. 158–63.

Baron-Cohen, S., Wheelwright, S., Stott, C., Bolton, P. and Goodyear, I. (1997) 'Is there a link between engineering and autism?' *Autism*, vol. 1, pp. 153–63.

Baron-Cohen, S., Wheelwright, S., Spong, A., Scahill, V. and Lawson, J. (2001) 'Are intuitive physics and intuitive psychology independent? A test with children with Asperger Syndrome', *Journal of Developmental and Learning Disorders*, vol. 5, pp. 47–78.

Barson, C. (1998) *Autism: Supporting the Family. A Report on the Short-term Care Needs of Children with Autism in Wales*, London, National Autistic Society.

Batten, A., Corbett, C., Rosenblatt, M., Withers, L. and Yuille, R. (2006) *Make School Make Sense: Autism and education, the reality for families today*, London, National Autistic Society. Available from: http://www.nas.org.uk/nas/jsp/polopoly.jsp? d=160&a=12846&view=print (Accessed 23 October 2009).

Bayat, M. (2007) 'Evidence of resilience in families of children with autism', *Journal of Intellectual Disability Research*, vol. 51, no. 9, pp. 702–14.

Beardon, L. and Edmonds, G. (2007) *ASPECT Consultancy Report: The needs of adults with Asperger syndrome*, Sheffield Hallam University.

Begeer, S. S., El Bouk, S. E., Boussaid, W., Terwoght, M. M. and Koot, H. M. (2009) 'Underdiagnosis and referral bias of autism in ethnic minorities', *Journal of Autism and Developmental Disorders*, vol. 39, no. 1, pp. 142–8.

Bettelheim, B. (1967) *Empty Fortress: Infantile Autism and the Birth of Self*, New York, Free Press.

Blake, R., Turner, L. M., Smoski, M. J., Pozdol, S. L. and Stone, W. L. (2003) 'Visual recognition of biological motion is impaired in children with autism', *Psychological Science*, vol. 14, no. 2, pp. 151–7.

Bogdashina, O. (2003) *Sensory Perceptual Issues in Autism and Asperger Syndrome: Different sensory experiences – different perceptual worlds*, London and Philadelphia, Jessica Kingsley Publishers.

Bolton, P., Macdonald, H., Pickles, A., Rios, P., Goode, S., Crowson, M. Bailey, A. and Rutter, M. (1994) 'A case-control family history study of autism', *Journal of Child Psychology and Psychiatry and Allied Disciplines*, vol. 35, no. 5, pp. 877–900.

Bondy, A. and Frost, L. (1998) 'The Picture Exchange Communication System', *Seminars in Speech and Language*, vol. 19, pp. 373–89.

Boucher, J. (2009) *The Autistic Spectrum: Characteristics, causes and practical issues*, London, Sage Publications.

Broach, S., Camgöz, S., Heather, C., Owen, G., Potter, D. and Prior, A. (2003) *Autism: Rights in reality*, London, National Autistic Society.

Bromley, J., Hare, D., Davison, K. and Emerson, E. (2004) 'Mothers supporting children with autistic spectrum disorders: social support, mental health status and satisfaction with services', *Autism*, vol. 8, no. 4, pp. 409–23.

Carr, D. and Felce, J. (2007) 'The effects of PECS teaching to Phase III on the communicative interactions between children with autism and their teachers', *Journal of Autism and Developmental Disorders*, vol. 37, no. 4, pp. 724–37.

Chakrabarti, S. and Fombonne, E. (2001) 'Pervasive developmental disorders in preschool children', *Journal of the American Medical Association*, vol. 285, no. 24, pp. 3093–9.

Chan, J. B. and Sigafoos, J. (2000) 'A review of child and family characteristics related to the use of respite care in developmental disability services', *Child and Youth Care Forum*, vol. 29, no. 1, pp. 27–37.

Charlop-Christy, M. H., Carpenter, M., Loc, L., Leblanc, L. A. and Kellet, K. (2002) 'Using the Picture Exchange Communication System (PECS) with children with autism: assessment of PECS acquisition, speech, social-communicative behavior, and problem behavior', *Journal of Applied Behavior Analysis*, vol. 35, no. 3, pp. 213–31.

Charman, T. (2003) 'Why is joint attention a pivotal skill in autism?' in Frith, U. and Hill, E. (eds) *Autism: Mind and brain*, New York, Oxford University Press, pp. 67–87.

Chawarska, K., Paul, R., Klin, A., Hannigen, S., Dichtel, L. E. and Volkmar, F. (2007) 'Parental recognition of developmental problems in toddlers with autism spectrum disorders', *Journal of Autism and Developmental Disorders*, vol. 37, pp. 62–72.

Claiborne Park, C. (2001) *Exiting Nirvana: A daughter's life with autism*, Boston, MA, Little, Brown and Company.

Cole, B. (1987) 'The story of two little sisters', *Communication*, vol. 21, no. 3, pp. 1–5.

Corbett, C. and Perepa, P. (2007) *Missing Out? Autism, Education and Ethnicity: The reality for families today*, London, National Autistic Society.

Courchesne, E., Pierce, K., Schumann, C. M., Redcay, E., Buckwalter, J. A., Kennedy, D. P. and Morgan, J. (2007) 'Mapping early brain development in autism', *Neuron*, vol. 56, no. 2, pp. 399–413.

Craig, J. and Baron-Cohen, S. (1999) 'Creativity and imagination in autism and Asperger syndrome', *Journal of Autism and Developmental Disorders*, vol. 29, pp. 319–26.

Craig, J. and Baron-Cohen, S. (2000) 'Story-telling ability in autism: a window into the imagination', *Israel Journal of Psychiatry*, vol. 37, pp. 64–70.

Craig, J., Baron-Cohen, S. and Scott, F. (2001) 'Drawing ability in autism: a window into the imagination', *Israel Journal of Psychiatry*, vol. 38, pp. 242–53.

Crane, L., Goddard, L. and Pring, L. (2009) 'Brief report: self-defining and everyday autobiographical memories in adults with autism spectrum disorders' [online], *Journal of Autism and Developmental Disorders* advance online publication, 24 September 2009, http://www.springerlink.com/content/944n507361424uwv (Accessed 4 October 2009).

Currie, G. and Ravenscroft, I. (2002) *Recreative Minds*, Oxford, Clarendon Press.

Daily Life Therapy: Higashi (2008) The National Autistic Society [online], http://www.autism.org.uk/nas/jsp/polopoly.jsp?d=1351&a=3295 (Accessed 30 October 2008).

Damasio, A. R. and Maurer, R. G. (1978) 'A neurological model for childhood autism', *Archives of Neurology*, vol. 35, pp. 777–86.

Darwin, C. (1872) *The Expression of the Emotions in Man and Animals,* London, John Murray.

Dawson, M. (2009) 'Notes on autism severity and the DSM-V', *The Autism Crisis: Science and ethics in the era of autism advocacy,* 15 June. Available at: http://autismcrisis.blogspot.com/2009/06/notes-on-autism-severity-and-dsm-v.html (Accessed 18 November 2009).

Dennett, D. (1978) *Brainstorms: Philosophical essays on mind and psychology,* Montgomery, VT, Bradford Books and Hassocks, Sussex, Harvester.

DfES (2001) *Inclusive Schooling: Children with special educational needs,* Crown Copyright 2001, Nottingham, DfES Publications.

DfES (2002) *Autistic Spectrum Disorders: Good practice guidance,* Crown Copyright 2002, Nottingham, DfES Publications.

DfES (2003) *Every Child Matters: Pointers to good practice,* Crown Copyright 2003, Nottingham, DfES Publications.

DfES (2004) *Removing Barriers to Achievement: The government's strategy for SEN,* Crown Copyright 2004, Nottingham, DfES Publications.

Dowty, T. and Cowlishaw, K. (2002) *Home Educating Our Autistic Spectrum Children,* London and New York, Jessica Kingsley Publishers.

Dyches, T. T., Wilder, L. K., Sudweeks, R. R., Obiakor, F. E. and Algozzine, B. (2004) 'Multicultural issues in autism', *Journal of Autism and Developmental Disorders,* vol. 34, no. 2, pp. 211–22.

Edmonds, G. and Worton, D. (2005) *The Asperger Love Guide: A practical guide for adults with Asperger's syndrome seeking, establishing and maintaining success,* London, Paul Chapman Publishing.

Education Act 1996, Office of Public Sector Information, Crown Copyright, London, HMSO.

Ehlers, S. and Gillberg, C. (1993) 'The epidemiology of Asperger syndrome – a total population study', *Journal of Child Psychology and Psychiatry and Allied Disciplines,* vol. 34, no. 8, pp. 1327–50.

Ekman, P. and Friesen, W. V. (1971) 'Constants across cultures in the face and emotion', *Journal of Personality and Social Psychology,* vol. 17, pp. 124–9.

Ferguson, J. N., Young, L. J., Hearn, E. F., Matzuk, M. M., Insel, T. R. and Winslow, J. T. (2000) 'Social amnesia in mice lacking the oxytocin gene', *Nature Genetics,* vol. 25, no. 3, pp. 284–8.

Filipek, P. A., Accardo, P. J., Ashwal, S., Baranek, G. T., Cook, E. H., Dawson, G. et al. (2000) 'Practice parameter: Screening and diagnosis of autism – Report of the Quality Standards Subcommittee of the American Academy of Neurology and the Child Neurology Society', *Neurology,* vol. 55, no. 4, pp. 468–79.

Folstein, S. and Rutter, M. (1977) 'Genetic influences and infantile autism', *Nature,* vol. 265, no. 5596, pp. 726–8.

Folstein, S. and Rutter, M. (1978) 'Infantile autism: a genetic study of 21 twin pairs', *Journal of Child Psychology and Child Psychiatry,* vol. 18, pp. 297–321.

Freitag, C. M. (2007) 'The genetics of autistic disorders and its clinical relevance: a review of the literature', *Molecular Psychiatry,* vol. 12, no. 1, pp. 2–22.

Frith, U. (1989) *Autism: Explaining the enigma,* Oxford, Blackwell Publishing.

Frith, U. and Happé, F. (1999) 'Theory of Mind and self-consciousness: what is it like to be autistic?' *Mind and Language,* vol. 14, no. 1, pp. 1–22.

Frith, U. and Soares, I. (1993) 'Research into earliest detectable signs of autism: what the parents say', *Communication,* vol. 27, pp. 17–18.

Geschwind, D. H. (2009) 'Advances in autism', *Annual Review of Medicine*, vol. 60, pp. 367–80.

Gillberg, C. (1991) 'Clinical and neurobiological aspects of Asperger syndrome in six family studies' in Frith, U. (ed.) *Autism and Asperger Syndrome*, pp. 122–46, Cambridge, Cambridge University Press.

Goin-Kochel, R. B., Abbacchi, A. and Constantino, J. N. (2007) 'Lack of evidence for increased genetic loading for autism among families of affected females. A replication from family history data in two large samples', *Autism*, vol. 11, no. 3, pp. 279–86.

Golan, O. and Baron-Cohen, S. (2006) 'Systemising empathy: teaching adults with Asperger Syndrome and High Functioning Autism to recognise complex emotions using interactive multi-media', *Development and Psychopathology*, vol. 18, pp. 591–617.

Golan, O. and Baron-Cohen (2008) 'Teaching adults with autism spectrum conditions to recognise emotions: systematic training for empathising difficulties' in McGregor, E., Nuñez, M., Cebula, K. and Gómez, J. C. (eds) *Autism: An integrated view from neurocognitive, clinical and intervention research*, Wiley Blackwell.

Golan, O., Baron-Cohen, S., Hill, J. J. and Golan, Y. (2006) 'The 'Reading the Mind in Films' task: complex emotion recognition in adults with and without autism spectrum conditions', *Social Neuroscience*, vol. 1, pp. 111–23.

Golan, O., Baron-Cohen, S. and Golan, Y. (2008) 'The 'Reading the Mind in Films' task [child version]: complex emotion and mental state recognition in children with and without autism spectrum conditions', *Journal of Autism and Developmental Disorders*, vol. 38, no. 8, pp. 1534–41.

Gorrod, L. (author) and Carver, B. (illustrator) (1997) *My Brother is Different*, London, National Autistic Society.

Gould, G. A., Rigg, M. and Bignell, L. (1991) *The Higashi Experience: The report of a visit to the Boston Higashi School*, London, National Autistic Society.

Grandin, T. (2000) *Sensory Challenges and Answers*, Future Horizons Inc.

Grandin, T. and Duffy, K. (2004) *Developing Talents: Careers for individuals with Asperger syndrome and high-functioning autism*, Shawnee Mission, KS, Autism Asperger Publishing Company.

Grandin, T. and Scariano, M. M. (1986) *Emergence: Labeled autistic*, Novato, CA, Arena Press.

Grandin, T., Barron, S. and Zysk, V. (2005) *The Unwritten Rules of Social Relationships*, Arlington, Texas, Future Horizons.

Gray, D. (2003) 'Gender and coping: the parents of children with high-functioning autism', *Social Science and Medicine*, vol. 56, pp. 631–42.

Greenspan, S. (1998) 'A developmental approach to relating and communicating in autistic spectrum disorders and related syndromes', *SPOTLIGHT on Topics in Developmental Disabilities*, vol. 1, pp. 1–6.

Greenspan, S. and Weider, S. (1999) 'A functional developmental approach to autism spectrum disorders', *Journal of the Association for Persons with Severe Handicaps*, vol. 24, pp. 147–61.

Gregory, C., Lough, S., Stone, V., Erzinclioglu, S., Martin, L., Baron-Cohen, S. and Hodges, J. (2002) 'Theory of Mind in patients with frontal variant fronto-temporal dementia and Alzheimer's disease: theoretical and practical implication', *Brain*, vol. 125, pp. 752–64.

Grinker, R. R. (2009) *Isabel's World: Autism and the making of a modern epidemic*, London, Icon Books.

Gubbay, S. S., Lobascher, M. and Kingerlee, P. (1970) 'A neurologic appraisal of autistic children: results of a western Australian survey', *Developmental Medicine and Child Neurology*, vol. 12, pp. 422–9.

Gutstein, S. and Sheely, R. K. (2002) *Relationship Development Intervention with Children, Adolescents and Adults: Social and emotional development activities for Asperger Syndrome and autism*, London, Jessica Kingsley Publishers.

Gutstein, S. E., Burgess, A. F. and Montfort, K. (2007) 'Evaluation of the Relationship Development Intervention program', *Autism*, vol. 11, no. 5, pp. 397–411.

Hadcroft, W. (2005) *The Feeling's Unmutual: Growing up with Asperger syndrome (undiagnosed)*, London and Philadelphia, Jessica Kingsley Publishers.

Haddon, M. (2003) *The Curious Incident of the Dog in the Night-Time*, Doubleday.

Happé, F. G. E. (1994) 'An advanced test of theory of mind: understanding of story characters' thoughts and feelings by able autistic, mentally handicapped and normal children and adults', *Journal of Autism and Developmental Disorders*, vol. 24, pp. 129–54.

Happé, F. G. E. (1997) 'Central coherence and theory of mind in autism: reading homographs in context', *British Journal of Developmental Psychology*, vol. 15, pp. 1–12.

Happé, F. G. E. and Frith, U. (2006) 'The Weak Central Coherence Account: detail-focused cognitive style in autism spectrum disorders', *Journal of Autism and Developmental Disorders*, vol. 35, pp. 5–25.

Hare, D. J., Pratt, C., Burton, M., Bromley, J. and Emerson, E. (2004) 'The health and social care needs of family carers supporting adults with autistic spectrum disorders', *Autism*, vol. 8, no. 4, pp. 425–44.

Hart, B. and Risley, T. R. (1975) 'Incidental teaching of language in the preschool', *Journal of Applied Behavior Analysis*, vol. 8, pp. 411–20.

Heaton, P. (2003) 'Pitch memory, labelling and disembedding in autism', *Journal of Child Psychology and Psychiatry*, vol. 44, pp. 543–51.

Herba, C. and Phillips, M. (2004) 'Annotation: development of facial expression recognition from childhood to adolescence: behavioural and neurological perspectives', *Journal of Child Psychology and Psychiatry*, vol. 45, no. 7, pp. 1185–98.

Hermelin, B. and O'Connor, N. (1970) *Psychological Experiments with Autistic Children*, Oxford, Pergamon Press.

Hill, E. L. (2004) 'Evaluating the theory of executive dysfunction in autism', *Developmental Review*, vol. 24, no. 2, pp. 189–233.

Hill, E. L. (2008) 'Executive functioning in autism spectrum disorder: where it fits into the causal model' in McGregor, E., Núñez, M., Cebula, K. and Gómez, J-C. (eds), *Autism: An integrated view from neurocognitive, clinical and intervention research*, Oxford, Blackwell Publishing.

Hobson, P. (2002) *The Cradle of Thought*, London, Macmillan.

Hobson, R. P. (1986) 'The autistic child's appraisal of expressions of emotion', *Journal of Child Psychology and Child Psychiatry*, vol. 27, pp. 321–42.

Hobson, R. P. (1993) *Autism and the Development of Mind*, Hove (UK) and Hillsdale (USA), Lawrence Erlbaum Associates.

Hobson, P. and Hobson, J. (2010) 'Cognitive flexibility in autism: a social-developmental account' in Roth, I. and Rezaie, P. (eds), *The Autism Spectrum: Research reviews*, Cambridge, Cambridge University Press.

Hocking, B. (1987) *The Independent*, 3 November, p. 15.

Honda, H., Shimizu. Y. and Rutter, M. (2005) 'No effect of MMR withdrawal on the incidence of autism: a total population study', *Journal of Child Psychology and Psychiatry*, vol. 46, pp. 572–9.

Howlin, P. (2000) 'Outcome in adult life for more able individuals with autism or Asperger syndrome', *Autism*, vol. 4, pp. 63–83.

Howlin, P. (2003) 'Outcome in high-functioning adults with autism with and without early language delays: Implications for the differentiation between autism and Asperger syndrome', *Journal of Autism and Developmental Disorders*, vol. 33, no. 1, pp. 3–13.

Howlin, P. and Yates, P. (1990) 'A group for the siblings of children with autism', *Communication*, vol. 24, no. 1, pp. 11–16.

Howlin, P., Goode, S., Hutton, J. and Rutter, M. (2004) 'Adult outcome for children with autism', *Journal of Child Psychology and Psychiatry*, vol. 45, no. 2, pp. 212–29.

Howlin, P., Gordon, K., Pasco, G., Wade, A. and Charman, T. (2007) 'The effectiveness of Picture Exchange Communication System (PECS) training for teachers of children with autism: a pragmatic, group randomised controlled trial', *Journal of Child Psychology and Psychiatry*, vol. 48, no. 5, pp. 473–81.

Howlin, P., Goode, S., Hulton, J. and Rutter, M. (2009) 'Savant skills in autism: psychometric approaches and parental reports', *Philosophical Transactions of the Royal Society, B,* vol. 364, pp. 1359–1367.

Hughes, C. and Russell, J. (1993) 'Autistic children's difficulty with mental disengagement from an object: its implications for theories of autism', *Developmental Psychology*, vol. 29, pp. 498–510.

Hurlbutt, K. and Chalmers, L. (2002) 'Adults with autism speak out: perceptions of their life experiences', *Focus on Autism and other Developmental Disabilities*, vol. 17, no. 2, pp. 103–11.

Jackson, L. (2002*) Freaks, Geeks & Asperger Syndrome: A user guide to adolescence*, London, Jessica Kingsley Publishers.

Jackson, J. (2003) *Multicoloured Mayhem: Parenting the many shades of adolescents and children with autism, Asperger syndrome and AD/HD*, London and New York, Jessica Kingsley Publishers.

Järbrink, K., Fombonne, E. and Knapp, M. (2003) 'Measuring the parental, service and cost impacts of children with autistic spectrum disorder: a pilot study', *Journal of Autism and Developmental Disorders*, vol. 33, no. 4, pp. 395–402.

Jarrold, C. (2003) 'A review of research into pretend play in autism', *Autism*, vol. 7, pp. 379–90.

Jolliffe, T. and Baron-Cohen, S. (2000) 'Linguistic processing in high-functioning adults with autism or Asperger syndrome: is global coherence impaired?', *Psychological Medicine* vol. 30, pp. 1169–87.

Jolliffe, T. and Baron-Cohen, S. (2001) 'A test of central coherence theory: can adults with high-functioning autism or Asperger syndrome integrate fragments of an object?' *Cognitive Neuropsychiatry*, vol. 6, pp. 193–216.

Jolliffe, T., Lansdown, R. and Robinson, C. (1992) 'Autism: a personal account', *Communication*, vol. 26, no. 3, pp. 12–19.

Jordan, R. (2004) 'Meeting the needs of children with autistic spectrum disorders in the early years', *Australian Journal of Early Childhood*, vol. 29, no. 3, pp. 1–7.

Kaminsky, L. and Dewey, D. (2002) 'Psychosocial adjustment in siblings of children with autism', *Journal of Child Psychology and Psychiatry and Allied Disciplines*, vol. 43, no. 2, pp. 225–32.

Kanner, L. (1943) 'Autistic disturbances of affective contact', *Nervous Child*, vol. 2, pp. 217–50.

Kanner, L. (1973) *Childhood Psychosis: Initial Studies and New Insights*, Washington DC, V. H. Winston.

Kaufman, B. N. (1994) *Son-Rise: The miracle continues*, Tiburon, CA, H. J. Krammer Inc.

Knapp, M., Romeo, R. and Beecham, J. (2009) 'Economic cost of autism in the UK', *Autism*, vol. 13, no. 3, pp. 317–36.

Larkin, A. and Gurry, S. (1998) 'Brief report: progress reported in three children with autism using daily life therapy', *Journal of Autism and Developmental Disorders*, vol. 28, pp. 339–42.

Lawson, W. (2006) *AS Poetry: Illustrated poems from an Aspie life*, London, Jessica Kingsley Publishers.

Lawson, W. (2008) *Concepts of Normality: The autistic and typical spectrum*, London, Jessica Kingsley Publishers.

Lehmann, D. and Siebzehner, B. (2006) *Remaking Israeli Judaism: The challenge of Shas*, London, Hurst.

Leslie, A. (1991) 'The theory of mind impairment in autism: evidence for a modular mechanism of development?' in Whiten, A. (ed.) *Natural Theories of Mind*, Oxford, Blackwell Publishing.

Lewis, V. and Boucher, J. (1988) 'Spontaneous, instructed and elicited play in relatively able autistic children', *British Journal of Developmental Psychology*, vol. 6, pp. 325–39.

Little, L. (2002) 'Middle-class mothers' perceptions of peer and sibling victimization among children with Asperger's syndrome and non-verbal learning disorders', *Issues in Comprehensive Pediatric Nursing*, vol. 25, no. 1, pp. 43–57.

Lombardo, M. V., Barnes, J. L., Wheelwright, S. J. and Baron-Cohen, S. (2007) 'Self-referential cognition and empathy in autism', *PLoS One*, vol. 2, no. 9, e883 [online]. Available from: http://www.plosone.org/article/info:doi%2F10.1371%2Fjournal.pone.0000883 (Accessed 18 November 2009).

Lopez, B. R., Lincoln, A. J., Ozonoff, S. and Lai, Z. (2005) 'Examining the relationship between executive functions and restricted, repetitive symptoms of autistic disorder', *Journal of Autism and Developmental Disorders*, vol. 35, pp. 445–60.

Lord, C., Risi, S., Lambrecht, L., Cook, E. H. Jr, Leventhal, B. L., DiLavore, P. C., Pickles, A. and Rutter, M. (2000) 'The Autism Diagnostic Observation Schedule-Generic: a standard measure of social and communication deficits associated with the spectrum of autism', *Journal of Autism and Developmental Disorders*, vol. 30, no. 3, pp. 205–23.

Lotter, V. (1966) 'Epidemiology of autistic conditions in young children, 1 Prevalence', *Social Psychiatry*, vol. 1, pp. 124–37.

Lovaas, O. I. (1987) 'Behavioural treatment and normal educational and intellectual functioning in young autistic children', *Journal of Consulting and Clinical Psychology*, vol. 55, pp. 3–9.

Loynes, F. (2001) *The Impact of Autism: A report compiled for the All Party Parliamentary Group on Autism*, London, APPGA.

Macintosh, K. E. and Dissanayake, C. (2004) 'Annotation: the similarities and differences between autistic disorder and Asperger's disorder: a review of the empirical evidence', *Journal of Child Psychology and Psychiatry*, vol. 45, no. 3, pp. 421–34.

Mackenzie, H. (2008) *Reaching and Teaching the Child or Young Person with Autism Spectrum Disorder: Using learning preferences and strengths*, London and New York, Jessica Kingsley Publishers.

Maestro, S. and Muratori, F. (2008) 'How young children with autism treat objects and people: some insight into autism in infancy from research in home movies in autism', in McGregor, E., Núñez, M., Cebula, K. and Gómez, J. C. (eds) *Autism: An integrated view from neuroscience, clinical, and intervention research*, Oxford, Blackwell Publishing, pp. 170–92.

Maestro, S., Muratori, F., Cavallaro, M.C., Pecini, C., Cesari, A., Paziente, A., Stern, D., Golse, B. and Palacio-Espasa, F. (2005) 'How young children treat objects and people: an empirical study of the first year of life in autism', *Child Psychiatry and Human Development*, vol. 35, pp. 383–96.

Malaton (2005), independent film, directed by Jeong Yunchul.

McCann, J., Peppé, S., Gibbon, F., O'Hare, A. and Rutherford, M. (2008) 'The prosody-language relationship in children with high-functioning autism' in McGregor, E., Núñez, M., Cebula, K. and Gómez, J. C. (eds), *Autism: An integrated view from neuroscience, clinical and intervention research*, Oxford, Blackwell Publishing, pp. 214–35.

McConachie, H., Randle, V., Hammal, D. and Le Couteur, A. (2005) 'A controlled trial of a training course for parents of children with suspected autism spectrum disorder', *Journal of Pediatrics*, vol. 147, pp. 335–40.

McDougle, C. J., Erickson, C. A., Stigler, K. A. and Posey, D. J. (2005) 'Neurochemistry in the pathophysiology of autism', *Journal of Clinical Psychiatry*, vol. 66, suppl. 10, pp. 9–18.

McEachin, J. J., Smith, T. and Lovaas, O. I. (1993) 'Long-term outcome for children with autism who received early intensive behavioral treatment', *American Journal on Mental Retardation*, vol. 4, pp. 359–72.

Minter, M., Hobson, R. P. and Bishop, M. (1998) 'Congenital visual impairment and "theory of mind"', *British Journal of Developmental Psychology*, vol. 16, pp. 183–96.

Moore, C. (2003a) 'Mind the gap', *The Guardian*, 14 May [online], http://www.guardian.co.uk/lifeandstyle/2003/may/14/familyandrelationships.features10 (Accessed 5 June 2009).

Moore, C. (2003b) 'Mind the gap', *The Guardian*, 19 February [online], http://www.guardian.co.uk/lifeandstyle/2003/feb/19/familyandrelationships.features101 (Accessed November 2009).

Mottron, L., Dawson, M., Soulières, I., Hubert, B. and Burack, J. (2006) 'Enhanced perceptual functioning in autism: An update and eight principles of autistic perception', *Journal of Autism and Developmental Disorders*, vol. 36, pp. 27–43.

Mukhopadhyay, T. R. (2000) *Beyond the Silence: My life, the world and autism*, London, National Autistic Society.

Mulder, E. J., Anderson, G. M., Kema, I. P., de Bildt, A., van Lang, N. D., den Boer, J. A. and Minderaa, R. B. (2004) 'Platelet serotonin levels in pervasive developmental disorders and mental retardation: diagnostic group differences, within-group distribution, and behavioral correlates', *Journal of the American Academy of Child and Adolescent Psychiatry*, vol. 43, no. 4, pp. 491–9.

Müller, R. A. (2008) 'From loci to networks and back again: anomalies in the study of autism', *Annals of the New York Academy of Sciences*, vol. 1145, pp. 300–15.

Munson, J., Dawson, G., Abbott, R., Faja, S., Webb, S. J., Friedman, S. D., Shaw, D., Artru, A. and Dager, S. R. (2006) 'Amygdala volume and behavioral development in autism', *Archives of General Psychiatry*, vol. 63, no. 6, pp. 686–93.

Murray, D. (2008) 'Whose normal is it anyway?' in Lawson, W. *Concepts of Normality: The autistic and typical spectrum*, London, Jessica Kingsley Publishers.

Murray, D. and Lawson, W. (2007) 'Inclusion through technology for autistic children', in Cigman, R. (ed.) *Included or Excluded? The challenge of the mainstream for some SEN children*, London, Routledge.

Myers, P., Baron-Cohen, S. and Wheelwright, S. (2004) *An Exact Mind: An artist with Asperger Syndrome*, London and New York, Jessica Kingsley.

NAS (2008) *'I Exist' report*, February 2008, National Autistic Society [online], http://www.autism.org.uk/nas/jsp/polopoly.jsp?d=1558 (Accessed 4 October 2009).

NAS (2009) [online], http://www.nas.org.uk/autism (Accessed 20 October 2009).

National Initiative for Autism: Screening and Assessment (NIASA) (2003) *National Autism Plan for Children: Plan for the identification, assessment, diagnosis and access to early interventions for pre-school and primary aged children with autism spectrum disorders (ASD)*, London, National Autistic Society.

Navon, D. (1977) 'Forests before trees: the precedence of global features in visual perception', *Cognitive Psychology*, vol. 9, pp. 353–83.

Nissenbaum, M. S., Tollefson, N. and Reese, R. M. (2002) 'The interpretative conference: sharing a diagnosis of autism with families', *Focus on Autism and other Developmental Disabilities*, vol. 17, no. 1, pp. 30–43.

Ofsted (2006) *Inclusion: Does it matter where pupils are taught?* [online], www.ofsted.gov.uk (Accessed 4 June 2009).

Paradiž, V. (2002) *Elijah's Cup*, New York, The Free Press.

Pardo, C. A. and Eberhart, C. G. (2007) 'The neurobiology of autism', *Brain Pathology*, vol. 17, pp. 434–47.

Parent (2009) Parent Perspectives [workshop as part of University of Cumbria course 'Principles and Practice of Working with Individuals on the Autism Spectrum'], 22 January.

Pellicano, L. (2010) 'Psycholological models of autism: an overview' in Roth, I. and Rezaie, P. (eds), *The Autism Spectrum: Research reviews*, Cambridge, Cambridge University Press.

Pellicano, E., Maybery, M., Durkin, K. and Maley, A. (2006) 'Multiple cognitive capabilities/deficits in children with an autism spectrum disorder: "Weak" central coherence and its relationship to theory of mind and executive control', *Development and Psychopathology*, vol. 18, pp. 77–98.

Pfeiffer, B. E. and Huber, K. M. (2009) 'The state of the synapse in fragile X syndrome', *The Neuroscientist* (in press).

Piven, J., Palmer, P., Landa, R., Santangelo, S., Jacobi, D. and Childress, D. (1997) 'Personality and language characteristics in parents from multiple-incidence autism families', *American Journal of Medical Genetics*, vol. 74, no. 4, pp. 398–411.

Powell, S. and Jordan, R. (eds) (1997) *Autism and Learning: A guide to good practice*, Oxford, David Fulton Publishers.

Rain Man (1988), film, directed by Barry Levinson, USA, MGM.

Randall, P. and Parker, J. (1999) *Supporting the Families of Children with Autism*, Chichester, John Wiley.

Reid, B. and Batten, A. (2006) *B is for Bullied: The experiences of children with autism and their families*, London, National Autistic Society. Available from: http://www.nas.org.uk/nas/jsp/polopoly.jsp?d=160&a=12849 (Accessed 23 October 2009).

Robinson, S. (1997) 'TEACCH in adult services: the practitioner's eye view', *Communication*, membership journal of the National Autistic Society, summer, pp. 8–10.

Rodrigue, J. R., Morgan, S. B. and Geffken, G. R. (1992) 'Psychosocial adaptation of fathers of children with autism, Down's syndrome, and normal development', *Journal of Autism and Developmental Disorders*, vol. 22, no. 2, pp. 249–63.

Rogers, S. J. and Vismara, L. A. (2008) 'Evidence-based comprehensive treatments for early autism', *Journal of Clinical Child and Adolescent Psychology*, vol. 37, no. 1, pp. 8–38.

Romkema, C. (2002) *Embracing the Sky: Poems beyond disability*, London, Jessica Kingsley Publishers.

Roth, I. (2007a) 'Autism and the imaginative mind', in Roth, I. (ed.) *Imaginative Minds*, London, Oxford University Press/British Academy.

Roth, I. (2007b) 'Imagination and awareness of self in autistic spectrum poets' in Osteen, M. (ed.) *Autism and Representation*, New York, Routledge.

Russell, J. (1997) 'How executive disorders can bring about an inadequate 'theory of mind', in J. Russell (ed.) *Autism as an Executive Disorder*, Oxford, Oxford University Press.

Rutter, M. (1999) 'Autism: two-way interplay between research and clinical work', *Journal of Child Psychology and Child Psychiatry*, vol. 40, pp. 169–88.

Rutter, M. (2005) 'Aetiology of autism: findings and questions', *Journal of Intellectual Disability Research*, vol. 49, pt 4, pp. 231–8.

Rutter, M., Andersen-Wood, L., Beckett, C., Bredenkamp, D., Castle, J., Groothues, C., Kreppner, J., Keaveney, L., Lord, C., O'Connor, T.G. and the English and Romanian Adoptees (ERA) study team (1999) 'Quasi-autistic patterns following severe global privation', *Child Psychology and Child Psychiatry*, vol. 40, pp. 537–49.

Sacks, O. (1993) 'An anthropologist on Mars: A neurologist's notebook', *New Yorker*, vol. 69, no. 44, pp. 106–25.

Sainsbury, C. (2000) *The Martian in the Playground: Understanding the schoolchild with Asperger's syndrome*, Bristol, Lucky Duck Publishing.

Sallows, G. O. and Graupner, T. D. (2005) 'Intensive behavioral treatment for children with autism: four-year outcome and predictors', *American Journal on Mental Retardation*, vol. 110, no. 6, pp. 417–38.

Schain, R. J. and Freedman, D. X. (1961) 'Studies on 5-hydroxyindole metabolism in autistic and other mentally retarded children', *Journal of Pediatrics*, vol. 58, pp. 315–20.

Schechter, R. and Grether, J. K. (2008) 'Continuing increases in autism reported to California's developmental services system: mercury in retrograde', *Archives of General Psychiatry*, vol. 65, no. 1, pp. 19–24.

Schopler, E., Mesibov, G. and Baker, A. (1982) 'Evaluation of treatment for autistic children and their parents', *Journal of the American Academy of Child Psychiatry*, vol. 21, no. 3, pp. 262–7.

Schultz, R. T. (2005) 'Developmental deficits in social perception in autism: the role of the amygdala and fusiform face area', *International Journal of Developmental Neuroscience*, vol. 23, no. 2–3, pp. 125–41.

Sciutto, M. J. and Cantwell, C. (2005) 'Factors influencing the differential diagnosis of Asperger's disorder and high-functioning autism', *Journal of Developmental and Physical Disabilities*, vol. 17, no. 4, pp. 345–59.

Segar, M. (1997) *A Survival Guide for People with Asperger Synd* http://www.autismandcomputing.org.uk/marc2.en.html (Accessed 1

Segar, M., *The Battles of the Autistic Thinker* [online], http://www. autismandcomputing.org.uk/marc1.en.html (Accessed 4 June 2009)

Seltzer, M. M., Krauss, M. W., Orsmond, G. I. and Vestal, C. (200 adolescents and adults with autism: uncharted territory' in Glidden *International Review of Research in Mental Retardation*, vol. 23, S Academic Press.

Slater-Walker, C. and Slater-Walker, G. (2002) *An Asperger Marri* New York, Jessica Kingsley Publishers.

Stuart-Hamilton, I. (2007) *An Asperger Dictionary of Everyday Ex* edn), London and Philadelphia, Jessica Kingsley Publishers.

Südhof, T. C. (2008) 'Neuroligins and neurexins link synaptic func disease', *Nature*, vol. 455, no. 7215, pp. 903–11.

Swedo, S. (2009) *Report of the DSM-V Neurodevelopmental Disor* American Psychiatric Association, http://www.psych.org/MainMenu DSMV/DSMRevisionActivities/DSM-V-Work-Group-Reports/Neuro Disorders-Work-Group-Report.aspx (Accessed 2 October 2009).

Tager-Flusberg, H. (2000) 'Language and understanding minds: co autism', in Baron-Cohen, S., Tager-Flusberg, H. and Cohen, D. (ec *Other Minds: Perspectives from developmental cognitive neuroscie* Oxford University Press.

Tammet, D. (2006) *Born on a Blue Day: Inside the extraordinary savant,* New York, Free Press.

Tarleton, B. and Macaulay, F. (2003) 'Better for the break? Short t children and teenagers with autistic spectrum disorders and their fa Shared Care Network.

Taylor, B., Miller, E., Farrington, C. P., Petropoulos, M., Favot-Mayaud, I., Li, J. and Waight, P. A. (1999) 'Autism and measles, mumps, and rubella vaccine: no epidemiological evidence for a causal association', *The Lancet*, vol. 353, pp. 2026–9.

Tinbergen, N. and Tinbergen, E. A. (1985) *Autistic Children, New Hope for a Cure,* 2nd edn, 1985, Taylor & Francis Books Ltd.

Tomanik, S., Harris, G. E. and Hawkins, J. (2004) 'The relationship between behaviours exhibited by children with autism and maternal stress', *Journal of Intellectual and Developmental Disability*, vol. 29, no. 1, pp. 16–26.

Treffert, D. A. (1989) *Extraordinary People*, London, Bantam Books.

Tréhin, G. (2006) *Urville*, London and Philadelphia, Jessica Kingsley Publishers.

Trevarthen, C. (1979) 'Communication and cooperation in early infancy: A description of primary intersubjectivity', in M. Bullowa (ed.), *Before Speech*, Cambridge, Cambridge University Press, pp. 321–47.

Tronick, E., Als, H., Adamson, L., Wise, S. and Brazelton, T. B. (1978) 'The infant's response to entrapment between contradictory messages in face-to-face interaction', *Journal of the American Academy of Child and Adolescent Psychiatry*, vol. 17, pp. 1–13.

Turner, M. (1999) 'Generating novel ideas: fluency performance in high-functioning and learning disabled individuals with autism', *Journal of Child Psychology and Psychiatry*, vol. 40, pp. 189–201.

Wakefield, A. J., Murch, S. H., Anthony A., Linnel, J., Casson, D. M., Malik, M., Berelowitz, M., Dhillon, A. P., Thomson, M. A., Harvey, P., Valentine A., Davies, S. E. and Walker-Smith, J. A. (1998) 'Ileal-lymphoid-nodular hyperplasia, non-specific colitis, and pervasive developmental disorder in children', *The Lancet,* vol. 351, pp. 637–41.

Walsh, F. (1998) 'The concept of family resilience: crisis and challenges', *Family Process*, vol. 35, pp. 261–81.

Walsh, F. (2003) 'Changing families in a changing world', in Walsh, F. (ed.) *Normal Family Processes: Growing diversity and complexity*, New York, Guilford, pp. 3–26.

Wang, K., Zhang, H., Ma, D., Bucan, M., Glessner, J. T., Abrahams, B. S. et al. (2009) 'Common genetic variants on 5p14.1 associate with autism spectrum disorders' [online], *Nature* advance online publication 28 April 2009, http://www.nature.com/ nature/journal/v459/n7246/full/nature07953.html (Accessed 2 June 2009).

Warnock Report (1978) *Special Educational Needs: Report of the committee of enquiry into the education of handicapped children and young people*, Cmnd 7212, London, HMSO; also available online at http://www.dg.dial.pipex.com/documents/ docs3/warnock00.shtml (Accessed 10 June 2009).

Wawro, R. (2009) [online] Available at: http://www.wawro.net/ (Accessed August 2009)

Wheelwright, S., Baron-Cohen, S., Goldenfeld, N., Delaney, J., Fine, D., Smith, R., Weil, L. and Wakabayashi, A. (2006) 'Predicting Autism Spectrum Quotient (AQ) from the Systemising Quotient-Revised (SQ-R) and Empathy Quotient (EQ)', *Brain Research*, vol. 1079, pp. 47–56.

Whitaker, P. (2007) 'Provision for youngsters with autistic spectrum disorders in mainstream schools: what parents say – and what parents want', *British Journal of Special Education*, vol. 34, no. 3, pp. 170–8.

Willey, L. H. (1999) *Pretending to be Normal: Living with Asperger's syndrome*, London, Jessica Kingsley Publishers.

Williams, D. (1992) *Nobody Nowhere: The remarkable autobiography of an autistic girl*, Doubleday Books.

Williams, D. (2003) *Exposure Anxiety – The Invisible Cage: An exploration of self-protection responses in the autism spectrum and beyond*, London and New York, Jessica Kingsley Publishers.

Williams, D. (2004) *Not Just Anything: A collection of thoughts on paper*, London and Philadelphia, Jessica Kingsley Publishers.

Williams, D. (2006) *The Jumbled Jigsaw: An insider's approach to the treatment of autistic spectrum 'fruit salads'*, London and New York, Jessica Kingsley Publishers.

Wimpory, D. C., Hobson, R. P., Williams, J. M. and Nash, S. (2000) 'Are infants with autism socially engaged? A study of recent retrospective parental reports', *Journal of Autism and Developmental Disorders*, vol. 30, no. 6, pp. 525–36.

Wing, L. (1981) 'Language, social and cognitive impairments in autism and severe mental retardation', *Journal of Autism and Developmental Disorders*, vol.11, no. 1, pp. 31–44.

Wing, L. (1991) 'The relationship between Asperger's syndrome and Kanner's autism', in Frith, U. (1991) (ed.) *Autism and Asperger Syndrome*, Cambridge, Cambridge University Press.

Wing, L. (1996) *The Autism Spectrum*, London, Constable.

Wing, L. and Gould, J. (1979) 'Severe impairments of social intera associated abnormalities in children: epidemiology and classificatio *Autism and Developmental Disorders*, vol. 9, pp. 11–29.

Woodbury-Smith, M., Klin, A. and Volkmar, F. (2005) 'Asperger's comparison of clinical diagnoses and those made according to the IV', *Journal of Autism and Developmental Disorders*, vol. 35, no.

World Health Organisation (2007) *International Classification of L Revision (ICD-10)*.

Yang, M. S. and Gill, M. (2007) 'A review of gene linkage, associ expression studies in autism and an assessment of convergent evid *Journal of Developmental Neuroscience*, vol. 25, no. 2, pp. 69–85.

Yoder, P. J. and Stone, W. L. (2006a) 'Randomized comparison of communication interventions for preschoolers with autism spectrun *Journal of Consulting and Clinical Psychology*, vol. 74, no. 3, pp.

Yoder, P. J. and Stone, W. L. (2006b) 'A randomized comparison (prelinguistic communication interventions on the acquisition of spc communication in preschoolers with ASD', *Journal of Speech, Lar Hearing Research*, vol. 49, pp. 698–711.

Acknowledgements

Grateful acknowledgement is made to the following sources:

Text

Poem extracts on page 83 and page 270: Tito Rajarshi Mukhopadhyay (2000) *Beyond the Silence*: *My life, the world and autism*, The National Autistic Society; poem extract on page 273: Romkema, C. (2002) 'Perspectives', *Embracing the Sky: Poems beyond disability*, Jessica Kingsley Publishers.

Figures

Figure 1.2: © Photos 12/Alamy; Figure 1.3: US National Library of Medicine/Science Photo Library; Figure 1.4: Courtesy of the Asperger Estate; Figure 1.5: Courtesy of Uta Frith; Figure 1.6: Courtesy of Sir Michael Rutter; Figure 1.7 left: Daniel Attia/Corbis; Figure 1.7 right: Photolibrary; Figure 2.1: Solus Veer/Corbis; Figure 2.2 Queensmill School; Figure 2.4 left: Rex Features; Figure 2.4 right: © Photos 12/Alamy; Figure 2.5: National Autistic Society; Figure 2.6: Western Psychological Services; Figure 3.3: Ian Hooton/Science Photo Library; Figure 3.5: Photolibrary; Figure 3.4 Adapted from Maestro, S. and Muratori, F. (2008) 'How young children with autism treat objects and people: some insight into autism in infancy from research in home movies in autism', in McGregor, E., Núñez, M., Cebula, K. and Gómez, J. C. (eds) *Autism: An integrated view from neuroscience, clinical, and intervention research*, Oxford, Blackwell Publishing, pp. 170–92; Figure 3.6: adapted from Hobson, R. P. (1986) 'The autistic child's appraisal of expressions of emotion', *Journal of Child Psychology and Psychiatry*, vol. 27, no. 3, Pergamon Journals Ltd; Figure 3.8: Stephen Wiltshire; Figure 3.9: Pure Vision Arts; Figure 4.1: Brian Harris; Figure 4.2: Robert Taylor; Figure 4.3: adapted from Frith, U. (1989) *Autism: Explaining the enigma*, Oxford, Blackwell Publishing; Figure 4.4: taken from the BBC Series *Antenna*, 1988; Figure 4.5: Andrew Atkinson; Figure 4.6: Axel Scheffler; Figure 4.7: ITN Archive (1999) *Lost for Words*; Figure 4.10: Tronick, E. (2007) *The neurobehavior and social emotional development of the infant*, Norton Press; Figure 4.13: Navon, D. (1977) 'Forests before trees: the precedence of global features in visual perception', *Cognitive Psychology*, vol. 9, pp. 353–83; Figures 4.14 and 4.15: Baron-Cohen, S. et al. (2001) 'Are intuitive physics and intuitive psychology independent? A test with children with Asperger Syndrome', *Journal of Developmental and Learning Disorders*, vol. 5, Interdisciplinary Council on Developmental and Learning Disorders; Figure 5.1: adapted from Taylor, B. et al. (1999) 'Autism and measles, mumps and rubella vaccine: no epidemiological evidence for a causal association', *The Lancet*, vol. 353, June 12 1999, Lancet Publications; Figure 5.2: adapted from Honda, H., Shimizu. Y. and Rutter, M. (2005) 'No effect of MMT withdrawal on the incidence of autism: a total population study', *Child Psychology and Psychiatry*, vol. 46, no. 6, Blackwell Publishing; Figure 5.3: adapted from Schechter, R. and Grether, J. K. (2008) 'Continuing increases in autism reported to California developmental services system', *Archives of General Psychiatry*, vol. 65, no. 1, January 2008, American Medical Association;

Index

Entries and page numbers in **bold** refer to glossary terms. Page numbers in italics refer to entries mainly, or wholly, in figures or tables.

W

X–Y